CHROMATOGRAPHIC METHODS

CHROMATOGRAPHIC METHODS

A. Braithwaite   F. J. Smith

*Department of Physical Sciences,
Trent Polytechnic, Nottingham*

London New York
Chapman and Hall

First published 1963
Second edition 1967
Third edition 1974
Reprinted 1977
Fourth edition 1985
Chapman and Hall Ltd
11 New Fetter Lane, London EC4P 4EE
Published in the USA by
Chapman and Hall
29 West 35th Street, New York NY 10001

© 1985 A. Braithwaite and F. J. Smith

Softcover reprint of the hardcover 1st edition 1985

British Library Cataloguing in Publication Data

Braithwaite, A.
    Chromatographic methods.—4th ed.
    1. Chromatographic analysis
    I. Title II. Smith, F. III. Stock, R.
    Chromatographic methods
    543'.089   QG79.C4

    ISBN-13: 978-94-010-8316-4   e-ISBN-13: 978-94-009-4093-2
    DOI: 10.1007/978-94-009-4093-2

Library of Congress Cataloging in Publication Data

Braithwaite, A., 1942–
    Chromatographic methods.

    Rev. ed. of: Chromotographic methods/R. Stock.
    3rd ed. 1974.
    Includes bibliographies and index.
    1. Chromatographic analysis. I. Smith, F. J.,
    1950–   . II. Stock, Ralph. Chromatographic methods.
    III. Title.
    QD79.C4B73   1985   543'.089   85–12746

CONTENTS

PREFACE

In recent years the techniques of chromatography have progressed rapidly. However, the aims and objectives of the First Edition, as quoted below, are just as relevant today as they undoubtedly were in 1963.

'The various methods of separating mixtures which are grouped under the general name *chromatography* are now well known and widely used. Since the inception of chromatography as a column technique in 1903, the principal landmarks in its progress have been its virtual rediscovery in the 1930s, the invention of synthetic resins in 1935, the introduction of paper chromatography in the early 1940s and finally, the development of gas solid and gas liquid chromatography in the late 1940s and early 1950s.

Subsequent expansion in the use of chromatographic methods has been rapid and continuous, with the result that in the last 15 years a substantial volume of literature on the subject has appeared, dealing not only with particular separations but also in much specific detail with improvements in technique.

Many specialist books have been published. Some are concerned only with particular aspects of the subject. Others are essentially literature surveys which are usually very comprehensive (though somewhat uncritical) and hence rather formidable to someone seeking an introduction to chromatography. The present book aims to present a short account of the techniques in current use.'

The new edition of *Chromatographic Methods* reflects the many changes that have occurred right across the field of chromatography. Development of new materials, for instance adsorbents and polymers, and advances in electronic instrumentation and computing techniques have radically changed the practice and implementation of the various chromatographic techniques.

The principles of chromatography remain the same however, and therefore several aspects of the earlier editions have been retained, but with a new emphasis. Thus, there is an updated but more condensed coverage of plane chromatography; an expanded chapter on gas chromatography to reflect the developments of the past ten years, particularly those advances in column and detector design; a new substantial chapter on high performance liquid chromatography, currently the most rapidly expanding analytical technique. Developments in spectroscopic instrumentation have enabled combination techniques such as GC–MS, GC–IR, HPLC–MS, HPLC–IR to increase in importance and these are discussed in Chapter 7.

The march of technology has included rapid developments in both analog and digital electronics, which is reflected in the changes in instrument design and capabilities. This includes control of instrument parameters and collection and processing of data. Chapter 8 presents an overview of the subject to assist the analyst's understanding and evaluation of modern instruments and data processing techniques. The final chapter comprises a considerably extended and modified series of experiments which reflect the current practice of chromatography.

The individual chapters have been written, in general, to be self-contained so that readers may dip into the text and pursue the study of particular topics without necessary reference outwith the particular chapter.

Although the chromatographic instrument capable of totally automated method development is now available in, for instance HPLC, there is no substitute for a sound understanding of the principles and practice of chromatography. The role of the chromatographer may have changed in recent years but his expertise is still a valuable essential in the analytical laboratory.

The authors gratefully acknowledge the help, advice and criticism from colleagues and particularly the preceding authors, R. Stock and C. B. Rice. Thanks are also due to the various manufacturers who have generously provided information and permission to use diagrams, etc, as noted in the text.

Finally we would like to acknowledge the patience and support shown by our wives during writing of the text, and particularly to May for preparation of the typescript.

A. BRAITHWAITE
F. J. SMITH
Trent Polytechnic

1 INTRODUCTION

1.1 INTRODUCTION TO CHROMATOGRAPHY

The first person to use the term chromatography was Tswett (1872–1919) the Russian chemist. He used chromatography, from the Greek for colour – chroma and write – graphein to describe his work on the separation of coloured plant pigments into bands on a column of chalk [1, 2]. It was not until the 1930s that chromatography in the form of thin-layer and ion-exchange chromatography became a regularly used technique. The 1940s saw the development of partition chromatography and paper chromatography with gas chromatography following in 1950. The 1960s saw a rapid rise in the routine use of chromatography as a universal technique, particularly in chemistry, biology and medicine. It is now used as a production process and yet is sensitive enough for trace analytical techniques.

Two Nobel prizes have been awarded to chromatographers, Tiselius (Sweden) in 1948 for his research on 'Electrophoresis and Adsorption Analysis', and Martin and Synge (UK) for the 'Invention of Partition Chromatography'. Recent developments and new technologies, such as microelectronics and microcomputers have enabled manufacturers to produce instruments that are reliable, with parameters that can be precisely set and measured, to give reproducible chromatograms.

Chromatography is a flexible yet powerful analytical procedure but remains a separation technique. However, the ideal instruments for complete analysis of complex mixtures are becoming more feasible with the coupling of rapid scanning spectroscopic instruments to chromatographs providing spectro-analytical information for each separated component.

1.1.1 Definition of chromatography
Tswett (1906) stated that: 'Chromatography is a method in which the compo-

nents of a mixture are separated on an adsorbent column in a flowing system'.

Recently the International Union of Pure and Applied Chemistry has defined chromatography as:

'A method used primarily for the separation of the components of a sample, in which the components are distributed between two phases, one of which is stationary while the other moves. The stationary phase may be a solid, or a liquid supported on a solid, or a gel. The stationary phase may be packed in a column, spread as a layer, or distributed as a film, etc.; in these definitions 'chromatographic bed' is used as a general term to denote any of the different forms in which the stationary phase may be used. The mobile phase may be gaseous or liquid.' [3].

1.2 HISTORICAL ASPECTS OF CHROMATOGRAPHY

Although chromatographic-like separation processes occur in nature – for example, migration of solutions through soils, clays and porous rocks – the value of such processes was not recognized until the 19th century. Runge (1850) developed methods for testing dyes and bleaches produced from coal tars used in dye chemistry [4]. He demonstrated the composition of dye colours by spotting the mixtures on to special paper producing colour separations. Examples of Runge's work are illustrated and discussed in a recent paper by Cramer [5]. Groppelsroder (1861) developed 'capillary analysis', a form of paper chromatography, using paper strips, with the ends dipping into an aqueous solution, to separate coloured materials in solution, but he was unable to explain the process [6]. It was to be 75 years before this work was followed up and paper chromatography as we know it developed [7, 8, 11].

Tswett's early papers are regarded as the first to describe the separation processes involved during the extensive studies on plant extracts and ligroin solutions using a range of over 100 adsorption media. More comprehensive descriptions are given in Tswett's own book, which was unfortunately only published in Russian.

The next major developments occurred in the 1930s when Lederer and co-workers (1931) separated lutein and zeaxanthine in carbon disulphide on a column of calcium carbonate powder and xanthophylls from egg yolk on a 7 cm diameter column [8, 9]. Further developments soon followed from Khun, Karrer and Ruzicka, who applied chromatography to their own fields of interest, the work being recognized by the award of the Nobel prize (1937, 1938, 1939 respectively). 'Flow Through Chromatography' rapidly gained acceptance and by the 1940s liquid adsorption column chromatography was an established laboratory separation technique on both preparative and analytical scales.

Tiselius (1940) and Claesson (1946) developed the classical procedures by observing the properties of solutions in the chromatographic process and classifying these into three groups, differing in the principle of the separation, *viz.* frontal analysis, displacement chromatography, elution chromatography [10]. Gradient elution was introduced at a later date (1952). Tiselius was awarded the Nobel Prize in 1948 for his contribution to chromatography. At about the same time Martin and Synge were developing a separation procedure for the isolation of acetylated amino acids from protein hydrolysates by extraction from an aqueous phase into a chloroform organic phase. A series of 40 extraction funnels were used in which the acetylated amino acids could be separated according to their distribution ratio and partition coefficients between a counter current of water and chloroform [11].

They soon replaced this with a chromatographic column filled with silica gel particles with water retained on the silica gel, and the chloroform flowing through the column. This system successfully separated the acetylated amino acids according to their partition coefficients and marked the beginning of partition chromatography. The silica gel was soon replaced by cellulose removing the need to derivatize the amino acids [12]. Martin and Synge were awarded the Nobel Prize in 1952 for this work.

Evidence of the importance of the technique was the method development work sponsored by the American Petroleum Institute for the analysis of constituents in petroleum products; for example, ASTM D-1319 (1954) details the procedure for the determination of saturates, alkenes and aromatics using a fluorescent indicator on silica gel adsorbent with isopropanol as eluent [13].

During the 1930s and 1940s chromatography progressed rapidly with several parallel developments of the earlier work which have resulted in the various chromatographic techniques we use today. A brief note on the historical developments of the main techniques is presented below.

Paper chromatography (PC)

This technique arose from the early work mentioned above with the developments due to Martin and co-workers [14]. Their work on partition column chromatography (*vide supra*) required an adsorbent that would hold water more efficiently than silica gel. This led to the use of cellulose, and hence filter paper as the 'column'. They were able to separate successfully over 20 amino acids by a two-dimensional technique using ninhydrin to locate the spots. The simplicity of paper chromatography ensured its rapid acceptance and reference texts were soon produced detailing organic and inorganic applications thus illustrating the importance of the new analytical technique [15, 16].

Thin layer chromatography (TLC)

TLC originated from the work of Izmailov and Shraiber (1938), who analysed pharmaceutical tinctures by spotting samples on to a thin layer of alumina adsorbent on a glass plate and applying spots of solvent to give circular chromatograms [17]. Later Meinhard and Hall (1949) used a starch binder with a mixture of celite and alumina on microscope slides, still obtaining circular chromatograms [18]. Kirchner *et al.* (1951) used an ascending development method analogous to paper chromatography [19]. It was, however the work of Stahl, and the development of standardized commercially available adsorbents that provided the impetus for the widespread use of TLC [20], as illustrated in his book, a reference text on TLC [21].

Ion exchange chromatography (IEC)

This technique came into prominence during the Second World War as a separation procedure for the rare earth and transuranium elements. The technique was first used by Taylor and Urey (1938) to separate lithium and potassium isotopes using zeolite resins [22], and Samuelson (1939) demonstrated the potential of synthetic resins [23]. A summary of developments that resulted from work on separation of the transuranium elements is described in Seaborg's book, based on the work he carried out with Thompson. Such texts assisted the general acceptance of the technique [24, 25].

Gel permeation chromatography (GPC)

GPC, sometimes called gel filtration, uses material with a controlled pore size as the stationary phase. The discovery by Flodin and Porath (1958) of a suitable cross-linked gel formed by reaction of dextran with epichlorohydrin provided the breakthrough [26]. Subsequently the commercial development of dextran and similar hydrophilic gels (e.g. agar), ensured rapid acceptance and application of GPC. Development of polystyrene and similar hydrophobic gels with their semi-rigid structure and wide range of pore sizes permitted organic solvents to be used [27]. Analysis by GPC of polymeric materials has revolutionized molecular weight analysis and preparative separation of high molecular weight synthetic polymers.

Affinity chromatography (AC)

This is a relatively recent development attributed to Porath *et al.* (1967) [28]. The stationary phase is a peptide or protein covalently bonded to a ligand such as a nucleic acid or an enzyme on an inert open matrix such as cellulose or agar and is used for the separation of protein molecules.

Gas chromatography (GC)

One of the most important techniques, GC evolved from earier work on the adsorption of gases on various materials which had been observed for many years, and the pioneering work of Martin on partition chromatography. Martin, with co-worker James, developed and refined this earlier work to develop gas–liquid chromatography (GLC), a technique that has revolutionized analytical chemistry. They used a gas (nitrogen) instead of a liquid mobile phase and stearic acid stationary phase on a celite support to separate C_2–C_4 fatty acids [29]. The apparatus for gas chromatography rapidly developed and by 1956 GLC was widely used as a routine analytical technique.

The theoretical aspects of chromatography were first studied by Wilson (1949), who discussed the quantitative aspects in terms of diffusion, rate of adsorption and isotherm non-linearity [30]. The first comprehensive mathematical treatment describing column performance (using the height equivalent to a theoretical plate HETP) in terms of stationary phase particle size and diffusion was presented by Glueckauf (1949) [31]. However, it was van Deemter and co-workers (1956) who developed the rate theory to describe the separation processes following on earlier work of Lapidus and Admunson (1952) [32]. Column efficiency was described as a function of mobile phase flow rate, diffusion properties and stationary phase particle size. It was many years before Giddings (1963) pointed out that if the efficiencies of gas chromatography were to be achieved in liquid chromatography, then particle sizes of 2–20 μm were required [33]. This would require high mobile phase inlet pressures. When such systems were demonstrated high column efficiencies were obtained and high performance (or pressure) liquid chromatography (HPLC) had arrived and was to have just as significant an effect on analytical chemistry as GC had a decade earlier.

There has been continuous development in chromatography, particularly techniques and practice, materials and refinement of instrumentation which has resulted in the efficient, reliable and sensitive chromatographic methods in use today and which form the backbone of modern analytical procedures and routine laboratory analysis.

1.3 CLASSIFICATION OF CHROMATOGRAPHIC METHODS

1.3.1 According to separation procedure

Chromatography encompasses a number of variations on the basic principle of the separation of components in a mixture achieved by a successive series of equilibrium stages. These equilibria depend on the partition or differential adsorption of the individual components between two phases; a mobile phase (MP) which moves over a stationary phase (SP) composed of small particles and therefore presenting a large surface area to the mobile phase. The sample mixture is introduced into the mobile phase and undergoes a series of partition or adsorption interactions between the mobile and stationary phases as it moves through the chromatographic system. The differences in physical and chemical properties of the individual components determine their relative affinity for the stationary phase and therefore the components will migrate through the system at differing rates. The least retarded component, having an equilibrium ratio which least favours the stationary phase, will be eluted first, i.e. moves fastest through the system. The most retarded component moves the slowest and is

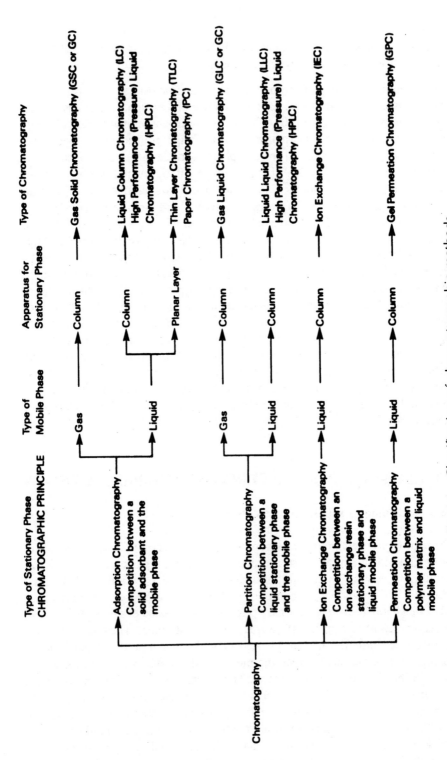

Fig. 1.1   Classification of chromatographic methods.

eluted last. A wide range of stationary and mobile phases can be used making it possible to separate components with only small differences in their properties.

The mobile phase can be a liquid or a gas and the stationary phase a liquid or a solid. Separation involving two immiscible liquid phases is referred to as partition or liquid–liquid (partition) chromatography and when physical surface forces govern the retention properties of the component on a solid stationary phase liquid–solid (adsorption) chromatography is involved; when the mobile phase is a gas we have gas–liquid chromatography (GLC) and gas–solid chromatography (GSC) respectively. The classification of chromatographic methods is shown in Fig. 1.1 and a simplified diagram of the apparatus of chromatography is shown in Fig. 1.2.

1.3.2 According to development procedure

Tiselius (1941) classified chromatography according to the separation principle, viz. elution development, displacement development and frontal analysis [10]. In

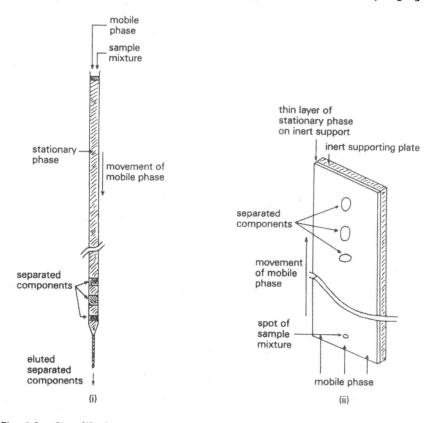

Fig. 1.2   Simplified apparatus for chromatography: (i) column chromatography; (ii) planar chromatography (tlc).

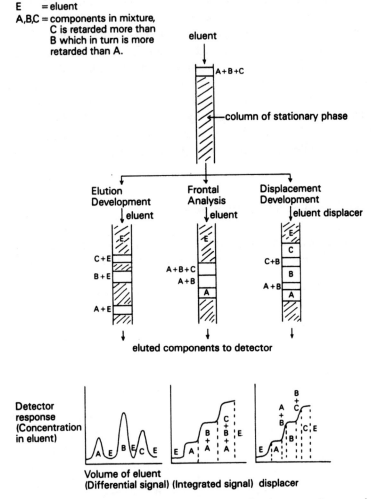

E   = eluent
A,B,C = components in mixture,
         C is retarded more than
         B which in turn is more
         retarded than A.

Fig. 1.3   Classification of chromatographic methods according to development procedure.

practice only elution and to a lesser extent, displacement development are commonly used (Fig. 1.3.).

Elution development

Elution development is the technique most widely used in the various methods of chromatography (GC, GLC, LLC and LSC). A small sample mixture is introduced on to the column and is eluted with a moblic phase which has a lesser affinity for the stationary phase than the sample components. The components therefore move along at a rate determined by their relative affinity for the stationary phase but at a slower rate than the eluent. The components are eluted in order of their affinities but their migration is determined by the ternary interaction between components, stationary phase and mobile phase. Since the components can be completely separated with a zone of mobile phase between them, elution chromatography is used for analytical separations, with some variation possible. In simple elution chromatography the column is eluted with the same solvent all the time. This is most suitable when the components have similar affinities for the stationary phase and are therefore eluted rapidly, one after another.

Stepwise elution is carried out by changing the eluent after a predetermined period of time. The eluents are chosen to have increasing eluting power, that is, increasing affinity of the mobile phase for the components remaining on the column, and therefore 'releasing' them from the stationary phase, enabling them to move through the system.

Gradient elution uses a gradual change in composition of the eluting solvent to achieve separation of components of widely varying affinities for the stationary phase. The ratio of two or more solvents is gradually changed to increase slowly the eluting power of the mobile phase. Thus the tailing part of a component zone or peak emerging from a column is eluted by a solvent of slightly higher eluting power than the leading part. This eluent gradient narrows the zones and reduces tailing. The solvent composition gradient may be linear, steadily increasing or decreasing, or logarithmic, and may be a concentration, pH, polarity or ionic strength gradient.

Displacement development

This consists of elution or development of the separation procedure by a solvent which has a greater affinity for the stationary phase than the sample components. The sample mixture is first introduced on to the column, and adheres to the stationary phase. Elution occurs when a displacing solvent is passed through the column, displacing the components on the stationary phase which also separate due to their varying partition or adsorption properties.

Generally displacement development does not produce completely separated components in bands separated by eluent. Between the zones of pure component there are adjacent zones containing mixtures and therefore the central parts are collected if preparative work is being carried out.

Frontal analysis

This consists of the continuous addition of a sample mixture on to the column. Initially the component with the least affinity for the stationary phase will pass along the column while a strongly adsorbed or attracted component builds up on the stationary phase at the beginning of the column. However, there is a limit to the capacity of the stationary phase and when this is exceeded this component also migrates along the column. Therefore the first component is eluted from the column, firstly in a pure form, then as a mixture with the next components to be eluted. This process can also occur with elution development if too much sample is placed on the column. Frontal analysis is clearly a preparative method primarily used for the separation of one readily eluted component from others with greater affinities.

REFERENCES

1. Tswett, M. S. (1906) *Ber. Dtsch. Bot. Ges.*, **24**, 316.
2. Tswett, M. S. (1906) *Ber. Dtsch. Bot. Ges.*, **24**, 384.
3. *Recommendations on Nomenclature for Chromatography, Rules Approved 1973*, IUPAC Analytical Chemistry Division Commission on Analytical Nomenclature, *Pure Appl. Chem.*, (1974) **37**, 447.
4. Runge, F. F. *Farbenchemie*, Vol. III, Berlin (1850).
5. Cramer, E. (1979) *J. High Res. Chrom. Comm.*, **2**, 7.
6. Goppelsroeder, F. (1861) *Verhandle. Naturforsch. Ges.* (Basel), **3**, 268.
7. Liesegang, R. E. (1943) *Z. Anal. Chem.*, **126**, 172.
8. L. S. Ettre and A. J. Zlatkis (eds) (1979), *75 Years of Chromatography – A Historical Dialog*, Chrom. Library, Vol. 17, Elsevier, Amsterdam.
9. Khun, R., Lederer, E. and Winterstein, A. (1931) *Z. Physiol. Chem.*, **197**, 141.
10. Tiselius, A. (1940) *Arkiv. Kemi. Mineral Geol.*, **14B**, 22, and Claesson S. (1946) *Arkiv. Kemi. Mineral Geol.*, **23A**, 1.
11. Martin, A. J. P. and Synge, R. L. M. (1941) *Biochem. J.*, **35**, 91.
12. Martin, A. J. P. and Synge, R. L. M. (1943) *Biochem. J.*, **37**, proc. xiii.
13. *Hydrocarbon Types in Liquid Petroleum Products by Fluorescent Indicator Techniques* (1954) American Society for Testing Materials. ASTM D-1319-77.
14. Consden, R., Gordon, A. H. and Martin, A. J. P. (1944) *Biochem. J.*, **38**, 224.
15. Lederer, M. (1948) *Anal. Chim. Acta*, **2**, 261.
16. Block, R. J., Strange, R. and Zweig, G. (1952) *Paper Chromatography, a Laboratory Manual*, Academic Press, New York; also *Chromatographic Methods for Inorganic Analysis with Special Reference to Paper Chromatography* (1953), Butterworths, London.
17. L. S. Ettre and A. J. Zlatkis (eds) (1979), *75 Years of Chromatography – A Historical Dialog*, Chrom. Library, Vol. 17, Elsevier, Amsterdam, pp. 413–417.
18. Meinhard, J. E. and Hall, N. F. (1949) *Anal. Chem.*, **21**, 185.
19. Kirchner, J. G., Miller, J. M. and Keller, G. T. (1951) *Anal. Chem.*, **23**, 420.
20. Stahl, E. (1956) *Pharmazie*, **11**, 633.
21. Stahl, E. (ed.) (1962) *Thin Layer Chromatography*, Academic Press, New York.
22. Taylor, T. I. and Urey, H. C. (1938) *J. Chem. Phys.*, **6**, 429.
23. Samuelson, O. (1939) *Z. Anal. Chem.*, **116**, 328.
24. Seaborg, G. T. (1968) *The Transuranium Elements*. In *Encyclopaedia of the Chemical Elements*, Reinhold, New York.
25. Salmon, J. E. and Hale, D. K. (1959) *Ion Exchange, a Laboratory Manual*, Academic Press, New York.
26. Flodin, P. and Porath, J. (1959) *Nature*, **183**, 1657; also Flodin, P. (1962) *Dextran Gels and their Application in Gel Filtration*, Pharmacia AB, Uppsala, Sweden.
27. Moore, J. C. (1964) *J. Polym. Sci.*, **A2**, 835.
28. Axen, R., Ernback, S. and Porath, J. (1967) *Nature*, **214**, 1302.
29. James, A. T. and Martin, A. J. P. (1952) *Biochem. J.*, **50**, 679.
30. Wilson, J. N. (1940) *J. Am. Chem. Soc.*, 1583.
31. Glueckauf, E. (1949) *Discuss. Faraday Soc.*, **7**, 12.
32. Lapidus, L. and Admunson, N. R. (1952) J. Phys. Chem., **56**, 984.
33. Giddings, J. C. (1963) *Anal. Chem.*, **35**, 2215.

2 THEORETICAL CONSIDERATIONS

Chromatography is a dynamic separation system consisting of two media, a stationary phase and a mobile phase. The stationary phase consists of small solid particles (usually less than 150 μm in diameter) with a microporous surface, which may be packed into a column or coated on to a plate. These particles are sometimes coated with an inert chemical agent to modify the surface properties. The mobile phase may be a gas or a liquid and serves to carry the sample component molecules through the chromatographic system. During this procedure the component or solute molecules in the mobile phase come into contact with the stationary phase. There is now competition between the two phases for the solute molecules which depends on their physical properties and affinity for the stationary phase. This process is termed partition with each component (A, B, C, etc) distributed between the stationary phase (s) and mobile phase (m) as they pass through the system. At any stage there is an equilibrium established with $[A_s]$ and $[A_m]$ the concentrations in the stationary and mobile phases respectively;

$$A_m \rightleftharpoons A_s$$

thus
$$D_A = [A_s]/[A_m]$$

where D_A is the distribution coefficient for component A. The larger the value of D the greater the affinity of the component for the stationary phase. Since D varies for different molecules the affinity will vary and so each component will proceed through the system at differing speeds as shown in Fig. 2.1(a), where $D_A < D_B < D_C$ (D_C has greater affinity for the stationary phase than D_B than D_A). The composition of the mobile phase as it emerges from the system, the eluent, is continually monitored by a detector, and the concentration of component molecules at any given time is plotted against time or volume of mobile phase to construct the chromatogram (Fig. 2.1(b)). Since the component molecules spread out during the separation, Gaussian peaks representing this spread are produced.

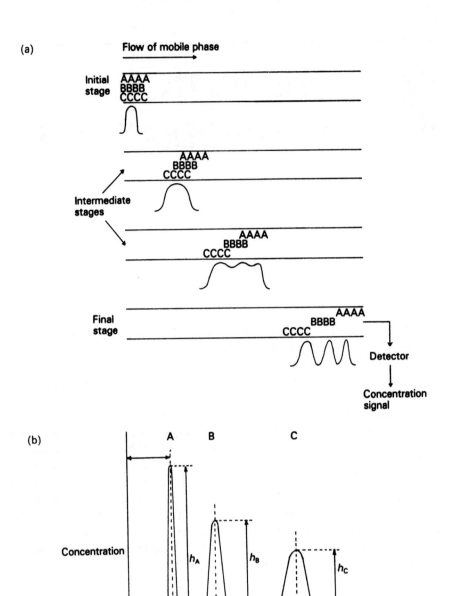

(Contd.)

t_0 = time for the solvent or mobile phase to pass through the system;
t_{RA} = retention time of component A, that is the time for A to pass through the system; V_A is the retention volume;
t_{RB} = retention time of B, V_B = retention volume;
t_{RC} = retention time of C, V_C = retention volume;
h = peak height, h_A for component A, h_B for B, h_C for C;
t_W = width at the base of a peak;
t_{W_x} = width of a peak at half height;
a and b are the width of the leading and trailing halves of a peak, used to determine asymmetry.

Fig. 2.1 (a) Separation of a three-component mixture ABC; (b) chromatogram, also used as Fig. 5.1.

Note that the longer the component takes to pass through the system the greater the spread, and hence C produces a broader peak than B than A.

2.1 FACTORS INFLUENCING RETENTION

The molecular interactions leading to the distribution of a component between the mobile phase and stationary phase are attributed to a combination of polar forces arising from induced and permanent electric fields and London's dispersion forces which are influenced by the relative molar masses of the solute and solvent [1]. Intermolecular forces predominate in chromatography with polar and dispersion forces having a major contribution to the overall interactions. The relative polarities of solvents are usually quoted as their dielectric constants.

Polar forces include dipole–dipole interactions and hydrogen bonding. Molecules that have permanent dipoles are more strongly attracted to like molecules than to non-polar ones. This leads to associations of molecules, and thus only components with similar dipoles will disperse in the solvent producing solute–solvent pairs. Dipole pairs in the liquid phase tend to orientate with mutual attraction. The average energy (E_{DD}) is dependent on the respective dipoles (μ) of the two molecules (A and B), the distance between centres (r) and is a function of temperature (T).

$$E_{DD} = -(2\mu_A^2 \mu_B^2 / r^6 \, K \, T)$$

A list of some dipole moments for common organic groups is given below.

There is in practice about a ten-fold range in dipole moments which corresponds to approximately a 10^4 range in dipole forces. It is this large range in the magnitude of dipole forces that gives rise to the selectivity of chromatographic separations.

Conversely non-polar solute molecules will not be attracted to polar solvent molecules but will disperse in a non-polar solvent. In addition to a single covalent bond hydrogen is able to form an associative or weaker bond with electron-rich molecules. Hydrogen bonding may occur via inter- or intramolecular

Dipole moments of some organic groups (Debye Units)

R–CH=CH$_2$	(alkene)	0.4
R–O–Me	(methyl ether)	1.3
R–NH$_2$	(amine)	1.4
R–OH	(alkanol)	1.7
R–COOH	(carboxylic acid)	1.7
R–Cl	(chloride)	1.8
R–COOMe	(methyl ester)	1.9
R–CHO	(aldehyde)	2.5
R–CO–R	(ketone)	2.7
R–CN	(nitrile)	3.6

association. The strength of the bond depends on stereochemistry, electronic effects of neighbouring atoms or groups and acid-base character. The solubility of a solute in water therefore depends on its ability to form H-bonds with the highly hydrogen-bonded water molecules. Hydrogen-bonded solvents in general will attract polar solute molecules but will exhibit varying degrees of repulsion to non-polar molecules. Thus in a chromatographic system the component or solute molecules will be attracted towards the phase of similar polarity.

Dispersion forces are the most universal intermolecular forces and therefore in non-polar solvents London's dispersion forces are the main interactions between molecules. They are produced as a result of dipoles formed between electrons and nuclei interacting on the polarizable electronic system of other atoms. They are approximately described as the attraction between induced phase coherent dipoles arising from zero point energy. Dispersion forces are relatively weak and therefore similar non-polar molecules are not repulsed, the net effect being a mixing of molecules. The London forces (E_L) are dependent on the ionization potentials (I), polarizability (α) and distance between centres (r) for a pair of atoms (A and B).

$$E_L = 3\alpha_A\alpha_B I_A I_B / 2r^6 (I_A + I_B)$$

Thus dispersion forces decrease very rapidly with increase in distance from the interacting centres. When extended to large complex organic molecules as encountered in chromatography the coherent dispersion forces must occur mainly at the surface of the molecule.

2.2 THEORY OF SEPARATIONS AND RETENTION CHARACTERISTICS

An optimized chromatographic separation is achieved by varying the mobile and stationary phase properties and operating parameters to give the required retention of the components in a sample. The overall partition and retention characteristics may be related to the thermodynamics and kinetics of the separation process. The volume of mobile phase required to carry the component solute molecules or band through the system to the detector is termed the retention volume (V_R) and is measured to the peak maxima (Fig. 2.1). It is frequently recorded as the retention time (t_R), the time taken by a solute band to move through the system. If the mobile flow rate is F_M then

$$V_R = t_R F_M$$

For a given chromatographic column of internal diameter (d), length L, the flow rate is given by:

$$F_M = (\pi d^2/4) \times \varepsilon$$

where ε is the total porosity of the column and is approximately 0.4 for solid packings and 0.8 for porous packings. The average linear velocity ($\bar{u}$) of the mobile phase is therefore:

$$\bar{u} = L/t_M = V_C \varepsilon/t_M$$

where V_C is the column or layer bed volume and t_M the transient time of the mobile phase. The volume involved is termed the dead volume (V_0) and includes contributions due to the injector and detector internal volumes.

The adjusted retention volume (V_R') and time (t_R') for a solute is therefore:

$$V_R' = V_R - V_0 \text{ and } t_R' = t_R - t_0$$

In gas chromatography the retention volumes must be corrected for the compressibility of the gaseous mobile phase due to the pressure differential along the column. A pressure gradient factor (j) must be used giving the net retention volume (V_N) for a given temperature and initial pressure as:

$$V_N = jV_R'$$

The observed retention characteristics for a solute depend on its distribution between the mobile and stationary phases and the relative affinity towards each. The relative amount of the solute in each phase is termed the partition ratio given by the partition coefficient K:

$$K = C_S/C_M$$

C_M = concentration in the mobile phase and C_S = concentration in the stationary phase.

The velocity of the centre of each band is determined by the partition coefficient. The total retention volume for a given solute is the volume of mobile phase (V_M) within the column and the volume of stationary phase (V_S) determined by the partition ratio, at the time of elution.

$$V_R = V_M + KV_S$$

or

$$V_R - V_M = KV_S$$

The volume of V_R may be obtained from the chromatogram by noting the flow rate of the mobile phase (F_M) and the retention time (t_R). Also, V_M the void volume (dead volume or interstitial volume of the column) is given by:

$$V_M = F_M t_0$$

where t_0 is the transient time of the mobile phase.

The relative retention (α) for two components A and B is determined by their respective partition characteristics, K_A and K_B, i.e.

$$\alpha = K_D/K_A = V_A/V_B$$

where V_A and V_B are the specific retention volumes. For a separation to occur α must be greater than unity. However values larger than 2 give analysis times which are rather too long for practical use. The capacity factor K' is a more practical quantity than K and can be determined from the chromatogram. It is proportional to V_S and V_m and is on indication of the increased retention volume or time for a given solute (V_R, t_R) relative to the transient volume or time of the mobile phase (V_0, t_0).

$$K' = (V_S/V_M)K \text{ and may be expressed as } K' = \frac{V_R - V_0}{V_0} \text{ or } \frac{t_R - t_0}{t_0} \text{ at constant flow}$$

2.3 COLUMN EFFICIENCY

Column efficiency describes the rate at which the solute molecules spread out as they travel through a column or across a TLC plate or paper. The rate at which they travel depends on their partition coefficients, and the resultant profile of the solute bands approximates to a normal Gaussian distribution profile or curve. The peak maxima represent the K' value of each component and approximate to the average rate of travel of the solute molecule. Small deviations from the peak maxima or mean value are due to the mass transfer or partitioning forces between the two phases, varying pathways through the column packing or thin layer material and diffusion processes. The solute bands therefore broaden and the concentration at peak maxima gradually decreases as they proceed through the column or along the plate or paper. Peak width (t_W) is therefore a measure of column efficiency and is reflected in the number of theoretical equilibrium steps that have occurred within the column. The column distance equivalent to each step or theoretical plate is termed the height equivalent to a theoretical plate (H) and is given by:

$$H = L/16(t_W/t_R')^2$$

where L is the column length, t_W the base width of the peak and t_R' the corrected retention time. The effective number of plates (N_{eff}) in the column is

$$N_{eff} = L/H = 16(t_R'/t_W)^2$$

It is frequently easier to measure the peak width at half height $(t_{w_{1/2}})$, thus:

$$N_{eff} = 5.54(t'_R/t_{w_{1/2}})^2$$

If no correction is made for transient time of the mobile phase, that is, retention time (t_R) is measured instead of t'_R, then N_{eff} becomes the number of theoretical plates, n

and

$$n = 5.54(t_R/t_{w_{1/2}})^2$$

$$N_{eff} = n(K'/1 + K')$$

N_{eff} is a more accurate measure of the separating power of a column, especially if capillary columns are being evaluated. Also, plate height H is the true measure of column efficiency since it determines the number of equilibrium steps and is independent of column length. The sharpness of a peak reflects the plate height.

2.4 BAND BROADENING

The work of Giddings et al. [2] has produced the generalized non-equilibrium theory of factors contributing to band spreading, thus enabling better chromatographic columns to be designed. The theory, sometimes called the Random Walk Theory, assumes the progress of molecules through a column as a succession of random stops and starts. The resulting dynamic non-equilibrium mass transfer of molecules in the stationary phase lags behind the mean equilibrium concentrations and in the mobile phase the molecules move more rapidly than the mean (Fig. 2.2). Dispersion and hence band broadening increases with the number of transfer steps and decreases as the flow rate of the mobile phase

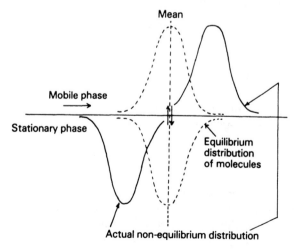

Fig. 2.2   Equilibrium process during separation.

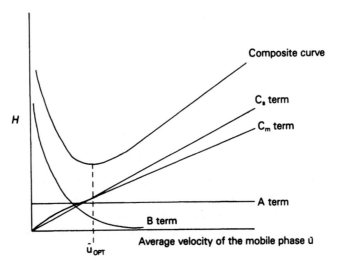

Fig. 2.3   Plot of the van Deemter equation showing the contributions of the various terms and the optimum velocity.

decreases. Dispersion is the result of four processes occurring as the solute band moves through the column or TLC plate. Step or plate height, H, is used to express in simple terms the net effect of the band broadening processes. The equation below is sometimes known as the van Deemter equation, relating plate height to diffusion and average linear velocity terms (Fig. 2.3).

$$H = A + (B/\bar{u}) + C_S \bar{u} + C_M \bar{u}$$

The average linear velocity $\bar{u}$ is used rather than flow rate since it is directly related to the speed of analysis, whereas flow rate depends on the internal volume of the column packing material.

$$\bar{u} = L/t_M$$

2.4.1 'Eddy' diffusion – A term

The A term describes the 'eddy' diffusion and relates to the variable, unequal pathways, hence path length, around the stationary phase particles or support material particles.

$$A = \lambda d$$

where d = mean particle diameter and λ is a constant reflecting the packing uniformity and column geometry. Molecules finding relatively easy pathways, including the more rapidly moving stream near the walls of the column, will elute first, whilst these following shorter more erratic paths will follow, leading to a spreading out of the solute band.

To prepare a good column the particles should be as small as practicable for uniform packing and acceptable pressure drop across the column. The A term is almost zero for open tubular GC columns.

2.4.2 Longitudinal diffusion – *B* term

The B term describes the band broadening due to longitudinal diffusion resulting from random motion of the molecules. It is related to the hindrance to the diffusion by the column packing, often termed the 'tortuousity or obstruction factor' (γ) and solute diffusion in the mobile phase (D_M).

$$B = 2\gamma D_M$$

The tortuousity factor for packed columns is approximately 0.6 and 1.0 for capillary columns. The contribution of the B term to the van Deemter equation is most important at low mobile-phase velocities. The B term is more important in gas chromatography than liquid chromatography since diffusion coefficients of solutes in gases are at least 10^4 greater than in liquids.

2.4.3 Mass transfer – *C* terms

The C terms describe the resistance to the mass transfer processes. C_S results from resistance to mass transfer at the solute–stationary phase interface. It is dependent on the diffusion coefficient of the solute in the stationary phase (D_S) and the effective film thickness of the stationary phase on the support particles ($d_{THICKNESS}$).

$$C_S = d_{THICKNESS}^2/D_S$$

Band broadening results from lower mass transfer rates and higher mobile phase velocities. Thinner stationary phase films produce higher mass transfer rates, but there is an accompanying decrease in solute capacity of the column. Fluid liquid stationary phases give acceptable D_S values, i.e. not too low.

The C_M term describes the resistance to radial mass transfer caused by the particles of packing material. It is related to the particle diameter ($d_{PACKING}$) and diffusion coefficient of the solute in the mobile phase (D_M).

$$C_M = d_{PACKING}^2/D_M$$

2.5 RESOLUTION

Resolution is the term used to describe the degree of separation of successive solute bands or peaks. For Gaussian peaks the separation is given by the ratio of the separation of the peak maxima to the broadness of the peaks, i.e. the mean peak widths.

$$R_S = (t_{RB} - t_{RA})/\tfrac{1}{2}(t_{WA} + t_{WB})$$

The separation is also dependent on the relative retention characteristics of the two components as defined by their respective partition ratios, α, often called the selectivity factor.

$$\alpha = K'_B/K'_A$$

Adjacent peaks which are unsatisfactorily resolved can be improved by increasing the separation of the peak or by reducing the width of the peaks, i.e. reducing band broadening. The former is accomplished by varying the mobile phase or stationary phase to give different relative partition characteristics, whilst the latter is achieved by using a more efficient column with more theoretical plates.

An alternative relationship for R is given by:

$$R_S = 1/4 N_{eff}^{1/2} [(\alpha - 1)/\alpha][\bar{K}'/(1 + \bar{K}')]$$

The equation has three parts: the α term is a measure of selectivity of the solute–stationary phase system for the component solutes; the $\bar{K}'$ term ($\bar{K}'$ is the mean of

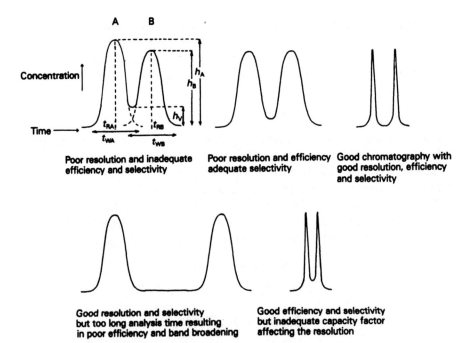

Fig. 2.4   Effects of efficiency, selectivity and partition ratios for a given pair of components.

K'_A and K'_B) which relates the rate of movement of the solutes through the column or TLC plate and N_{eff} which is a measure of column efficiency. Generally an increase in N_{eff}, α or $\bar{K}'$ will give better resolution. However, as K' increases so transit time for the solutes through the system increases, giving increased band broadening. In practice a good efficient column is used and then either the mobile phase or stationary phase is varied to achieve better resolution.

The criteria for resolving two peaks are difficult to quantify accurately. In general terms the peak separation should be greater than 4σ, i.e. greater than $2t_{w_{1/2}}$ apart with better than a 10% valley between peaks. The valley height is then less than 10% of the mean peak height for adjacent peaks (Fig. 2.4). A value for R of 1.0 corresponds to about 3–5% overlap of peaks whilst higher values of R represent progressively smaller overlaps. Values of $R >$ about 1.2 are desirable. Figure 2.4 summarizes the effects of selectivity, efficiency and partition ratios for a given pair of solutes.

A further factor affecting peak shape and hence resolution is related to the capacity of the stationary phase and sample size. Exceeding the sample capacity causes overloading and therefore results in unsymmetrical peak shapes, modification of retention times and loss of resolution. Sample capacity is defined as the amount of solute (in mg) per g of stationary phase and will depend on the surface area and available volume of stationary phase.

2.6 QUANTITATION IN CHROMATOGRAPHY

Data from chromatograms may be used to obtain the relative concentrations of components in a mixture, providing good resolution is achieved. Peak area, from integration of the detector signal during elution of a component, is proportional to concentration of that component. However, the response of detectors varies from one compound to another; for example, the HPLC UV detector depends on molar absorptivity and the GC electron capture detector depends on electron affinities. Thus a set of response factors needs to be determined for a particular analysis. These may be obtained by normalizing peak areas or by using an internal standard.

2.6.1 Normalizing for relative response factors

Relative response factors are obtained by repeated (11 +) analysis of a mixture containing equal (or known) amounts of all the components. One component is chosen as the reference and the relative responses of the other components are determined by dividing the peak areas by that of the reference component. The response factors may then be used to calculate corrected peak areas for other analyses involving these components and hence their ratios in the mixture may be determined.

Response factor for a component $R = \dfrac{A_{\text{COMPONENT}}}{A_{\text{REFERENCE}}}$

and the corrected peak area $A_{\text{CORRECT}} = R \times A_{\text{CHROM}}$

where A_{CHROM} is the area measurement from the chromatogram.

2.6.2 Internal standard

This method is a variation on the above, and is recommended for accurate quantitation. An additional compound is chosen as the reference standard for determination of the relative response factors, a known amount (usually the same amount) being added to all sample mixtures for analysis. An internal standard is found which has a retention time such that it is eluted in a suitable 'gap' in the chromatogram. The procedure involves analysing a test sample containing known amounts of each component plus a predetermined amount of the internal standard. Peak area is proportional to the amount of an eluted component and will also depend on the response factor (R). Therefore, for peak area A and concentration (C):

$$A = R \times C$$

For an individual component:

$$A_{\text{C}} = R_{\text{C}} \times C_{\text{C}}$$

For the internal standard:

$$A_{\text{IS}} = R_{\text{IS}} \times C_{\text{IS}}$$

The relative response of a component (R_{R}) to the internal standard is therefore:

$$R_{\text{R}} = A_{\text{C}}/A_{\text{IS}} = (R_{\text{C}} \times C_{\text{C}})/(R_{\text{IS}} \times C_{\text{IS}})$$

Response factors for all components are calculated in the same way. Analysis of an unkown mixture is achieved by adding an accurately known amount of the internal standard and then running the chromatogram. All peak areas are recorded and the concentration of each component calculated using the equation above rearranged to give:

$$C_{\text{C}} = (A_{\text{C}} \times C_{\text{IS}})/(A_{\text{IS}} \times R_{\text{C}})$$

The precision of the analysis is not dependent on the injection of an accurately known amount of sample, but accuracy does depend on accurate measurement of peak areas. This is not a problem with electronic integrators.

2.6.3 Standard addition

Standard addition is used in many techniques in analytical chemistry. It is of limited use in chromatography because of the difficulty of injecting accurately known amounts of sample. A sample mixture is analysed for the component of interest, using a known sample quantity. A specified amount of this component is then added to the sample thus increasing its concentration. The analysis is then repeated and the resulting increase in peak area due to addition of the standard amount is noted. Hence, the concentration of the component originally in the sample may be calculated.

If the peak area for the first analysis is A_1 and with the standard addition of x mg is A_2 then the peak area corresponding to x mg is $(A_2 - A_1)$. Thus the original concentration of the component in the sample is given by:

$$C = (x \times A_1/A_2 - A_1)$$

Allowance for any dilution due to addition of the standard amount has to be made unless it is negligible. The main difficulty with this method concerns the reproducibility of the sample injection. A precision of better than $\pm 1\%$ should be achieved if valid quantitative results are to be obtained. This precision is possible in HPLC using sample loops. If syringe injections are used then up to 11 or more samples should be injected to define the overall precision by calculating the standard deviation and covariance.

REFERENCES

1. Littlewood, A. B. (1970) *Gas Chromatography*, Academic Press, New York, Chapter 3, pp. 71–85.
2. Giddings, J. C. (1965) *Dynamics of Chromatography*, Part 1, Principles and Theory, Marcel Dekker, New York.

3 PLANE CHROMATOGRAPHY

3.1 THIN-LAYER CHROMATOGRAPHY (TLC)

The idea and fundamentals of using a chromatographic adsorbent in the form of a thin layer fixed on an inert rigid support seem to have been suggested by Izmailov and Shraiber in 1938 [1]. Meinhard and Hall [2] in 1949 developed this notion of an 'open column', and in 1951 Kirchner, Miller and Keller [3] reported the separation of terpenes on a 'chromatostrip', prepared by coating a small glass strip with an adsorbent mixed with starch or plaster of Paris, which acted as a binder.

Several years passed before the method became widely used, probably because at that time the development of paper and gas chromatography was proceeding rapidly. In the late 1950s, however, Stahl [4(a), (b)] devised convenient methods of preparing plates, and showed that thin-layer chromatography could be applied to a wide variety of separations. He introduced a measure of standardization, and since the publication of his work and the appearance of commercial apparatus based on his designs, TLC has been accepted as a reproducible analytical technique. As usually happens, once the initial stimulus had been given, many variations of the original procedures were proposed, and though TLC has been applied predominantly in the adsorption mode it has been employed using other sorption processes, such as partition and ion exchange. In fact, TLC is now regarded as an indispensable tool in both quality control and research laboratories. The apparatus required is relatively inexpensive and the technique is easy to learn and is fast and versatile.

3.1.1 Outline of the method

In thin-layer chromatography a solution of the sample in a volatile solvent is applied *via* a pipette to the bottom of a uniform layer of inert adsorbent, such as silica or alumina, which has been uniformly spread over a suitable supporting plate of a material such as glass or plastic and dried under standard conditions. When the spot has dried the plate is placed vertically in a suitable tank with its lower edge immersed in the selected mobile phase. The solvent rises by capillary action and an ascending chromatographic separation is thus obtained, resolving the sample mixture into discrete spots. At the end of the run the solvent is allowed to evaporate from the plate and the separated spots are located and identified either by physical methods such as sight, fluorescence or radiation monitoring, or by treating chemically with a developing reagent: the method chosen is dictated by the composition of the starting mixtures.

In its simplest form a TLC plate can be prepared in the laboratory, placed in any suitably sized container and the resultant chromatogram scanned visually. At its most sophisticated there is a large variety of plates, sample application aids, developing chambers, visualization aids [5] and adsorbents commercially available. TLC can be an excellent qualitative and quantitative method. The practical techniques required have much in common with those employed in paper chromatography and more detailed descriptions will follow.

3.1.2 Comparison of thin-layer with other forms of chromatography

To assess the relative value of the thin-layer method, it is necessary to compare it first with adsorption column chromatography, because the same sorption system is being used in both cases, and second with paper partition chromatography, because the same experimental techniques are used in both. Conventional column chromatography is a fairly slow process which requires large amounts of adsorbent and sample. The major disadvantages of the technique are with speed, scale and characterization.

In recent years the method of choice for the rapid analysis of complex samples has been the analytical technique of HPLC (see Chapter 6), though the necessary instrumentation is expensive. However, despite this trend, TLC has a number of advantages.

(a) Simultaneous analysis of multiple standards and samples can be carried out under identical conditions in a time comparable to HPLC.
(b) Strongly retained compounds in comparison to HPLC form the most compact chromatographic zones and therefore can be detected with the highest sensitivity; in addition the bands can be removed and purified.
(c) All components can be located, unlike in HPLC, where highly polar materials may be overlooked as the peaks are very broad and difficult to discern.

In thin-layer chromatography only small amounts of adsorbent and minute samples are needed. The separated spots are located on the plate using a variety of visualization techniques in common with paper chromatography, so that normally no collection of fractions is necessary. There is, however, no difficulty about preparative separations which are achieved by increasing the thickness of the layer and using a higher loading of sample. After separation, it is easy to recover an individual substance by scraping off and collecting the part of the layer on which it is adsorbed. The substance can then be extracted with a suitable solvent.

Compared with paper chromatography, the main advantages of the thin-layer method are greater speed, and in most cases, better resolution. The average time for a 10 cm run in thin-layer chromatography on silica gel is 20–30 minutes (depending on the nature of the mobile phase), whereas the same separation on a fast paper might take two hours. Rough qualitative separations on small plates may take as little as five minutes. The better resolution arises from the fact that the adsorbent in thin-layer chromatography has a higher capacity than the paper in paper chromatography and the particle size of the adsorbent layer materials is very small compared to the large cellulose fibres from which the paper matrix is formed. The separated spots therefore retain fairly closely the shape and size of the original applied spot, without the spreading associated with partition chromatography on paper. This advantage is largely lost when a partition system is used on a thin layer. A further, and very important, advantage of the adsorption system is that it can be used to separate hydrophobic substances, such as lipids and hydrocarbons, which are difficult to deal with on paper, even with a reversed-phase system. Thin-layer separations have been applied, however, in most fields of organic, and some of inorganic chemistry. Location of separated substances on thin layers is done in the same way as it is on paper, but more reactive reagents, for example concentrated sulphuric acid, can be applied on thin layers, provided that the thin-layer material is an inert substance such as silica gel or alumina.

3.1.3 Adsorbents

The general properties of adsorbents for thin-layer chromatography should be similar to those described for adsorbents used in columns, and the same arguments about 'activity' apply. Two important properties of the adsorbent are its particle size and its homogeneity, because adhesion to the support plate largely depends on them. A particle size of 1–25 μm is usually recommended. A coarse-grained material will not produce a satisfactory thin layer, and one of the reasons for the greatly enhanced resolution of thin-layer chromatography is this use of a fine-grained adsorbent. Whereas in a column a very fine material will give an unacceptably slow flow rate, on a thin layer the fine grain gives a faster and more even solvent flow. Some examples of adsorbents which have been used for representative separations by thin-layer chromatography are given in Table 3.1.

Silica gel

Silica gel is the most commonly used adsorbent in TLC studies. It is prepared [44] by the hydrolysis of sodium silicate to polysilicic acid which on further

Table 3.1   Adsorbents for thin-layer chromatography

Solid	Used to separate
Silica gel	Amino-acids [4 a, b], alkaloids [6], sugars [7], fatty acids [8,9], lipids [10], essential oils [11], inorganic anions and cations [12], steroids [13,14], terpenoids [15]
Alumina	Alkaloids [6], food dyes [16], phenols [17], steroids [14, 18], vitamins [19], carotenes [20], amino-acids [59]
Kieselguhr	Sugars [7], oligosaccharides [21], dibasic acids [22], fatty acids [23], triglycerides [24], amino-acids [25], steroids [26]
Celite	Steroids [27] inorganic cations [12]
Cellulose powder	Amino-acids [28, 29], food dyes [30], alkaloids [31], nucleotides [32]
Ion-exchange cellulose	Nucleotides [33], halide ions [34]
Starch	Amino-acids [35]
Polyamide powder	Anthocyanins [36], aromatic acids [36], antioxidants [37], flavonoids [38], proteins [39]
Sephadex	nucleotides [40], proteins [41,42], metal complexes [43]

condensation and polymerization yields silica gel material. The synthesis can be controlled so as to yield silicas of high purity and of the required specification with regard to pore volume, pore size and specific surface area. A binder is commonly added to the silica gel to confer greater mechanical strength to the layer and to enhance adhesion to the backing plate. The suffix G is used universally to denote silica gel with a gypsum binder, namely calcium sulphate hemi-hydrate $(CaSO_4(0.5H_2O))$. The presence of calcium ion does not affect most separations, however, there are available silica gels which adhere sufficiently without the use of a binder. Another binder which has found a limited use is starch, though it places restrictions on the use of corrosive location agents. The binder is present at about 10% w/w. The resolution and separating efficiency achieved are dependent, as in other forms of chromatography, upon particle size and particle size distribution. The resolution improves as particle size becomes smaller and particle-size distribution narrower. The trend towards smaller and more uniform particles continues and the silica gel now commonly in use for TLC studies has a mean particle size of 15 μm with a particle size range of 5–40 μm. Commercially available precoated plates have a mean particle size of 10 μm with a correspondingly narrower particle size range, wth thinner layers of 250 μm for increased speed and resolution. The newer technique of high-performance TLC (HPTLC) uses silica gel with a particle size of 5–6 μm.

Plates are available with a fluorescent indicator commonly a phosphor, which emits a green fluoresence when irradiated with UV light (Hg lamp) of 254 nm. The absorbing substances appear as dark spots against the green fluorescent background due to quenching of the fluoresence. It is also possible to modify the adsorption properties of the silica gel by incorporating substances such as bases or buffers enabling coatings with accurately defined pH to be prepared. Similarly silver nitrate can be added; this admixture changes the adsorptive properties to permit increased discrimination and separation of unsaturated compounds, especially alkenes. The technique is commonly known as 'Argentation TLC'.

The sorption mechanism predominant on silica gel is adsorption and the plates with suitable choice of eluent can be used to separate neutral, basic and acidic hydrophilic substances. The silica gel can be further modified to afford reverse-phase chromatography. Reverse-phase plates have a long chain hydrocarbon impregnated into the support giving packings of defined composition and uniform coverage which behave similarly to octadecylsilane (ODS) modified silica (Chapter 6). These materials are of use for the analysis of lipophilic substances, fats and waxes, steroids and fat-soluble vitamins and dyes. However, simple impregnation of the silica gel support with the stationary phase liquid is unsatisfactory as it can be washed off which consequently lowers the capacity and effectiveness of the partition separation. As in HPLC these failings have been largely overcome by chemically bonding the stationary phase to the support.

The synthesis of TLC reverse-phase sorbents uses procedures similar to those employed for HPLC packings. Plates coated with C_2, C_8 and C_{18} are commercially available and have shown good correlation with their HPLC column counterparts [45].

Silanised silica gel

This material is prepared by treating silica gel with a silanising agent, for instance dimethyldichlorosilane. The silanol groups of the silica gel are mainly transformed to dimethylsilyl groups with little adsorptive capacity.

This silanised material can be used to advantage as a lipophilic stationary phase in reverse-phase chromatography. The principal advantage of these materials compared with those formed by impregnations of adsorbent with other organic materials, are the uniform and defined degree of hydrophobation and the chemical bonding of the silanising agent to the silica gel. The range of applications is similar to those enumerated above.

Kieselguhr (celite)

Kieselguhr and celite are diatomaceous earths composed of the silica-rich fossilized skeletal remains of microscopic sea organisms. The material exhibits

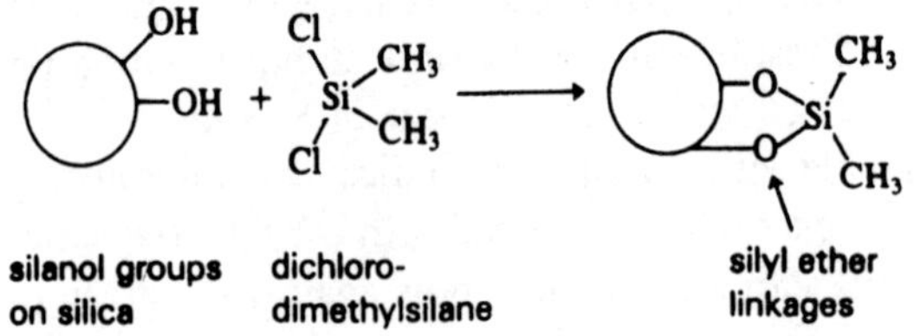

Fig. 3.1   Preparation of silanised silica gel.

very little adsorptive property and for this reason is used primarily as a support for the stationary phase in partition chromatography. The adsorptive capacity can be further reduced by treatment with acids or alkali or by silanising.

Celite when mixed with clay forms firebrick which can subsequently be crushed and sieve-graded. The firebrick has good flow and packing characteristics with an increased adsorptive capacity.

Alumina

Alumina (aluminium oxide) can be synthesized to the same degree of purity and specification as silica gel by a series of non-uniform dehydration processes on various crystalline modifications of aluminium hydroxide [46]. Furthermore the reaction conditions can be adjusted to produce aluminium oxide with a surface either acidic, basic or neutral; it can be used with or without a binder and the use in the latter form is more common than with silica. Alumina is a strong adsorber and can function as an amphoteric ion exchanger depending upon the nature of the surface and the solvent; for instance, basic aluminium oxide when used with organic eluants will adsorb aromatic and unsaturated hydrocarbons, carotenoids, steroids, alkaloids, and other natural products. In aqueous or aqueous-alcoholic solutions its exchanger properties become more pronounced and it can adsorb basic dyes, basic amino acids as well as inorganic cations. Neutral aluminium oxide is principally employed with organic eluants and is suitable for use with substances that are either labile or bound to strong alkalis. Acidic aluminium oxide is used for the separation of neutral or acid materials which are not acid-labile. In aqueous and alcoholic media it serves as an anion exchanger.

Cellulose powders

At first it may seem unnecessary to go to the trouble of preparing cellulose powder plates when paper could be used more conveniently, but there are important advantages for the thin-layer method. In paper the cellulose is fibrous, and the fibres, however closely they are matted together, inevitably form a network with large gaps. The solvents flow along the surface of the fibres, and the gaps become filled with liquid, with the result that excessive diffusion of solutes takes place, and the separated zones tend to be larger than the original spot. If the fibres are too tightly compressed the flow rate becomes unacceptably slow. Layers of cellulose powder, on the other hand, are aggregations of very small particles, all of much the same size. The interstices are therefore much smaller and more regular, and the adsorbent surfaces are more evenly distributed. In consequence there is a much more even flow of mobile phase, with less diffusion of the dissolved substances. The flow is also much faster.

Cellulose contains adsorbed water which is held in the glucopyranose structure by hydrogen bonding, and hence the separation proceeds via a partition mechanism [47]. Cellulose materials are used almost exclusively for separating hydrophilic substances, for instance, amino acids and sugars. Similar eluants to those used for the paper chromatography application, can be selected.

Diethylaminoethyl (DEAE)-cellulose carries positive charges at neutral and acidic pH. It is commonly employed for separation of negatively charged molecules by ion exchange chromatography. Due to the hydrophilic nature of the cellulose substrate, DEAE-cellulose is particularly well suited to ion-exchange separations of delicate biomolecules such as proteins and nucleic acids.

Modified cellulose powders can be used to obtain ion-exchange separations of thin layers, with similar advantages over column or paper sheet methods. Both normal and modified cellulose powders can be used without binder.

Molecular sieve layers

Thin layers on glass plates can be made from Sephadex gel chromatography media, with a superfine grade having a particle size 10–40 μm. The layers range in thickness from 0.4 to 1.00 mm. Chromatography with these layers is rather slower and more troublesome than other forms of TLC, but it may be faster and more convienient than gel chromatography in a column. Separation is achieved by partition augmented by size exclusion in the solvent-filled pores of the swollen gel.

PEI-cellulose

The chromatographic layer is formed by impregnating the 'support', microcrystalline cellulose, with polyethyleneimine (PEI). The latter is prepared by the co-polymerization of aziridine in the presence of an acid catalyst and the resultant product is highly branched and has primary, secondary and tertiary amino groups [48]. The PEI-cellulose behaves as a strong anion exchanger with high capacity and is of considerable utility in the analysis of nucleotides, nucleosides, nucleobases and sugar phosphates. The layers can be obtained with the common fluorescent indicators and should be stored at 0–5°C to prevent (minimize) deterioration.

Polyamide layers

A number of polyamides, for instance, polycaprolactam and Nylon 6.6 (poly-hexamethylenediaminoadipate) can be coated on to plates in the conventional manner to give a chromatographic material [49]. These materials are particularly useful for the separation of closely related phenols which interact with the chromatographic layer by hydrogen bonding. These bonds are weak and reversible and the adsorbed solutes can be displaced by elution with solvents capable of H-bonding. The desorptive power of commonly used solvents is of the order: dimethylformamide > formamide > acetone > methanol > water.

All the materials so far mentioned can be used for adsorption chromatography, but some of them, such as silica gel, celite, kieselguhr and cellulose, can be used for thin-layer partition chromatography (as they can be used for partition chromatography in columns), if an appropriate mobile phase is selected. If the plate is dried so that it retains very little adsorbed water, and the mobile phase is a non-polar mixture, separation will be by adsorption chromatography. If, however, the plate retains an appreciable amount of water, or the solvent mixture contains a highly polar constituent, separation will be largely by partition chromatography.

3.1.4 Preparation of plates

The adsorbent is spread on a suitable firm support, which may be quite rigid, or flexible. Glass plates were the original support; however, flexible plates have become increasingly popular. The size used depends on the type of separation to be carried out and on the type of chromatographic tank and spreading apparatus available. Most of the commercial apparatus is designed for plates of 20 × 5 or 20 × 20 cm, and those are now regarded as 'standard'. It is important that the surface of the plate is flat, and without irregularities or blemishes. Glass plates are cleaned thoroughly before use, washed with water and a detergent, drained and dried. A final wash with acetone may be included, but it is not essential. It is important not to touch the surface of the cleaned plates with the fingers. The first step is to make the adsorbent into a slurry with water, usually in the proportion 1:2, for example 10 g of adsorbent to 20 cm³ of water. The slurry is thoroughly stirred, and spread on the plate by one of the methods described below. If a binder is used, the time available from mixing the slurry to completion of spreading is about four minutes (after which setting will have begun). The properties of the adsorbent can be modified by using buffer solutions instead of water, to give a layer of desired acidity, or to modify the water-retaining properties of the layer. Similarly, complexing agents or fluorescent indicators can be incorporated in the layer by mixing the slurry with solutions of the appropriate substances. An important example is the use of silver nitrate in the separation of lipids and related materials.

The film thickness is a most important factor in thin-layer chromatography. The 'standard' thickness is 250 μm, and there is little to be gained by departing very much from that in analytical separations (thinner layers may give rise to erratic R_f values) [50]. Thicker layers (0.5 to 2.0 mm) are used for preparative separations, with a loading of up to 250 mg on a 20 × 20 cm plate.

There are in principle four ways of applying the thin layer to its support: spreading, pouring, spraying and dipping.

Spreading

It is possible to spread the adsorbent in a number of ways, but the main objective is to produce an absolutely even layer with no lumps or gaps, which adheres evenly and securely to the support. Commercial spreaders are in general of two types, the 'moving spreader' and the 'moving plate'. The difference is shown diagramatically in Fig. 3.2. Both types are made in varying degrees of sophistication (and cost), and since each maker supplies detailed instructions for the use of

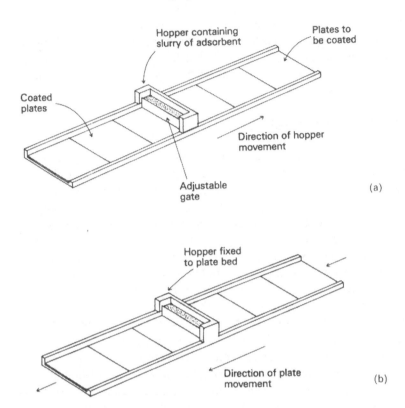

Fig. 3.2 Commercial plate spreaders: (a) moving spreader apparatus; (b) moving plate type.

his equipment, only the general principles are mentioned here.

In the 'moving spreader' type, the glass plates (usually five of size 20 × 20 cm, or an equivalent number of smaller size) are held in a flat frame, and a rectangular hopper containing the slurry is passed over them. The hopper has no bottom (or the bottom can be opened when required), and its trailing face has an accurately machined lower edge to give an even layer of the required thickness. In some appliances the thickness is adjustable. The lower edge of the leading face of the hopper rests on the glass plates. In the moving plate apparatus the hopper containing the slurry is fixed and the plates are pushed through under the hopper as indicated.

Makers have produced spreading 'beds' in which the long sides have an overhanging lip (Fig. 3.3). The plates are pushed from below against the lip, by means of spring strips, or by an inflatable air-bag, so that the upper surfaces of the plates are at the same level, regardless of their thickness. A foam-rubber base on which the plates are laid has also been suggested (van Damm and Maas [51]) as another way of getting an even spreading surface. With a little practice the 'moving spreader' method is a very satisfactory way of making thin-layer plates.

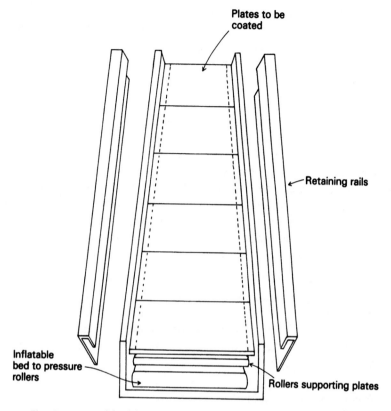

Fig. 3.3   Modified bed for moving spreader apparatus.

Pouring

Many workers prefer not to use mechanical spreading methods at all. If the adsorbent is very finely divided and of homogeneous particle size, and if no binder is used, a slurry can be poured on a plate and allowed to flow over it so that it is evenly covered. Some manual dexterity is required to do this properly. Preparation of plates by pouring is particularly easy with certain types of alumina, but water alone is not usually suitable for making the slurry; a volatile liquid such as ethanol (or an ethanol–water mixture) or ethyl acetate is preferable. The appropriate amounts of liquid and solid adsorbent needed to cover a plate have to be found by trial and error, and exactly those quantities should be used to ensure that the thickness of the layer is reproducible. Good, even plates can be made by this method, but the thickness of the layer is not known.

Spraying

Descriptions or details of methods of making plates by spraying with a slurry of adsorbent have been published (for example, by Bekersky [52], and by Morita and Harata [53]). The methods do not seem to have any particular advantage over spreading, and are open to the objections usually associated with spraying, among which are the difficulty of getting even coverage, and the fact that there is no easy way of ensuring reproducible thickness from batch to batch.

Dipping

Small plates, such as microscope slides, can be spread by dipping in a slurry of the adsorbent in chloroform, or other volatile liquid. Again, the exact thickness of the layer is not known and the evenness of the layer may not be very good, but this is a most convenient method for making a number of plates for rapid qualitative separations. After spreading, the plate is allowed to dry for 5–10 minutes, and, if it has been made with an aqueous slurry, is further dried and 'activated' by heating at about 100° C for 30 minutes. Plates made with volatile organic liquids may not need this further drying. It is important to standardize this part of the preparation of plates, because the activity of the adsorbent may depend rather critically on it.

Plates may be kept for short periods in a desiccator, but long storage is not recommended. When inspected for imperfections before use, they should appear uniform in density when viewed by transmitted or reflected light, and there should be no visible large particles. Gentle stroking with the finger should not remove the layer, and there should be no loose particles on the surface.

3.1.5 Application of samples

Samples must be applied to thin layers with extreme care and minimal disturbance of the adsorbent layer. Normally samples are applied *via* a capillary tube or a micropipette so that the emerging drop just touches the surface of the plate with the appliance tip remaining just above the sorbent layer. A hole in the sorbent causes an obstruction to even solvent flow, with distortion of the moving spots culminating in a loss of resolution.

Spots should not be nearer than 1 cm centre to centre; they should be 2–5 mm in diameter and should not be nearer to the edge of the plate than 1.5 cm on a 20 × 20 cm plate. A volume of 0.1–0.5 mm^3 should be applied, and if a larger volume of the sample solution is needed to give the required loading, it should be applied in portions. TLC is a microanalytical method and the loading should not be more than about 12 μg per spot on a layer 250 μm thick, 10 μg being the optimum amount for most substances.

In semi-preparative work the sample is often applied as a streak along the start line; up to about 4 mg may thus be loaded on a 20 × 20 cm plate 250 μm thick. Mechanical devices can be obtained for use in conjunction with a syringe to give rapid and even streaking. A line can be drawn across the plate with a sharp pencil. The pencil removes a fine line of adsorbent down to the glass.

The solvent flow is forced to stop when the front reaches the line, a useful feature which enables conditions to be standardized very easily. The plate should not, however, be left standing in the tank for a long time after the front has reached the stop line, as diffusion and evaporation may cause spreading of the separated spots. The edges of the plate should be rubbed clear with a finger before spotting to a width of about 0.5 cm, to give a sharper edge to the adsorbent layer.

The solvent in which the sample is dissolved for spotting should be as volatile as possible, and also have as low a polarity as possible. If the spotting solvent is strongly adsorbed by the layer, marked irregularities may be observed as the mobile phase passes the position of the spots, and the separated spots may be seriously distorted.

3.1.6 R_f values

The property of a component which determines the distance it moves on elution is its distribution coefficient (D_x). Distribution coefficients, however, are difficult to evaluate, certainly on routine analysis, and a more practical evaluation of the

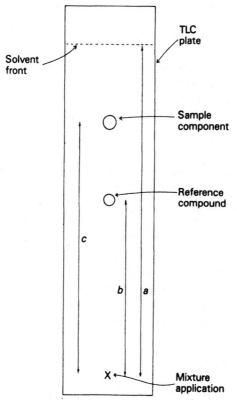

Fig. 3.4   Determination of R_f and R_{st} from TLC chromatoplate.

chromatogram is required. In TLC and paper chromatography the results obtained are described by quoting the R_f values. An R_f value is defined as:

$$R_f = \text{distance moved by solute/distance moved by solvent front}$$

R_f stands for relative to (solvent) front and was shown by Martin and Synge [54] to be related to the distribution coefficient of the component.

While the R_f value is not an absolute physical value for a component, it can aid identification with careful control of conditions. Due to the large number of variables, however, which can influence the R_f value – for instance, minute differences in solvent composition, temperature, size of tank, the sorbent layer and the nature of the mixture – coincidence of R_f values, even in more than one solvent system, should never be taken as unequivocal proof of the structure of a component.

An alternative approach which minimizes differences in R_f values due to the influence of the variables enumerated above, is to quote the R_f value relative to a carefully chosen standard which is run on the same plate. This relative value, R_x or R_{st}, should be constant since under any given conditions the relative R_f values remain the same.

$$R_{st} = \text{distance to centre of component spot/distance to centre of standard spot}$$

As with the R_f value, however, coincidence of R_{st} values should not be taken as absolute proof of identification and for complete structural characterization the component should be eluted from the sorbent layer and spectroanalytical studies, such as infrared ultraviolet, nuclear magnetic resonance (^{13}C and ^1H) and mass spectroscopy carried out to aid identification.

3.1.7 Documentation

It is obvious from the above discussion that in any description of a chromato-graphic procedure the fullest possible details should be presented. Not only are R_f values important, but the shape and colour of spots give valuable information also. A minimum record of the chromatogram would be to sketch the chromatoplate and annotate the diagram fully, for instance, colour of spots, locating reagent, solvent used, etc. Alternatively, the pre-prepared plastic-coated plates may themselves be retained and detail entered on the plate in pencil or with a suitable marker. The most successful method is to photograph the plate and commercial apparatus is available. The procedures for photographic document-ation of thin-layer chromatograms have been reviewed by Scholtz [55].

3.1.8 Development

Once the chromatographic plate has been prepared and the samples have been applied to it, it is placed in a suitable chamber with the lower edge immersed in the eluant to a depth of 0.5–1.0 cm. A suitable solvent should give R_f values of between 0.3 and 0.7 for the sample components of analytical interest.

The purpose of allowing equilibration time is to achieve homogeneity of the atmosphere in the tank, thus minimizing evaporation of the solvent from the TLC plate during development. It has been shown that equilibration is more important in thin-layer than in paper chromatography, and therefore it is important to keep the atmosphere in the tank saturated with solvent vapour. Saturation can be assisted by lining the walls with filter paper soaked in solvent. With these precautions, however, it is not usually necessary to allow any 'equilibration time' before the start of the chromatographic run. The size of the tank and the actual volume of a mixed solvent used have an effect on R_f values, because these two factors control the composition of the vapour in the tank. The smallest tank possible should be used, so that the enclosed atmosphere has the smallest possible volume. This in turn controls the rates of evaporation of solvent from the plate during the run. Standardization of the geometrical parameters of the plate is desirable; for instance, length of run, distance of the start line from the solvent surface (or position of solvent feed), and positions of initial spots, should be kept constant. An indication that the atmosphere in the tank is not saturated with vapour, when a mixed solvent is being used, is the development of a concave solvent front (the mobile phase advancing faster at the edges than in the middle). This condition should be avoided.

It is not essential to use a tank at all. A sandwich can be made consisting of a second glass plate clamped firmly over the sorbent surface (Fig. 3.5). This

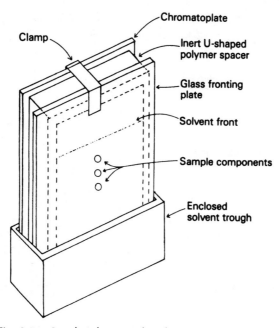

Fig. 3.5   Sandwich-type development apparatus.

sandwich can then be placed in a normal development chamber or into a special trough designed to prevent solvent loss.

Regardless of the procedure used it must be documented in its entirety. A few important parameters are: solvent composition; tank volume; position of application; and migration distance.

A number of methods of development have been investigated in TLC studies. Those still commonly employed are detailed below.

Ascending

In the ascending technique the TLC plate is positioned in the development tank after it has come to equilibrium with the solvent; the application of sample spots should be above the solvent level. The solvent percolates through the sorbent material by capillary action moving the components to differing extents, determined by their distribution coefficient, D_x, in the direction of flow of the eluant. This is the simplest technique and remains the most popular.

Descending

The descending technique though more common in paper chromatography, can be used in TLC. The top of the plate, where the spots are located, has solvent from a trough fed into it *via* a wick; some solvent of the same composition is placed in the bottom of the tank but the plate is supported above the solvent level. In order

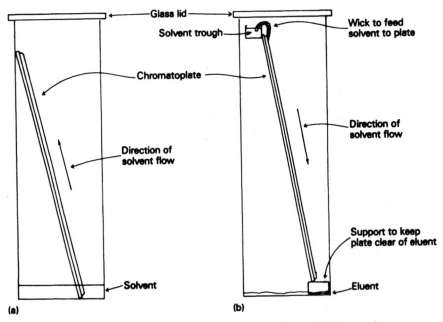

Fig. 3.6   TLC plate development: (a) ascending; (b) descending.

to improve the resolution for particularly difficult separations a number of modifications to the above technique have been developed.

Continuous development

It is not necessary in either ascending or descending techniques to remove the plate once the solvent front has traversed the sorbent layer. In ascending chromatography the eluant is allowed to wash off the top of the plate and a continuous flow of solvent is obtained. Descending chromatography readily lends itself to this modification, the eluant simply being allowed to wash off the plate into the bottom of the tank. Descending development has the advantage of quicker solvent flow, due to the action of the capillary and gravity forces on the eluant, though it has the disadvantage of requiring additional equipment and additional expertise to set up. Continuous development can be used to good effect for the resolution of compounds using low polarity solvents.

Stepwise development

There is no reason why the development process cannot be interrupted, the plate removed from the tank, solvent allowed to evaporate off and the whole sequence repeated. The subsequent elution procedure can be modified: for instance, different solvent systems can be used and the solvents allowed to migrate each to a different extent. The sequential use of a series of eluants of differing elutropic strength can be used for the separation of mixtures of wide-ranging polarity. Depending upon the nature of the mixture either an increasing or decreasing series of solvent may be used.

Multiple development

This method is a particular variant of stepwise development where the same solvent system is used successively.

Two-dimensional development

Sometimes, particularly in the case of large groups of compounds of similar chemical constitution, such as amino acids, the R_f values are too close together to give a good separation using one-dimensional linear development techniques. In these instances, improved resolution can be obtained with two-dimensional development, a technique developed by Martin, which employs a second eluant system run at right angles to the first. The sample is spotted in the normal manner and developed with the edge (AB) of the plate in contact with the first solvent system. The plate is then removed and allowed to dry. It is then developed with a second solvent at right angles to the first, edge AC of the plate in the solvent. The diagram shows the form of chromatogram obtained and the use of standards and identification of the components of the unknown by constructing tie-lines as illustrated (Fig. 3.7). Where the pure components of a mixture are not available or

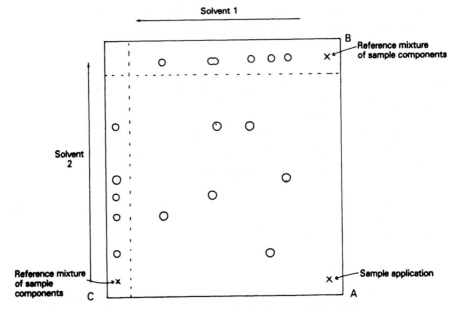

Fig. 3.7   Two-dimensional development in TLC.

are unknown then the chromatogram obtained may serve as a fingerprint/map in identifying and characterizing the sample.

Radial development

The technique of radial development, sometimes referred to as horizontal chromatography and also known as the Rutter method [56], involves a slightly different principle from those so far described. In this method the sample spot is applied to the centre of the plate (a disc) and the solvent is supplied through a hole in the plate *via* a wick which dips into a solvent reservoir. In a variation proposed by Litt and Johl [57] the plate is placed with the sorbent layer facing downward with its centre in contact with a porous 'spring loaded' wick standing in the solvent. As development proceeds the components move out radially forming circles of increasing diameter. There is an inherent advantage here, since there is a concentration effect, as the annular zones are formed, due to the solvent moving the trailing edge faster than the leading edge. Because of this concentration effect the resolution of components of low R_f with linear development is much improved. The relationship between linear R_f values and circular RR_f is

$$R_f = (RR_f)^2$$

All of the development techniques, except two-dimensional, are equally applicable to qualitative and quantitative studies.

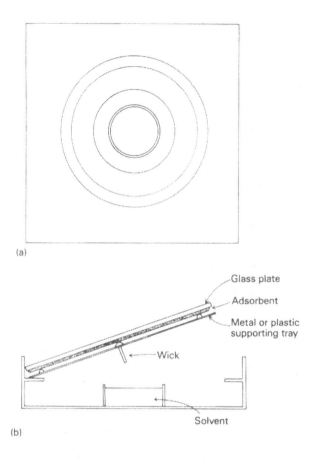

(a)

(b)

Fig. 3.8   (a) Radial chromatogram; (b) radial development system for TLC.

Gradient Elution

The technique of gradient elution (see Chapter 4, Section 4.1.4(b)) in which the composition of the mobile phase is modified as the chromatographic development is in progress, has been applied to TLC. The plate stands as usual in one solvent, and the second is added slowly, with magnetic stirring. A constant level device is necessary. Examples of the use of this method are given by Wieland *et al.* [58] and by Rybicka [59] (for the separation of glycosides).

3.1.9 Solvents

The choice of eluant as in column chromatography is determined by the sorption process employed and by the nature of the sample components. The polarity of

Table 3.2   Elutropic series of solvents

Solvent	Dielectric constant (at 25° C)
Hexane	1.89
Cyclohexane	2.02
1,4-Dioxan	2.21
Carbon tetrachloride	2.24
Benzene	2.28
Toluene	2.38
Acetonitrile	3.88
Diethyl ether	4.34
Chloroform	4.87
Formic acid	5.0
2-Methylbutan-2-ol	5.82
Ethyl acetate	6.02
Acetic acid, glacial	6.15
Tetrahydrofuran	7.58
Dichloromethane	9.14
2-Methylpropan-2-ol	10.9
Pyridine	12.3
Butan-2-ol	15.8
2-Methylpropan-1-ol	17.7
Butan-1-ol	17.8
Propan-2-ol	18.3
Propan-1-ol	20.1
Acetone	20.7
Ethanol	24.3
Methanol	33.6
Water	78.3

solvents is typically expressed in an elutropic series in which they are arranged in order of increasing polarity as indicated by their dielectric constant (Table 3.2).

Generally, a solvent or a solvent mixture of the lowest polarity consistent with a good separation should be employed. Suitable mixing gives mobile phases of intermediate eluting power, but it is best to avoid mixtures of more than two components as much as possible, chiefly because more complex mixtures readily undergo phase changes with changes in temperature. When mixtures are used, greater care is necessary over equilibration. The purity of the solvents is of much greater importance in thin-layer than in most other forms of chromatography, because of the small amounts of material involved.

Principal requirements

The solvents used should be reasonably cheap, since large amounts are often consumed. They must be obtainable in a high level of purity. It is now possible to buy pure solvents for chromatography which for most purposes need no further

Table 3.3 Solvent mixtures employed in TLC for various representative separations

Coating material	Dominant sorption process	Substances separated	Solvent system	Method of location	Remarks	Ref.
Silica	Adsorption	Amino acids	1. BuOH/AcOH/H_2O (4:1:1) 2. PhOH/H_2O (3:1)	Ninhydrin or densitometer	2-way development	60
		Fatty acids	1. MeCN/Me_2CO/$C_{12}H_{26}$ 2. Pr_2O/n-C_6H_{14}	pH indicator or 50% H_2SO_4	2-way development, adsorbent with binder and $AgNO_3$	10
		Unsaturated fatty acids	Light petrol/Et_2O	I_2 or diphenylcarbazone		61
		Lipids	Pet. ether/Et_2O/AcOH (80:20:1)	I_2 or 50% H_2SO_4	Suitable for neutral lipids	62
		Lipids	$CHCl_3$/MeOH/H_2O (65:25:4)	I_2 or 50% H_2SO_4	Suitable for phospho and neutral lipids	63
		Hydrocarbon oils	Hexane/Et_2O (4:1)	Fluorescence or conc. H_2SO_4	2-way development in same direction	64
		Synthetic ester oils	$CHCl_3$/C_6H_6	50% H_2SO_4		
		Sterols	$CHCl_3$/Me_2CO (95:5)	α-Naphthol–sulphuric acid	Adsorbent with binder + $AgNO_3$	65
		Sugars	EtOAc/AcOH/MeOH/H_2O (60:15:15:10)	α-Naphthol–sulphuric acid		66
Alumina	Adsorption	Amino acids	BuOH/EtOH/H_2O	Ninhydrin		67
		Vitamins	Hexane-acetone	Antimony chloride in AcOH	Adsorbents with $AgNO_3$	68
Kieselguhr	Adsorption or partition	Sugars	PrOH/H_2O/$CHCl_3$ (6:2:1)	α-Naphthol–sulphuric acid		69
		Carotenoids	PrOH/EtOAc (65:35)	Visual		70
Cellulose	Partition	Amino acids	PrOH/Pet. ether/Et_2O	Ninhydrin		71
		Carbohydrates	BuOH/AcOH/H_2O (60:15:25)	p-Anisidine phthalate		72
PEI-cellulose	Ion exchange	Nucleic acid components	BuOH/Pyridine/H_2O (6:4:3)	Autoradiography		73
DEAE-cellulose	Ion exchange	Amino acids	Dil. HCl (0.01–0.1 M) 0.01–1 N aq. NaCl	Ninhydrin	Also 2-way development see ref.	
Reverse-phase silica	Partition	Nucleo bases	Acetonitrile/H_2O (20:80)	UV 254 nm	C_8 alkyl-bonded phase	74
	Ion-pair	Alkaloids	$C_8H_9SO_3Na$ in $(CH_3)_2CO$/H_2O (40:60)	UV 254 nm	C_{18} alkyl-bonded phase	75
Sephadex gels	Exclusion	Serum proteins	Phosphate buffers	UV absorbance		

treatment. Mixtures of isomers, such as xylene, pyridine homologues, or petrol tend to be of variable composition, and are best avoided. Traces of metals are undesirable, even for organic separations. The solvent should not be too volatile, because of the necessity for more meticulous equilibration; on the other hand, high volatility makes for easy removal of the solvent from the sheet after the run. Its rate of flow should not be greatly affected by changes in temperature.

The choice of solvent for a particular purpose is still to a large extent empirical. So many separations have been reported, however, that it is not usually difficult to find a suitable one to use as a starting point for new work, but a knowledge of the chemical properties of the substances to be separated is clearly desirable.

Some examples of the types of solvent mixture which have been used in various representative separations are shown in Table 3.3. They are given simply as examples, and are not necessarily the best for the separations quoted, although they are all perfectly satisfactory; it is not really possible to recommend a 'best' solvent for any particular purpose, as the views and requirements of authors vary considerably, even when they are working in closely-related fields.

3.1.10 Location of separated substances

The success of a chromatographic separation depends ultimately on the location process. Coloured substances are, of course, visible as separate patches at the end of the run. Colourless substances require chemical or physical detection.

Chemical methods

Chemical methods of detection involve the application of a derivatising agent, commonly referred to as a locating reagent, or chromogenic reagent, to the TLC plate. The reagent in a suitable solvent is applied as a spray to the plate, when a coloured derivative is formed *in situ*. The reagents may be classified as non-specific if they produce coloured spots with a wide range of compound classes – for instance, iodine, sulphuric acid, Rhodanine B and fluorescein – or they may be specific and only react with compounds containing a particular functional group e.g. dinitrophenylhydrazine for carbonyl compounds. Thus specific chromogenic reagents can be applied successively and judicious choice will not only make the spots visible but will also aid in component identification.

It is frequently necessary to heat the plate after spraying to accelerate the chemical reaction between reagent and components and this requires specialized heating chambers to provide uniform conditions for even spot development. An alternative to spraying is to dip the TLC plates into a solution of the reagent; however, though this may give a more uniform application of reagent to the plate, sample can be lost from the plate and spreading of the spots may occur which leads to a loss in resolution and sensitivity.

As a rule these methods of location are 10–100 times more sensitive on TLC than on paper chromatography with the added advantage that more corrosive

Table 3.4 Locating agents for TLC

Reagent	Colour of spots	Component detected
Iodine vapour	Brown	General organic, Unsaturated compounds
2,7-fluorescein	Yellow-green	Most organic compounds
Ninhydrin	Pink/purple	Amino acids and amines
2,4-DNP	Orange/red	Ketones and aldehydes
Antimony chlorides	Various characteristic	Steroids, alicyclic vitamins and carotenoids
Bromophenol blue or bromocresol green	Yellow	Carboxylic acids
Diphenylcarbazide	Various characteristic	Metals

agents can be employed. Comprehensive lists of spray reagents for TLC and PC are available from manufacturers and in the chemical literature [76–79].

Physical methods

(a) UV detection

The most common method of location uses an adsorbent layer containing a fluorescent indicator. Commercially available plates use an indicator which absorbs light at 254 nm and re-emits or fluoresces light at the green end of the spectrum; thus the plate when irradiated at 254 nm takes on a striking green colour. If a spot of compound is present which itself absorbs at 254 nm, this will quench the fluorescence and the component will show up as a dark spot against the green background. While this is not a specific identification the technique has the advantage, since the indicator is insoluble in common solvents and the location is non-destructive, of allowing isolation of the component for subsequent spectroanalytical analysis. This is achieved by scraping the sorbent where the spot is positioned from the plate and extracting with a suitable solvent. Removal of solvent under reduced pressure leaves the pure component. Other reagents used fluoresce at 370 nm.

(b) Densitometers

Spectrodensitometers or TLC scanners are available for the quantitative evaluation of thin-layer chromatograms based on measuring transmittance, fluorescence or reflectance intensity.

(i) *Absorption measurements*

Compounds which absorb UV or visible light can be quantified from absorption measurements. Absorption measurements can be obtained in either the

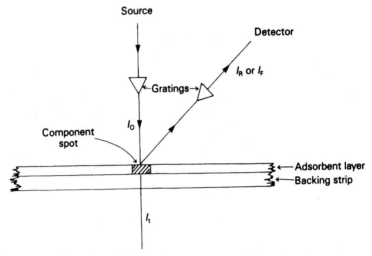

Fig. 3.9   Schematic diagram of a densitometer.

reflectance or transmission modes. The instrumentation required for these techniques is shown schematically in Fig. 3.9.

The vast majority of compounds absorb in the ultraviolet or visible region of the spectrum and deuterium and tungsten lamp sources can be used with prisms or gratings; cheaper instrumentation uses band-pass filters for monochromation.

(ii) Transmission

For transmission measurements the chromatoplate is scanned. The intensity of the beam transmitter through the adsorbent is taken as I_0 while the intensity of the beam transmitted through the adsorbent-components zone is I_t. However, quantitation using transmission values is not simply governed by the Beer Lambert Law because: (A) there is considerable scatter of the incident radiation; (B) there is variable thickness and irregularity of the surface. Quantitative studies involve the use of calibration graphs based on measurements of standards of known concentration.

(iii) Reflectance

The instrument components required for reflectance measurements are as for transmission. There are two standard geometric configurations of the components, an incidence angle of $0°$ with the detection instrumentation at $45°$ or *vice versa*. Reflectance measurements are not so sensitive to variation in thickness and uniformity of surface layer, and give more precise and accurate measurements. A modified form of the Rubella–Munk function [80] relates intensity of reflectance beam to concentration. However, for routine work calibration curves would be used.

(c) Fluorescence measurements

Compounds which emit light after irradiation are said to fluoresce. The intensity of the fluorescence is related to the concentration and the measurement of this intensity is the basis of quantitation. As with absorption studies fluorescence measurements can also be carried out in the transmittance or reflectance modes, and the arrangement of the instrumental components is similar to that depicted in Fig. 3.9. The differences are minor. Mercury or xenon lamps are used because of their high intensity and the detection monochromator is adjusted for the appropriate fluorescence wavelength.

Where sources of this type are used the beam of incident radiation is sufficiently intense to excite all the molecules and measurements in either the reflectance or 'transmittance' mode are similar. As fluorescence measurements are absolute this affords high signal amplification and fluorescence studies are 10^3 times more sensitive than absorbance. In practice, calibration graphs are used.

Measurement of fluorescence quenching relies on the uniform distribution of a fluorescent indicator throughout the matrix. Substances which absorb UV light (most organic compounds), thus appear as dark spots. The difference in the fluorescence intensity is measured and can be related to concentration. The advantage of the technique lies in the fact that it does not rely on the compounds themselves fluorescing or being derivatised with fluorescent labels; however, though it is used routinely in qualitative work the lack of homogeneity of the fluorescent indicator restricts its use in quantitative analysis.

A variety of instrumentation ranging in complexity and sophistication is commercially available including combined reflectance-transmission systems and double beam instruments. The systems are capable of giving quantitative accuracy to $\pm 2\%$.

(d) Radiochemical detection

Radiolabelled compounds are widely used in radio-tracer methods for following the course of chemical and biochemical reactions. For instance, the study of metabolic pathways of drugs involves adding a substrate, analysing the reaction mixture by taking aliquots at various times, separating the products by chromatography, then detecting the radioactive compounds by autoradiography, liquid scintillation counting or *in situ* measurement of radioactivity.

(i) *Autoradiography*

In this technique the thoroughly dried and developed chromatoplate is laid on top of a piece of film sensitive to X-rays. The film is exposed to the chromatogram for a precise period of time, determined by the type of film being used, and the type of radiation given off by the isotope. The film is then developed by normal photographic procedures. Spots appear as dark areas and can be quantified by densitometric procedures. The major disadvantage of this technique is that, depending on the activity of the isotope, suitable exposure times can vary from seconds to weeks.

(ii) *Liquid scintillation counting*

This method is also referred to as scintillation autoradiography. In TLC, portions of the sorbent, where the components are located, are scraped off, placed in a phial and mixed with scintillation solution. The radiation emitted, for instance by ^3H nuclei, is converted into light, and can be detected either with photographic film or with a scintillation counter. The technique for paper chromatography is somewhat different in that the paper chromatogram is attached to a similarly sized piece of photographic film and dipped into a tank containing the scintillator.

(iii) In situ *measurements*

In situ or direct measurements are carried out by scanning the chromatogram with a radiation sensitive device such as a thin end-window Geiger–Muller tube, with automated instrumentation which can be calibrated to give a quantitative evaluation of the spots. This produces a trace similar to a densitometer result.

The result can be confirmed by elution of the substances and measurement of the active material in the eluate. In paper chromatography the area of a paper containing each spot can then be cut out, put on an ordinary planchette and counted accurately in a lead castle.

Perhaps the major advantage of radio-tracer methods lies in their sensitivity. Due to the low concentration of metabolites present in biological samples then radiolabelling of the sample followed by thin-layer radiochromatography (TLRC) is often the only reasonable method for following the course of biochemical reactions.

A major consideration in the use of TLRC techniques is adherence to the numerous safety aspects detailed in various regulations and codes of practice. Furthermore, to practise radiochemical techniques it is necessary to obtain a licence for handling radioisotopes from the Department of the Environment.

A more detailed discussion of isotope techniques and the detection of radioisotopes is outside the scope of this text. The interested reader is directed to the excellent exposés presented by Roberts [81], Snyder [82] and Prydz [83].

3.1.11 Preparative TLC

Thin-layer chromatography can be scaled up and used for the isolation of large ($10–10^2$ mg) quantities of pure component. The practice of the technique is similar to that for analytical, qualitative scale work. The main difference lies in the plates used. Almost all preparative scale work is carried out, in the adsorption mode, principally on silica gel plates of varying thickness, 1–5 mm, and of 20×20 cm dimensions. The sample is applied as a streak, either by a pasteur pipette, syringe or a motorised 'streak applicator'. Advantage can be taken of multiple development techniques, which allow efficient separation of

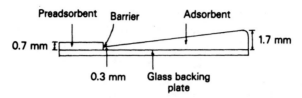

Fig. 3.10 Cross-section of taper plate (Analtech).

components of markedly different polarities. Bands incompletely resolved can be applied to a fresh plate and rechromatographed with a suitable solvent and development procedure. Once development is complete the 'bands' of component can be scraped off with a razor blade or spatula and the component washed off the adsorbent with a suitable solvent. Plates ior preparative chromatography are available with added fluorescent indicator which facilitates non-destructive location of the components. The fluorescent indicator is irreversibly bound to the silica.

Preparative TLC is an ideal quantitative technique for radioactive and toxic substances and for feasibility studies of reactions of expensive pharmaceutical and 'fine' chemicals, and allows isolation of products from complex reaction mixtures. A recent innovation has been the introduction of taper plates (*Analtech*) for use in preparative TLC work. The dimensions and features of the taper plate are illustrated in Fig. 3.10. Sample concentration prior to separation occurs in the pre-adsorbent zone. The tapered adsorbent layer causes low R_f bands to separate further than on a preparative plate of constant thickness. A more uniform mobile phase flow pattern reduces vertical band spreading, further enhancing the performance.

3.1.12 Recent advances in TLC

Normal TLC plates, i.e. those spread from adsorbent 5–40 μm particle size distribution, are capable of giving 1000–2000 theoretical plates per 5 cm migration. A recent advance has been the use of 5 μm silica gel plates in TLC studies which gives an extremely smooth homogenous surface. A consequence of the reduced particle size is that sample capacity is also reduced and sample loadings of 5–100 nl are recommended. The latter can prove to be disadvantageous where lengthy clean-up involving dilution of the samples is required and restricts precision and accuracy in quantitative studies. It has been shown that 5000–10 000 theoretical plates can be achieved over migration distances of ~ 5 cm.

The technique has a number of advantages; for instance, improved detection due to smaller degree of zone diffusion, reduced solvent consumption and higher efficiency. Optimum particle size is 1–5 μm as predicted from the study of the van

Deemter equation. The initial spot size is critical and must be as small as possible. The improvement in speed, efficiency and sensitivity which can be achieved has led to it being dubbed High Performance TLC (HPTLC). The technique can be operated using linear or radial development techniques and the instrumentation required is similar to that for conventional TLC. There are now plates coated with microcrystalline cellulose commercially available for HPTLC, and a range of reverse-phase materials based on commercially available HPLC packings. These plates when used in conjunction with *in situ* detection (densitometry) are a very powerful qualitative analytical tool capable of extreme sensitivity.

Though HPLC has been to the fore as the method of chromatography for qualitative and quantitative studies improvements in detection and in accuracy and precision of sample application for HPTLC could lead to it becoming the method of choice for analysis of many classes of compound. In addition multiple analysis can be carried out under identical conditions and more quickly compared to HPLC.

3.2 PAPER CHROMATOGRAPHY (PC)

3.2.1 Origin

Various types of simple separation on paper have been described as forerunners of paper chromatography, among them a method of Runge in 1850 for separating inorganic mixtures, and the process called 'capillary analysis' (Goppelsroder, 1909). However, chromatography and specifically paper chromatography, was not established until the late 1940s, arising from the pioneering work of Consden, Gorden and Martin [84]. Following their studies of the separation of amino acids using cellulose powder columns, they used paper in the expectation that the bound water in the paper would serve as a basis for partition chromatography. Using a two-way development technique they achieved the separation of 18 amino acids and peptides in wool protein hydrolysates. The paper chromatographic technique devised was rapidly and successfully applied to the analysis of amino acids and peptides in a wide variety of matrices and was quickly adapted and modified for the analysis of numerous classes of organic compound and inorganic ions – both cationic an anionic.

The use of paper as a chromatographic medium is usually regarded as a typical partition system, where the stationary phase is water, held by adsorption on cellulose molecules, which in turn are kept in a fixed position by the fibrous structure of the paper. It is now realised, however, that adsorption of components of the mobile phase and of solutes, and ion-exchange effects, also play a part, and that the role of the paper is by no means merely that of an inert support. The technique devised by Consden, Gordon and Martin has not undergone any fundamental changes, but there has been considerable improvement in detail, resulting partly from the wide variety of commercial apparatus which is available.

Elaborate or expensive equipment is not essential, however, and very good results can be obtained with quite simple apparatus and materials.

The literature relating to PC and its application is extensive and there are numerous reviews and bibliographies containing detailed information on the techniques of paper chromatography; a current listing of papers published appears in the bibliography section of the Journal of Chromatography.

3.2.2 Overview of the technique

Paper chromatography may be described as the technique for the separation of substances using paper as the chromatographic sorbent with a liquid mobile phase.

A drop of the sample solution is applied to the paper and allowed to dry out. There are two techniques commonly used for development of the chromatogram, ascending and descending. In the former the solvent is placed in the bottom of a sealed container and allowed to saturate the chamber with its vapour. The paper is then suspended in the chamber so that the bottom edge is in contact with the solvent. The sample spot(s) should be just above the level of the solvent. The solvent moves up through the paper drawn by capillary action and moves the components of the mixture to an extent determined by their distribution coefficients. In the descending development technique, the end of the paper at which the sample(s) is spotted is located in a suspended trough of solvent. The solvent then flows down the paper being carried by a combination of capillary and gravity forces, carrying the components of the sample mixture with it to differing extents.

When the solvent front has moved a suitable distance, or after a pre-determined time, the paper is removed from the apparatus, the position of the solvent front is marked, and the sheet is allowed to dry. If the substances are coloured they are now visible as separate zones or spots. If the substances are colourless they must be detected by physical or chemical means. The usual procedure is to apply a reagent or reagents, referred to as the locating reagent, which give a colour with some or all the substances. Examination by ultraviolet light, or radiochemical techniques (where applicable) can also be used.

The extent of migration both in PC and TLC is commonly described by its R_f or R_{st} value as previously discussed in TLC:

$$R_f = \text{Distance moved by solute/Distance moved by solvent}$$

Under standard conditions, including the type of development, this value is characteristic for a given compound and is a measure of the distribution coefficient for that compound under the specific experimental conditions.

The forces retarding the components and preventing them being located at the solvent front derive from the special chemical and structural properties of the paper used as chromatographic medium, and are in part due to partition, adsorption and ion-exchange sorption phenomena.

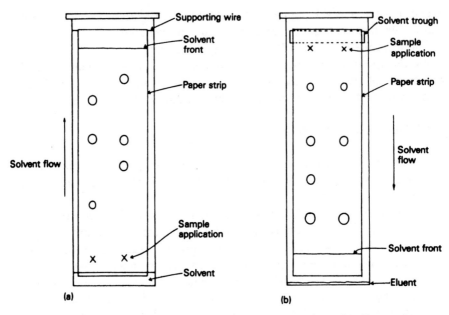

Fig. 3.11   Development methods in PC: (a) ascending; (b) descending.

3.2.3 Sample preparation

Preparation of specimens

The mixture to be separated is applied to the paper as a solution. The solution should be ~ 0.5% of which 10 μl are applied to the paper. The precise amount and concentration will depend on the complexity of the sample mixture and the sensitivity of the detection system. The nature of the solvent is immaterial, as long as it will evaporate completely without leaving a residue, and without attacking the paper. Solid samples, such as oils, or biological cell or tissue material, are macerated with the solvent, or submitted to some standard extraction procedure, such as Soxhlet. Many important samples, such as urine or other biological fluids, are already in an aqueous medium. In many other cases water can be used as the solvent.

Removal of matrix interferants

The extraction procedures used in sample preparation inevitably extract more than just the mixture to be analysed; in addition biological materials frequently contain substances not of analytical interest, which when present in large amounts may have a deleterious effect on the chromatography. For instance aqueous biological extracts, urine, neutralised protein hydrolysates, and other solutions which may have to be examined for amino acids and sugars always contain appreciable amounts of inorganic material which impair the separation process. Removal of these is called 'desalting'; it is important, and should always be carried out if it can be done without affecting the organic compounds.

A number of techniques have been developed for removal of ionic substances from sample matrices. The earliest method was electrolytic, using a mercury cathode to remove metal ions. Two later processes are based on the use of ion-exchange materials; one is a column technique using Zeokarb 225 resins and the other is electrodialysis with an ion-exchange membrane. Solvent extraction is sometimes preferred for desalting non-ionic substances, in cases where undesirable losses or changes occur when the other methods are used. The choice of method depends on the apparatus available and on the electrochemical nature of the substances to be separated. The ion-exchange method seems to be the more popular. Electrolytic desalting which is more generally useful and convenient, requires the use of expensive apparatus. A detailed discussion of the techniques of desalting techniques is outside the scope of this text and the interested reader is directed towards the following references [85–88].

Organic interferants can be removed by extraction or ultrafiltration.

3.2.4 Types of paper

The majority of paper chromatography has been carried out on standard filter paper. In order to appreciate more fully the processes occurring during development, it is necessary to look closely at the structure of paper itself.

Paper is a random pile of cellulose fibres, each fibre made up by a number of chains of ~ 2000 anhydroglucose units. The structure of a cellulose chain which is comprised of $\beta(1 \rightarrow 4)$ linked glucose residues is shown below. As indicated, there

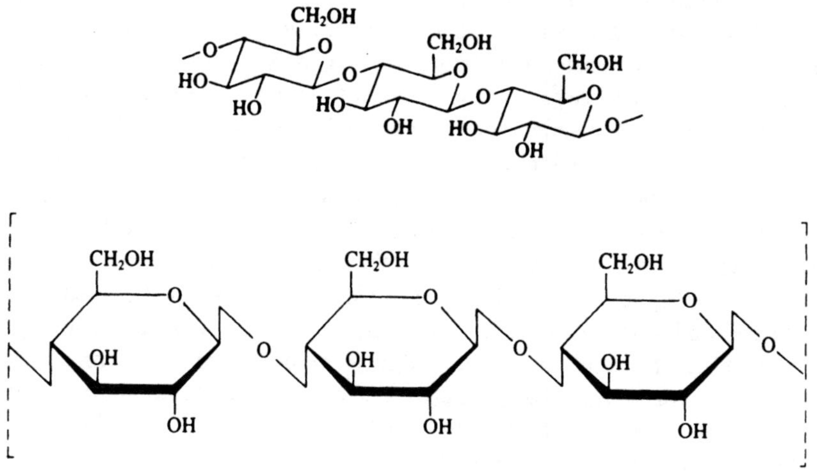

Fig. 3.12   Partial structure of cellulose molecule.

may be up to three hydroxyl groups per glucose monomer but during the manufacturing process many of these undergo oxidation to carbonyl and carboxyl functional groups. As paper for chromatography is made from cotton cellulose it will contain a number of impurities, including inorganic ions bound to the 'ion exchange' sites, adsorbed salts and organic impurities. The levels of these materials does not normally interfere in most separations.

These polymeric chains can then interact *via* hydrogen bonding to give a film with highly ordered regions, crystalline regions, and some non-interacting amorphous regions. Cellulose material exhibits a strong affinity for water and adsorbs between 5–20% by weight depending on the nature of the paper, the humidity and temperature. It is estimated that about 7% of the water is strongly held *via* H-bonding probably in the crystalline region, the remainder being present as more loosely-bound surface water. Initially the sorption mechanism suggested was solely partition with the bound water acting as the stationary phase and the liquid mobile phase being drawn through the fibrous structure of the paper by capillary action. However, the many free hydroxyl groups in the cellulose molecule render the surface hydrophilic, and thus give it an affinity for the more polar solvent molecules. There must also be other adsorption effects, since the cellulose has a similar affinity for the more polar solutes, and there will usually be ion-exchange effects due to carboxyl groups, of which a few are always present in cellulose molecules.

Each manufacturer supplies chromatography paper in several different grades, the differences being principally in the density and thickness. The grade chosen for a particular separation will depend on the loading and rate of flow required. The primary role of the paper is to act as a support for the stationary phase. In this role the chemical nature of the paper is probably of first importance, and there is little, if any, chemical difference between the various grades of pure cellulose paper. The rate of flow of the mobile phase depends on the viscosity of that phase, and for a given solvent mixture the rate depends on the physical nature of the paper. Paper consists of a mass of small cellulose fibres randomly matted together to form a three-dimensional network with relatively large open spaces. The stationary phase is adsorbed on the surface of the fibres; the mobile phase flows over the surface and the adsorbed layer and fills the voids. If the fibres are more closely packed, to give an increased density, the area of free surface and the size of the voids are reduced, and the flow rate decreases. Conversely, making the paper thicker without changing the density tends to increase the flow rate. (Flow rate in this context is the rate of movement of the solvent front, and not the volume flowing in unit time.) There is, however, no simple relationship between density, thickness, and flow rate, because the various grades of paper have slightly different fibre characteristics built in during manufacture. Thus the choice of paper influences the rate of development and the amount of sample which can be applied. Furthermore, during manufacture a slight grain is introduced in the washing process, the rate of solvent flow being greater with the grain than against and thus in description of the method the direction of development should be specified. Variations in all the above properties can also be encountered with the same type of paper and thus procedures for the storage, pre-treatment and handling of the paper should be standardized in order to minimize variations in the R_f values obtained.

Ion-exchange papers

A combination of the specificity of ion-exchange with the convenience of paper chromatography is afforded by ion-exchange papers. There are two kinds. One consists of cellulose where acidic groups have been introduced by chemical modification of the –OH groups. These papers have a much higher carboxyl content and are suitable for the separation of cations, amines and amino acids.

Treatment of cellulose fibres with aqueous sodium hydroxide followed by chloracetic acid converts some of the hydroxyl groups to the ethoxy acid, $-O-CH_2-COOH$. Careful control gives an ion-exchange material with a capacity of ~ 1 meq/g. Phosphoric acid functionality can be introduced by treatment of the cellulose with phosphorous oxychloride. Using alternative reagents strong cation exchangers ($-O-C_2H_4SO_3H$) and weakly basic materials [$O-C_2H_4N(C_2H_5)_2$] can be produced. Reaction of cellulose fibres with epichlorohydrin and triethanolamine produces Ecteola cellulose, a weakly basic product whose structure has not been fully characterized.

The properties of these resins are summarized in Table 3.5. Alternatively, ion-exchange capability may be introduced by blending an ion-exchange resin with cellulose, and making sheets with the mixture in the normal way. Paper so obtained contains, about 45% of resin by weight. By using the appropriate ion-exchange resin, papers with strong and weak acid character and strong and weak basic character can be produced. These papers have been used successfully for the chromatography of inorganic anions and cations.

Other modified forms of paper have been utilized in which the paper has been

Table 3.5 Whatman modified cellulose ion-exchange materials

No.	Type	Name	Ion-exchange group	Flow rate water (upwards) mm/30 min	Ion-exchange capacity mmol H^+ cm^{-2}
P81	Strongly acid	Cellulose phosphate	$-O-PO_3H$	125	18.0
CM82	Weakly acid	Carboxymethyl cellulose	$-CO_2H$	110	2.5
DE81	Strongly basic	Diethylamino-ethyl cellulose	$-C_2H_4\ NEt_2$	95	3.5
ET81	Weakly basic	Ecteola cellulose	*tert*-amino	125	2.0

impregnated with alumina, silica, and organic stationary phases giving improved separations for a number of applications.

Reversed phase methods

If the substances being chromatographed are only very sparingly soluble in water, they merely move with the solvent front, and thus no separation results. In such a case it may be advantageous to impregnate the paper with a non-aqueous medium, to act as the stationary phase. In 'normal' chromatography, the stationary phase, being aqueous, is more polar than the mobile phase. The technique where the mobile phase is the more polar is called 'reversed phase' chromatography. The mobile phase is not necessarily water, although the mixtures used normally contain some water.

A number of substances have been employed as supports for the stationary phase, among them rubber latex, olive oil and silicone oils and similar materials. A number of papers impregnated with these materials is now available commercially. If the paper is treated with rubber latex or silicones it is rendered water-repellent, and absorbs the organic component of the solvent mixture, which then becomes the stationary phase, in preference to the water. Where liquids such as olive oil are used they perform a similar function, but may also act as the stationary phase themselves. There must also be some modification of the adsorption and ion-exchange effects of the paper.

Reversed phase methods can be applied to all the various forms of paper chromatography. The general procedure is the same as for normal methods. The solvent for the locating reagent must be one in which the stationary phase support is not soluble.

Examples of the uses of ion-exchange papers include the separation of amino acids [89, 90], metals [89] and other ionic species. The apparatus used is that of ordinary paper chromatography, and the methods are in general the same. In some cases it is necessary to use the paper in a different form from that in which it is supplied. For instance, carboxymethyl cellulose paper is supplied in the sodium form, but for the separation of some mixtures of metals it is best to convert it to the magnesium form [90]. The conversion is done in a descending chromatography tank, by allowing a solution of magnesium chloride to flow down the paper overnight.

When the ion-exchange properties of the paper are being used, the eluting solution must contain some ion which can displace those to be separated. Choice is made in the same way as in ion-exchange resin chromatography on columns. One-way separations of amino acids and of metals have been reported on both anion- and cation-exchange paper with aqueous buffers; pH is important, particularly in the case of the weakly acidic and basic papers. The ion-exchange papers still retain the cellulose matrix, however, and if the exchange properties can be suppressed, the sheet can be used to give the same sort of separation as does ordinary paper. Two-way separations with different buffers in each direction do not give useful results, but the combination of ion-exchange separation in one direction with a conventional chromatographic separation in the other seems to have considerable potentialities. As an illustration of the technique, the following conditions were reported by Knight [91] for the separation of a number of amino acids.

(a) Cellulose phosphate paper – H^+ form.
Solvent 1: 0.02 mol dm^{-1} sodium buffer, pH 4.7.
Solvent 2: 99% m-cresol/1% ammonia.
(b) DEAE cellulose paper – free base form.
Solvent 1: 0.02 mol dm^{-1} acetate buffer, pH 7.5.
Solvent 2: m-cresol/1% ammonia.

The locating reagent in each case was ninhydrin, which is not entirely satisfactory for use on some anion-exchange papers, where the paper itself is a weak ninhydrin reactor and gives a high background colour. In the first solvent for each separation the amino acids were in the cationic form in the pH 4.7 buffer in cellulose phosphate paper and the anionic form in the pH 7.5 buffer on DEAE-cellulose. In the second solvent they were in the anionic form in both cases, and thus on cellulose phosphate paper no ion-exchange occurred, and the compounds behaved as they do on ordinary paper. On the DEAE-cellulose the partition solvent probably inhibits the ionization of the exchange groups, giving a separation mainly of the ordinary chromatographic type. The separation obtained is illustrated in Fig. 3.13. It will be observed that the resolution is much

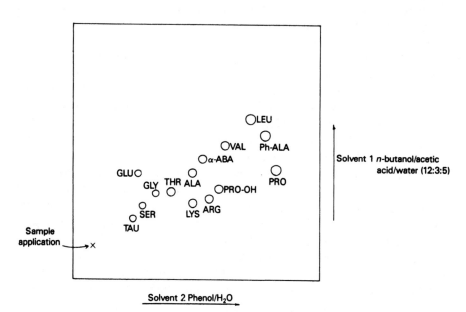

Fig. 3.13   Separation of amino acids.

better on the strongly acidic cation-exchange paper, and that the acids are more evenly spread over the sheet.

Knight [92] described an even better separation, on paper impregnated with Zeo-Karb 225 (W. R. 1.5–2.0). In this case none of the separated acids appeared on the diagonal of the paper through the origin, and some acids which are usually difficult to deal with, such as leucine and isoleucine were separated.

The advantages of the ion-exchange paper method appear to be increased resolution, which makes the use of smaller sheets convenient, and a saving in time. A two-way separation may be done in one day, or in one day and one overnight run, as against the usual two overnight runs of conventional paper chromatography.

3.2.5 Solvents

The mobile solvent is normally a mixture consisting of one main organic component, water, and various additions, such as acids, bases or complexing agents, to improve the solubility of some substances or to depress that of others. An anti-oxidant may be included to stabilize the solvent. The choice of eluant is largely empirical and is dictated by the complexity of the mixture and whether the stationary phase is hydrophilic or hydrophobic; however a few general principles can be highlighted.

For polar organic substances more soluble in water than in organic liquids, there will be little movement if an anhydrous mobile phase is used; adding water to the solvent will cause those substances to migrate. Thus butan-1-ol is not a suitable solvent for amino acids unless it is saturated with water; addition of acetic acid allows more water to be incorporated, and hence increases the solubility of amino acids, particularly basic ones; the addition of ammonia increases the solubility of acidic materials. t-Butanol and water mixtures are the primary solvents for the separation of many polar anionic species, and many other polar substances with solubility characteristics similar to those of amino acids, such as indoles, guanidines and phenols, can be separated with this mixture. For hydrophobic stationary phases, various mixtures of benzene, cyclohexane and chloroform have been used to good effect as eluants.

Inorganic ions are usually separated as complex ions or chelates with some solubility in organic solvents; for instance, iron forms a complex chloride ion which is very soluble in aqueous acetone, whereas nickel does not so readily form such an ion; iron and nickel can therefore be separated with this solvent, so long as hydrochloric acid is present to stabilize the complex ion.

Similar arguments can be applied to aid the choice of solvent system for any particular application. However, a suitable choice of eluant for new work can usually be made from the mass of applications literature. Whilst there have been a vast number of solvent systems developed many are simply modifications of the primary solvents listed in Table 3.6.

Table 3.6   Solvent systems for PC applications

Compound class	Solvent	Proportions	Sample
Hydrophilic compounds	Phenol/water	Sat. soln.	
	Phenol/water/ammonia	200:1	
	Butanol/water/acetic acid	4:1:5	Amino acids
	Butanol/water/pyridine	1:1:1	
	Isopropanol/water/ammonia	9:1:2	
	Butanol/ammonia	Sat. soln	Fatty acids
Moderately hydrophilic substances	Pyridine/EtOAc/water	2:1:2 – 12:5:4	
	Formamide/chloroform	1:9–9:1	Sugars
	*Formamide–CHCl$_3$/benzene	1:9–9:1	
Inorganic	Acetone/water/conc. HCl	87:8:5	Co, Mn, Ni, Cu, Fe (chlorides)
	Pyridine/water	9:1	F, Cl, Br, I (Na salts)
	n-Butanol/HCl (3 mol/l)	Sat. soln.	Hg, Pb, Cd, Cu, Bi (chorides)
	Pentan-2,4-dione (sat. soln. in water)/ acetone/conc. HCl	149:1:50	As, Sb, Sn (chlorides)

*Paper impregnated with 60% ethanolic formamide prior to use.

In general a solvent system with as low a polarity as possible consistent with an adequate separation should be used. Polar components of the eluant can be strongly adsorbed on to the cellulose matrix forming a stationary phase which may not give the desired properties.

3.2.6 Equilibrium

Study of the literature of paper chromatography reveals many views on the establishment of 'equilibrium' in the tank and some authors have given it special attention [93–95]. It is not possible to generalize because the degree of equilibration needed depends on the size of the apparatus, the solvent system and the nature and purpose of the separation. The object is to prevent evaporation of the solvent from the paper.

Since the basis of the paper chromatography process is distribution between cellulose-bound water and a moving organic solvent, it has been usual to choose as the mobile phase an organic liquid which is only partly miscible with water, and to saturate it with water before use. The simple picture of a water-solvent boundary as is seen in solvent extractions cannot exactly represent the situation on paper, because it has been found that solvents completely miscible with water can be used, and that partly miscible ones need not be saturated. It is probably

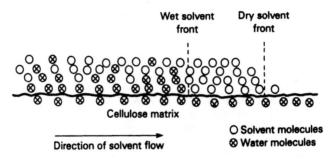

Fig. 3.14   Schematic diagram of the solvent layers in a paper chromatogram.

best to consider that there is a layer of water molecules held on the cellulose by hydrogen bonding, and that this (the stationary phase) absorbs the solute molecules from the moving solution. There is thus no definite solvent–solvent interface, but there is a gradual change in composition from polar solvent (water) to the less polar organic solvent in the direction away from the surface of the cellulose molecules (Fig. 3.14). This is only possible if the layers concerned are fairly thin, and explains why an excess of either phase ('flooding') prevents separation by causing extensive diffusion.

As the mobile phase flows through the fibres of the paper the cellulose will tend to adsorb more water from it. The result is that the moving solvent tends to become denuded of water as it advances, and its composition is not constant along the sheet [96] (Fig. 3.14). Sometimes there is a definite boundary where the solvent composition changes. For example, in some inorganic separations where acetone/water/hydrochloric acid mixtures are used as the solvent there is a 'dry' solvent front, and, some distance behind it, a 'wet' solvent front. The forward area consists of acetone from which the water has been removed, and the area behind the wet solvent front consists of aqueous acetone, and therefore contains all the acid.

This purely descriptive analysis reveals a situation of great complexity. If the composition of the solvent varies continuously along the paper, the composition of the vapour with which it is in equilibrium also varies. As it is not possible to arrange a corresponding concentration gradient in the atmosphere in the tank, there may tend to be further changes in solvent composition due to evaporation of the more volatile constituents. A further complicating factor is the amount of water held by the paper initially. It is thus necessary to consider to what extent the original solvent mixture and the paper must be equilibrated with the atmosphere before the run starts. For most applications it seems that it is not necessary to go to extreme lengths, and some of the meticulous and elaborate equilibration carried out by earlier workers was probably not really necessary. Some authors recommmend that for a particular separation (such as DNP–amino acids [89]) the paper should be equilibrated for a long time with the solvent atmosphere. Others recommend, for example in some inorganic separations (Pollard [96]), putting the paper into an already equilibrated tank and allowing the run to begin immediately.

The time taken for the atmosphere to reach equilibrium with the solvent depends on the size of the tank and the volatility of the solvent. If very volatile mixtures, such as those containing lower alcohols, ethers or ketones, are used evaporation from the paper will be more rapid, and equilibration is important. Reducing the volume to be saturated with vapour will clearly make equilibration easier and more efficient, and it is a general rule that the tank should be of the smallest possible size to hold paper of the desired dimensions. This is partly responsible for the general reduction in size of apparatus to which reference has already been made. It is also the reason why the gas jar and horizontal methods, with their very small surrounding atmosphere, are so effective.

It will be observed that in most cases the paper is allowed to be in contact with the solvent vapours for a time before the run begins. During this period the atmosphere will approach saturation with the vapour, and it may be that after a certain time equilibrium in this respect is attained. It is, however, arguable whether the paper attains equilibrium with the atmosphere. The cellulose will tend to adsorb water from, or give it up to, the atmosphere, and it may also adsorb organic solvent constituents. In extreme cases the paper may adsorb so much that no clear solvent boundary can be seen during the chromatographic run. This leads to excessive diffusion of the solutes and inefficient separation. Probably all that is needed is a short period (say, up to one hour) in which the disturbance caused by the insertion of the paper can settle down, and in many cases even this short wait is superfluous. It should be established whether careful equilibration makes any important difference if all the other factors are standardized, and if the separation is reproducible and satisfactory without it, equilibration can well be omitted.

It might at first sight seem attractive to eliminate the influence of the atmosphere in the tank by sandwiching the paper between glass plates. This, however, usually causes uneven solvent flow because of irregular contact between paper and glass, and is not often used, except in some separations of volatile substances, for example, in the separation of peroxides [97].

Associated with the problem of equilibrium is that of temperature control. If accurate control of temperature is wanted, one of the very small types of apparatus can be used in an oven or incubator. Special apparatus has been designed for this purpose, such as the *Chromatocoil* [98, 99].

Changes in temperature can set up convection currents in the tank, giving local inhomogeneity in the atmosphere and causing changes in the relative rates of evaporation of solvent components from the paper; the partition coefficients of the various solutes will alter with temperature, and the viscosity of the solvent, and hence the rate of flow, may be markedly affected by temperature changes. The combined effect of these factors may make the separation virtually useless. If the solvent is a mixture saturated with water a reduction in temperature may cause it to separate into two phases; this will spoil the chromatogram, but can be avoided by using non-saturated solvent mixtures. It must be emphasised that these difficulties apply to temperature changes during the run. It has been proposed that chromatography at controlled elevated temperatures (up to about 60°) might be used to give quicker separations.

The concentrations in the two phases at equilibrium depend on the partition coefficient. How nearly these concentrations approach the equilibrium values depends upon the rate of flow of the mobile phase, which in turn depends partly on the viscosity of the liquid. Since both viscosity and partition coefficient are temperature dependent the temperature has an important effect on the R_f values. On fast papers a rise in temperature improves the efficiency of separation considerably, providing the loading is low. The effect on slow papers is very much less significant.

3.2.7 Development

The range of development techniques available in paper chromatography is similar to those employed in TLC i.e. ascending, descending, radial, two-

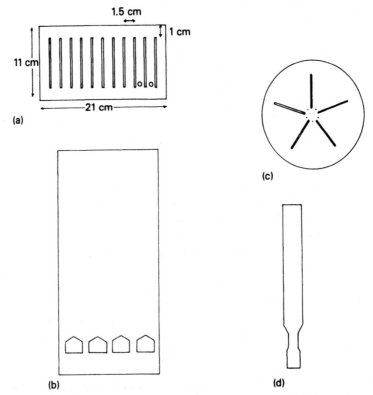

Fig. 3.15   Various designs of chromatographic papers: (a) slotted paper for multiple developments; (b) multiwedge strip; (c) paper with radial slots for sector circular development; (d) constriction of the paper strip to reduce the rate of solvent flow.

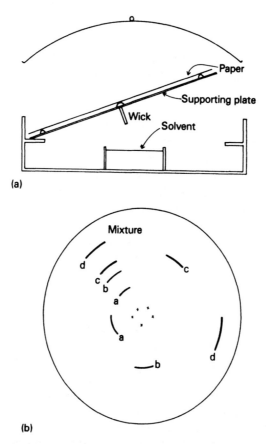

Fig. 3.16 (a) Radial development system for PC; (b) radial chromatogram of a simple mixture.

dimensional, multiple and stepwise methods. The principles of the techniques are identical: the only differences arise from the difference in design of the various equipment, for instance, special frames are commercially available for supporting the papers. In vertical paper chromatography there is a variety of paper sheet designs available. In its simplest form a rectangular sheet of paper is used and the sample(s) applied as in TLC. To minimize the diffusion of sample spots into one another a sheet with slits cut into it can be used; the effect is thus of a set of separate strip chromatograms. Wedge-shaped strips have been designed with a view to reducing the rate of solvent flow. A special paper for radial chromatography, developed by Kawerau has five radial slits, which help to homogenise the atmosphere in the container and keep the migrating zones separate from each other. The modifications of vertical development techniques such as two-dimensional, stepwise and multiple are as for TLC and will not be discussed further. Typical apparatus and experimental set-up for ascending and descending development have been illustrated previously (Fig. 3.11). The system for radial development is shown in Fig. 3.16.

Choice of technique

For many applications the choice of development technique (ascending, descending or radial) may be one of personal preference. There is little difference in the chromatograms obtained from upward and downward development though the time taken varies.

The descending method is the most popular technique and is faster than the ascending method as the movement of the mobile phase is assisted by gravity. The time of flow of a downward chromatogram can be extended by turning the strip to give a constriction between the reservoir and the position of the sample spot. A further advantage of the descending method is that genuine continuous development can take place if desired, thus extending the effective length of the run and improving separation, whereas with the ascending method the development ceases when the solvent reaches the top of the paper. The main advantage of ascending chromatography is that it requires no special apparatus and gives better results with very volatile solvent systems.

Radial development techniques

As previously discussed radial development has an inherent advantage in that due to the solvent moving the trailing edge faster than the leading edge there is a concentration effect which effectively gives improved resolution. As in TLC the sample is applied to the centre of the sorbent material and solvent is applied from a reservoir by a wick. As development proceeds the components of the mixture move out radially, forming circles of increasing diameter. Multiple samples can be run on the same paper by applying the samples around a circle approximately 2 cm in diameter. The solvent is applied to the centre of this circle and as development proceeds segments are formed as the components of the mixture move out. As mentioned earlier, special paper discs with radial slits cut in them can be used, which help to keep the migrating zones separate from one another.

One of the major restrictions to the wider application and advancement of paper chromatography as an analytical separation technique has been the lengthy development times (several hours). A recent development/modification of horizontal radial chromatography has attracted considerable attention. The technique, known as centrifugally accelerated chromatography, uses circular paper; the sample(s) are applied at the centre and the solvent is allowed to drip on to the paper from above. The innovation was to spin the paper at 300–1500 rpm, thus reducing the development time for many applications to a few minutes [100], due to the centrifugal acceleration of the solvent flow. The centrifugal method has been found useful in the separation of compounds labelled with radioactive isotopes with short half-lives [101, 102].

3.2.8 Sample application

The solution of the test mixture is applied to the paper, in the form of a spot or streak, the point of application being marked with a pencil. The zones do not exactly maintain their original shape as they migrate, but the better the shape at the start, the better it will be at the end. The standard method of applying the solution to the paper is *via* calibrated micropipettes of 10, 20 or 25 μl capacity. For very accurate quantitative work a syringe with a micrometer screw can be used (Agla); this allows accurate and precise variable volumes of test solutions to be applied. Larger volumes should be applied as a series of applications to the same spot, the solvent being allowed to evaporate in between the individual application. Solvent evaporation can be accelerated by blowing a gentle draught of hot air from a fan or domestic hairdryer. The size of the spot depends on the scale of the experiment, but a diameter of about 0.5 cm should not be exceeded. This diameter is related to the thickness and the absorption characteristics of the paper, but generally the smaller the spot, the better the separation.

The minimum quantity of any components which should be present depends on the sensitivity of the locating reagent; the maximum is the amount which will migrate as a discrete zone. Excess of any component may mean that, because the rate of flow is fixed at a constant temperature by the solvent system, this component cannot achieve equilibrium partition as it migrates, and thus the spot becomes distorted, forming a streak due to tailing and/or fronting which may obscure the position of other less abundant components.

Spots very near the edge of a strip may spread along the edge; the diffusion may be due to local higher concentration of the mobile phase in that area, or it may be due to higher local rate of evaporation of solvent from the edge, giving abnormal partition effects.

3.2.9 Detection

The majority of the techniques employed in TLC for the location of sample components can be used with the minimum of modification in paper chromatography; for instance, chemical derivatization (though the more corrosive agents such as sulphuric acid cannot be used on paper), physical methods, eg. UV, fluorescence and densitometer techniques and radiochemical methods. Due to the more diffuse spots encountered in paper chromatography compared to TLC, detection sensitivities are ~ 100 times less sensitive on the former. Methods of quantitation similar to those used in TLC and based on the development techniques mentioned above, have been developed for paper chromatography.

3.2.10 Identification

As in TLC studies the accepted method of evaluating paper chromatograms is by determination of retardation factors. These can be obtained with equal facility for vertical and horizontal development techniques and the underlying principles and concepts are as for TLC. However, coincidence of R_f values should never be taken as absolute identification and for complete and unambiguous structural characterization the components should be eluted from the sorbent layer, isolated and further spectroanalytical studies carried out.

3.2.11 Quantitative methods

Chromatography is a method of separating substances in a mixture. Quantitative use of the technique requires not only a quantitative separation, but also quantitative location and evaluation of the substances present. If a good chromatographic separation can be obtained, then the quantitative application depends solely on the last factor. A satisfactory qualitative separation is not necessarily useful quantitatively. The quantitative finish can be either by estimation of the amount of substance in the spot on the paper *in situ*, or by removal of the substance from the paper, and analysis of the separate fractions by conventional quantitative techniques.

It cannot be emphasised too highly that rigid standardization of procedure is essential if good, reproducible quantitative results are to be obtained. The original spot is applied with a calibrated capillary tube, a micropipette or an Agla syringe; $10 \mu l$ is usually a convenient volume. Drying of the spot must be done under standard conditions of time and temperature. The solvent must be made up with extreme care as to proportions and equilibration must be in a standard manner, the length of run must be the same each time, the temperature must remain constant throughout, and there must be a standard time and temperature for drying the sheet. The locating reagent, if the coloured spot is being used for the measurement, must be applied in an exactly reproducible way, and any after-treatment must be for a standard time.

The amount of substance which should be put on the paper for a chromato-graphic separation varies considerably. For instance, the minimum amount for some amino acids is about $0.1 \mu g$, but for others it is about $20 \mu g$. For sugars 30–$40 \mu g$ may be needed. The quantities have to be somewhat larger for two-way separations. Separation of metals can be done with as little as $0.1 \mu g$ in some cases, but larger amounts, up to about $200 \mu g$, may be needed in others, particularly if the substances are to be eluted.

Visual comparison of spots

In this procedure a number of chromatograms are run on the same sheet, the reference solutions contain known amounts of each and every substance present in the test solution. Normally several reference solutions of different con-centrations are used. After development is complete the intensity of the spots are compared with the series of standards. The accuracy and precision of this method depends ultimately on the reproducibility of solution application which should be carried out with calibrated micropipettes or syringes. Quantities of metals $(0.2–2 \mu g)$ can be estimated to about 3–5%. For organic separations colour matching is usually only possible to about 10%.

Photometric method

A range of spectrophotometric methods has been developed for detection and quantitation in paper chromatography. The range and type of instrumentation available is as for TLC. Densitometers of various types are commercially available and some designs undertake two-dimensional scanning of the spot. Many are fitted with dedicated integrators which further reduces the total analysis time. Densitometric measurement of the intrinsic spectrophotometric properties of the components gives better results than measurements determined on chemical derivatives after spraying.

Measurement of the area of the spot

The area of the spot is proportional to the logarithm of the concentration of the substance in the original solution. Measurement of the area is made difficult by the lack of a sharp boundary, but this method of estimation has been used in a few cases.

Radiochemical detection

The principles of combining chromatographic techniques with radiochemical detection have previously been discussed. The three main methods of locating radiolabelled compounds on paper chromatograms are as in TLC, i.e. autoradiography (film registration), liquid scintillation counting, and direct scanning, each of which has previously been reviewed. Though the technique requires specialized apparatus and demands extreme care and rigour when working with radiolabelled compounds it affords great sensitivity in qualitative studies.

3.2.12 Removal of the substances from the paper

Unless the components of the mixture are ultraviolet absorbing, fluorescent or radiolabelled, then location requires the application of a chemical reagent usually in the form of a spray. For compounds of the latter class the procedure for isolation is as follows.

It is necessary to run two chromatograms under identical conditions, to apply the locating reagent to one only and to use that to mark the position of the substance on the other, which is then eluted. The method of Pollard [103] is to use a strip cut longitudinally into two or three parts (Fig. 3.17(a)). The same volume of test solution is applied to each origin, in the form of a narrow line. After development the strips are separated; the locating reagent is applied to one, which is used as a guide in cutting the other for elution of each piece separately. For larger quantities a sheet, with a tracer strip at each side, can be used. In that case the tracer spots will contain only a fraction of the amount in the main part of the paper, but the method works quite well (Fig. 3.17(b)). The accuracy of the quantitation depends on the effectiveness of recovery of the substances from the paper.

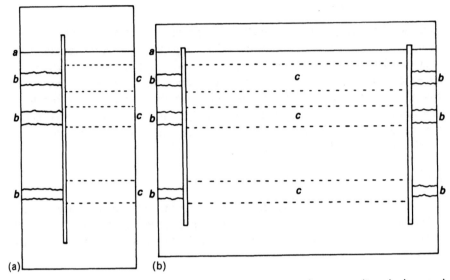

Fig. 3.17   Method of using sheets in quantitative work; a—start line, b—located
spots, c—areas cut out.

The recovery can be done by immersing the piece of paper in a solvent, by extraction in a Soxhlet apparatus, or by using some special arrangement giving in effect a downward chromatographic flow through the paper. For inorganic separations the pieces of paper can be ashed, and the residue can be taken up in acid. This method does not give as good results as elution. The solutions thus obtained can be analysed by any conventional method; those most used to follow chromatography are colorimetry and polarography.

It is not absolutely necessary to find a chromatographic method which will separate quantitatively all the components of a mixture. For instance, if a metal A is to be estimated by polarography, and the only metal present in the mixture which will interfere is B, it is only necessary to separate the mixture into two groups, one of which contains all the A but no B; the fact that A is still mixed with other metals is now immaterial, as long as its position can be found. In other cases it may be possible to arrange that only the desired substance moves from the origin, or is the only which does not move.

Quantitative estimation of organic substances is rather more difficult than that of metals because there are fewer available methods for examination of an eluate. Organic estimations are usually done on the paper, and thus require that each substance shall be quantitatively separated from all the others.

3.2.13 Preparative chromatography

Though paper chromatography is considered to be and is used primarily as an analytical technique a range of preparative procedures have been developed. The use of these procedures has declined dramatically in favour of thin layer preparative techniques. However, for completeness a brief review will be presented.

Chromatographic cardboards are commercially available on to which can be loaded up to 200 mg of mixture depending on its complexity. The sample is applied as a streak. Development is by either descending or ascending techniques. The position of non-fluorescent or UV absorbing bands can be located by treating a 'side cutting' of the cardboard with a suitable chemical reagent, similar to the process described by Pollard [96].

Alternatively a number of individual paper sheets each separated by a plastic lining sheet can be compiled and the chromatogram developed using ascending, descending or radial development, the sample being applied either as a streak or a concentrated spot. A modification of the above procedures is to form the chromatographic medium by passing a large number of individual papers together.

Finally systems have been developed in which discs of paper are compressed to form a column. Depending upon the mode of development the sample mixture is applied to the top or bottom of the column, and then eluted, using a suitable solvent, by established column techniques. Individual papers can be treated with chemical developing agents to establish the location of non-absorbing or fluorescing components.

3.2.14 Applications of paper chromatography

The literature on analytical methods and on the investigation of natural compounds shows that there are hardly any fields in which paper chromatography has not found some use, although it is most widely employed in separations of a biochemical nature.

Since the early '70s paper chromatography has gradually given way to TLC although it still offers a few advantages, for instance, in cost, and effectiveness in separating polar and water soluble compounds. Also without elaborate modification continuous development techniques can lead to the separation of compounds of low R_f. Some of the principal uses, with examples, are summarized below. It is emphasized that the actual separations mentioned are given merely for illustration, and it is not suggested that the list is in any way comprehensive.

Clinical and biochemical

Separation of amino acids and peptides is regularly carried out to aid the investigation of protein structures; routine examination of urine and other body fluids for amino acids and sugars (this is most important, as it can be used for diagnosis of a number of pathological conditions, with the 'standard map' technique); separation of purine bases and nucleotides in the examination of nucleic acids; separation of steroids.

General analytical

Analysis of polymers [104]; detection and estimation of metals in soils and geological specimens [105]; investigation of phenolic materials in plant extracts [106]; separation of alkaloids; separation of radio-isotopically labelled compounds.

It is perhaps only fair to mention fields in which paper chromatography has not been very successful, and where other forms of chromatography have been found to be better. One is the separation of volatile unreactive substances such as hydrocarbons. Another is the separation of the more volatile fatty acids. Quantitative and preparative separations are mostly more efficient when carried out by other forms of chromatography.

Although published work in which paper chromatography is used continues to appear use of the method has passed its peak. Developments in thin-layer chromatography and gas chromatography, and the renaissance of column methods (HPLC) with the increased speed and degree of instrumentation and automation that they offer, have diverted attention from the cheaper and less sophisticated paper methods. Paper chromatography is a technique in which the individual worker must devise the best solution for his own problems, because there are so many variables and no 'standard' procedure of universal application. It is therefore not surprising that it should be replaced by methods which lend themselves more readily to automation and instrumental operation, even though some large-scale users have been able to automate certain parts of the paper chromatography process [107].

3.3 ELECTROPHORESIS

The basis of electrophoresis rests in the differential rate of migration of ion molecules in an electrolyte solution when under the influence of an applied electric field. Although not in principle a chromatographic technique, electrophoresis used in conjunction with paper chromatography, proves an extremely useful method for the separation of charged substances, ranging from small ions to large charged macromolecules, of biological and biochemical interest. Many of

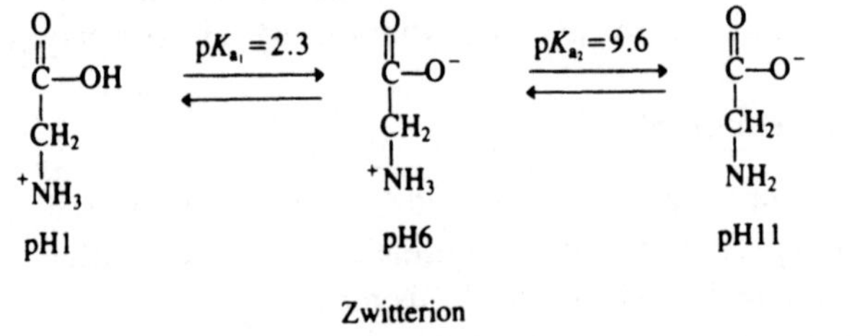

Fig. 3.18   The different ionic forms of glycine and the pH at which the form predominates.

these compounds contain acidic and basic groups which are readily ionizable, the extent of ionization being dependent upon the composition or pH of the matrix: for instance amino acids have two distinct pK_a values and the actual form of any amino acid depends upon the pH of the solution. The ionic forms of glycine which predominate at various pH are illustrated.

The dipolar form of the amino acid is known as the zwitterion, and the pH at which the net charge on the amino acid is zero as the isoelectric point (p*I*). At other pH, amino acids and like species can exist in solution either as cations or anions, the charge carried depending upon the solution pH. When placed in an electric field these charged species will migrate to the appropriate electrode. The driving force of migration is the resultant of the electrostatic forces of attraction, between the electric field and the charged molecule, and the retarding forces due to friction and electrostatic repulsion from molecules of the transport medium. The electrostatic forces of attraction are proportional to the mass/charge ratio and thus molecules of different mass/charge ratio will migrate at different rates when placed in an electric field. The technique can be extended to non-polar compounds such as carbohydrates and sugars by derivatization to the borate and phosphate [108]. Migration usually takes place in a buffered medium to ensure constant pH as changes could result in alteration of the charges borne by the species under examination.

Electrophoresis may be conducted in free solution, where the species are free to move as soon as the applied field is in force. Migration is rapid as there is minimal frictional resistance. This technique is known as moving boundary or frontal electrophoresis, and was pioneered by Tiselius and co-workers [109]. The method found initial application in the separation of proteins. However, it requires sophisticated scanning optics to detect changes in the refractive index at boundary interfaces, and is further limited by convective instabilities and by the development of 'false' salt boundaries. Diffusion begins after the voltage is removed, resulting in rapid remixing. Of greater utility is zone electrophoresis, in which the separation, according to electrophoretic mobility, is carried out on relatively inert supporting media, such as paper, agarose gels, cellulose acetates and acrylamides. The frictional resistances are considerably increased resulting in the components migrating and separating out as distinct zones or bands. The position of spots on the electrophoretogram can be readily located by procedures previously discussed for paper chromatography.

3.3.1 Procedure of zone electrophoresis

A paper strip, suitably supported, dips at its ends into electrode vessels containing a buffer solution which acts as the electrolyte. The paper is soaked in the buffer, and the sample is applied at some point on the strip as a thin transverse streak (by the same method as used in paper chromatography). The electrodes are connected to a D.C. source, and a field applied for a predetermined time. The strip

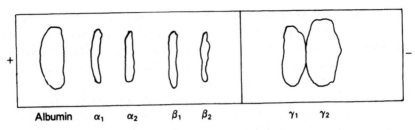

Fig. 3.19   Electrophoretogram of plasma proteins on cellulose acetate at pH
8.6 (0.5 M barbitone).

is removed from the apparatus, dried, and bands located – again as in paper
chromatography.

The separated substances are then apparent as a series of bands, whose
distance from the origin depends on the charge on the ion, its mobility in the field
applied (and thus on the applied voltage and the current) and the pH of the buffer
(see Fig. 3.19).

Whereas in chromatography the separation is achieved by means of a flowing
solvent which moves the various solutes differentially, in electrophoresis the
electrolyte is stationary and the flow of ions occurs by virtue of their charge. The
only movement of solvent is the electro-osmotic flow (produced by ionic charges

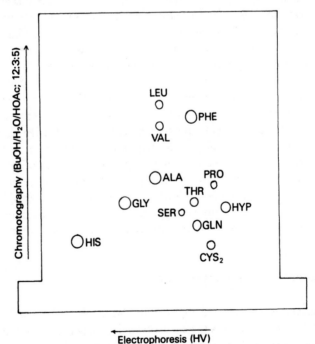

Fig. 3.20   Arrangement of paper sheet for combined electrophoresis and
chromatography.

induced on the supporting medium), which is only slight, but which may restrain the movement of some of the ions of lowest mobility.

This technique, with its similarity to paper chromatography, is called 'paper electrophoresis'. The paper acts as a support for the electrolyte, and also for the separated substances. It restrains their diffusion in the buffer solution, and holds them on drying so that the locating reagent can be applied.

The nature of the paper has very little bearing on the separation, and, since other supports are now available the terms 'zone electrophoresis' or 'electro-chromatography' are commonly used. Electrophoresis can be used in conjunction with conventional chromatography. A paper sheet cut as shown in Fig. 3.20 can be used, in suitable apparatus, to give useful two-way separations of substances such as amino acids and similar polar species.

3.3.2 Factors affecting migration rates

Electric field

The movement of ions on the paper is caused by the potential difference applied across the paper. The important parameter determining the extent of migration (d) is the voltage gradient, i.e., the applied voltage (V) divided by the distance (L) between the electrodes:

$$d \propto (V/L)$$

The extent of the migration increases with the increase in the voltage gradient. The speed of migration has been found to attain a constant value quickly, the terminal velocity, when no net force acts on the charged ion, the frictional forces arising from movement through the medium being exactly balanced by the applied electrical force. For species of the same charge, the terminal velocity achieved is determined by their size and shape.

The larger the molecule, the greater the frictional and retarding electrostatic interactions and hence the more slowly it will move. However, molecules of similar size can have different shapes, for instance. Secondary and tertiary interactions in protein macromolecules lead to fibrous and globular proteins, which because of the differential effect of frictional and electrostatic forces can result in different migration characteristics. The characteristics of each species, such as net charge, shape and size, overall charge distribution, electrostatic interactions, and their influence on the extent of electrophoretic migration are embodied in its electrophoretic mobility, μ. Thus the distance moved, d, is related to the voltage gradient applied and the time of migration by the compound's electrophoretic constant (μ):

$$d = \mu t(V/L)$$

The separation of two species of different electrophoretic mobility after time t is given by:

$$(d_1 - d_2) = (\mu_1 - \mu_2)t(V/L)$$

During the course of electrophoresis, current flows and as in electrolysis the products are oxygen and hydrogen.

$$H_2O + 2e \rightarrow 2OH^- + H_2\uparrow \qquad \text{Cathode}$$
$$2H^+ + 0.5O_2 + 2e \rightarrow H_2O \qquad \text{Anode}$$

(The applied voltage is normally removed before the ions of analytical interest reach the electrodes). The current flowing generates heat in the chromatostrip which results in evaporation of the solvent. The effective increase in electrolyte concentration results in a decrease in electrical resistance, in part due to the increased mobility of ions because of reduced electrostatic repulsion from solvent molecules. Consequently the current flowing will increase, resulting in greater heat generation and solvent evaporation. In paper electrophoresis, the heat generated is relatively small and easily dissipated at small voltages (~ 100–400 V). Evaporation is reduced to a minimum by enclosing the apparatus under an air-tight cover. Other media, such as layers of cellulose acetate, are preferable for work under constant current condition, and also for certain separations, e.g. for components of low molecular weight.

A further procedure which can minimize heat generation is to use organic buffers, for instance, aqueous pyridine and acetic acid solutions, as these ionic species are not nearly as conducting as their inorganic counterparts. High voltage electrophoretic studies require cooling plates to aid dissipation of heat.

Buffer

The importance of buffer pH on the mode of ionization of organic compounds has previously been discussed. Amino acids (and ampholytes) at their isoelectric point exist as the zwitterion and will not migrate in an electric field; however, if the pH is made slightly more acidic the protonated form of the amino acid dominates and migration to the cathode will occur. The converse is true if the pH of the buffer solution is slightly increased, i.e. migration to the anode occurs. The extent and direction of migration of many compounds of biological interest is thus pH dependent.

A range of buffers is available, both inorganic and organic, for instance, EDTA, phosphate, Tris, citrate, barbitone, acetate and pyridyl. In addition the use of borates as the electrolyte has allowed the technique to be extended to carbohydrates and polyhydric alcohols. These compounds form ionized complexes with borate reagents (e.g. cetyltrimethylammonium borate)[108]. Organic buffers as well as producing less heat during development of the electrophoretogram are also easily removed prior to location of the components on the chromatostrip.

The migration rate of the solutes is controlled not only by the pH of the electrolyte but also by its concentration, normally referred to as its ionic strength. As the ionic strength of the buffer solution increases, it carries a higher proportion of the current, with a concomitant reduction in the proportion carried by the sample. Although this gives compact bands, the time required to develop the electrophoretogram is excessive and the problems encountered with heat generation and solvent evaporation, prevent high concentrations being used. On the other hand, if too low a concentration is used, migration times are very short and this, with extensive diffusion of the solute bands, results in a loss of resolution. Therefore as a compromise buffer concentrations used normally lie in the range 0.05–0.1 M.

3.3.3 Supporting media

Several different supports and numerous designs of apparatus can be used for electrophoresis. The supports can be classified broadly as strips, gels, and thin layers; they may be totally inert, or they may have a physical effect on the separation. Materials such as filter paper, cellulose acetate, gels made from starch, agar or polyacrylamide and thin layers of silica and alumina have been used as the supporting medium for the electrolyte solution and sample.

Paper

Whatman No. 1 and No. 3 MM in strips 3 or 5 cm wide are most often used. 3 MM has a slightly greater wet strength, which is an advantage when aqueous solutions are being used. Since the paper is thicker it will pass a higher current than No. 1 for a given voltage. Apart from the use of still thicker papers for preparative separations there is nothing to be gained by changes in the type of paper, except that ion-exchange papers can be used to improve separations of some mixtures by the two-way electrophoresis–chromatography technique [110].

   While paper offers the advantages of economy and ease of use, certain classes of compound, such as proteins and other large hydrophilic molecules, cannot be adequately resolved because of the adsorptive and ionogenic properties of paper which results in tailing and distortion of component bands.

Cellulose acetate

Due to the limitations of paper enumerated above, cellulose acetate has been developed as an alternative. Cellulose acetate contains 2–3 acetyl groups per glucose unit and its adsorptive capacity is substantially less than paper. Thus, for many purposes strips of cellulose acetate are preferred, since they give sharper bands, and are more easily rendered transparent for photoelectric scanning.

   The low solvent capacity of cellulose acetate chromatostrips enables higher voltages to be used, further enhancing the resolution. In practice, no tailing of proteins or hydrophilic materials occurs. They are available in a range of particle size and layer thickness.

Gels

Gels, which are semi-solid colloids are commonly prepared from starch, agar, or polyacrylamide for use as supports in electrophoresis. The resolving power obtained in electrophoretic studies by using these materials is considerably enhanced due to the molecular filtration or sieve effect. The first successful gel electrophoretic study was carried out on a starch medium with human serum and showed about 15 bands. The paper electrophoretogram showed only five zones.

(a) Starch

For the preparation of a starch gel, a suspension of granular starch should be boiled in a buffer to give a clear colloidal suspension. The suspension on cooling sets as a semi-solid gel due to the intertwining of the branched chains of amylopectin. The porosity varies with the percentage of starch in the buffer solution; 15% solutions give low porosity gels, 2% solutions afford high porosity gels. Although some molecular sieving is achieved with starch gels, difficulty is encountered in obtaining consistency of pore size from batch to batch.

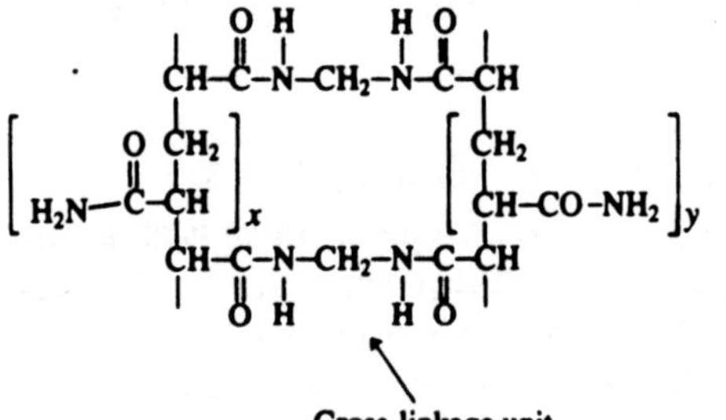

Fig. 3.21   Part structure of a polyacrylamide gel.

(b) Polyacrylamide gels

Polyacrylamide gels are synthesized by cross-linking with N,N-methylenebisacrylamide, the chain polymer of acrylamide ($CH_2 = CHCONH_2$). The extent of cross-linkage is oxygen dependent and thus enables gels of varied but precise porosity to be synthesized.

Cross-linkage may also be carried out using N,N'-bisacrylcystamine. The co-polymer contains disulphide cross-linkage units which may be cleaved after hydrolysis, thus allowing the gel to be solubilized and facilitating recovery of the separated components. Other solubilizable polyacrylamide media are commercially available which have suitable properties for isoelectric focusing, isotachophoresis and gradient work.

Though proteins are more stable in starch gels, acrylamide based gels have a number of advantages. They are superior to starch gels with respect to versatility, R_f reproducibility and ease of handling. They may be synthesized with a high degree of reproducibility and the extent of porosity can be varied within wide limits to enhance the separation of molecules of similar charge, but different size and shape, so that macromolecules can either be allowed access to the gel or excluded.

The applicability of acrylamide gels is wide and they have been used in a variety of techniques, for example, pore-gradient electrophoresis, molecular weight characterization and isoelectric focusing. Arguably the most important application is in the molecular weight characterization of proteins. The sample pre-treatment required, however, to produce similar mass/charge ratios is involved; detailed information of the subunit structure of the proteins is essential and furthermore standards composed of the proteins of analytical interest must be available for calibration studies.

(c) Agarose

Agarose is the name given to a mixture of polysaccharides, principally agarose and agaropectin, and commonly referred to as agar. The porosity is determined by the percentage of agarose in the gel. The methods of preparation of agar gels are principally concerned with removing those polysaccharides with charged and highly polar substituent groups, as these confer undesirable adsorptive effects and can cause denaturation of protein. Agarose gels are not covalently cross-linked but are stabilised by helical formation between individual polymer molecules; they have large pore size, low resistance to macromolecular measurement and hence exert little, if any, molecular sieving effect. The latter feature makes it especially suitable for the separation of high molecular weight proteins and nucleic acids. High gel strength and gel clarity of agar gels make them suitable for varied applications: for instance, immunoelectrophoretic and isotachophoretic study of antigenic proteins.

(d) Sephadex

The starting material, dextran, is a natural linear polysaccharide, in which the glucose residues are predominantly 1,6 linked. The individual 'dextran chains' are cross-linked with glyceryl bridges when reacted in alkaline medium with a dispersion of epichlorohydrin in an organic solvent. Though the extent of cross-linkage can be varied by controlling the relative proportions of epichlorohydrin and dextran, the position of cross-linkage is random, which results in a wide distribution of pore sizes in each gel type. Sephadex gels are commercially available with molecular weight exclusion limits of < 1000 to $\sim 5 \times 10^6$ daltons.

Agarose and sephadex gels are discussed further in Chapter 4.

Thin layers

Electrophoretic studies can also be carried out on thin layers of silica, kieselguhr and alumina. As in TLC electrophoretic studies with thin layers of these materials offers the same advantages of speed and resolution when compared with paper, and produces smaller more discrete bands. However, it is difficult to impregnate the dry plate with an adequate quantity of buffer reproducibly. These materials find their greatest application in combined electrophoretic–chromatography studies in the two-dimensional separations of proteins and nucleic acid hydrolysates.

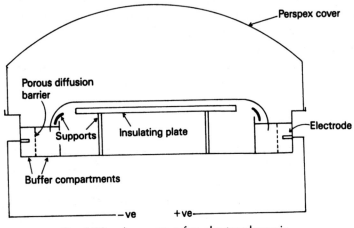

Fig. 3.22   Apparatus for electrophoresis.

3.3.4 Techniques of electrophoresis

Low voltage

The general principle of the design of low-voltage electrophoresis (LVE) apparatus is shown in Fig. 3.22. The essentials are two compartments to hold the buffer and electrodes and a suitable carrier for the support medium, such that its ends are in contact with the buffer compartments. The design of the carrier depends on the medium (strip, gel block, thin-layer plate) and Fig. 3.22 illustrates the use of paper strips. It will be noted that the paper does not dip into the electrode compartments, but into separate compartments connected by wicks with the anode and cathode cells. The purpose is to restrain diffusion of buffer electrolysis products along the paper, and to maintain the pH at the ends of the strip. In more recent designs a labyrinth construction replaces the wicks. The apparatus is enclosed to avoid evaporation from the paper, and sometimes provision is made for external cooling. The strip is not supported throughout its length, but is stretched as tautly as possible across the end supports. A power pack supplying up to 500 V or even 1000 V and 0–150 mA, is needed to provide voltage gradients of $\sim 5\,\mathrm{V\,cm^{-1}}$. It can be of the constant current or constant voltage type, but the former gives better results.

Horizontal electrophoresis units of similar design are available for gel slabs and thin layers of cellulose acetate. Low voltage units for vertical electrophoresis are available for work on paper and gel slabs. Low-voltage electrophoresis can be used in principle to separate any ionic substances. In practice its main application is in the examination of biological and clinical specimens for amino acids and proteins. The latter, until recently, were more easily separated by electrophoresis than by chromatography. There are numerous research and routine examinations of serum, plasma, and other similar specimens which are done in this way. The preferred support media for these separations are cellulose acetate strips or one of the various forms of gel. The proteins are located by staining with a dye, and they can be estimated with fair accuracy with an automatic or manual scanner. Sugars can be separated in a borate buffer, in which they form complex ions. They are located with the usual chromatographic reagents.

High voltage electrophoresis (HVE)

Electrophoresis of medium to low molecular weight compounds with LVE techniques met with limited success due to the loss in resolution attributable to diffusion effects over the long development times, typically several hours. It was appreciated by many workers that improved resolution in much reduced analysis times could be achieved by using high-voltage gradients. However, though the rate of migration increases linearly with increase in voltage gradient the heat generated increases quadratically. Thus heat dissipation for the control of evaporation was of crucial importance to the development and application of HVE techniques. There are three approaches. The first is the incorporation of direct cooling systems into the electrophoresis unit. A typical system is shown below (Fig. 3.23). The water cooled plates are insulated from the electrophoresis medium by two polythene sheets; with this procedure it is possible to use gradients of up to $100\,V\,cm^{-1}$. The second approach is simply to reduce the concentration of buffer solution. A reduction of one-tenth allows gradients of $30\,V\,cm^{-1}$ to be used. In the third method the sheet is immersed in a non-conducting liquid and heat exchanger such as petroleum

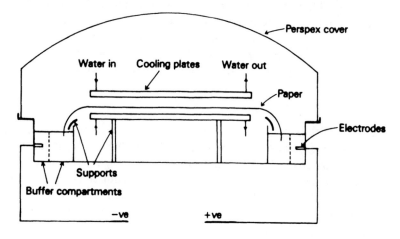

Fig. 3.23   HVE apparatus.

ether, fluorinated hydrocarbons and silicone oils. Here again, however, voltage gradients of only 30–40 V cm^{-1} can be used. Typical run times of less than one hour can be achieved. This technique works best with small ions, for instance, those derived from small peptides and amino acids. In protein- structure studies two-dimensional techniques have allowed fingerprinting of various protein hydrolysates [111, 112]. The hydrolysate is developed by high voltage electrophoresis in one direction followed by chromatography at right angles to the direction of the applied field.

Isoelectric focusing (IEF)

This technique, also referred to as electrofocusing, has similar underlying principles to those discussed for chromatofocusing (Chapter 4) and may be considered as a combined technique of the latter with electrophoresis [113]. The technique is applicable to ampholytic compounds, for instance, amino acids, whose charge is determined by the matrix pH. Separation is carried out on gels on which a stable pH gradient, increasing in the direction of the cathode, has been established. As previously discussed each ampholytic compound has a pH at which it is neutral, its isoelectric point (pI). The pH gradient is achieved by impregnating the gel with polyamino-polycarboxylic acids, which are chosen such that their individual pI covers the pH range of interest. When subjected to an electric field these migrate and come to rest in order of pI, each maintaining a local pH corresponding to its pI due to their strong buffering capacity. Thus each ampholyte migrates in the applied field until it reaches a position on the plate where the pH of the medium is equal to the component's pI. At this point the ampholyte is in its zwitterion form and is neutral; thus it loses its electrophoretic mobility and becomes focused in a narrow zone at this point. Regardless of the point of application on the plate the ampholyte always migrates to the location of its pI and then remains stationary.

As spreading of the bands is minimized by application of the applied field and the pH gradient, high resolution can be achieved and proteins that differ by as little as 0.01 pH units can be adequately resolved. Analytical applications of IEF are concerned with the determination of pI values, assay of purity and also preparative scale procedures for the isolation of purified fractions.

Immunoelectrophoresis

The resolution of electrophoresis can further be enhanced by using the specificity of antigen–antibody reactions. Low voltage electrophoresis is carried out in a barbitone-impregnated gel for 1–2 hours. A pre-cut trough in the electrophoretogram is then filled with antisera. The antisera diffuses out of the trough laterally and on contact with the electrophoretographed antigen zones reaction occurs resulting in the precipitation of the antigen-antibody complexes, so forming curved lines of precipitation.

A number of developments to improve the resolution and specificity of the method further have been reported [114–117], namely cross-over electro-phoresis, rocket electrophoresis, two-dimensional immunoelectrophoresis, and radioimmunoassay.

Discontinuous electrophoresis

By introducing discontinuities in both buffer pH and voltage gradient in the chromatographic bed, sample ions can be concentrated as thin discs in a preliminary large pore gel prior to passage through a small pore gel where further separation is achieved in order of mass/charge ratio and also shape and size of sample components.

In discontinuous disc electrophoresis, the system used comprises a vertical cylindrical column, containing two discrete gel layers each maintained initially at a specific pH. The upper third of the column contains a wide-pore acrylamide gel in a Tris–HCl buffer of pH 6.7. The lower two-thirds is packed with a small-pore acrylamide gel in Tris-HCl at pH 8.9. The gels are prepared and the buffer located *in situ*.

After the sample has been applied the upper chamber of the electrophoretic apparatus is filled with Tris-glycine buffer (pH 8.3). The lower reservoir (cathode) already contains this buffer. On applying an electric field to the system the glycinate ions migrate very slowly through the spacer gel while the chloride ions are considerably more mobile. This charge separation produces a zone of lower conductivity between the leading (Cl^-) ions and the trailing ions (glycinate). This voltage gradient sweeps through the sample spacer gel and separates the components of the protein mixture into very narrow bands ($\sim 10 \, \mu$m) in order of their mobilities.

As the bands move into the separating gel, the mobility of the glycinate ions which is pH dependent, increases markedly and they migrate through the protein bands to move with the chloride. The bands of protein molecules now move through the separating gel according to their electrophoretic mobility which is modified by the molecular sieving effect of the gel.

The above is a simple qualitative description. More exhaustive treatments of this and the related technique of isotachophoresis can be found in the following references [118, 119].

REFERENCES

1. Izmailov, N. A. and Shraiber, M. S. (1938) *Farmatsiya*, **3**, 1.
2. Meinhard, J. E. and Hall, N. F. (1949) *Anal. Chem.*, **21**, 185.
3. Kirchner, J. G. Miller, J. M. and Keller, J. G. (1959) *Anal. Chem.*, **23**, 420.
4(a) Stahl, E. (1965) *Thin Layer Chromatography*, Academic Press, London; (b) Stahl, E. (1964) *Thin Layer Chromatography*, (ed. G. B. Martini-Bettolo), Elsevier, London.
5. Heathcote, J. G. (1979) *Densitometry in Thin Layer Chromatography* (eds. J. C. Touchstone and J. Sherma), Wiley, New York.
6. Waldi, D., Schnackerz, K. and Munter, F. (1961) *J. Chromatogr.*, **6**, 61.

7. Stahl, E. and Kaltenbach, V. (1961) *J. Chromatogr.*, **5**, 351.
8. Padley, F. B. (1964) *Thin-layer Chromatography*, (ed. G. B. Martini-Bettolo), Elsevier, London, p. 87.
9. Bergelson, L. D., Dyatlovitskaya, E. V. and Voronkova, W. V. (1964) *J. Chromatogr.*, **15**, 191.
10. Malins, D. C. and Mangold, H. K. (1960) *J. Am. Oil Chemists' Soc.*, **37**, 383 and 576.
11. Stahl, E. and Trennheuser, L. (1960) *Arch. Pharm.*, **293/65**, 826.
12. Gasparic, J. and Churacek, J. (1979) *Laboratory Handbook of Paper and Thin Layer Chromatography*, Halstead: J. Wiley & Sons, New York.
13. Wortmann, B., Wortmann, W. and Touchstone, J. C. (1972) *J. Chromatogr.*, **70**, 199.
14. Neher, R. (1964) *Steroid Chromatography*, Elsevier, Amsterdam.
15. Evans, F. J. and Kinghorn, A. D. (1973) *J. Chromatogr.*, **87**, 443.
16. Mottier, M. and Potterat, M. (1955) *Anal. Chim. Acta*, **13**, 46.
17. Bark, L. S. and Graham, R. J. T. (1966) *J. Chromatogr.*, **25**, 347.
18. Cerny, V., Joska, J. and Labler, L. (1961) *Coll. Czech. Chem. Comm.*, **26**, 1658.
19. Blattna, J. and Davidek, J. (1961) *Experientia*, **17**, 474.
20. Davidek, J. and Blattna, J. (1962) *J. Chromatogr.*, **7**, 204.
21. Weill, C. E. and Hanke, P. (1962) *Anal. Chem.*, **34**, 1736.
22. Knappe, E. and Peteri, D. (1962) *Z. Anal. Chem.*, **188**, 184 and 352.
23. Kaufmann, H. P., Makus, Z. and Khoe, T. H. (1961) *Fette u. Siefen*, **63**, 689.
24. idem, ibid. (1962), **64**, 1.
25. Honegger, C. G. (1961) *Helv. Chim. Acta*, **44**, 173.
26(a) Peereboom, J. W. C. and Beekes, H. W. (1962) *J. Chromatogr.*, **9**, 316:(b) Monroe, R. E. (1971) *J. Chromatogr.*, **62**, 161.
27. Vaedlke, J. and Gajewska, A. (1962) *ibid.*, **9**, 345.
28. Smith, I., Rider, L. J. and Lerner, R. P. (1967) *J. Chromatogr.*, **26**, 449.
29. Bujard, El. and Mauron, J. (1966) *ibid.*, **21**, 19.
30. Wollenweber, P. (1962) *ibid.*, **7**, 557.
31. Teichert, K. Mutschler, E. and Rodelmeyer, H. (1961) *Z. Anal. Chem.*, **181**, 325.
32. Randerath, K. and Struck, H. (1961) *J. Chromatogr.*, **6**, 365.
33. Tomasz, J. (1973) *J. Chromatogr.*, **70**, 407.
34. Berger, J. A., Meyniel, G. and Petit, J. (1962) *Compt. Rend*, **225**, 1116.
35. Petrovic, S. M. and Petrovic, S. E. (1966) *J. Chromatogr.*, **21**, 313.
36. Mosel, H. D. and Hermann, K. (1973) *J. Chromatogr.*, **87**, 280.
37. Davidek, J. (1962) *J. Chromatogr.*, **9**, 363.
38. Davidek, J. and Davidkova, E. (1961) *Pharmazie*, **16**, 352.
39. Hofmann, A. F. (1962) *Biochim. Biophys. Acta*, **60**, 458.
40. Tortolani, J. G. and Colosi, M. E. (1972) *J. Chromatogr.*, **70**, 182.
41. Johansson, B. G. and Rymo, L. (1964) *Acta Chem. Scand.*, **18**, 217.
42. Morris, C. J. O. R. (1964) *J. Chromatogr.*, **16**, 167.
43. Shibukawa, M. and Ohta, N. (1980) *Chromatographia*, **13**, 531.
44. Scott, R. P. W. (1978) *Analyst*, **103**, 37.
45. Gonnet, C. and Marichy, M. (1979) *Analysis*, **7**, 204.
46. Snyder, L. R., (1975) *Chromatography*, (ed. E. Heftmann), 3rd edn, Reinhold, New York.
47. Sherma, J. and Zweig, G. (1971) *Paper Chromatography*, Academic Press, New York.
48. Randerath, K. and Randerath, E. (1965) *Anal. Biochem.*, **13**, 575.
49. Wang, K. -T., Lin, Y. -T. and Wang, I. S. Y. (1974) *Adv. Chromatogr.*, **11**, 73.
50. Pataki, G. and Keleman, J. (1965). *J. Chromatogr.*, **20**, 605.
51. van Damm, N. J. D. and Mass S. P. J. (1964) *Chem. and Ind.*, 1192.
52. Bekersky, I. (1963) *Anal. Chem.* **35**, 261.
53. Morita, K. and Harata, F. (1963) *J. Chromatogr.*, **12**, 412.

54. Martin, A. J. P. and Synge, R. L. M. (1950) *J. Biochem.*, **50**, 679.
55. Scholtz, K. H. (1974) *Dt. Apoth. -Ztg.*, **114**, 589.
56. Rutter, L. (1948) *Nature*, **161**, 435.
57. Litt, G. L. and Johl, R. G. (1965) *J. Chromatogr.*, **20**, 605.
58. Wieland, T., Lüben B. and Determan, H. (1962) *Experientia*, **18**, 430.
59. Rybicka, S. M. (1962) *Chem. and Ind.*, 308.
60. Harbone, J. B. (1973) *Phytochemical Methods – A guide to Modern Techniques of Plant Analysis*, Chapman and Hall, London.
61. Mangold, H. K. and Kammereck, R. (1961) *Chem. and Ind.*, 1032.
62. Mangold, H. K. (1969) *Thin Layer Chromatography*, (ed. E. Stahl), 2nd edn, Springer Verlag, New York.
63. Fried, B. and Shapiro, I. L. (1979) *J. Parasitol.*, **65**, 243.
64. Crump, G. B. (1962) *Nature*, **193**, 674.
65. Morris, G. D. (1966) *J. Lipid Res.*, **7**, 717.
66. Menzies, I. S., Mount, N. N. and Wheeler, M. J. (1978) *Ann. Clin. Biochem.*, **15**, 65.
67. Mottier, M. (1958) *Mitt. Gebiete Lebensm. u. Hyh.*, **49**, 454; (1956), **47**, 372.
68. Huang, H. S. and Goodman, D. S. (1965) *J. Biol. Chem.*, **240**, 2839.
69. Ghebregzabher, M., Rufini, S., Monalde, B. and Lato, M. (1976) *J. Chromatogr.*, **127**, 133.
70. Goodwin, T. W. and Williams, R. J. H. (1965) *J. Biochem.*, **94**, 5c.
71. Bailey, R. S. and Fried, B. (1977) *Int. J. Parasitol*, **7**, 497.
72. Vomhof, D. W. and Tucker, T. C. (1965) *J. Chromatogr.*, **17**, 300.
73. Randerath, E., Yu, C. -T. and Randerath, K. (1972) *Anal Biochem.*, **48**, 172.
74. *Reversed Phase Pre-Coated Plates* (1983) E. Merck, Darmstadt, Germany.
75. Johansson, B. G. and Rymo, L. (1964) *Acta. Chem. Scand.*, **18**, 217.
76. Bobbitt, J. M. (1963) *Thin Layer Chromatography*, Van Nostrand Reinhold, New York.
77. Kirchner, J. G. (1967) *Thin Layer Chromatography: Technique in Organic Chemistry*, Vol 12, (eds. E. S. Perry, A. Weissberge), Interscience, New York.
78. Stahl, E. (ed.) (1969) *Thin Layer Chromatography – A Laboratory Handbook*, Springer, New York.
79. Maier, R. and Mangold, H. K. (1964) *Advances in Analytical Chemistry and Instrumentation* Vol III, (ed. C. N. Reilly), Interscience, New York, p. 369.
80. Ebel, S. *et al.* (1974) *Chromatographia*, **7**, 197.
81. Roberts, T. R. (1978) *Radiochromatography*, Elsevier, New York.
82. Snyder, F. (1969) *Isotop. Radiat. Technol.*, **6**, 381.
83. Prydz, S. (1973) *Anal. Chem.*, **45**, 2317.
84. Consden, R., Gordon, A. H. and Martin, A. J. P. (1944) *J. Biochem.*, **38**, 224.
85. Sargent, J. R. (1975) *Methods in Zone Electrophoresis* 2nd edn, BDH, Poole.
86. Archer, R., Jutisz, M. and Fromageot, C. (1952) *Biochim. Biophys. Acta*, **9**, 339.
87. Wood, T. (1956) *J. Biochem.*, **42**, 611.
88. Zweig, G. and Hood, S. L. (1957) *Anal. Chem.*, **29**, 438.
89. Smith, I. (1960) *Chromatographic and Electrophoretic Techniques*, Heinemann, London.
90. Macek, K. and Becvarova, H. (1971) *Chromatogr. Revs.*, **15**,
91. Knight, C. S. (1959) *Nature*, **184**, 1486.
92. Knight, C. S. (1960) *Nature*, **188**, 739.
93. Hanes, C. S. (1961) *Canad. J. Biochem. Physiol.*, **39**, 119.
94. Cassidy, H. G. (1952) *Analyt. Chem.*, **24**, 1415.
95. Clayton, R. A. (1956) *Analyt. Chem.*, **28**, 904.
96. Pollard, F. H. and Banister, A. J. (1956) *Analyt. Chim. Acta.*, **14**, 70.
97. Cartlidge, J. and Tipper, C. F. H. (1959) *Chem. and Ind.*, 852.
98. Schwarz, V. (1953) *Chem. and Ind.*, 102.

99. Schwarz, V. (1953) *J. Biochem.*, **53**, 148.
100. Tata, V. R. and Hemmings, A. W. (1960) *J. Chromatogr.*, **3**, 225.
101. McDonald, H. J. *et al.* (1958) *J. Chromatogr.*, **1**, 259.
102. Parlicek, M., Rosmus, J. and Deyl, Z. (1964) *Chromatogr. Rev.*, **6**, 19.
103. Pollard, F. H., McOmie, J. F. W. and Martin, J. V. (1956) *Analyst*, **81**, 353.
104. Clasper, M., Haslam, J. and Mooney, E. F. (1957) *Analyst*, **82**, 101.
105. Hunt, E. C., North, A. A and Wells, R. A. (1955) *Analyst*, **80**, 172.
106. Hughes, E. B. (1957) *Modern Analytical Chemistry in Industry*, Heffer, Cambridge, p. 90.
107. Weaver, V. C. (1968) *Advances in Chromatography*, Decker, New York, Vol. 7, p. 87.
108. Eisenberg, F., Jr. (1971) *Carbohyd. Res.*, **19**, 135.
109. Tiselius, A. (1937) *Trans. Faraday Soc.*, **33**, 524.
110. Street, H. V. and Niyogi, S. K. (1961) *Analyst*, **86**, 671.
111. Bennett, J. C. (1967) *Methods in Enzymology*, Vol XI, (eds. S. P. Colowick and N. O., Kaplan) Academic Press, New York, p. 330.
112. Michl, H. (1967) *Chromatography*, (ed. E. Heftmann), 2nd edn. Van Nostrand Reinhold, New York, p. 252.
113. Catsimpoolas, N. (ed.) (1976) *Isoelectric Focusing*, Academic Press, New York.
114. Verbruggen, R. (1975) *Clin. Chem.*, **21**, 5.
115. Laurell, C. -B. (ed.) (1972) *Scan. J. Clin. Lab. Invest.*, **29**, (Suppl. 124).
116. Axelson, N. H., Krøll, J. and Weeks, B. (eds) (1973). A manual of quantitative immunoelectrophoresis. Methods and Applications, *Scand. J. Immunol.* **2**, (Suppl. 1)
117. Greenhalgh, B. (1983) *Lab. Eq. Digest.*, **Jan**, p. 56–59.
118. Jovin, T. M. (1973) *Biochemistry*, **12**, 871.
119. Gaal, O., Medgyesi, G. A. and Vereczkey, L. (1980) *Electrophoresis in the Separation of Biological Macromolecules*, Wiley, Chichester.

4 LIQUID PHASE CHROMATOGRAPHY ON OPEN COLUMNS

In this chapter we will consider the principal methods of chromatography in which a packed column is used with a liquid moving phase. We are here grouping together a number of different physical systems, in which the common feature is the practical technique used; the broad sub-divisions were described in Chapter 1. The technique is best described as open-column or open-tubular chromatography in order to distinguish it from the newer technique of high performance or pressure liquid chromatography (HPLC).

The solid column packing may be itself the stationary phase as in adsorption or ion-exchange chromatography, or the packing may be the support for a liquid stationary phase (partition chromatography). In particular the term 'adsorption chromatography' is restricted to cases where adsorption is principally by van der Waals forces, and 'ion-exchange chromatography' is used when the packing is an ion-exchange material and adsorption is principally by electrostatic forces.

The technique of gel chromatography, where the stationary phase is a porous gel and the separation is according to size, and the newer techniques of affinity chromatography and chromatofocusing are included in this chapter because the methods used are commonly those of conventional open-column chromatography. The apparatus and experimental set-up shown in Fig. 4.1 can be used for all the above procedures with minor modification.

Many of the qualitative uses of open-column chromatography have been replaced by paper chromatography and TLC and now that preparative-scale HPLC systems are available the technique is not so widely used. It does, however, find continued application for the large scale separation(s) (> 10 g) of reaction mixtures encountered in synthetic organic chemistry, especially as with minor modifications to the basic apparatus, extremely inexpensive systems (c.f. HPLC) with moderate resolution ($\Delta R_f > 0.10$) can be set up [1].

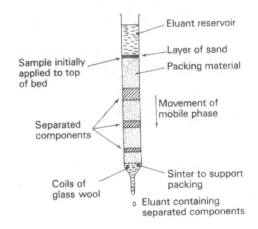

Fig. 4.1 Basic experimental set-up for column chromatography.

4.1 PRACTICAL ASPECTS/CONSIDERATIONS

4.1.1 Columns

Open-column chromatography is commonly carried out with simple glass columns. The dimensions of the column depend on the quantity of material to be separated. The smallest columns are only a few millimetres in diameter and a few centimetres long, while the largest may be several centimetres in diameter and of correspondingly greater length.

Some model experiments are described in Chapter 9, where column sizes are specified. The lower end of the column is drawn out so that it can be connected to a stopcock or a piece of flexible tubing which can be pinched with a screw-clip. The adsorbent can be supported on a plug of glass wool or on a porous plate which rests on lugs (Fig. 4.2). The latter is preferable if it is desired to remove the column packing after separation.

4.1.2 Packing the column

In order to obtain maximum efficiency the column must be evenly packed. The influence of particle size and regularity of packing on column performance has been discussed elsewhere (Chapter 2). While open-tubular chromatography using gravity feed of solvent is restricted to packing particles $> 150 \, \mu m$ (in order to obtain acceptable flow rates), the column must be packed as uniformly as possible to minimize distortion of the chromatographic boundaries.

Channelling is usually caused by the inclusion of air bubbles during packing.

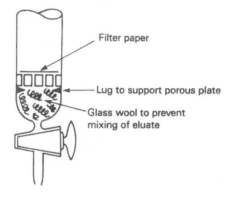

Fig. 4.2   Supporting the column packing.

To prevent these effects, so far as possible, the packing material should be slurried with the solvent and poured as a thin stream into the tube, which should be about one-third full of solvent. If the adsorbent is allowed to settle gradually – which can be arranged by maintaining gentle agitation while there is solvent flow through the column – reasonably homogeneous packing will result. If the particle size of the adsorbent is uniform, it is easier to get homogeneous packing. On no account should any part of the column be allowed to run dry, during packing or during a separation.

4.1.3 Sample application

The sample should be applied to the top of the column as evenly as possible, and in as concentrated a solution of the eluting solvent as possible, avoiding disturbance of the column packing. The top of the column can be protected with a thin layer of sand, glass wool, filter paper or ballotini beads. When all the sample has been adsorbed the void can be filled with solvent and the chromatogram developed. The supply of solvent can be replenished as required.

4.1.4 Elution procedures

There are three principal elution procedures; isocratic (from the Greek, isochros, meaning equal strength); stepwise (or fractional); and gradient. The isocratic procedure is the operation of the chromatographic column by allowing a solvent mixture of unvarying composition to run through the column until separation is complete.

If the separated constituents of the mixture can be observed on the column (either by their colour, their reaction with an indicator previously or subsequently applied to the column, or, perhaps, by their fluorescence in ultraviolet light), the development can be stopped. The contents of the column can now be extruded and the separated constituents extracted by means of suitable solvents.

Isolation of the bands is facilitated by the use of transparent nylon tube as the column container. When the separated constituents have been located the whole tube is cut into sections and the separate parts of the column are removed. An alternative and more commonly used method is to allow the column to run until the separated components can be detected in the column effluent (eluate).

The importance of mobile phase flow rate has previously been discussed. If solvent flow has to be accelerated it is better to apply pressure to the top of the column by means of compressed gas rather than to reduce pressure at the bottom. Reduction of pressure is liable to cause channelling by allowing dissolved gases to come out of solution.

Stepwise or fractional elution

If only one solvent is used ready elution of only some of the components of the original mixture from the column may result. To remove those which are more firmly held a stronger eluting agent will be required. Sometimes it may be necessary to use several different solvents of gradually increasing strength for the successive desorption of different components. This is known as stepwise elution. It has the advantage that sharper separations may be obtained than if only one strongly eluting solvent, capable of moving even the most firmly bound of the components of the mixture, is used – apart from the possibility of displacement development. One danger of this technique, however, is that a given compound may give rise to more than one peak by appearing in the eluates of successive steps.

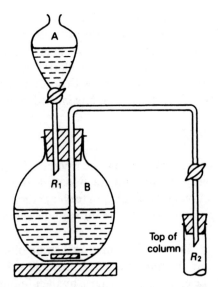

Fig. 4.3   Mixing device for gradient elution.

Gradient elution

The technique of gradient elution analysis was first described in detail by Alm, Williams and Tiselius [2]. It involves the use of a continuously changing eluting medium. The effect of this gradient is to elute successively the more strongly adsorbed substances and at the same time to reduce tailing. This means that the chromatographic bands will tend to be more concentrated and thus occupy less of the column. This desirable effect may be ascribed to the 'straightening' of the isotherms by the concentration gradient; that is, the adsorption isotherms are becoming more nearly linear as the use of concentration gradient ensures that the tail of a particular chromatographic band is always in contact with a more concentrated solution (therefore more strongly eluting) than the front. The tail will therefore tend to move more rapidly to catch up the front.

In Fig. 4.3 is shown a simple apparatus for obtaining the gradient; the whole device may be under pressure if necessary. The flask, B, which contains a magnetic stirrer, initially contains the pure solvent used to make up the column, and the solvent whose concentration is to be increased is added from A at rate R_1. R_2 is the rate at which the mixture is added to the column. The rates R_1 and R_2 can be adjusted to give concentration curves similar to those depicted in Fig. 4.4.

Type (I) curves (R_2 greater than $2R_1$) give the best separations with the minimum tailing.

By using the equation

$$C = 1 - \left(\frac{a}{(a + bt)} \right) \sim \frac{1}{b}$$

in which $a = V_o/R_1$, where V_o = volume of pure solvent in vessel B and $b = 1 - R_1/R_2$, the concentration C of the stronger eluting agent in B can be calculated at any time, t. Shallow concentration curves can conveniently be obtained by adding to the mixing chamber a solution instead of pure solvent.

There are available microprocessor controlled solvent delivery modules which can generate the required gradient profile, be it stepwise, linear, convex, concave or simply isocratic. Up to four solvents can be selected. A detailed discussion of

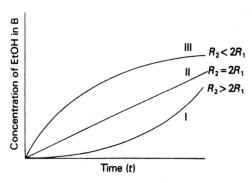

Fig. 4.4   Concentration gradients.

the instrumentation is presented in Chapter 6. The pumping systems and accessories are equally adaptable to use with open-tubular chromatography as with high-pressure systems.

4.2 MODES OF CHROMATOGRAPHY

The exact mode of chromatography operating in a given application is determined principally by the nature of the packing, though it must be appreciated that, while there may be one dominant mechanism, the modes are not mutually exclusive.

4.3 ADSORPTION CHROMATOGRAPHY

The lattice of the common porous adsorbents e.g. alumina and silica, is terminated at the surface with polar hydroxyl groups, and it is these groups which provide the means for the surface interactions with solute molecules. (Alumina has additional structural features which can influence solute retention; these will be discussed later in the chapter.)

The eluant systems used in adsorption chromatography are based on non-polar solvents, commonly hexane, containing a small amount of a polar additive, such as 2-propanol. When the sample is applied, solute molecules with polar functionality will bond to the active sites on the packing; they will subsequently be displaced by the polar modifier molecules of the eluant, as the chromatogram is developed and will pass down the column to be re-adsorbed on fresh sites. The ease of displacement of solute molecules will depend on their relative polarities. More polar molecules will be adsorbed more strongly and hence will elute more slowly from the column. A system as described in Fig. 4.1 may be used. It was the type of apparatus first used for chromatographic separation of the kind familiar today.

After its introduction (in about 1903 by Tswett) there was little or no application of adsorption chromatography until it was again successfully employed in 1931 by Kuhn, Winterstein and Lederer [3] for the separation of xanthophyll pigments on columns packed with calcium carbonate. From that time much more use was made of adsorption chromatography and there were minor improvements in technique. It was left to Tiselius and his school, however, to make the most of the major advances, such as the perfection of the elution method of separation and the devising of apparatus for the continuous analysis of the eluate by, for example, measuring changes in refractive index. One advantage of this is that the use of such adsorbents as active carbon for column packing becomes convenient since it is no longer necessary to detect the separated components while they are still on the column.

Other advances, such as frontal analysis, displacement development, and gradient elution analysis, also invented by Tiselius and his co-workers, aim at the reduction or elimination of the 'tailing' always associated with adsorption chromatography, and help to achieve more efficient columns. A brief description of these methods has already been presented in Chapter 1.

4.3.1 Solvents

As already indicated the solvent plays an active part in the adsorption process and competes with the sample molecules for active sites on the adsorbent. Thus the stronger the binding of solvent molecules the greater the amount of time the solute molecules spend in the mobile phase, and hence the faster they are eluted. Retention is therefore not so much influenced by sample solubility in the eluent as by the strength of solvent adsorption. It is advisable for a given application to choose an initial solvent of indifferent eluting power so that stronger agents can be tried successively. 'Strength' of the eluting agent means the adsorbability on the column packing. Generally, for polar adsorbents such as alumina and silica gel, the strength of adsorption increases with the polarity of the adsorbate. For carbon the order is reversed.

One of the first 'elutropic' series was recorded by Trappe [4], who found that the eluting power of a series of solvents for substances adsorbed in columns such as silica gel decreased in the order:

pure water > methanol > ethanol > propanol > acetone > ethyl acetate > diethyl ether > chloroform > dichloromethane > benzene > toluene > trichloroethylene > carbon tetrachloride > cyclohexane > hexane.

This order is also the order of decreasing dielectric constant. The eluting power of different solvents has also been studied by Williams et al., [5], who found that on an active carbon column the eluting power for amino acids and saccharides decreased in the order:

ethyl acetate > diethyl ether > propanol > acetone > ethanol > methanol > pure water.

This order is of increasing polarity or decreasing chain length of homologues. The reverse order was true for alumina and silica gel. Other series have been given by Snyder [6], Strain [7], Bickoff [8] and Knight and Groennings [9].

Practically speaking the solvent is the controlling variable in adsorption chromatography. With the aid of the above series it is possible to select a solvent or solvent mixture with the appropriate eluting power. It should be appreciated that the eluting power of a solvent can be markedly affected by the presence of small amounts of impurity, e.g. methanol in benzene, and hence the purity of the solvents used should be as high as possible. If necessary, further purification can be achieved by running the solvent through a column of the adsorbent to be used.

4.3.2 Adsorbents

Many solids have been used as adsorbents (Tswett himself tried over 100 different compounds), some of which are listed in Table 4.1 with the types of compounds separated with their aid. It may be noted that in the table there is little reference to inorganic separations, which are usually more conveniently carried out with the aid of ion-exchange resins or by paper chromatography.

A term which is used in connection with adsorbent is 'activity'. It usually relates to the specific surface of the solid; that is, the surface area measured in square metres/gram, in which case carbon, silica gel, and alumina can be made the most active of solids, possessing specific surfaces of many hundreds of square metres. Others, such as calcium carbonate and lime, have specific surfaces measured in tens of square metres and less, and can therefore be considered relatively inactive. This definition of activity relates to the amount of substance adsorbed at a given concentration and says nothing about the tenacity with which it is held. On the other hand, the term 'activity' is often used to denote the strength of adsorption; this is usually the sense referred to in chromatography and the one that will be employed here. The term 'chromatographic activity' will be used.

Often, of course, the two types of activity are found together, that is, a solid with a large surface area adsorbs tenaciously, but the situation where a substance is firmly held on the surface of a 'low area' solid is not uncommon. Thus it might be expected that substances possessing some acidic character should be strongly adsorbed on say, lime or magnesia.

As might be expected, chromatographic activity is the more specific and it is found that the strength of adsorption of polar groups on polar compounds increases in the order:

$$-CH{=}CH- < -OCH_3 < -CO_2R < {=}C{=}O < -CHO < -SH < -NH_2$$
$$< -OH < -COOH$$

Table 4.1 Adsorbents for chromatography

Solid	Used to separate
Alumina	Sterols, dyestuffs, vitamins, esters, alkaloids, inorganic compounds
Silica gel	Sterols, amino acids
Carbon	Peptides, carbohydrates, amino acids
Magnesia	Similar to alumina
Magnesium carbonate	Porphyrins
Magnesium silicate	Sterols, esters, glycerides, alkaloids
Calcium hydroxide	Carotenoids
Calcium carbonate	Carotenoids, xanthophylls
Calcium phosphate	Enzymes, proteins, polynucleotides
Aluminium silicate	Sterols
Starch	Enzymes
Sugar	Chlorophyll, xanthophyll

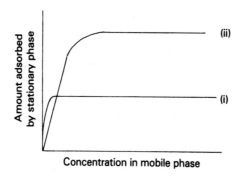

Fig. 4.5   Adsorption isotherms.

This order is approximately reversed for carbon (see also under 'solvents').

The shape of the isotherm associated with 'active' adsorption is illustrated in Fig. 4.5, curve (i). Since it is more strongly curved than (ii) it will give rise to more pronounced tailing, and therefore the specificity mentioned above, though desirable, is often associated, in the case of the more polar compounds at least, with steep isotherms and hence pronounced tailing. Two undesirable chromatographic features may arise as consequences: first, very slow movement of the adsorbate on the column; and second, wide chromatographic bands of low concentration with a tendency to overlap. For these reasons it is often desirable to deactivate the adsorbent or to use the stepwise or gradient elution techniques mentioned above.

Preparation of adsorbents

An indication has been given above (Table 4.1) of the wide range of materials that have been exploited as adsorbents in chromatography. Because of the breadth and detail associated with the preparation and activation of procedures, the following section will of necessity be devoted to the selective examination of the more common adsorbents.

(a) Silica

Silica, silica gel and silicic acid are terms applied to the material prepared by acidification of sodium silicate with sulphuric acid followed by washing and drying of the gel. The final pH of the solution largely determines the specific surface area. For example, at pH 3.72 the specific surface is $830 \, \text{m}^2 \, \text{g}^{-1}$ while a pH of 5.72 gives a value of $348 \, \text{m}^2 \, \text{g}^{-1}$. Provided that the same pH is reached during preparations and the same drying procedure is followed, then the surface properties are remarkably consistent from batch to batch. The batch size has some influence, but this effect can be eliminated [10] if an acetic acid/sodium acetate buffer is used. In this case only the final pH is important, especially if it is about 4.64, the maximum buffer capacity of the system.

The active sites on the surface consist of silanol groups which are spaced approximately 5 Å apart. The procedures used to modify the surface activity depend on the addition or removal of water. Surface adsorbed water which 'masks' the active sites is removed simply by heating; this is a reversible process and the surface can be deactivated by rehydrating the silica. Heating at higher temperatures ($\sim 400°$ C) leads to a permanent loss of surface activity due to the elimination of a molecule of water from two adjacent silanol groups resulting in the formation of a siloxane linkage (silyl ether) which is chromatographically inactive.

The activity is tested by the relative adsorbability of a number of azodyes and assigned a Brockmann number [11]. The higher the grade number the less active the surface. The surface interacts with polar solutes chiefly by means of H-bonding and thus, for example, alkenes are more strongly retained than alkanes, and further, due to the acidic nature of the surface basic substances are held particularly strongly. The principal problem associated with silica (and adsorbents in general) is the tendency to cause peak tailing.

An additional hazard is that irreversible adsorption may take place on columns and for this reason complete recovery of the adsorbates is not always achieved. Isomerization of various compounds such as terpenes and sterols has been reported to occur on silica gel.

(b) Alumina

The alumina surface is capable of exhibiting different types of solute–sorbent interaction. This may be attributed to, first, the very strong positive fields surrounding the Al^{3+} which allow interaction with easily polarizable molecules, such that alumina would be preferred to silica for the resolution of aromatics from olefins; and second, the pressure of basic sites (probably O^{2-}) which allow interaction with proton donors.

The preparation and activation procedures for alumina are markedly different from silica in that the activity increases with the temperature of activation. Highly active alumina can be produced by heating at $400°$ C overnight. The surface can be deactivated by addition of water and then graded and assigned a Brockmann number as with silica [12]. Alumina is less widely used than silica due to its propensity to catalyse reactions with base-labile molecules and to cause rearrangements and even ring expansions in unsaturated and alicyclic compounds [13].

4.4 PARTITION COLUMN CHROMATOGRAPHY

In partition chromatography the solid adsorbent is replaced by a packing comprising a support material coated with a stationary phase. The stationary phase should be insoluble or at the most sparingly miscible in the mobile phase.

Partition chromatography is a technique which utilizes the ability of a solute to distribute itself between the two phases, to an extent determined by its partition coefficient. The basis of this method is that because of differences in the partition coefficients of the various components, the mixture will be resolved.

The stationary phase is supported on a solid which is inert to the substances to be separated. The coated solid is packed in columns as in adsorption chromatography. There is, in fact, very little visible difference between the two types of column. The support material must adsorb and retain the stationary phase, and must expose as large a surface of it as possible to the flowing phase. It must be mechanically stable and easy to pack into the column when loaded with the stationary liquid, and it must not impede the solvent flow.

Needless to say, there is no support which has all these properties to the desired extent. The greatest difficulty (more or less unavoidable when a solid has to be used) is the incursion of adsorption effects. Even if the surface of the support is completely covered with liquid, adsorption effects can still make themselves felt. As complete coverage of the surface is not easy to achieve adsorption may be a major influence on the separation. As far as liquid-phase chromatography on columns is concerned it is probably true to say that the division into adsorption and partition methods is of practical, rather than theoretical, significance. The importance of adsorption varies from system to system and is mentioned briefly in connection with the different supports described below. The moving phase in partition chromatography may be a liquid or a gas, and the general principles are the same in each case.

4.4.1 Solid supports

The supports most commonly used are silica gel (sometimes referred to as silicic acid), diatomaceous earths (kieselguhr, celite, etc) and cellulose. Other solids such as starch or glass beads have found more limited use.

Silica gel

The preparation and surface characteristics of silica gel have been discussed previously. Silica gel is almost always used with water or a buffered aqueous solution as the stationary phase. The amount of liquid held (or loading of stationary phase) is about $0.6 \, \text{cm}^3 \, \text{g}^{-1}$ of gel.

It is fairly certain that adsorption plays a large part in all separations employing silica gel, but it is, nevertheless, extensively used. The same kinds of chemical reactions can occur in partition systems as in adsorption systems, although they may be less marked due to the diminished influence of the surface of the solid support caused by the stationary liquid. Silica gel used for chromatography is in the form of a fine white powder; a fairly narrow range of particle sizes is desirable (about the same as for an adsorption column) although swelling may occur when the gel is mixed with the stationary phase.

Diatomaceous earths

These are all similar, being available commercially as kieselguhr, celite, or other proprietary products. The amount of liquid phase used with these solids is about $0.8 \, cm^3 \, g^{-1}$. They are usually pure enough for use, but if necessary they can be freed from iron by boiling with 3% hydrochloric acid, washed free from chloride and dried at 80° C. Kieselguhr has very little adsorptive capacity and therefore makes an ideal support for partition chromatography.

Cellulose powder

This is supplied ready for use and usually requires no further treatment, not even the addition of the stationary phase, since this is acquired from the aqueous solvent. The use of cellulose in columns is an alternative to the use of cellulose in the form of paper sheets or in thin layers coated on glass plates (Chapter 3). Cellulose columns are essential if a preparative separation is required, and they have also been found more convenient for quantitative estimations. The separations achieved on columns and thin layers are similar to those on paper, but are not necessarily identical, since the cellulose fibres have some sort of regular orientation in paper sheets, whereas in cellulose powder they have a completely random arrangement. Another difference, which, like the first, may affect the solvent flow, is that in a column the support and stationary phase are in contact with mobile phase before the separation starts, whereas on paper and thin layers the mobile phase has a definite boundary which moves ahead of the solutes.

While the separation on cellulose is mainly due to partition, adsorption again plays some part and ion-exchange is also possible. The extent of adsorption is uncertain, but is partly due to the polar nature of the hydroxyl groups of the cellulose molecule, and varies according to the polarity of the solutes. The ion-exchange effects are also due to the hydroxyl groups and to the small number of carboxyl groups in the cellulose (see Chapter 3). These groups act as weak acid ion-exchangers, the protons exchanging with cations in the solution. The same factors influence separations on paper.

Apart from the methods of handling, the main difference between the use of cellulose as powder in columns and as sheets of paper or thin layers is that in the last two cases the separated substances are detected and identified in their final positions on the sheet or layer, whereas in the column method the substances are normally eluted and identified in the eluate. Cellulose powder should be stored and treated in the same way as paper sheets (Chapter 3).

4.4.2 Solvents

It is normal to choose a system so that there is a considerable difference between the solvent strength parameters of the mobile and stationary phases, e.g. with water as stationary phase, pentane would be the optimum choice as eluent.

Table 4.2 Some typical separations on partition columns

Separation	Support	Stationary phase	Mobile phase	Ref.
C_1–C_4 alcohols	celite	water	$CHCl_3$ or CCl_4	14
C_2–C_8 fatty acids	silica gel	water (buffered)	$CHCl_3$/BuOH	15
C_1–C_2 fatty acids	silica gel	water	Skellysolve/Bu_2O	16
Acetylated amino-acids	silica gel	water	$CHCl_3$/BuOH	17
Acetylated amino acids	kieselguhr	water	$CHCl_3$/BuOH	18
Amino acids	starch	water	PrOH or BuOH/HCl	19
Proteins (ribonuclease)	kieselguhr	water	$(NH_4)_2SO_4$/H_2O/ cellosolve	20
Purines	starch	water	PrOH/HCl	21
17-Oxo-steroid glucuronides	silica gel	aqueous sodium acetate	$CHCl_3$/EtOH/ AcOH	22
Corticosteroids	celite	water	EtOH/CH_2Cl_2* 40–60 petrol/ CH_2Cl_2*	23, 24
Methoxy aromatic acids	silica gel	$0.25 \, mol \, dm^{-3}$ H_2SO_4	BuOH/$CHCl_3$	25
Phenols	cellulose	water	MeOH/BuOH/ $CHCl_3$	26
DNP amino-acids	chlorinated rubber	butanol	aqueous buffers	27
17-Oxo-steroids	silica gel	water	CH_2Cl_2/petrol*	27
Inorganic	cellulose	water	acetone/HCl	28
Dibasic acids	silica gel	water	BuOH/$CHCl_3$ (stepwise in three mixtures)	29
Alkanes and cycloalkanes	silica gel	aniline	iso-PrOH/benzene	30
Organic acids	silica gel	aqueous sulphuric acid	$CHCl_3$/BuOH*	31
Lanthanides	kieselguhr	tributyl phosphate	(i) $15.8 \, mol \, dm^{-3}$ HNO_3† (ii) $15.1 \, mol \, dm^{-3}$ HNO_3 (iii) $11.5 \, mol \, dm^{-3}$ HNO,	32
			(iv) methylene bis-(di-n-hexyl)-phosphine oxide	33
Lipids	silica gel	water	various	34

*Gradient elution
†Stepwise elution

However, over a long period of time the stationary phase will be stripped/washed from the column. This is referred to as solvent stripping, which led to the development of chemically-bonded stationary phases for HPLC (Chapter 6). This problem can be overcome by pre-saturating the eluent with the stationary phase before it contacts the packing. This can be achieved either by stirring the two phases together until equilibration is achieved or by placing a pre-column at the chromatographic-column inlet. The pre-column contains a support with a high specific surface area coated with a high loading of the stationary phase to be used in the analytical column.

Some typical applications and separations achieved with partition columns are shown in Table 4.2.

4.5 ION-EXCHANGE CHROMATOGRAPHY

Ion exchange is a process wherein a solution of an electrolyte is brought into contact with an ion exchange resin and active ions on the resin are replaced by ions (ionic species) of similar charge from the analyte solution.

A cation exchanger is one in which the active ions on the ion-exchange material are cations and the exchange process involves cations. The polar groups in cation-exchangers are acidic, commonly $-SO_3H$, $-CO_2H$, $-OH$ or $-PO_4H_3$. They are attached to the polymer molecule in a regular way and are accessible to the solution containing the ions to be removed or separated. The polar groups in anion exchangers are tertiary or quaternary ammonium groups ($-CH_2-NR_2$ or $-CH_2-\overset{+}{N}R_3$) and they function in an analogous manner. Anion exchangers are usually supplied in the chloride form rather than the hydroxide because of the greater stability of the former.

Ion-exchange chromatography on columns was initially restricted to the use of resins, mainly because of their desirable properties such as mechanical and chemical stability. Initially the resins were prepared by polycondensation of

Table 4.3   The general characteristics of various ion-exchange resins

	Type	Exchanging group	Effective in the pH range	Exchange capacity*
Cation-exchange	Strong acid	$-SO_3H$	1–14	$4\,mmol\,H^+\,g^{-1}$
	Weak acid	$-CO_2H$	5–14	$9–10\,mmol\,H^+\,g^{-1}$
Anion-exchange	Strong base	$-CH_2-\overset{+}{N}R_3$	1–15	$4\,mmol\,OH^-\,g^{-1}$
	Weak base	$-CH_2-NR_2$	1–9	$4\,mmol\,OH^-\,g^{-1}$

$R = -CH_3$ (usually).
*The capacity quoted is for the dry resin

phenols and aromatic amines with formaldehyde. Alternative ionogenic groups were introduced by condensation of formaldehyde with sulpho and carboxy derivatives. Though these synthetic procedures allowed the introduction of the ionogenic groups in a single step they have been replaced by resin materials based on styrene – divinylbenzene copolymers and polyacrylates. The synthesis of these materials is more easily controlled and gives materials of improved chemical and physical stability, with the necessary uniformity of particle size and shape,

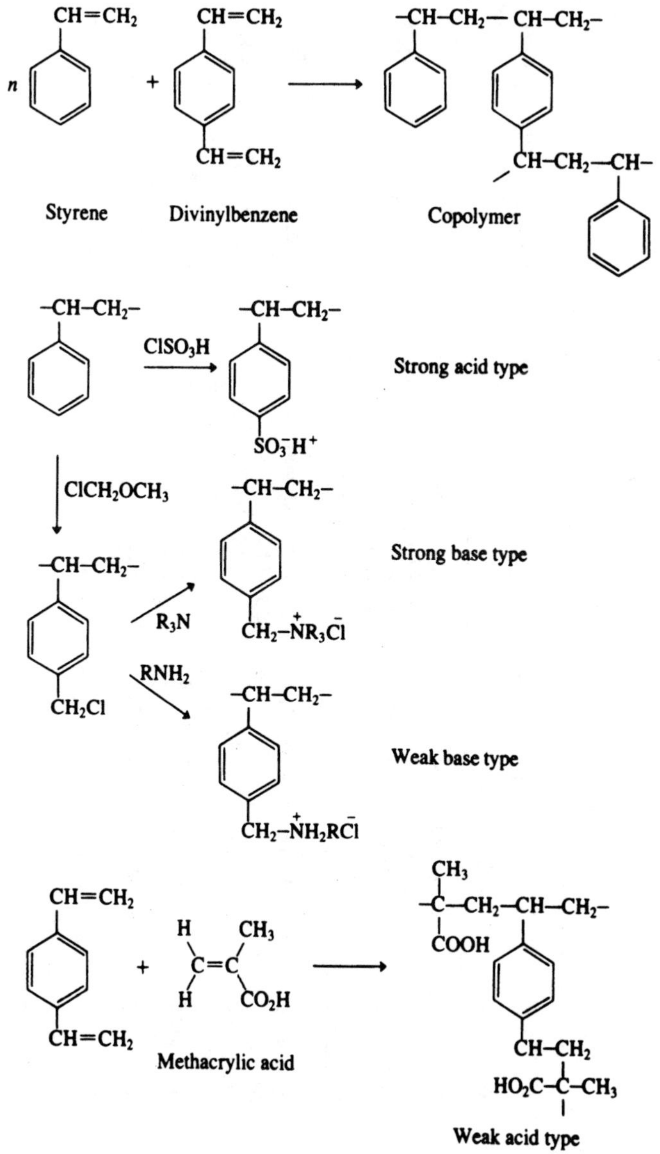

Fig. 4.6   Synthetic routes to ion-exchange resins.

Table 4.4   Some commercially available resins suitable for chromatography

Name	Type	Functional group	Bead sizes (mesh)	% cross-linking	Exchange capacity g^{-1} (dry resin)	Form supplied	Working pH range	
Zeo-Karb 225	Strong acid	$-SO_3H$	14-52, 52-100, 100-200, > 200*	4, 8, 12 20	4.5-5.0 mmol H^+	Na^+	1-14	
Amberlite CG 120	Strong acid	$-SO_3H$	100-200, 200-400 400-600†	8	5.0 mmol H^+	Na^+	1-14	
Zeo-Karb 226	Weak acid	$-CO_2H$	14-52, 52-100*	2.5, 4.5	9-10 mmol H^+	H^+	6-9	
Amberlite CG 50	Weak acid	$-CO_2H$	100-200, 200-400 400-600†		10.0 mmol H^+	H^+	5-14	
Deacidite FFIP	Strong base	$-CH_2\overset{+}{N}R_3$	14-52, 52-100*	2-3, 3-5, 7-9	4.0 mmol OH^-	Cl^-	1-14	R = alkyl
Amberlite CG 400	Strong base	$-CH_2\overset{+}{N}R_3$	100-200† 200-400	8	3.8 mmol OH^-	Cl^-	0-12	R = alkyl
Amberlite CG 45	Weak base	$-CH_2NR_2$	100-200† 200-400		5.0 mmol OH^-	OH^-	0-9	R = alkyl

*British Standard Screens
†US Standard Screens

porosity and chemical composition. These resins find wide application in demineralization, water treatment and ion-recovery from wastes.

The insoluble polymeric resin is synthesized by the suspension-radical copolymerization of styrene with divinylbenzene (DVB) (see Fig. 4.6). The polymerization results in a three-dimensional column framework which is porous in character and can thus allow diffusion of ions to take place through it. By conducting the polymerization in an aqueous medium beads of definite size can be produced. The extent of cross-linkage and hence pore size can be varied by altering the proportion of DVB. Sulphonic acid $(-SO_3H)$ exchange units are introduced in a controlled fashion by reacting the solvent swollen resin with chlorosulphonic acid, which results in mainly *para*-substitution of the benzene rings. The sulphonic-acid resin is described as a strong cation exchanger, is fully dissociated over a wide range of pH, and will exchange its protons for other cations under a wide range of pH (Tables 4.3 and 4.4).

Weak acid exchangers $(-COOH)$ are restricted in use between pH 5 and 14. The exchange groups are introduced directly by the polymerization of DVB and methacrylic acid. Phosphate groups commonly bonded to cellulose form ion exchangers of intermediate strength. Common exchange units on anion exchange resins are:

(a) $-CH_2-\overset{+}{N}-(CH_3)_3X^-$; $X^- = Cl, OH, NO_3$ etc.   quaternary ammonium resin
(b) $-CH_2-N-(CH_3)_2$ tertiary amino resin
(c) $-CH_2-NH-CH_3$ secondary amino resin
(d) $-CH_2-NH_2$ primary amino resin

The resins are prepared by chloromethylating the polymer matrix followed by treatment with the appropriate amine. The quarternary resin in both hydroxyl and salt forms is ionic, and hence may be described as a strongly basic resin which may be regarded as an insoluble polymeric cation associated with an equivalent number of active exchangeable hydroxide or halide ions.

The amino resins are weakly basic and are generally too weak to attract a proton from water to form a stable cation. They are therefore not commonly found in the hydroxide form. Salt forms are obtained by interaction of the base with an acid and these are ionic, containing the stable ammonium-type ion which is associated with an equivalent number of anions.

The wet form of the resin is denser than water and thus the resin beads may be packed into a column and conveniently eluted with water or aqueous solutions. Column operation is the usual procedure, though batch operation is possible where the resin and aqueous solution are stirred together to effect exchange.

4.5.1 Properties desirable in resins

For most applications using ion-exchange resins an important factor is the accessibility of the exchange sites to the ions in solution. The exchange takes place partly in the thin film of solvent adsorbed on the surface of the beads, and partly within the resin matrix; it is normally assumed that for small ions (including all metallic ions and simple inorganic anions, and many small organic ions) all the sites are equally accessible to the displacing ions in solution. This accessibility within the lattice depends partly on the degree of cross-linking of the polymer chains. If this varies in different parts of the resin, the exchange properties will be variable also, which is not desirable for efficient chromatography. With small amounts of cross-linkage exchange equilibria are established more quickly, due to the extra swelling of the resin, so that the diffusion of ions becomes more rapid. The degree of cross-linking is controlled in the manufacturing process; a larger range of cross-linking can be achieved in the polystyrene–divinylbenzene acidic resins than in basic polymethacrylate resins. By altering the degree of cross-linkage in the polymerization the resin pore size may be varied and the resin made selective for ions of a given size. If the pore size is small (a high degree of cross-linkage) the resin becomes selective towards smaller ions, the larger species being excluded from the resin. For acceptable chromatography a resin must also possess the following properties.

1. It must possess mono-functional exchange groups. There is no difficulty about this with modern resins, but earlier products made from phenol were polyfunctional (–OH and –COOH groups) and their exchange properties depended on the pH of the solution in which they were immersed. They were not, on this account, suitable for chromatography.
2. It must have a controlled degree of cross-linking; 4–8% is best for chromatography.
3. The range of particle sizes must be as small as possible.
4. The particle size must be as small as practicable.

4.5.2 Particle size

For large-scale (industrial plant) operation a fairly high flow rate through the resin bed is desirable, which requires the use of fairly large particles. The standard size for analytical purposes is about 50 mesh BSS. Analytical grades of resin differ from the standard industrial grades in being washed free of fines and water-soluble traces of polymerization intermediates. The useful bead sizes for chromatography are.

1. 200–600 mesh: only two types of resin, both cation-exchangers, are obtainable in this size.
2. 200–400 mesh: lower limit of practicable size for manufacture of anion-exchange and some cation-exchange resins. Even with this size flow rates are slow, but useful for microscale work.
3. 100–200 mesh: macroscale separations; quantitative.
4. 50–100 mesh: preparative separations.
5. 14–50 mesh: industrial scale separations.

In Table 4.4 the products of two principal manufacturers of resin are listed. Only the resins supplied in chromatographic grades are shown. There are other products with similar properties and the list is not intended to be exhaustive. Comprehensive lists are available elsewhere [35] and extensive literature is available from the manufacturers and suppliers of chromatographic materials.

4.5.3 Ion-exchange capacity

The ion-exchange capacity of a resin is a quantitative measure of its ability to take up exchangeable ions. The total capacity is defined as the amount of charged and potentially charged groups per gram of dry resin. The available capacity is the actual capacity obtained under specified experimental conditions and will be influenced by accessibility to functional groups, eluent concentration, ionic strength and pH, the nature of the counter ions, and the strength of the ion exchanger and its degree of cross-linkage.

For a cation exchanger the available capacity is determined by converting the resin to the hydrogen form, and using a neutral solution of a sodium salt to displace H^+ ions which are then titrated as free acid by a standard solution of sodium hydroxide. Then if: wt. of dry resin $= Wg$; NaOH titre $= Tml$; Molarity of NaOH $= A$; Dry wt. capacity $= TA/W$ milliequivalents gm^{-1}.

The available capacity of an anion exchanger is determined by converting it to the chloride form and using a neutral nitrate or sulphate solution to displace the chloride ions which are then estimated using a standard silver nitrate solution. As previously mentioned resins absorb water, causing the beads to swell, and hence ion-exchange capacities are determined on the basis of dry weight.

4.5.4 Selectivity of resins

The affinity between a resin and an exchangeable ion is a function both of the resin and the ion. Ion exchange is an equilibrium process which for a cationic process can be represented by the equation:

$$n(R^-H^+) + M^{n+} \rightleftharpoons (R^-)_n M^{n+} + nH^+$$

where R represents the resin matrix. The equilibrium distribution coefficient (K_d) also known as the selectivity coefficient, is given by:

$$K_d = [M^{n+}]_R [H^+]^h / [M^{h+}][H^+]_R^n$$

where $[M^{n+}]_R$ and $[H^+]_R$ are the concentrations of the exchanging ion and hydrogen ion within the structure. The greater the affinity for a particular ion, relative to hydrogen, the greater the value of K_d. For solutions which depart from the ideal concentration should strictly be replaced by activity. However, there is no entirely satisfactory way of measuring the activities of ions on a resin.

To illustrate how different cations may be separated let us consider a column which is packed with a cation exchanger in the hydrogen form. As a solution containing M^+ ions flows through the column the M^+ ions will replace H^+ ions on the resin according to the value of K_d. If only a small amount of the solution is used and it is washed down the column with pure water, all the M^+ ions will eventually replace hydrogen ions, and will form a stationary adsorbed band. The distribution of the ions within this band will depend on the value of K_d; if large, the band will be narrow and concentrated; if small, wide and diffuse. Thus if a few ml of 0.1 mol dm^{-3} sodium chloride are placed on a column which is then washed with distilled water, the sodium ions will remain in a more or less narrow band near the top of the column and an equivalent amount of hydrochloric acid will be liberated to be eluted from the column. (In fact it is possible to standardize a solution of caustic soda by using it to titrate the hydrochloric acid eluted when a solution of a known weight of sodium chloride is passed through a column in the hydrogen form.) In order to make the adsorbed band of ions (M^+) move down the column it is obviously necessary to elute with a solution of an acid (or a solution containing another cation) so that exchange can take place. The M^+ ions will then be washed out of the column, leaving it in its original form. The rate at which the band of ions moves will depend on the pH of the eluting acid and the value of K_d. Thus, two ions having different affinities for the resin will move at different rates down the column and a separation will be achieved.

4.5.5 Nature of the resin

The selectivity coefficient (K_d) is influenced by a number of factors operating in the resin; most obvious is the acid or base strength, i.e. the polarity of the exchange groups. Since in cation-exchangers the exchange groups are either $-SO_3H$ or $-COOH$ there is little scope for differences within each class (strong or weak).

The selectivity can also be affected by the degree of cross-linking. Small amounts reduce the selectivity while large amounts may totally or partly exclude larger (particularly organic) ions. Selectivity is also slightly influenced by temperature.

The affinity of cations for the resin in dilute aqueous solution increases with increasing charge; for cations of the same charge the affinity is inversely proportional to the radius of the hydrated ion. This may be explained in terms of the polarizing power of the cation, i.e. the greater the polarizing power of the cation, the greater its affinity for the resin and the more strongly will it be retained. (The polarizing power of a cation is proportional to Z^2/r where Z is the charge on the ion and r is the radius of the hydrated ion).

Some affinity sequences are given below:

1. Na^+ (aq.) $< Ca^{2+}$ (aq.) $< Al^{3+}$ (aq.) $< Th^{4+}$ (aq.).
2. Li^+ (aq.) $< Na^+$ (aq.) $< NH^+$ (aq.) $< K^+$ (aq.) $< Ti^+$ (aq.) $< Ag^+$ (aq.).
3. Mg^{2+} (aq.) $< Ca^{2+}$ (aq.) $< Sr^{2+}$ (aq.) $< Ba^{2+}$ (aq.).
4. Al^{3+} (aq.) $< Sc^{3+}$ (aq.) $< Lu^{3+}$ (aq.) $< \ldots$ lanthanides $\ldots < La^{3+}$ (aq.).

The orders above, however, are only true for solutions whose strength is about $0.1 \, mol \, dm^{-3}$ in the exchanging ion. At higher solution strengths the tendency is for the most concentrated ion to be most firmly bound, the others remaining in the same relative order. It is difficult to achieve separations of mixtures of multivalent cations solely on differences in affinities. Mixtures of this type are usually resolved by taking advantage of the ability of the ions to form complexes.

Anion-exchange resins, however, allow of more variation because the exchange groups are either $-\overset{+}{N}R_3$ or $-NR_2$ and the nature of the R group can be changed. The ionic form of a resin will also have some influence; the nitrate form of an anion resin will behave slightly differently (though not markedly so) from the chloride form; a series of K_d values is valid for only one specific ionic form of the resin.

In dilute solution the affinity of anions for an anion-exchange resin depends on the degree of polarization of the anion by the exchanger cation; i.e. the greater the degree of polarization the more firmly the anion is held, and the greater the affinity of the anion for the resin. Polarization of the anion increases with increasing negative charge and increasing size of the anion. In general, polyvalent anions have greater affinity than monovalent anions and for anions of the same charge the larger have the greater affinity.

$$F^- < HCO_3^- < Cl^- < HSO_3^- < CN^- < Br^- < NO_3^- < I^- \ll SO_4^{2-}$$

In terms of elution of anions from the resin the anions of least affinity will be eluted first.

4.5.6 Separation methods

The strong acid and strong base resins find much wider application than the weak varieties because of the wide pH range over which they retain their exchange properties. The weak acid and weak base types are highly ionized only when in a salt form, which is why their operation is restricted to the pH ranges indicated in Table 4.4. They may be preferred for certain separations however; for instance, polymethacrylic acid has more than twice the exchange capacity of the sulphonic acids at pH values greater than 7. Both weak acid and weak base resins may show a greater selectivity in certain circumstances. A weak base resin will adsorb strong acids but not weak ones and, conversely, weak acid resins will adsorb strong bases but not weak ones. Again, weak acid resins show greater selectivity for certain divalent ions.

Exchange isotherms measured in dilute solutions are approximately linear; that is, the amount of a particular ion held by a resin is directly proportional to the concentration of the ions in the solution in contact with it. At higher concentrations the uptake by the resin begins to fall off, with the result that the isotherm becomes concave to the concentration axis in a manner similar to that depicted in Fig. 4.5. Tailing can therefore be expected when the elution technique is used to separate concentrated solutions, otherwise symmetrical peaks, familiar in partition chromatography, will be obtained (see Chapter 9).

In chromatography the solutions used are mostly dilute; hence the elution technique is much employed and frequently gives highly satisfactory separations. In addition, all the other methods described in Chapter 1 have been used, although frontal analysis is not often encountered. Displacement development and stepwise and gradient elution are all employed; reference to Table 4.5 and 4.6 will provide examples.

A modification of the elution technique, already referred to under 'Selectivity' (section 4.2.3(d)), is also used to good advantage. It depends on alteration of the activities of the ions being separated by means of an eluting agent which will complex with them. A simple example is provided in Experiment 15 in Chapter 9, where copper(II) and iron(III) ions are separated by elution with phosphoric acid. If this separation is tried with hydrochloric acid as the eluant, the copper(II) ions tend to move more rapidly down the column than the iron(III) because they carry a smaller charge and are therefore not so firmly held by the resin. A good separation will not be obtained. If, however, phosphoric acid is used the iron(III) ions are rapidly removed from the column, and a sharp separation results. Subsequently the copper(II) ions can be removed with hydrochloric acid. Clearly

Table 4.5   Ion-exchange resins: inorganic separations

Separation	Ion-exchanger	Method	Ref. No.
Lanthanides	Sulphonated polystyrene	Elution with citrate buffers	36
Lanthanides	Dowex 1-X10 in nitrate form − 325 mesh	Stepwise and gradient elution with $LiNO_3$ solution	37
Actinides	Dowex 50 in ammonium form	Elution with ammonium lactate or ammonium α-hydroxy-isobutyrate	38
Lanthanides from actinides	Dowex 1-X8	Elution using $10 \, mol \, dm^{-3}$ LiCl in $0.1 \, mol \, dm^{-3}$ HCl	39
Ca, Al, Fe	Dowex 2 in citrate form	Stepwise elution with (a) water, (b) conc. HCl, (c) dil. HCl. (Also involves backwashing with conc. HCl)	40
Ca, Sr, Ba, Ce	Dowex 50-X8	Stepwise elution with ammonium α-hydroxy-isobutyrate	41
Zr, Hf	Dowex 1-X8	Elution with 3.5% H_2SO_4	42
Zr, Ti, Nb, Ta, W, Mo	Dowex 1-X8 200–400 mesh	Stepwise elution with mixtures involving HCl, oxalic acid, H_2O_2, citric acid and ammonium citrate	43
Many simple mixtures of metal ions	Dowex 50W-X8 100–200 mesh (in polythene columns)	Stepwise elution with dil. HF followed by a mineral acid such as HCl or HNO_3	44

Table 4.6   Ion-exchange resins: organic separations

Separation	Ion-exchanger	Method	Ref. No.
Amino-acids	Dowex 50-X4	Stepwise and gradient elution with citrate and citrate/acetate buffers	45
Phosphate esters	Dowex 1-X2 200–400 mesh in chloride or formate form	pH gradient elution (HCl)	46
Folic acid analogues	Diethylaminoethyl cellulose 100–250 mesh	Gradient elution $0.1-0.4\,mol\,dm^{-3}$ phosphate	47
Chlorophenols	Dowex 2-X8 200–400 mesh in acetate form	Gradient elution: acetic acid in ethanol	48
Aminobenzoic acid, aminophenols, and related substances	Dowex 1-X10 200–400 mesh in chloride form	Stepwise elution: water; $1\,mol\,dm^{-3}$, $5\,mol\,dm^{-3}$, and $8\,mol\,dm^{-3}$ HCl	49
Proteins	Diethylaminoethyl cellulose	Elution	
Separation of acids from bases both of which are freely water soluble	Sulphonated polystyrene in H form	Stepwise elution: water to remove acids: dil. HCl for bases	50

the phosphate ions form a much more stable complex with iron(III) ions, (which are rendered colourless) than with copper(II).

Complex formation is undoubtedly an important factor in other types of chromatography, particularly in inorganic separations on paper, but in no other technique has it been exploited to quite the same extent as in ion-exchange chromatography.

One of the earliest and most spectacular successes of ion-exchange chromatography was the separation of the lanthanides on a strong acid resin with a buffered citrate solution for elution. Straightforward elution with hydrochloric acid brings about little separation, but the citrate ions complex with the metal ions, thus reducing their activity, which then depends largely on the stability of the various citrate complexes. The equilibrium constants for the formation of the complexes (stability constants K_s) vary more than the affinities (K_d) of the free ions for the resin. Separation is therefore largely due to differences in K_s rather than those in K_d. Similar operations have been carried out on the actinides with Dowex 50 in the ammonium form and elution with ammonium lactate or ammonium-α-hydroxy-isobutyrate.

In Tables 4.5 and 4.6 some typical chromatographic separations performed on ion-exchange resins are listed.

4.6 SALTING OUT CHROMATOGRAPHY

In the technique of 'salting out' chromatography ion-exchange resins are used for the separation of non-electrolytes by elution from columns with aqueous salt solutions. The method has been reviewed by Rieman [51], who has also done most of the work in this field. He found that a mixture of methanol, ethanol, and propanol was scarcely separated at all when eluted through a column of Dowex 1-X 8 with water, but when the experiment was repeated on the same column using $3 \, mol \, dm^{-3}$ ammonium sulphate solution as the eluant, a good separation was obtained, the components appearing in the order of increasing molecular weight. In the presence of the salt the alcohols travel more slowly down the column because their solubilities are decreased and their affinities for the resin are increased. The solubility effect therefore considerably enhances the van der Waals adsorption, although the elution curves are symmetrical and show little sign of tailing. Other substances separated by this technique include ethers, aldehydes, ketones and amines.

As far as resin type is concerned there appears to be little difference between Dowex-1 (anion) and Dowex-50 (cation), but the presence of an exchange group (preferably strong) seems to be necessary, in order to confer the correct physical properties on the resin. Smaller than normal exchange capacities do improve the resolving power of a resin, but reduction below about $4 \, mmol \, M^+ \, g^{-1}$ reduces the rate at which equilibrium is established because the uptake of water by the resin is reduced; tailing may then occur.

Certain organic compounds of low solubility in water can be separated by a method which is almost the converse of that just described. Instead of an eluant which depresses the solubility in water, one which increases the solubility is used. For example, Rieman separated the alcohols, t-amyl, amyl, hexyl, heptyl, octyl and nonyl on a column of Dowex 50-X 8 in the hydrogen form, with aqueous acetic acid as the eluant. The particle size of the resin was 200–400 mesh and the column dimensions $39.0 \, cm \times 2.28 \, cm$.

4.7 INORGANIC ION-EXCHANGERS

It was mentioned at the beginning of the section on ion-exchange resins that certain inorganic salts had been used to impregnate paper thus enabling it to be used for separations involving ion-exchange. Considerable work was carried out to develop inorganic ion-exchange materials. Apart from clays and zeolites, which were in fact the first ion-exchange materials to be investigated, substances recently studied include heteropolyacid salts, zirconium salts, tin(IV) phosphate, tungsten hexacyanoferrate, and others. A general account of inorganic ion-exchangers was published by Amphlett [52] and chromatographic aspects were reviewed by Marshall and Nickless [53].

One of the reasons for the interest in inorganic materials is that resinous ion-exchangers are susceptible to radiation damage and are therefore not suitable for use with highly active solutions, although they have been successfully used for the separation of mixtures of actinides for example. Inorganic materials possess other advantages including a much greater selectivity for certain ions such as rubidium and caesium, and the ability to withstand solutions at high temperatures. In addition, inorganic ion-exchangers do not swell appreciably when placed in water and there is no change in volume when the ionic strength of the solution in contact with them is changed. On the other hand, some inorganic materials possess disadvantages such as solubility or peptization at certain pH values at which resins are normally stable, or they may be soluble in solutions in which resins are insoluble. Zirconium molybdate, for example, dissolves in EDTA, oxalate, and citrate solutions. Again, they may exist in microcrystalline forms which are not very convenient for packing columns since they tend to impede the flow of mobile phase, although there are ways of overcoming this problem.

Inorganic ion-exchangers fall roughly into two groups, crystalline, such as the ammonium salts of the 12-heteropolyacids, and amorphous, such as zirconium phosphate. One example from each group will be described.

Of the crystalline variety, perhaps the most thoroughly investigated compound is ammonium molybdophosphate, $(NH_4)_3PO_4.12MoO_3$ (AMP). As ordinarily prepared (see for example Thistlethwaite [54]) this salt is precipitated as very fine crystals which are unsuitable for packing columns. The problem was overcome by van R. Smit, Robb, and Jacobs [55], who used mixtures of AMP and asbestos. When equal weights of AMP and Gooch asbestos are mixed in water the AMP crystals adhere to the asbestos fibres. Columns packed with the coated asbestos thus obtained possess good flow characteristics. A method for the preparation of coarsely crystalline ammonium heteropolyacid salts including AMP was described by van R. Smit [56]; these crystals may be used to pack columns with good flow characteristics. Briefly, the process is to immerse large crystals of the heteropolyacid in saturated ammonium nitrate solution. The exchange capacity of AMP for caesium is about $1 \, mmol \, H^+ \, g^{-1}$ i.e. less than the theoretical value, but still comparable with the resinous ion-exchangers.

AMP can only be used in neutral or acid solutions because of its solubility in dilute alkalis. In acid solution (pH less than 2), only metal ions which form heteropolyacid salts insoluble in water exchange significantly with the ammonium ion, namely K^+, Rb^+, Cs^+, Ag^+ and Tl^+ [55]. Those ions are therefore selectively adsorbed from solutions containing other ions and very sharp separations are possible. In addition, very good separations of sodium from potassium, potassium from rubidium, and rubidium from caesium have been carried out, and more complicated separations are undoubtedly possible [55]. Under acid conditions polyvalent ions do not exchange readily, but at pH 2–5, they are fairly strongly adsorbed, especially if a suitable buffer solution is used [57]. Simple group separations are possible, for example Sr^{2+} from Y^{3+}, a quite strong acid solution being necessary to elute the Y^{3+}.

Zirconium phosphate, which is easily prepared by the addition of a solution of zirconyl nitrate or chloride to a phosphate solution is extremely insoluble and will not dissolve in solutions of high or low pH. It is an inorganic polymer with a relative molecular mass of about 880 [58]. It has a high exchange capacity (about 4 mmol OH^- g^{-1} in alkaline solution) and behaves as a weak acid cation-exchanger. It can be prepared in bead form [59] but does not show the very high selectivity of AMP. For example, the separation factor for caesium and rubidium on zirconium phosphate (α_{Rb}^{Cs}) is 1.3–1.5; in the case of AMP the corresponding figure is 26. Nevertheless zirconium phosphate shows adsorptive properties for a large number of cations and has been recommended for separations involving radioactive solutions.

4.8 LIQUID ION-EXCHANGERS

There are a number of liquids, exemplified by such compounds as trioctylamine (TNOA) and bis-(2-ethylhexyl)-phosphoric acid (HDEHP) which are immiscible with aqueous solutions and yet possess the property of ion-exchange, the former with anions and the latter with cations. These liquids have been used for liquid–liquid extraction but they may also be used to impregnate solid supports such as cellulose powder and polytrifluorochloroethylene (Kel-F) powder which are then packed into columns in the same way as for partition chromatography. Such columns operate in much the same way as columns of ion-exchange resins and it is thus possible to combine the advantages of partition chromatography (reversed phase) with the selectivity of ion-exchange. The subject of liquid ion-exchangers has been comprehensively reviewed by Coleman, Blake and Brown [60] and by Cerrai [61].

Early work was carried out with liquid anion-exchangers only, their capacity for extracting cations from solution being dependent on the ability of the cation to form anion complexes such as $[FeCl_6]^{3-}$. Liquid cation-exchangers, mainly mono- and di-esters of phosphoric acid, were used later.

4.8.1 Coating the solid support

The method of coating the solid support is somewhat different from that used for the preparation of ordinary partition columns. If cellulose is to be used as the support it is first dried in an air oven at about 80° C and allowed to cool in a desiccator. TNOA or HDEHP is dissolved in benzene or cyclohexane to give an approximately 0.1–0.3 mol dm^{-3} solution and equilibrated with the aqueous eluant by vigorously shaking the solutions together. The cellulose is then immersed in the organic solution and vigorously shaken for a prolonged period. The excess of liquid is decanted and the wet powder almost completely dried with filter paper, any remaining solvent finally being removed in an air oven.

Kel-F powder may be coated in a similar way, although the preliminary drying is not necessary. Because of its highly porous nature Kel-F has a greater capacity for the liquid ion-exchanger than has cellulose. The method of packing the column is similar to that described for partition columns.

4.8.2 Applications

A column in which TNOA is the stationary phase behaves in a similar fashion to a column packed with a strong anion-exchange resin (except that the capacity is somewhat lower), and therefore similar separations may be carried out. Mostly, however, TNOA columns have been used for separating cations, usually as their chloride or nitrate complexes. Eluting agents therefore tend to be aqueous hydrochloric acid or nitric acid, the eluting power of such solutions increasing with decreasing concentration of acid. Cations of transition metals clearly lend themselves to this treatment and a number of separations have been described [61] on TNOA-cellulose columns, for example iron, cobalt, and nickel. Nickel is eluted first with $8 \, mol \, dm^{-3}$ HCl, cobalt is eluted next with $3 \, mol \, dm^{-3}$ HCl, and finally iron with $0.3 \, mol \, dm^{-3}$ HNO_3. Uranium, thorium, and zirconium have been similarly separated with $8 \, mol \, dm^{-3}$ HCl plus 5% concentrated HNO_3.

HDEHP columns may be used to separate simple cations and it has been found possible to resolve mixtures of lanthanides, for example, lanthanum, cerium, neodymium, gadolinium, terbium, and thulium, by stepwise elution with hydrochloric acid. Lanthanum and cerium are eluted with $0.25 \, mol \, dm^{-3}$ HCl, neodymium, gadolinium, and terbium with $0.8 \, mol \, dm^{-3}$ HCl, and thalium with $6 \, mol \, dm^{-3}$ HCl. In this case the eluting power of the acid solution increases with increasing strength. It will be recalled that on a cation-exchange resin, little, if any, separation of lanthanides is possible with straightforward elution by hydrochloric acid and a complexing technique has to be employed.

4.9 GEL ION-EXCHANGERS

The separation of biological molecules from complex mixtures requires the use of high resolution techniques. It is, however, not normally practical to separate such molecules on conventional ion-exchange materials because the molecules cannot penetrate the resin matrix, even if cross-linking is as little as 1%. Most of the exchange sites are therefore inaccessible and, since the molecules do not use the full exchange capacity of the material, the separation is very inefficient. Ion-exchange using gels modified with ionogenic groups [62] has overcome this problem and made possible the ion-exchange separation of large polar and charged biological molecules.

In many cases it is clear whether an anion or cation exchanger is required for a separation, but this is not so with some important macromolecules (such as proteins) of biological origin which are amphoteric electrolytes. At a pH above the isoelectric point they are in the anionic form, and are separated on an anion exchanger; below the isoelectric point they are cationic, and a cation exchanger is used. The pH of the buffer is chosen according to the nature of the substances to be separated, and this then dictates the gel type to be employed. If, at the pH to be selected, the ampholyte has a high affinity for the exchange group of the resin, the appropriate weak ion-exchanger should be used.

Ion-exchange gels are used and handled in much the same way as are the unmodified gels, combined with some of the techniques used for conventional ion-exchange materials. Allowance must be made for changes in the gel condition when the ionic strength of the eluant is changed. Ion-exchange gels are supplied in the sodium form (cation-exchangers) or the chloride form (anion-exchangers) and they are usually converted before a separation is started into the H_3O^+ or the OH^- form respectively.

4.9.1 Dextrans

One of the first commercially available gel ion-exchangers was produced by introducing ionogenic units on to a cross-linked dextran.

The ionogenic groups were introduced by esterifying specific hydroxyl groups in the monosaccharide units of the gel. The alkylating reagents used for the esterification contain either a terminal acidic or basic group, this affording cationic and anionic exchangers respectively. Some of the properties of ion-exchange dextrans are listed in Table 4.7.

Gel ion-exchangers based on dextran have proved particularly useful since they have little tendency to denature or adsorb biological molecules because of their hydrophilic character and low adsorptivity. Furthermore, due to the high degree of substitution in the dextran matrix by ion-exchange groups, high sample

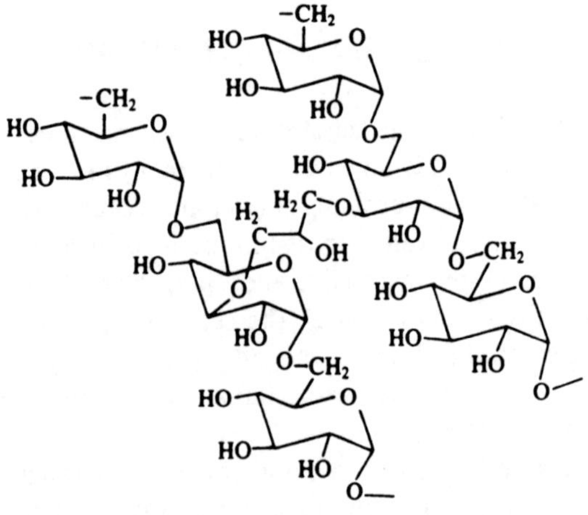

Fig. 4.7   Partial structure of a cross-linked dextran (Sephadex).

Table 4.7   Commercially available dextran ion-exchangers

Name	Type	Functional group	Exchange capacity $mmol\,H^+(OH^-)g^{-1}$ (approx.)
SP-Sephadex	Strong acid	Sulphoxyl	2.3
CM-Sephadex	Weak acid	Carboxymethyl	4.5
QAE-Sephadex	Strong base	Diethyl-(2-hydroxy propyl)aminoethyl	3.0
DEAE-Sephadex	Weak base	Diethylaminoethyl	3.5
DEAE-Agarose	Weak base	Diethylaminoethyl	1.5
CM-Agarose	Weak acid	Carboxymethyl	2.5
DEAE-Sephacel	Weak base	Diethylaminoethyl on cellulose	1.4

capacities are obtained, and also the material has good packing characteristics as the gel is bead-formed.

Physical properties

Ion-exchange dextrans are physically very similar to ordinary dextrans, and have similar chemical stability. However, the extent of swelling in aqueous buffers is very much more dependent on the ionic strength of the solute. When the ionic strength of the solution is lowered, the gels swell considerably; they shrink again when the ionic strength is raised. This is of practical importance in the operation of a column since if a considerable shrinkage occurs when a buffer is changed, cavities and irregularities may appear in the bed. Again, excessive swelling may clog the column. Swelling is most likely to happen during regeneration, and in consequence it is often better to regenerate the resin in a Büchner funnel, and then to repack the column.

Ion-exchange dextrans are supplied in two degrees of porosity, the less porous being recommended for separations where the relative molecular mass (M_r) is less than 3×10^4 or greater than 2×10^5 (in the latter case the molecules will be totally excluded from the gel and little ion-exchange will take place). The more porous gel is recommended for separations between the two M_r limits stated. The bead size in all cases is 40–120 μm.

Applications

The number of reported uses of ion-exchange dextrans is increasing rapidly. Examples are the use of DEAE-Sephadex for the separation of mucopolysac-charides by stepwise elution with NaCl [63] in dilute HCl, soluble RNAs [64], and the separation of myoglobin and haemoglobin [65]. Cation-exchange dextrans have been used for the separation of β and γ-globulin [66], alkaloids [66], and for the purification of enzymes [67].

4.9.2 Agarose gels

Agarose is a mixture of charged and neutral polysaccharides. The agarose repeating sub-unit is shown in Fig. 4.8(a). A gel is formed from the neutral fraction of agar and the agarose units cross-linked with 2,3-dibromopropanol (Fig. 4.8(b)). This process gives a bead-form gel with a very rigid structure arising from the alignment of the polysaccharide chains, which are stabilized by hydrogen bonding, while further rigidity is conferred on the chain by intrachain cross-linking. Ion-exchange capability is conferred by the introduction of carboxymethyl and diethylaminoethyl functionality, these groups being bonded to the monosaccharide sub-unit *via* an ether linkage. This preparation process gives a highly rigid gel material with a similar porosity, and molecular weight exclusion limit to dextran gels, but with improved mechanical strength and capacity. Further benefits arising from the rigid structure are: consistency of bed-volume, which is relatively unaffected by changes in the ionic strength and pH of the eluant; and the improved flow properties and high flow rates which can be achieved. Table 4.7 lists the properties of some agarose ion-exchange gels.

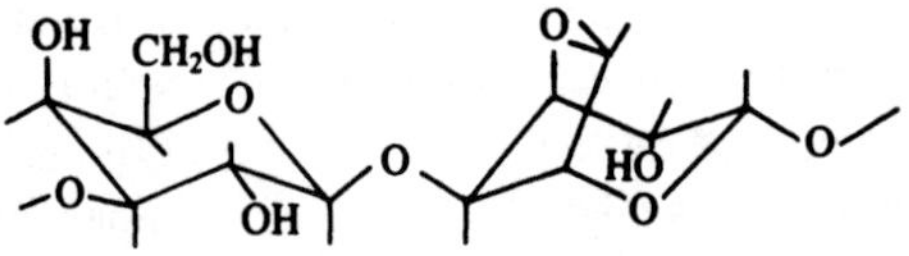

(a)

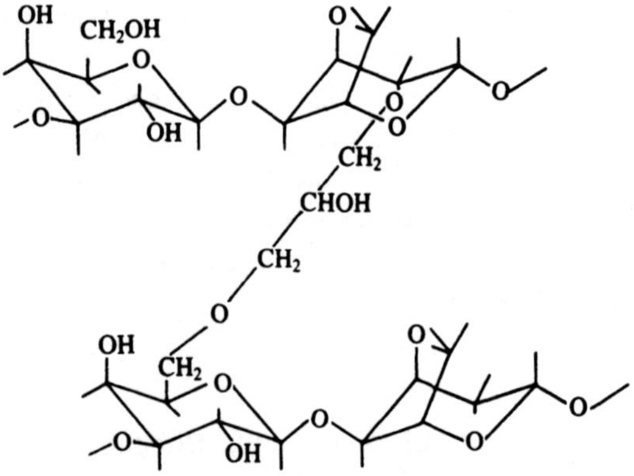

(b)

Fig. 4.8   (a) Partial structure of agarose; (b) partial structure of Sepharose, a cross-linked agarose.

4.9.3 Cellulose

The first ion-exchangers designed for the separation of biological molecules utilized a cellulose matrix [68]. Though cellulose, because of its hydrophilic properties, had little tendency to denature proteins, these packings suffered from low sample capacities and poor flow characteristics, both defects stemming from the irregular shape of the particles.

It was not until the mid-' 60s that cellulose gels were produced in the optimal bead form. In the production of commercial gels the polysaccharide gel is broken down and during the regeneration bead process it is cross-linked for added strength with epichlorohydrin. The resulting macroporous bead ($40–120\,\mu m$ diameter) has good hydrolytic stability with an exclusion limit of $\sim 1 \times 10^6$ for proteins. The only commercially available material, DEAE (diethylaminoethyl)-Sephacel can be used in the pH range 2–12. However, hydrolysis can occur in strongly acidic solutions while strongly alkaline media can cause breakdown of the macromolecular structure. These packings have excellent flow characteristics and increased physical strength and stability arising from the cross-linked bead structure. Re-equilibration is also facilitated as the bed volume is stable over a wide range of ionic strengths and pH. The above material is used in the ion-exchange separation of proteins, nucleic acids, hormones and other biopolymers.

4.10 GEL CHROMATOGRAPHY

Adsorption studies on silica gel and active carbon had shown molecular sieve effects with materials of high relative molecular mass, and in 1954 Mould and Synge [69] showed that separations based on molecular sieving could be performed on uncharged substances during electro-osmotic migration through gels. This formed a basis for separations based on the relative sizes of molecules, and the systematic use of the principle was introduced in 1959 by Porath and Flodin [70], who used the term 'gel filtration' to describe their method of separating large molecules of biological origin in aqueous systems by means of polysaccharide gels. In a pioneering paper on non-biochemical uses Moore [71] used the term 'gel permeation chromatography' (GPC). Both of these terms are still used in their respective fields, and others have been proposed, but in 1964 Determann [72] suggested that 'gel chromatography' was the most general name for the technique, and this is the one that will be used here.

The stationary phase is a porous polymer matrix whose pores are completely filled with the solvent to be used as the mobile phase. The pore size is highly critical, since the basis of the separation is that molecules above a certain size are totally excluded from the pores, and the interior of the pores is accessible, partly or wholly, to smaller molecules.

The flow of mobile phase will cause larger molecules to pass through the column unhindered, without penetrating the gel matrix, whereas smaller

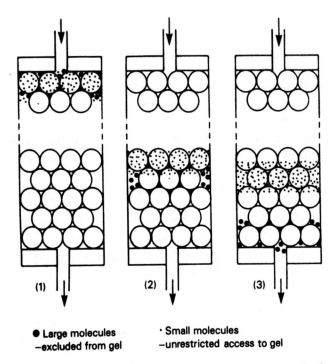

● Large molecules   · Small molecules
 −excluded from gel   −unrestricted access to gel

Fig. 4.9 Principle of gel chromatography: (1) mixture applied to top of column; (2) partial separation; (3) complete separation, excluded substance emerges from column.

molecules will be retarded according to their penetration of the gel. The principle is illustrated in Fig. 4.9. The components of the mixture thus emerge from the column in order of relative molecular mass, the larger first. Any compounds which are completely excluded from the gel will not be separated from each other, and similarly, small molecules which completely penetrate the gel will not be separated. Molecules of intermediate size will be retarded to a degree dependent on their penetration of the matrix. If the substances are of a similar chemical type they are eluted in order of relative molecular mass.

Adsorption effects caused by the surface of the gel particles can usually be ignored, and thus gel chromatography can be looked upon as a kind of partition chromatography. The liquid stationary phase is the liquid within the gel matrix, and the mobile phase is the flowing eluant which fills the rest of the column. We have, in other words, a partition column where the two liquid phases, mobile and stationary, are of the same composition.

The model proposed above suggests that the differential exclusion of the solute molecules was achieved on the basis of their hydrodynamic volumes, that is, their size and shape. This model has been extended by Porath [73] who considered the pores in dextran gels to be conical in nature. A further approach [74], which considers the gel to be composed of randomly arranged rigid rods, shows good correlation between the molecular radius and retention volume of the solute.

Gel chromatography was originally used for separation of biological materials, because the earliest gel media, cross-linked dextrans, were suitable for use only with an aqueous system. In 1964 cross-linked polystyrene gels suitable for use with organic solvents were first produced [71], and this made possible the extension of gel chromatography to the separation and characterization of synthetic polymers. Application of the method, not only to a large variety of separations but also to determination of relative molecular mass proceeded rapidly.

Early accounts of the use of gel chromatography were given by Porath [75], Tiselius, Porath, and Albertsson [76], Gelotte [77], and Granath [78]. In addition, the manufacturers and suppliers of many commercially available gel media provide an extensive information service.

4.10.1 Column parameters and separations

A number of theoretical treatments of gel chromatography have been published, including applications of the theoretical plate concept similar to those outlined in Chapter 2. It is appropriate here to mention only a few simple parameters of most value in practical work.

A column is made up by pouring a slurry of swollen gel particles, suspended in the solvent used to swell the gel, into a suitable tubular container. The total volume of the column, V_t (which can be measured) is the sum of the volume of liquid outside the gel matrix, V_0, the volume of liquid inside the matrix, V_i, and the volume of the gel matrix, V_M i.e.:

$$V_t = V_0 + V_i + V_m$$

V_0 is also known as the void or dead volume: it is the volume of mobile phase which will elute a totally excluded molecule. The volume required to elute a particular molecule is the elution volume (or retention volume) V_e. The use of these volumes is not very satisfactory in describing the behaviour of particular

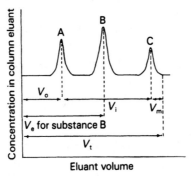

Fig. 4.10 Separation parameters for gel columns.

solvents because although they are characteristic of the gel and the solutes they also depend on the volume and packing density of the column. As in other forms of partition chromatography the elution volume (V_e) can be related to the column dead volume (V_0) and the volume of stationary phase (V_i) through the following equation:

$$V_e = V_0 + K_d V_i$$

where K_d is the volumetric distribution coefficient. Thus:

$$K_d = (V_e - V_0)/V_i$$

K_d is a constant for a given solute and gel under constant operating conditions of eluent composition and temperature. Thus the determination of K_d characterizes the retention behaviour of the solute independently of the dimensions of the chromatographic bed.

K_d represents the fraction of the gel volume that is accessible to the molecule concerned, and is thus zero for a totally excluded molecule ($V_e = V_0$), and unity for a molecule which has access to the gel equal to that of the solvent ($V_e = V_0 + V_i$). The relationship between these various parameters is shown in Fig. 4.10.

In practice, not all these volumes are readily determined. V_0 can be measured as the volume required to elute a completely excluded solute, and V_e for a particular solute is equally readily measured. On the other hand the methods which can be used for determining V_i (requiring, for example, observation of the elution of tritiated water) give only approximate results, since exchange reactions on the sephadex gel cause the ^3H peak to emerge after the bed volume [79]. K_d is often, therefore, replaced by an alternative distribution coefficient, K_{av}, which is defined [80] as:

$$K_{av} = (V_e - V_0)/(V_i + V_m)$$

that is:

$$K_{av} = (V_e - V_0)/(V_t - V_0)$$

where ($V_i + V_m$) approximates to the stationary phase volume V_s. Although all the volumes in this expression can be determined without difficulty, K_{av} has the disadvantage (because of the inclusion of a term for the gel volume, V_m) of not approaching unity for small molecules.

If K_d or K_{av} is plotted against the logarithm of the molecular weight for a series of solutes similar in molecular shape and density, an s-shaped curve is obtained. Over a small range of K_{av}, the fractionation range, the curve approximates to a straight line (Figs. 4.11 and 4.12):

$$K_{av} = A + B \log M$$

the fractionation range.

The first plot shows the fractionation range of the gel, which is defined as the approximate range of M_r (relative molecular mass) within which a separation can be expected, provided that the molecules concerned are in different parts of

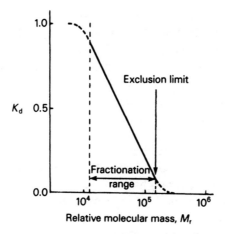

Fig. 4.11   Fractionation ranges.

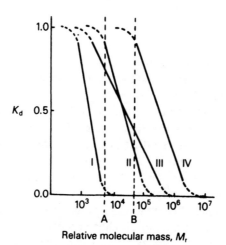

Fig. 4.12   Choice of gel.

the range. The upper end of the range $(K_d \rightarrow 0)$ is the exclusion limit, the M_r of the smallest molecule which cannot penetrate the pores of the matrix. The plot of K_d against log M_r diverges from linearity as K_d approaches 0 or 1, and the fractionation range is the range of M_r over the linear part of the curve. For most gels the lower limit of the range $(K_d \rightarrow 1)$ is about one tenth of the exclusion limit.

Since M_r is not directly related to the size or shape of the molecule, it is necessary to state, in publishing fractionation ranges for gels, what type of molecule has been used in the determinations. Most commercial gels are made in a number of grades of different fractionation range.

A gel is selected such that the M_r values of the substances to be separated lie on the straight part of the curve. This is illustrated in Fig. 4.12, where

$A(M_r \sim 5 \times 10^4)$ and $B(M_r \sim 6 \times 10^3)$ are the substances to be separated. It can be seen that either of the gels II or III could be used. It would be better to use gel II because the K_d values are in that case further apart, and the fractions of the eluate containing A and B would be further apart also. More complex mixtures would require the use of gels of wider fractionation range, but in general it is best to use a gel of as narrow a range as possible.

Sorption effects by the gel matrix may alter the values of K_{av} and K_d for certain solutes. Using K_d against log M_r plots to select a gel does not take into account either those effects or zone spreading in the column and variations in flow rate (which could arise, for example, from differences in viscosity of sample and eluant). Taken together these may have an important effect on the separation, and hence on the choice of the best gel for a particular purpose. The behaviour of small molecules on tightly cross-linked gels is profoundly influenced by adsorption, ion exclusion, ion exchange and various other processes which dominate the size differences between solutes.

4.10.2 Nature of the gel

Separation by gel chromatography is influenced by the properties of the pores in the three-dimensional network, and the nature of the pore-forming material itself. The gel must be chemically inert, mechanically stable and have a carefully formed and reproducible porous structure, with a fairly uniform particle size.

The fractionation range is governed by the range of pore sizes in a given gel. A wide range of pore sizes gives rather poor resolution, though a narrow range, while giving improved resolution, has a more limited molecular weight range of application. Normally, a series of sorbents is used which separates solutes over a characteristic molecular weight range, commonly one order of magnitude.

The chemical stability of commercially available gels is good though they are not resistant to strongly acidic or alkaline conditions. For high flow rates the sorbents must have good physical stability. However, the large pore structure contains only moderate amounts of the solid matrix; the gels are thus mechanically weak and are distorted even when moderate pressure is applied, and hence attainable flow rates are limited. As in other modes of chromatography the optimum particle shape is spherical. The bead size should be as small as possible, while still affording the desired flow rate, the limit of which is effectively determined by the rigidity of the structure – compressible gels would give impracticably low flow rates. Some examples of commercially available gels are given in Table 4.8. Two main types of gel material may be distinguished – xerogels and aerogels. Xerogels are gels in the classical sense; they consist of cross-linked polymers which swell in contact with the solvent to form a relatively soft porous medium, in which the pores are the spaces between the polymer chains in the matrix. If the liquid is removed the gel structure collapses, although it can sometimes be restored by replacing the liquid. Aerogels, on the other hand,

Table 4.8 Some commercially available media for gel chromatography

Name	Type	Chemical nature	Eluant (mobile phase)	Maximum exclusion limit M_r	Calibration	Number of fractionation ranges	Bead size	Notes
Sephadex G	Xerogel	Dextran	Aqueous	6×10^5 2×10^5	Peptides/proteins Dextrans	12 8	10–40,* 40–120, 50–150, 100–200	Superfine grade for very high resolution and thin layers
Sephadex LH	Xerogel	Dextran hydroxypropyl ether	Polar organic	5×10^3		1	25–100*	Exclusion limit varies according to solvent
Bio-Gel P	Xerogel	Polyamide	Aqueous	4×10^3	Peptides/proteins	10	50–100,† 100–200, 200–400	
Enzacryl Gel K	Xerogel	Polyacryloyl-morpholine	Aqueous Polar organic	1×10^5	Polyethylene-glycols	2		Little swelling in lower alcohols
Bio-Beads SX	Xerogel	Polystyrene	Organic	14×10^3	Polystyrenes	7		
Styragel	Hybrid	Macroporous polystyrene	Non-polar organic	4×10^8	Polystyrenes	12		
Bio-Gel A	Hybrid	Agarose	Aqueous	15×10^7	Dextrans	6	50–100,† 100–200, 200–400	1, 2, 4, 6, 8, 10% agarose
Sepharose	Hybrid	Agarose	Aqueous	4×10^7 2×10^7	Proteins Polysaccharides	3	60–250,* 40–190, 40–210	2, 4, 6% agarose
Merck-O-Gel	Hybrid	Polyvinyl acetate	Polar organic	1×10^6	Polystyrenes	6		
Porasil	Acrogel	Silica	Aqueous Organic	2×10^6	Polystyrenes	6		Calibration in organic solvents
Bio-Glas	Aerogel	Glass	Aqueous Organic	9×10^6	Polystyrenes	5		Calibration in toluene

*μm; †US standard Screens; M_r = relative molecular mass.

are rigid materials which are not really gels at all; they are porous solids which are penetrated by the solvent, and they do not collapse when the solvent is removed; porous glass and porous silica are examples. Some gel materials, such as polystyrene, are xerogel-aerogel hybrids. These have a fairly rigid structure, but swell to some extent on contact with solvents, in the same way as ion-exchange resins. An exception is agarose (see below), which behaves in an unusual way. Much greater care is needed in handling and using the relatively soft xerogels and agarose than in handling the much more rigid polystyrene hybrids and aerogels, particularly in controlling column conditions to prevent particle break-down and coagulation of the particles, both of which will retard the flow of mobile phase.

Dextran gels

The original gel chromatography medium which is still widely used, was Sephadex G, a cross-linked dextran. The starting material, dextran, is a natural linear polysaccharide, i.e., a polyglucose, in which the glucose residues are predominantly α-1,6 linked; it is insoluble in aqueous media.

The individual polysaccharide chains of dextran can be cross-linked, with glyceryl bridges between the hydroxyl groups, on reaction under alkaline conditions with a dispersion of epichlorohydrin in an organic medium (Fig. 4.7). The resulting product is a water-insoluble solid in bead form, which is hydrophilic due to the many residual hydroxyl groups, a feature that causes the gel to swell in water/aqueous solutions; the water regain is $1-20 \, \text{ml g}^{-1}$ of dry resin. The extent of cross-linkage can be varied by controlling the relative proportions of epichlorohydrin and dextran. Thus a range of sephadex gels of varying porosity have been obtained which are useful over different molecular weight ranges. The random distribution of cross-linkages also produces a wide distribution of pore sizes in each type of gel, thus providing a wide linear working range. The sephadex gels are insoluble and stable in water, salt and alkaline solutions and organic media.

Little swelling occurs in non-polar solvents, and thus dextran gels are only useful in aqueous media. Traces of carboxyl ($10-20 \, \text{mmol H}^+ \, \text{g}^{-1}$ of dry gel) remain, which may affect the separation of some polar species; this property is exploited in aromatic adsorption studies. High chemical stability is conferred on the gels due to the covalent cross-linking of the individual polysaccharide chains; they can be safely used between pH 2 and 12, though at very low pH hydrolysis of the glycosidic linkages may occur.

Dextran hydroxypropyl ether

Sephadex LH-20 is the hydroxypropyl ether of Sephadex G-25 (the number indicates the porosity of the gel). It will form a gel in both aqueous and organic solvents, and is particularly effective in solvents such as dimethyl sulphoxide, pyridine, and dimethyl-formamide.

Polyacrylamide gels

Bio-Gel P is a wholly synthetic polyacrylamide gel made by suspension co-polymerization of acrylamide and the cross-linking agent N, N'-methylenebisacrylamide. (Lea and Schon [81]; Hjerten [82]). The pore size is regulated by variation of the proportions of the monomers. Polyacrylamide gels behave in a similar way to dextran gels, with a water regain of $1.5–18\,\mathrm{ml\,g^{-1}}$ of dry resin. Polyacrylamide gels are less resistant to alkali than Sephadex and hydrolysis of the amide residues to carboxylic acid groups occurs on exposure to solvents of extreme pH.

Polyacryloylmorpholine

Suspension co-polymerization of acryloylmorpholine and N, N'-methylenebisacrylamide gives the medium known as Enzacryl Gel. This material swells to a gel in water, and also in pyridine and chloroform, although not in lower alcohols.

Polystyrene

Styrene-divinylbenzene polymers, as used in ordinary ion-exchange resins, but without ionizing groups, will form gels in less polar organic solvents. One form of this polymer is Bio-Beads S. Unfortunately this type of polymer has a very small pore size, which rather restricts the range of uses.

If styrene and divinylbenzene are co-polymerized in a solvent mixture in which the polymer is sparingly soluble, a macro-porous form of the polymer bead is obtained. One such material is Styragel, which can be used very effectively in the gel chromatography of organic polymers in organic solvents. Introduction of a few $-SO_3H$ groups into a macro-porous resin (Aquapak) makes the gel hydrophilic, and thus usable in aqueous solvents, although the presence of the strongly acidic group may be a disadvantage.

Polyvinyl acetate

Co-polymerization of vinyl acetate and 1,4-divinyloxybutane gives a material which forms a gel in polar organic solvents, including alcohols (Merck-O-Gel OR).

Agarose gels

All the xerogels described are characterized by extreme softness of the swollen gel when the pore size is large. Larger pore sizes with mechanical stability are obtainable in the aerogels glass and silica, but with a penalty of incursion of adsorption effects. To overcome this adsorption difficulty, and to obtain larger pore sizes, agarose gels were developed.

Agarose is a polysaccharide (alternating 1,3-linked β-D-galactose and 1,4-linked 3,6-anhydro-α-L-galactose) obtained from seaweed (Fig. 4.8). Above 50° C it dissolves in water, and if the solution is cooled below 30° C a gel is formed, which is insoluble below 40° C. Above that temperature the gel 'melts' or collapses; freezing also causes irreversible changes in the structure of the gel. The chemical stability of agarose gels is similar to that of dextran gels, and is derived from the helical formation between individual polymer molecules. Residual sulphate groups may be eliminated by alkaline hydrolysis of the cross-linked agar and agarose under reducing conditions [83]. The charged hydroxyl groups can be reduced to the corresponding alcohol on reaction with lithium aluminium hydride [84].

Several forms of agarose are obtainable commercially (Sepharose, Bio-Gel A, Gelarose, Sagavac), which indicates the usefulness of this gel. It can be made with a very large pore size, and it is mechanically much more stable than a dextran gel of similar pore size.

Porous silica

Silica is commercially available in bead form (Porasil, Merck-O-Gel Si) with a range of porosities. This is an aerogel, with a very rigid structure. It can be used in some organic solvents, but it is best used in water. It is rather highly polar, and can tend to retard polar molecules by adsorption.

Porous glass

Various grades of granular porous glass (Corning; Bio-Glas) are available. Glass can be used for gel chromatography in both aqueous and organic media, but there may be undesirable adsorption effects, as with silica, due to the presence of negatively charged sites. These groups can be temporarily 'capped' with polyethylene oxide [85] or polyethylene glycol [86]. The gels are derived from borosilicate by heat treatment followed by acid leaching; this process gives a gel of accurately controlled pore size and very narrow distribution. Porous glasses have numerous advantages arising from their rigid structure. They have good mechanical strength, are heat stable and can be used in aqueous and non-aqueous solvent systems.

4.10.3 Methodology

Column preparation

Columns for gel permeation studies are generally packed with a suspension of the gel material in the appropriate solvent. The gel suspension is adjusted to the consistency of a thick slurry, though sufficiently mobile to allow trapped air to bubble freely through it. The 'fines' can be decanted at this stage and the well-mixed slurry is poured into the column. The gel bed is then equilibrated by passing through two to three volumes of the eluant at a flow rate slightly higher than that to be used in the experiment. The column is then tested by running through a totally excluded coloured solute, commonly Blue Dextran 2000, in a sample volume less than 10% of the column volume. If the column is properly packed and stabilized the coloured substance should be eluted as a compact horizontal band. This test also gives a measure of the void volume, V_0, i.e. the volume required to elute the unretained coloured substance.

During packing of the column and development of the chromatogram the top of the column must not be allowed to run dry and must not be disturbed. Generally the most crucial factor in operation of the column is control of the flow rate. Operating the column at pressures greater than specified in the manu-facturers' literature can lead to diminution of the flow rate due to compression of the chromatographic bed arising from fracture and deformation of the gel particles.

The sample preparation

Solid particles and any substances which may be strongly adsorbed on the gel should be removed from the sample. The mass and concentration of the solutes are only important in so far as they affect the viscosity. Sample viscosity of more than about twice that of the eluant leads to poor resolution. The sample capacity, in terms of volume, is also important.

The sample volume is also important. The largest volume which can be handled for complete separation in one run through a column is $(V_{e1} - V_{e2})$ where these are the elution volumes of the two most closely related components (from the chromatographic point of view). For group separations where $(V_{e1} - V_{e2})$ is large, the sample volume can be 10–30% of the bed volume, V_t. For separation of closely related components i.e. if $(V_{e1} - V_{e2})$ is small the sample volume should only be 1–3% of V_t. No useful gain in resolution is obtained by further reduction of the sample volume. The smaller the sample volume, the greater will be the reduction of the component concentration in the eluate; this dilution effect may have to be taken into account in deciding upon column and sample sizes.

For very small samples, (approximately 1 mm^3), gel chromatography may well be more effective on gel thin-layer plates than on columns (Chapter 3). The thin-layer technique can often be used in a 'pilot' experiment to discover the best conditions for a larger-scale separation on a column.

With simple laboratory columns the sample is applied to the top of the gel bed by any of the usual methods. Application of sample to the drained bed, though requiring little specialist equipment, is difficult to achieve without disturbing the surface of the packing. A technique suitable for samples which are denser than the eluant, such as blood serum, involves sample application through a fine capillary to the top of the column under a layer of the eluant. If required, the sample density can be increased by the addition of glucose, buffer salts or other suitable inert material.

The sample can best be applied to the column using three-way valves in conjunction with a loop or syringe. In the former, the loop can be isolated from the eluant flow and filled with sample. The loop contents are then flushed on to the column by switching the valve position, so bringing the loop in series with the solvent delivery from the reservoir. Loop-valve systems afford very reproducible sample volume application. Syringe-valve systems, as illustrated in Fig. 4.13 necessitate interruption of the solvent delivery during sample application. This latter technique, however, allows for variation in the sample loading. The eluant flow can be generated either by gravity feed or by a pump. In the system illustrated (Fig. 4.13) the sample is applied from a syringe *via* a three-way valve to the bottom of the column. This system provides a constant hydrostatic pressure, which corresponds to the vertical distance between the lower end of the flask air-inlet tube and the free end of the column outlet tubing.

Development of the chromatogram is strikingly simple. Only isocratic techniques are used and the solutes are eluted in order of decreasing molecular weight and/or size. The number of solutes which can be resolved is normally less than 10 as the maximum elution volume in the absence of adsorption forces can be no greater than the total volume of mobile phase $(V_0 + V_i)$ present in the column. Resolution in gel chromatography is subject to the same theoretical considerations as in other forms of liquid chromatography (LC). The important variables for control of resolution are column length (l), particle size (dp) and

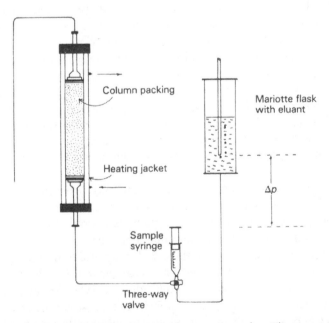

Fig. 4.13   Experimental set-up for gel chromatography. The operating pressure (Δp) is the height between the air inlet and the eluant outlet. The 3-way valve connects either the sample or the eluant to the column.

homogeneity of packing. The influence of flow rate on column performance has previously been discussed. While the column performance increases as the $\sqrt{1}$, the column length which can be used in practice is limited due to compressibility of the gel. Alternatively the resolution can be improved by using a smaller particle size, though again this is limited by the back pressure and the restriction on flow.

Homogeneity of column packing is essential for good column performance, as irregularities in packing will cause additional peak broadening, Peak resolution is generally little affected by solvent composition. However, where the solutes are electrolytes retention behaviour can be modified by varying the ionic strength of the eluant. The effect is especially marked where the solute configuration is influenced by electrolyte solutions. Furthermore, partition can be controlled by adding small amounts of materials such as dextran, polyvinylalcohol and polyethyleneglycol to the eluant. Small amounts of these additives have a significant effect on the K_{av} values. Of course, where adsorptive interactions occur between solute molecules and the gel packing eluant strength has a pronounced effect on resolution.

4.10.4 Applications

Since 1959 literally thousands of papers have been published on the use of gel chromatography and related applications. This section will therefore be restricted to a broad but necessarily selective examination of the areas of application, and only some instructive examples will be described.

Group separations and desalting

The simplest application of gel permeation chromatography is the separation of two groups of solutes of widely-differing sizes. By choosing a suitable gel, high molecular weight material may be totally excluded ($K_{av} \to 0$) and will wash through in the void volume, while low molecular weight materials ($K_{av} \to 1$) will be strongly retained. For example, low molecular weight materials such as urea, sugars and peptides, liberated during chemical modification of proteins, can be separated from the high macromolecular molecular weight products. The particular application where large molecules of biological origin are separated from inorganic or ionizable species is known as desalting. A typical example is the separation of haemoglobin and sodium chloride on a sephadex gel [87].

Fractionation of mixtures

Fractionation of mixtures of biopolymers is the most widespread application of gel chromatography and can be carried out on the analytical and preparative scale. When the molecular weight and sizes of the components of the sample do not differ greatly a gel of the appropriate fractionation range should be chosen.

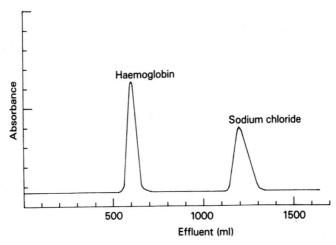

Fig. 4.14   Group separation of haemoglobin and sodium chloride [87].

Choice of suitable gels allowed various peptides [88], nucleic acid [89], enzyme [90] and polysaccharide [91] mixtures to be separated and purified.

Molecular weight determinations

Gel chromatography was first used to separate large molecules of biological origin such as proteins, polysaccharides, nucleic acids and enzymes. The initial observation that substances were eluted in order of decreasing molecular weight initiated studies exploring the relationship between the chromatographic behaviour of the molecules and their molecular weight (M) [70]. On sephadex the relationship has been reported [92]:

$$\log M = A - B(V_e/V_0)$$

where A and B are constants. Before applying such a relationship to the estimation of molecular weights, the column must be calibrated using several materials of similar type and of known molecular weight. Where the molecules concerned are chemically related the fractionation curve can be used as the basis for determining the M_r and M_r ranges. Though the studies were initially of naturally occurring macromolecules [93, 94], the separation and examination of synthetic polymers [95] has been added to the field of application, and the method has become an important part of polymer technology.

Protein-ligand binding

A recent area of study of increasing interest and importance is the examination of the equilibrium binding of small ligands to proteins [96, 97]. A sample of protein equilibrated with the ligand is applied to the gel column containing free ligand.

The normal processes of molecular sieving disturb the ligand-protein equilibrium concentrations of the applied sample and elution results in the appearance of a protein front followed by a mixture of free and bound material. The binding ratio can be estimated from peak area measurements obtained from the chromatogram.

4.11 AFFINITY CHROMATOGRAPHY

Ordinary chromatographic techniques depend for their effectiveness on differences (often small) in adsorption, partition, ionic charge, or size, between solute molecules of similar chemical character. A modified gel technique in which use is made of the high specificity of biochemical reactions is affinity chromatography [98, 99].

4.11.1 Principles

A ligand, which exhibits a specific binding affinity for a particular compound, is covalently bonded to the gel matrix and the material is packed into the column in the normal manner. The sample is applied to the top of the column in a suitable buffered eluant. On development components with a specific affinity for the ligand become bound (though not irreversibly) and are retarded. The unbound material washes straight through the column.

The composition or pH of the eluant is then altered to weaken the component-ligand bonding, thus promoting dissociation and facilitating elution of the retained compounds. The conditions which must be fulfilled are therefore: the gel–ligand bond must be stable under the conditions of the experiment; the ligand–substrate bond must be specific, and reversible under the conditions of the experiment; and the gel–ligand bonding must be such that the specific adsorption properties of the ligand are not interfered with by the gel matrix.

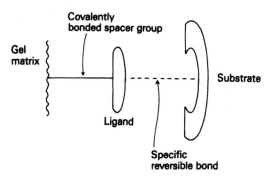

Fig. 4.15 Principle of affinity chromatography.

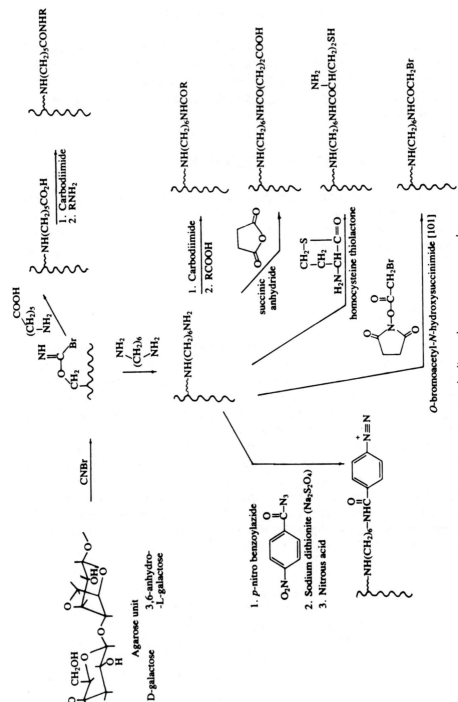

Fig. 4.16 Reactions to couple ligands to agarose gels.

4.11.2 Column materials

Sepharose, a bead-formed gel derived from agarose, possesses many of the properties necessary for a matrix for affinity chromatography. The residual hydroxyl groups on the gel can be readily derivatized by reaction with cyanogen bromide (CNBr) [100]. The CNBr-activated matrix can be coupled with a range of ligands giving packings with various specificities. The open pore structure makes the interior of the matrix available for ligand attachment and ensures good binding capacities. In addition sepharose exhibits extremely low non-specific adsorption and thus separation is achieved principally by the specific interactions of affinity chromatography.

Several intermediates are available commercially; for instance, CNBr-Sepharose; Sepharose and Bio-Gel P (polyamide) intermediates with reactive spacer groups attached; and Sepharose already coupled to a ligand specific for polysaccharides and glycoproteins. An outline of the reactions developed to couple ligands to sepharose is illustrated in Fig. 4.16; dextran and cellulose matrices can be derivatized in a similar manner.

To accommodate steric interferences, associated with the binding between the ligand and substrate, it has been found necessary to insert short alkyl chains between the ligand and gel matrix for retention of ligand activity, thus facilitating interaction of the ligand with the active site of the substrate. Bifunctional amines, for instance hexamethylenediamine, coupled to CNBr activated sepharose, are useful reagents in this respect and also furnish a free amino group, often suitable for bonding the affinity ligand. These 'spacers' can be lengthened by attaching succinic acid by its anhydride. The resulting free carboxyl group can then be bonded to affinity compounds containing an amino group via the intermediacy of N,N'-disubstituted carbodiimides. The latter have proved an important synthetic intermediate in promoting condensation between free amino and carboxylic acid groups.

4.11.3 Applications

The complexity and physicochemical similarity of many compounds of biological interest, such as nucleic acids and proteins, make affinity chromatography, because of its high specificity and concentrating effects, an indispensable separation technique in biochemical research.

Affinity chromatography has considerable potential and has already found extensive application in biochemical and chemical studies requiring the purification of antigens, enzymes, proteins, viruses, and hormones. It provides an elegant method for high yield purification in a single step under mild conditions of pH and ionic strength. The selectivity of the technique derives both from the ligand interactions and the use of selective elution conditions. An example of the use of affinity chromatography is the isolation of whole genes. A further example uses CNBr-activated sepharose to immobilise DNA, which can then be employed to bind specific enzymes and proteins. A detailed discussion of the applications is outside the scope of this text and the interested reader is directed to the papers already cited and description by Turkova [102].

4.12 COVALENT CHROMATOGRAPHY

Covalent chromatography is a technique used for the specific isolation and purification of thiol-containing proteins and peptides. Sepharose is commonly used as the gel matrix and the packing is prepared in a two-step synthesis which involves, for instance, the coupling of a thiopropylsepharose derivative with 2,2'-dipyridyl-disulphide to give pyridyl-disulphide; the hydroxylpropyl residue is effective as a spacer arm.

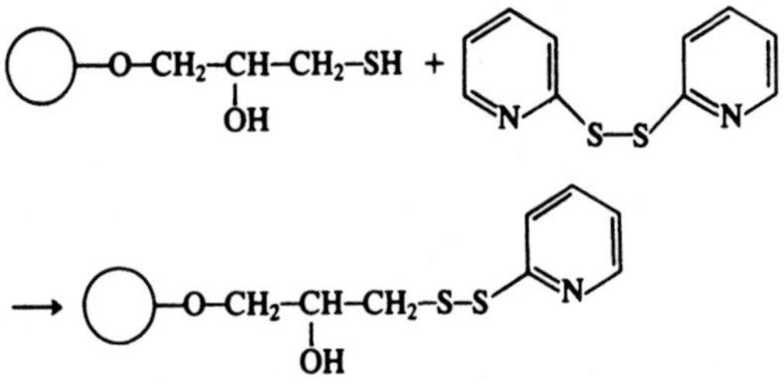

On application of the sample to the column, thiol-containing components become bound to the column. The disulphide linkage can then be reduced in a controlled fashion, normally with an excess of the activated thiol, thus freeing the thiol compounds which can be collected in the eluant. The technique thus allows the separation of thiol-containing proteins from non-thiol and disulphide functionalities.

4.13 CHROMATOFOCUSING

Chromatofocusing is a unique column chromatographic method for the separation of proteins on ion-exchange resins according to their isoelectric

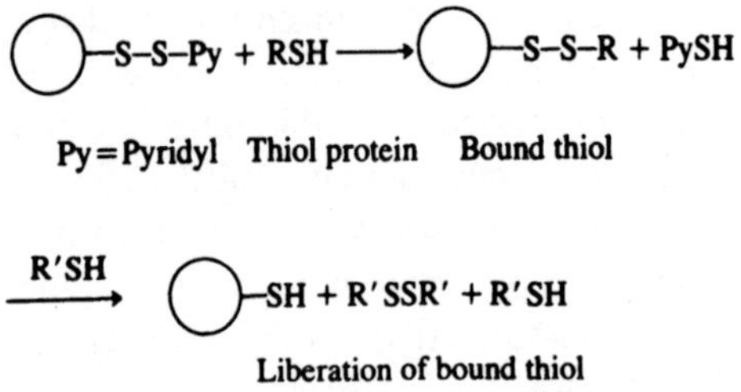

Fig. 4.17   Reaction scheme showing binding and liberation of thiol protein.

points. The technique, first described by Sluyterman [103], proposed that a pH gradient could be produced internally in an ion exchange column by taking advantage of the buffering action of the ion exchanger and running a buffer initially adjusted to one pH, through a column initially adjusted to another pH. If such a pH gradient is used to elute proteins bound to an ion exchanger, the proteins are eluted in order of their isoelectric points. This technique has a number of advantages. A protein is not subjected to a pH more than its isoelectric pH value, and focusing effects result in band sharpening, sample concentration and very high resolution. The pH range is chosen so that the isoelectric points of the proteins of interest fall in the region of the middle of the pH gradient.

For a descending pH gradient i.e. where the column is at higher pH than the eluant, a basic buffering group is required on the ion exchanger and thus an anion exchanger is used. As the eluant, which contains a mixture of differently charged species, migrates down the column, the most acidic components bind to the anion exchanger. The pH of the eluent leaving the column is gradually lowered to that of the eluting buffer solution.

4.13.1 Ionic properties of amino acids and proteins

Amino acids have two distinct pK_a values, and the actual ionic form of any amino acid depends on the pH of the solution. The ionic forms of glycine which predominate at various pH are illustrated in Fig. 3.18. Because of the presence of the charged groups, an amino acid in solution will have a positive charge at low pH. As the pH is raised, a point will be reached where the amino acid exists exclusively in the dipolar form, known as the Zwitterion. This pH is known as the isoelectric point (pI).

In a system using a descending pH gradient, the pH of the initial eluant, being less than the isoelectric point, ensures that the amino acid carries a positive charge and thus will migrate down the column of anion exchanger in the eluant. However, as it migrates down the column, the pH of the solvent surrounding the protein/amino acid increases. Eventually the pH is greater than the pI of the protein, and the equilibrium readjusts; the protein reverses its charge and binds to the ion exchanger. The protein remains bound until the passing eluant pH is less than the pI of the compound. The process is repeated continuously until the amino acid is washed from the column at its isoelectric point.

The theoretical considerations indicating the possibility of producing focusing effects, as with electrophoretic methods, in the ion-exchange chromatography of proteins in a pH gradient were soon confirmed experimentally. In chromato-focusing, protein molecules at the rear of the zone (i.e. acidic pH) are repelled from the ion exchanger. The protein remains bound until the passing eluant pH is less sample of the same protein is applied to the column after development of the first has commenced, it will catch up and co-elute with the first. If a second sample of greater pI is applied, it will overtake the first zone and elute before it.

The techniques and practice relating to column packing, sample preparation and sample application are similar to those described for affinity chromatography, as indeed is the apparatus employed. Chromatofocusing is a generally applicable technique for separation problems in biochemistry. For example, the genetic variants of haemoglobin (responsible for several blood disorders, such as sickle cell anaemia) can be readily resolved from carboxyhaemoglobin by chromatofocusing over a narrow pH interval (pH 8–7).

A more detailed treatment of the principles and practice of chromatofocusing is outside the scope of this text and the interested reader is directed to the handbook by Pharmacia [104].

REFERENCES

1. Still, W. C., Kahn, M. and Mitra, A. (1978) *J. Org. Chem.*, **43**, 2923.
2. Alm, R. S., Williams, R. J. P and Tiselius, A (1952) *Acta Chem. Scand.*, **6**, 826.
3. Kuhn, E., Winterstein, A. and Lederer, E. Z. (1931) *Physiol. Chem.*, **197**, 141.
4. Trappe, W., (1940) *Biochem. Z.*, **305**, 150.
5. Williams, R. J. P., Hagdahl, L. and Tiselius, A. (1954) *Arkiv Kemi.*, **7**, 1.
6. Snyder, L. R. (1968) *Principles of Adsorption Chromatography*, Dekker, New York.
7. Strain, H. H. (1942) *Chromatographic Adsorption Analysis*, Interscience, New York.
8. Bickoff, E. M. (1948) *Analyt. Chem.*, **21**, 20.
9. Knight, H. S. and Groennings, S. (1954) *Analyt. Chem.*, **26**, 1549.
10. Madeley, J. W. (1957) PhD. Thesis., London.
11. Hernandez, R., Hernandez, R. Jr and Axelrod, L. R. (1961) *Analyt. Chem.*, **33**, 370.
12. Brockmann, H. and Schodder, H. (1941) *Chem. Ber.*, **74**, 73.
13. Frew, A. J., Proctor, G. R. and Silverton, U. V. (1980) *J. Chem. Soc.*, 1251.
14. Neish, A. C. (1951) *Can. J. Chem.*, **29**, 552.
15. Moyle, V., Baldwin, E. and Scarisbrick, R. (1948) *J. Biochem.*, **43**, 308.
16. Zbinovsky, V. (1955) *Analyt. Chem.*, **27**, 764.
17. Martin, A. J. P. and Synge, R. L. M. (1941) *J. Biochem.*, **35**, 1958.
18. Moore, S. and Stein, W. H. (1949) *J. Biol. Chem.*, **178**. 53.
19. Smith, G. H. (1952) *J. Chem. Soc.*, 1530.
20. Martin, A. J. P. and Porter, R. R. (1951) *J. Biochem.*, **49**, 215.
21. Daly, M. M. and Mirsky, A. E. (1949) *J. Biol. Chem.*, **179**, 981.
22. Edwards, R. W. H. and Kellie, A. E. (1956) *Chem. and Ind.*, 250.
23. Weber, D. J., Ennals, T. R. and Mitchner, H. (1972) *J. Pharm. Sci.*, **61**, 689.
24. Cavina, G., Moretti, G. and Cantafora, A. (1973) *J. Chromatogr.*, **80**, 89.
25. Hathway, D. E. (1958) *J. Chem. Soc.*, 520.
26. Grassman, W., Deffreer, G., Schuster, E. and Pauckner, W. (1956) *Chem. Ber.*, **89**, 2523.
27. Partridge, S. M. and Swain, T. (1950) *Nature*, **166**, 272.
28. Burstall, F. H., Davies, G. R. and Wells, R. A. (1950) *Discuss. Faraday Soc.*, **7**, 149.
29. Smith, A. I. (1959) *Analyt. Chem.*, **31**, 1621.
30. Sauer, R. W., Washall, T. A. and Melpolder, F. W. (1957) *Analyt. Chem.*, **29**, 1327.
31. Wager, H. G. and Isherwood, F. A. (1961) *Analyst*, **86**, 260.
32. Siekierski, S. and Fidelis, I. (1960) *J. Chromatogr.*, **4**, 60.
33. Phillips, A. M. (1971) *Anal. Chem.*, **43**, 467.
34. Werthessen, N. T., Beall, J. R. and James, A. T. (1970) *J. Chromatogr.*, **46**, 149.

35. Mikes, O. (ed.) (1979) *Chromatographic and Allied Methods.*, John Wiley and Sons, New York.
36. Spedding, F. H. (1949) *Discuss. Faraday Soc.*, **7**, 214.
37. Marcus, Y. and Nelson, F. (1959) *J. Phys. Chem.*, **63**, 77.
38. Thompson, S. C., Harvey, B. G., Choppin, G. R. and Seaborg, G. T. (1954) *J. Am. Chem. Soc.*, **76**, 6229; Choppin, G. R., Harvey, B. G. and Thompson S. C. (1956) *J. Inorg. Nucl. Chem.*, **2**, 66.
39. Hulet, E. K., Gutmacher, R. G. and Coops, M. S. (1961) *J. Inorg. Nucl. Chem.*, **17**, 350.
40. Samuelson, O. and Sjoberg, B. (1956) *Anal. Chim. Acta.*, **14**, 121.
41. Wish, L. (1961) *Anal. Chem.*, **33**, 53.
42. Hague, J. L. and Machlan, L. A. (1961) *J. Res. Nat. Bur. Stand.*, **65A**, 75.
43. Bandi, W. R., Buyok, E. G., Lewis, L. L. and Melnick, L. M. (1961) *Anal. Chem.*, **33**, 1275.
44. Fritz, J. S., Garralda, B. B. and Karraker, S. K. (1961) *Anal. Chem.*, **33**, 882.
45. Moore, S. and Stein, W. H. (1951) *J. Biol. Chem.*, **192**, 663 (1954) **211**, 893.
46. Wade, H. E. (1960) *Biochem. J.*, **77**, 534.
47. Oliviero, V. T. (1961) *Anal. Chem.*, **33**, 263.
48. Skelly, N. E. (1961) *Anal. Chem.*, **33**, 271.
49. Tomsett, S. L. (1961) *Anal. Chim. Acta.*, **24**, 438.
50. Peterson, E. A. and Sober, H. A. (1956) *J. Am. Chem. Soc.*, **78**, 751.
51. Rieman, W. J. (1961) *J. Chem. Ed.*, **38**, 339.
52. Amphlett, C. B. (1964) *Inorganic Ion-Exchange Materials*, Elsevier, Amsterdam.
53. Marshall, G. R. and Nickless, G. (1964) *Chromatogr. Revs.*, **6**, 180.
54. Thistlewhaite, W. P. (1947) *Analyst.*, **72**, 531.
55. Smit, J. van R., Robb, W. and Jacobs, J. J. (1959) *J. Inorg. Nucl. Chem.*, **12**, 104.
56. Smit, J. van R. (1965) *ibid.*, **27**, 227.
57. Smit, J. van R. and Robb, W. (1964) *ibid.*, **26**, 509.
58. Bactslé, L. and Paelsmaker, J. (1961) *ibid.*, **21**, 124.
59. Amphlett, C. B., MacDonald, L. A., Burgess, J. S. and Maynard, J. C. (1959) *ibid.*, **10**, 69.
60. Coleman, C. F., Blake, C. A. and Brown, K. B. (1962) *Talanta.*, **9**, 297.
61. Cerrai, E. (1964) *Chromatogr. Revs.*, **6**, 129.
62. Porath, J. and Linden, E. B. (1961) *Nature*, **191**, 69.
63. Schmidt, M. (1962) *Biochim. Biophys. Acta.*, **63**, 346.
64. Kawade, Y., Okamoto, T., and Yamamoto, Y. (1963) *Biochem. Biophys. Res. Commun.*, **10**, 200.
65. Gondko, R., Schmidt, M. and Leyko, W. (1964) *Biochim. Biophys. Acta.*, **86**, 190.
66. Björling, C. O. and William-Johnson, B. (1963) *Acta. Chem. Scand.*, **317**, 2638.
67. Mathews, C. K., Brown, F. and Cohen, S. S. (1964) *J. Biol. Chem.*, **9**, 2957.
68. Peterson, E. A. and Sober, H. A. (1956) *J. Am. Chem. Soc.*, **78**, 751.
69. Mould, D. L. and Synge, R. L. M. (1954) *Biochem. J.*, **58**, 571.
70. Porath, J. and Flodin, P. (1959) *Nature*, **183**, 1657.
71. Moore, J. C. (1964) *J. Polymer Sci.*, **A2**, 835.
72. Determann, H. (1964) *Agnew. Chemie, Int. Edn.*, **3**, 608.
73. Porath, J. (1963) *J. Pure Appl. Chem.*, **6**, 233.
74. Laurent, T. C. and Killander, J. (1964) *J. Chromatogr.*, **14**, 317.
75. Porath, J. (1963) *Pure and Appl. Chem.*, **6**, 233.
76. Tiselius, A., Porath, J. and Albertsson, P. A. (1963) *Science*, **141**, 13.
77. Gelotte, B. (1964) *New Biochemical Separations*, (eds A. T. James and L. J., Morris), van Nostrand, New York, p. 93.
78. Granath, K., *ibid.*, p. 110.
79. Marsden, N V. B. (1971) *J. Chromatogr.*, **58**, 304.

80. Laurent, T. C. and Killander, J. (1961) *J. Chromatogr.*, **5**, 103.
81. Lea, D. J. and Schon, E. H. (1962) *Canad. J. Chem.*, **40**, 159.
82. Hjerten, S. (1962) *Archiv. Biochem. Biophys.*, Suppl. 1., p. 147.
83. Porath, J., Janson, J. -C. and Låås, T. (1971) *J. Chromatogr.*, **60**, 167.
84. Låås, T. (1972) *J. Chromatogr.*, **66**, 347.
85. Hiatt, C. W., Shelokov, A., Rosenthal, E. J. and Galimore, J. M. (1971) *J. Chromatogr.*, **56**, 362.
86. Hawk, G. L., Cameron, J. A. and Dufault, L. B. (1972) *Prep. Biochem.*, **2**, 193.
87. Flodin, P. (1961) *J. Chromatogr.*, **5**, 103.
88. Kusnir, J. and Meloun, B. (1973) *Coll. Czech. Chem. Comun.*, **38**, 143.
89. Petrovic, S. L., Petrovic, J. S. and Markovic, R. A. *et al.* (1974) *Prep. Biochem.*, **4**, 509.
90. Gelotte, B. (1964) *Acta Chem. Scand.*, **18**, 1283.
91. Barth, H. G. and Smith, D. H. (1981) *J. Chromatogr.*, **206**, 410.
92. Determan, H. and Michel, W. (1966) *J. Chromatogr.*, **25**, 303.
93. Zeichner, M. and Stern, R. (1977) *Biochemistry*, **16**, 1378.
94. Ansari, A. A. and Mage, R. G. (1977) *J. Chromatogr.*, **140**, 98.
95. Heitz, W. and Ullner, H. (1968) *Macromol. Chem.*, **120**, 58.
96. Colman, R. (1972) *Anal. Biochem.*, **46**, 358.
97. Wood, G. C. and Cooper, P. F. (1970) *Chromatogr. Revs.*, **12**, 88.
98. Friedberg, F. (1971) *Chromatogr. Revs.*, **14**, 121.
99. Turkova, J. (1974) *J. Chromatogr.*, **91**, 267.
100. Porath, J., Axen, R. and Ernback, S. (1967) *Nature*, **215**, 1491.
101. Cuatrecasas, P. (1970) *J. Biol. Chem.*, **245**, 3059.
102. Turkova, J. (1979) *Chromatographic and Allied Methods.*, (ed. O. Mikes), Chapter 7, John Wiley and Sons, New York.
103. Sluyterman, L. A. A. E. and Elgersma, O. (1978) *J. Chromatogr.*, **150**, 17.
104. *Affinity Chromatography – Principles and Methods* (1984) Pharmacia Fine Chemicals, Uppsala.

5 GAS CHROMATOGRAPHY (GC)

It was nearly 50 years from Tswett's description of chromatographic separations (1906) to the development of gas-liquid chromatography by Martin and James (1952). Since that time gas chromatography has developed rapidly, particularly during the 1960s, producing sweeping changes in analytical chemistry and in many areas of research and development. It was now possible to separate, quantify, and subsequently identify, components in a mixture, from permanent gases, and hydrogen isotopes to fatty acids and waxes. Although direct analysis is limited to compounds with a molecular weight up to 400–500, derivatives of involatile materials can readily be made which have some measure of volatility without thermal degradation. Preparative-scale gas chromatography offers a method of obtaining very pure compounds and is used commercially in the manufacture of laboratory reagents, drugs and flavours. It is also possible to obtain physicochemical measurements using GC, such as surface properties, kinetics and thermodynamics of separation and adsorption processes which have application in, for example, the development of catalysts.

5.1 PRINCIPLES OF GC

The general principles of chromatography have been discussed in Chapter 2. However, for completeness, the theoretical aspects of gas chromatography will be outlined. It is not intended to cover the subject in depth, but to present a summary of terms used to evaluate a chromatographic separation in order to enable the practising analyst to obtain maximum efficiency and performance from the GC system being used.

In order to assess the performance and separation efficiency of a column it is necessary to determine the number of theoretical separation steps that occur in the column (N). This is calculated by obtaining the height equivalent to a theoretical plate (HETP), H, which is the main measure of peak broadening:

$$H = L/16(t_W/t'_R)^2$$

where L = column length, t_W is the peak width at the base of the peak (given by the intersection of the tangents at the inflection points with the base line [1]); t'_R is the retention time for a peak of a non-retained component. It is usually difficult to measure t_W and therefore width at half the peak height $t_{W_{\frac{1}{2}}}$ is used.

$$H = L/5.54(t_{W_{\frac{1}{2}}}/t'_R)^2$$

A diagram of chromatographic peaks and the measurements obtained is shown in Fig. 5.1. The efficiency of a column is measured as the effective plate number N (or N_{eff}) but is often described by the number of theoretical plates, n. (Column

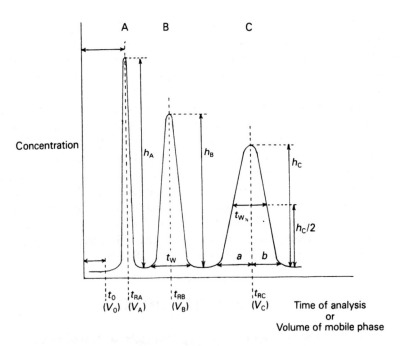

t_0 = time for the solvent or mobile phase to pass through the system;
t_{RA} = retention time of component A, that is the time for A to pass through the system; V_A is the retention volume;
t_{RB} = retention time of B, V_B = retention volume;
t_{RC} = retention time of C, V_C = retention volume;
h = peak height, h_A for component A, h_B for B, h_C for C;
t_W = width at the base of a peak;
$t_{W_{\frac{1}{2}}}$ = width of a peak at half height;
a and b are the width of the leading and trailing halves of a peak, used to determine asymmetry.

Fig. 5.1   Chromatogram.

efficiency N (or N_{eff}) $= L/H$.

$$N = 5.54(t'_R/t_{w_{\frac{1}{2}}})^2 \quad \text{and} \quad n = 5.54(t_R/t_{w_{\frac{1}{2}}})^2$$

and therefore in practice $N \approx n$.

However N and n, the effective and theoretical plate numbers respectively, are related by the efficiency of the partitioning process.

$$N = n(K'/(1 + k'))^2$$

where K' is the partition ratio of the component between the mobile and the stationary phases.

Peak symmetry

The normal gas chromatographic peak is Gaussian in shape, representing the distribution of molecules in the eluted component band. Non-uniform shapes are caused by a number of factors, including kinetic effects, non-linearity of the partition isotherm, column overloading, and poor injection techniques. A simple comparison of the peak half-widths for the forward and backward halves of the peak at 10% peak height may be used (Fig. 5.1). Asymmetry ratio (A_S) is given by:

$$A_S = b/a$$

A good, uniformly packed column should give an asymmetry ratio of 0.9 to 1.1.

Column efficiency

Column efficiency is measured on a well-retained peak which has a capacity ratio (K') of at least 5.0, and should be taken into account when comparing columns for a given separation.

$$K' = (t_0 - t_R)/t_R$$

where t_0 is the retention time of an unretained component and t_R is the retention time of a well-retained peak

Resolution

Adjacent bands or peaks are only resolved if their widths are less than the separation between the maxima. The ratio of the peak separation to the main peak width of adjacent peaks is thus a measure of their resolution R.

$$R = (t_{RB} - t_{RA})/\tfrac{1}{2}(t_{WA} - t_{WB}) = 2\Delta t_R/(t_{WA} - t_{WB})$$

For reasonable accuracy of peak areas and hence quantitative data:

$$t \geq \tfrac{1}{2}(t_{WA} - t_{WB}) \text{ or } \approx t_{WB}$$

This means that the peak maxima separation must be at least the peak width of the second peak. If $R = 1$ (4σ width) there is a 2 to 3% overlap, whereas at $R = 5$

(6σ width) there is only about 0.2% overlap. A further factor which affects resolution is where one component of an adjacent pair is in much greater concentration (larger peak). In this case higher values of R may be required for adequate resolution.

5.2 GC INSTRUMENTATION

The instrumentation for gas chromatography incorporates the features common to all forms of chromatography, namely a mobile phase, a stationary phase and a detection system. GC utilizes a column containing the stationary phase, but requires a gaseous mobile phase, the carrier gas, and a sample introduction or injection system. The detectors require an amplifier for signal processing; the variable parameters, for example, column and injection temperature, are electronically controlled. The GC instrument therefore consists of five sections (Fig. 5.2):

1. carrier gas supply and controls;
2. sample introduction/injector system;
3. chromatographic column and oven;
4. detector;
5. amplifier and signal processing, and control electronics.

5.2.1 Carrier gas supply and control

The carrier gas acts as the mobile phase and transports the sample components through the column to the detector. The individual partition or adsorption

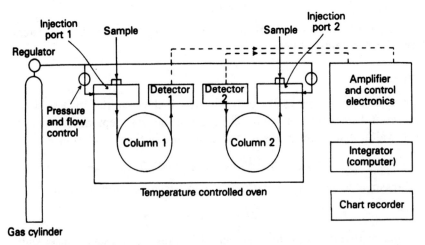

Fig. 5.2   Schematic diagram of a dual column gas chromatograph.

Table 5.1 Viscosity and thermal conductivity of common carrier gases

Gas	Mol. wt	Viscosity μP, $\eta \times 10^6$	Thermal conductivity cal/sec. cm $((°C/cm) \times 10^{-6})$
CO_2	44.01	189	49
Ar	39.95	269	50
O	32.00	256	77
N	28.01	219	73
He	4.00	228	388
H	2.02	108	490

equilibrium properties of the components determine the rate at which they move through the system. The selection of the best carrier gas is important, because it affects both the column separation processes and the detector performance. Unfortunately the carrier gas that gives the optimum column performance may not be the one most suitable for the detector used. The carrier gas has to be inert to the column materials and sample components; the gases with the smallest diffusion coefficients will give the best column performance; for example, high molecular weight gases, N_2, CO_2, Ar, give lower flow rates than hydrogen or helium. Viscosity dictates the gas pressure required for a given flow rate. For rapid analysis the ratio of viscosity to diffusion coefficient should be a minimum, and therefore H_2 and He would be ideal carrier gases (Table 5.1). However, these are not practicable for some detectors. Impurities such as air and water vapour can cause sample reactions, column deterioration and affect detector performance. For example, water is often retained for longer than the sample components, and therefore is eluted as a rather broad flat peak, affecting the baseline zero standard detector signal. In practice, a compromise is employed and N_2 is used for the flame ionization detector (FID) and nitrogen-phosphorus detector (NPD), argon for electron capture detectors (ECD) and H_2 or He for katherometer detectors. The carrier gas for most instruments is supplied from a high pressure gas cylinder, being stored therein at pressures up to 3000 psi, 200 bar. Additional gases may be required for the detectors, e.g. air and H_2 for FIDs. In many laboratories the use and storage of hydrogen cylinders is restricted due to safety regulations. An alternative supply of hydrogen and oxygen can be obtained from the electrolysis of water using commercially available units. These can supply up to 6 FIDs at 0–60 psi (4 bar) pressure and 0–250 ml min^{-1}. Small variations in the carrier gas flow rate will affect column performance and retention times. Therefore to achieve optimum separations, good accuracy and precision it is necessary to keep the flow rate constant. Good regulation is therefore required to obtain a pulse-free gas flow at preset pressures and flow rates.

Flow control is necessary, since if the carrier gas pressure remains constant during temperature programming of the column, the flow rate will change as the viscosity of most carrier gases increases with temperature. Hence the flow rate would decrease thus affecting the performance. In addition to the cylinder regulator, secondary instrument pressure and flow regulators are fitted, enabling several instruments to be supplied from a common gas line. The simplest control consists of a pressure regulator and gauge, but this is really only suitable for straightforward isothermal chromatography. Flow controllers to maintain the flow rate accurately over all the temperature operating range of 40–450° C are therefore necessary particularly if temperature programming is used. These controllers may be in the form of restrictors, consisting of fine-bore capillary tubing in the gas supply line, or for accurate variable control, a needle valve column inlet gas regulator with micrometer dial setting is used [2]. Completely automatic setting and read-out of carrier gas flow rate is now a feature of modern instruments using digital flow controllers. One form of these consists of a number of flow restriction lines arranged in series; the flow rate is controlled by selecting the appropriate lines to give the required flow. Column flow rates are generally checked using a soap bubble flow meter and a stop watch (Fig. 5.3). The flow meter is connected to the column outlet by the side arm and soap bubbles are introduced into the gas stream by squeezing the bulb at the bottom. The bubbles move up the calibrated tube and the time taken for a bubble to travel between the calibration marks (e.g. 10 ml) is measured. The flow per minute can thus be calculated. Additional regulators are required for the gas supplies to FID, NPD, and ECD detectors.

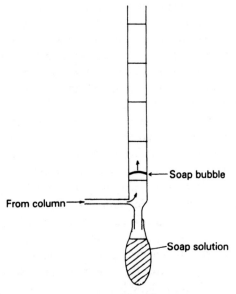

Fig. 5.3   Soap bubble flow meter.

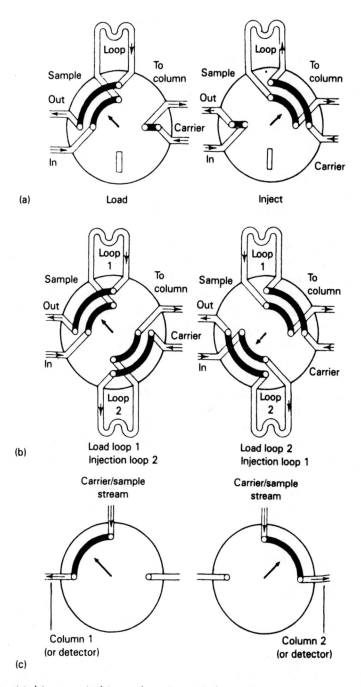

Fig. 5.4 Multiport switching valves. Part (c) shows the application of a 3-port switching valve to detector or column selection. The carrier-sample stream may be directed to either of two columns or two detectors, depending on the location of the valve in the chromatograph.

5.2.2 Venting and column switching

Column switching enables analyses to be carried out which are either impossible or do not yield the required information using conventional methods.

The switching of the carrier gas is achieved using multiport gas switching valves [3]. These are used to switch the carrier gas through sample loops as described later, and also for venting, back-flushing, peak or heart cutting, dual column operations and to achieve column switching (Fig. 5.4).

Frequently the sample to be analysed contains major components, such as solvents which can lead to column overloading, masking of minor peaks and possibly affect the equilibrium separation process of the solutes, and overload the detector. Venting or fore-flushing permits the rapidly eluting solvent to be removed from the system before the analytical column by using a pre-column in parallel with the main column. The major components are vented after the pre-column and when eluted the valve is turned to direct the components of interest on to the main column. Similarly, when the main components have been eluted from the main column any slow-moving and high boiling components which would either prolong the analysis time or might accumulate on the column, can be flushed backwards off the column.

Column switching is also used for peak or heart cutting. Separation of components is mainly influenced by polarity of the stationary phase and column temperature and these are characteristic of various classes of compounds. It is therefore possible to use one column for the main separation of a mixture and to separate further poorly resolved peaks by directing the column eluent containing this fraction on to a second column of different polarity to effect a better separation [4].

Column switching is particularly useful in capillary GC, since the small column capacities can easily be overloaded with a solvent band.

5.2.3 Sample inlet systems

The introduction of a sample into a gas chromatograph is the first stage in the chromatographic process and its efficiency is reflected in the overall efficiency of the separation procedure and the accuracy and precision of the qualitative and quantitative results.

The sample may be introduced as a gas using a gas sampling valve or as a liquid introduced into the chromatograph via a septum seal. The septum is a penetrable self-sealing barrier between the laboratory outside and the carrier gas supply placed just before the column. The resealing capability of the septum depends on temperature, flexibility of the silicone rubber, sharpness of the syringe needle and position of the injector. Automatic injection systems which repeatedly inject through the same hole give a longer septum life than manual injection methods, which lead to more rapid mechanical breakdown. The septum holder

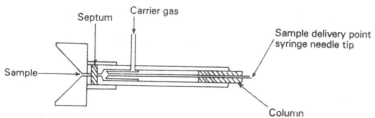

Fig. 5.5   On-column injector.

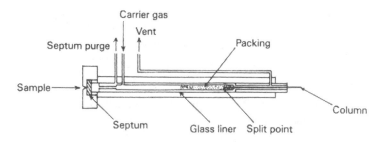

Fig. 5.6   Split/spiltless injector.

usually incorporates a needle guide to reduce the mechanical damage (Figs 5.5, 5.6).

The high injection temperatures can gradually lead to loss of flexibility of the silicone septum due to degradation, particularly at temperatures above 210°. This is accompanied by septum bleed of low molecular weight and depolymerized material which results in ghost peaks and baseline drift. Another phenomenon with similar results is the memory effect, a consequence of the ability of silicone rubber to absorb compounds which are later desorbed. These problems can be reduced by the use of a film of PTFE or PTFE-coated septa. Typically, septa are formed from 0.05–0.125 in. thick silicone rubber with 0.002–0.01 in. PTFE surface coating.

The sample should be introduced on to the beginning of the column with the minimum of dispersion in the mobile phase, so that it enters the column as a narrow band containing all the sample components. Some features of inlet systems are:

1. Rapid clean switching or injection of the sample into the mobile phase with no tailing or dispersion of sample;
2. Correct inlet temperatures high enough to vaporize instantaneously all components in a sample without decomposition and condensation;
3. minimum dead volumes to avoid diffusion (dispersion) of the sample in the mobile phase;
4. design of the overall inlet system for good precision (better than $\pm 1\%$);
5. no contamination of samples or catalytic effects;
6. no loss of sample in the inlet system;
7. no septum bleed or leak.

The ideal sample inlet system should allow instantaneous injection of the sample into the mobile phase and on to the beginning of the column. This operation is achieved in one of two ways, depending on whether the sample is gaseous or liquid.

5.2.4 Sample preparation

Gaseous samples can either be pumped into a GC sampling system or introduced from a pressurized container into a gas sampling valve. Liquid and solid samples can be introduced directly but are often contained in solution. This may be made up directly or obtained from an extraction process. The solvent needs to be carefully chosen to avoid problems in the chromatography. Some of the solvent requirements are:

1. it must not react with the sample or column stationary phase;
2. it must completely dissolve the sample and must be fully miscible with it;
3. there should be no interference of sample peaks by solvent peaks, i.e. sample and solvent should not elute from the column with similar retention times;
4. no involatile material should remain in the column;
5. overloading the column with large solvent volumes should be avoided.

5.2.5 Gaseous samples

Gaseous samples are generally introduced on to the column using a multiport switching valve (Fig. 5.4). The sample is introduced into the sample loop while the valve is in the LOAD position. It is important that excess volume of sample is used to ensure that the sample loop is completely flushed through. The sample may be drawn through the sample loop, injected into it using a gas-tight syringe, or introduced under pressure. Typical sample loop volumes are 0.5 to 20.0 ml and the loops are readily interchangeable.

The overall inlet system is carefully designed to minimize carrier gas pressure fluctuations as the valve is turned to the INJECT position when the carrier gas is directed on to the column via the sample loop. An alternative method of gas sampling is to use a gas-tight syringe available for injection volumes ranging from 1 ml to 50 ml. The sample is injected into the carrier gas *via* the rubber septum of the liquid injection port. Great care is required to avoid mishaps due to back pressure of carrier gas in the syringe.

5.2.6 Liquid sample inlet systems

To obtain maximum performance from a GC system it is important to use the correct injector and injection technique for a particular application. Most present-day instruments incorporate interchangeable injector blocks so that a conventional glass-lined injection port can be replaced with an on-column, capillary column injector or auto-sampler injection port. Flash vaporization injectors are mounted in a heated block which is maintained at a temperature 10–50° C higher than the column itself. Most are of straight-through design which incorporates a replaceable glass liner. The liner can be used to collect involatile residues and also provides an inert non-catalytic vaporizing surface for metal-sensitive compounds. The glass liner can be replaced by an extension to the end of a glass column, which can also contain column packing material, thereby minimizing sample dispersion problems (Fig. 5.6).

Capillary columns require much smaller samples than packed columns (approximately a factor of 10 less) due to the small column loadings required. It is technically difficult to introduce such small samples on to the end of the column and therefore a modified interchangeable injector is used, which allows split or splitless techniques to be employed (Fig. 5.6). The capillary column projects into the glass liner providing an all-glass system with minimum dead volume.

The reduced sample size may be achieved by splitting the injected sample allowing only a small fraction on to the column; split ratios of approximately 1:100 are required to achieve good linearity and reproducibility. In the splitless or direct injection technique the volatile, carefully chosen solvent travels on to the end of the column together with the sample. The solvent separates very rapidly from the solutes which then separate according to their chromatographic properties. Further details on capillary GC are given in Section 5.6.

Liquid and solid samples in a volatile solvent are manually introduced into the injection port using a syringe. These have capacities varying from 1 μl to 100 μl or more. A sample of 0.1 to 5 μl is normally used for packed columns with the components of interest typically 1% of the injected sample. Two types of syringe are available; those with the graduated glass barrel acting as the sample retaining and measuring reservoir and in which the sample is clearly visible. The main problem with this type of syringe is that some sample always remains in the needle. It is therefore essential that between samples the syringe is thoroughly flushed out with solvent and then with the new sample. The second type is the needle barrel syringe, where the sample reservoir is the stainless steel needle. This is swept by a stainless steel plunger wire which just protrudes from the end of the needle in the empty position. Both needle and barrel are accurately constructed and since almost all the sample is expelled from the syringe there is a minimum dead volume and sample retention, thus avoiding as far as possible cross-contamination of samples.

The syringes are fully loaded, carefully checked to make sure that no air bubbles are present, and adjusted to the required volume. The needle is introduced into the injection port through a self-sealing elastomeric septum, the sample rapidly expelled and the syringe quickly withdrawn to avoid vaporization of additional sample which may be retained in the needle. An overall reproducibility of ± 5% is obtainable for the sample introduction if care and technique are optimized, e.g. flushing out the syringe between samples, checking that no air bubbles are present, and consistent injection technique. A check on the purity of all solvents used in GC is essential and, as in any analysis, a blank should be analysed.

5.3 SAMPLING TECHNIQUES

5.3.1 Derivatization of sample

There are many compounds which cannot be readily analysed by GC, either because they are too involatile or because they tail badly and are too strongly attracted to the stationary phases. Derivatization before analysis enables many more compounds to be analysed by GC and an extensive literature is available [5]. The main reasons for derivatization are:

1. to increase volatility of the sample;
2. to reduce thermal degradation of the sample by increasing thermal stability;
3. to increase detector response by incorporating into the derivative functional groups which produce higher detector signals, e.g. CF_3 for electron capture detectors;
4. to improve separation and reduce tailing.

Derivatization methods may be classified into three groups according to the reagents used and the reaction achieved, namely silylation, acylation and alkylation. In many cases the derivatives are formed as soon as the sample dissolves; few require heating. Alkylation usually occurs quickly, but many compounds must be heated for the reaction to occur. Thus derivatization times will vary and in order to find if the reaction is completed, a sample is analysed at selected time intervals until no further increase in the derivative peak(s) is detected. Most derivatives are thermally stable, although trimethylsilyl derivatives may be decomposed on the stainless steel of an injector port at $> 210°$ C. The hydrolytic stability varies considerably with acid derivatives being the most stable and those of amines the least stable. Therefore solvents with active hydrogens, e.g. water, alcohols, enolizable ketones, cannot be used and non-polar solvents such as hexane tend to produce slow reactions. Pyridine is the commonly used solvent, and acts as an acid scavenger and basic catalyst if required. DMF, toluene and methanol are also used. All solvents are specially purified and stored under nitrogen.

Silylation

Silylation is the most widely used derivatization technique. It involves the replacement of an acidic hydrogen on the sample molecule with an alkylsilyl group, e.g. SiMe$_3$. The derivatives are generally less polar, more volatile and more thermally stable. Two examples are shown below:

1. using trimethylchlorosilane (TMS);

$$R-OH + Cl-SiMe_3 \longrightarrow R-O-SiMe_3 + HCl$$

2. using hexamethyldisilazane (HMDS);

$$2R-OH + Me_3Si-N=N-SiMe_3 \longrightarrow 2(R-O-SiMe_3) + N_2$$

Silylation reactions generally proceed very rapidly (within five minutes) with pyridine being the most frequently used solvent. GC columns used for analysis of silyl derivatives are conditioned by HMDS before use to block any acidic sites and avoid possible reactions with silyl derivatives.

Many varied and improved silylation reagents have been developed [4, 6]. Examples are the substituted acetamides e.g. BSTFA, (N, O-bis(trimethylsilyl)-trifluoroacetamide) (i) and BSA (the non-fluorinated analogue) (ii)

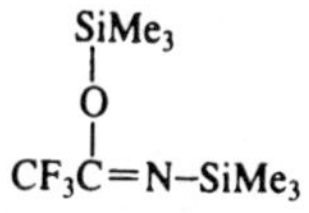

$$\underset{\text{(i)}}{\overset{\displaystyle \overset{SiMe_3}{\underset{|}{\overset{|}{O}}}}{CF_3C=N-SiMe_3}} \qquad\qquad \underset{\text{(ii)}}{\overset{\displaystyle \overset{SiMe_3}{\underset{|}{\overset{|}{O}}}}{CH_3C=N-SiMe_3}}$$

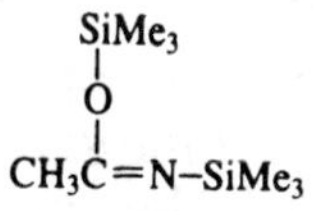

Both react rapidly and quantitatively under mild conditions using pyridine or DMF as solvent, forming esters, ethers, or N-TMS derivatives. The main advantage of BSTFA over BSA is that the by-products are more volatile and often elute with the solvent front.

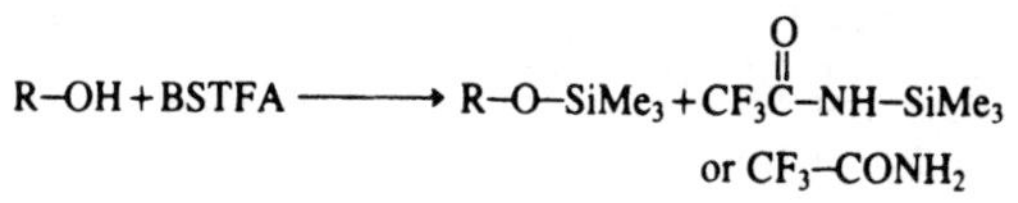

$$R-OH + BSTFA \longrightarrow R-O-SiMe_3 + CF_3\overset{\displaystyle O}{\overset{\|}{C}}-NH-SiMe_3$$
$$\text{or } CF_3-CONH_2$$

Acylation

Acylation is used to form perfluoroacyl (e.g. trifluoroacetyl from trifluoroacetic anhydride, TFAA) derivatives of alcohols, phenols or amines, mainly for enhanced detector performance using an electron-capture detector. An added benefit is the increased volatility.

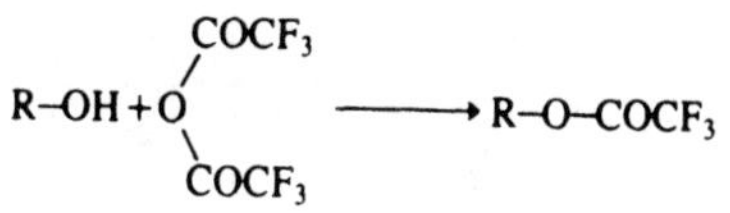

$$R-OH + O\overset{\displaystyle COCF_3}{\underset{\displaystyle COCF_3}{<}} \longrightarrow R-O-COCF_3$$

N-Fluoroacyl-imidazoles react smoothly to acylate hydroxy groups and second-ary or tertiary amines. No acids are produced which could hydrolyze the products. The imidazole produced as byproduct is relatively inert. A reaction using N-trifluoroacetylimidazole is shown below:

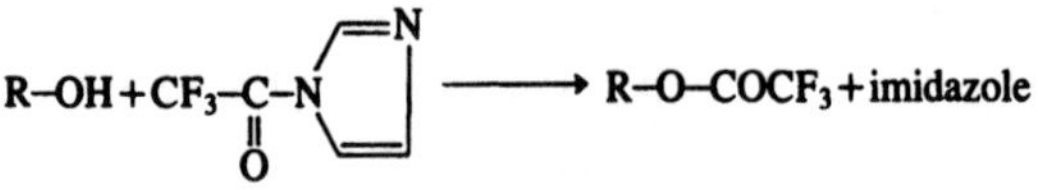

$$R\text{-}OH + CF_3\text{-}C\text{-}N \longrightarrow R\text{-}O\text{-}COCF_3 + imidazole$$

Alkylation

Alkylation is the addition of the alkyl group to an active functional group. Esterification to form methyl esters is the most useful reaction since they are the most volatile. A number of reagents are available but boron trifluoride in methanol is most commonly used.

$$RCOOH + BF_3/MeOH \longrightarrow RCOOMe_3$$

During the last two years, flash alkylation has been developed, in which the high temperature of the injection port is used to form the derivative on injection of the sample together with an appropriate reagent. Two major classes of alkylation reagents have been used; the quaternary alkylammonium hydroxides, e.g. tetrabutylammonium hydroxide (TBAH) (as an 0.2 M solution in methanol), which is used mainly for low molecular weight acids to increase retention times, and the general purpose reagent trimethylanilinium hydroxide (TMAH). This is also used where normal methylation might cause confusion with naturally occurring methyl derivatives in biological systems.

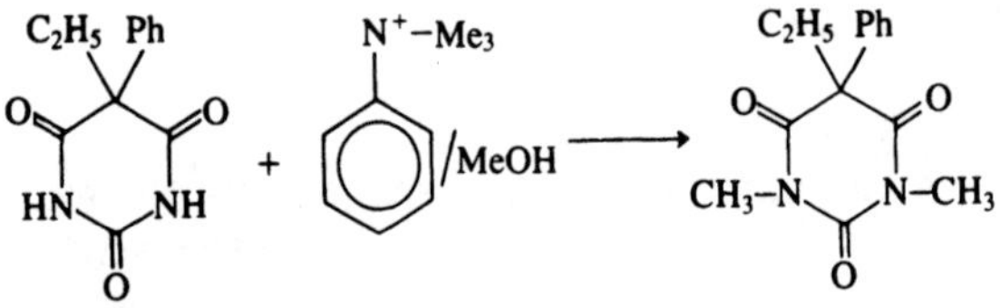

Phenobarbitone

Other reagents commonly used include pentafluorobenzyl bromide developed for the analysis of acids, amides and phenols using an electron capture detector for enhanced sensitivity. Organics in surface waters have been successfully analysed by this procedure [6].

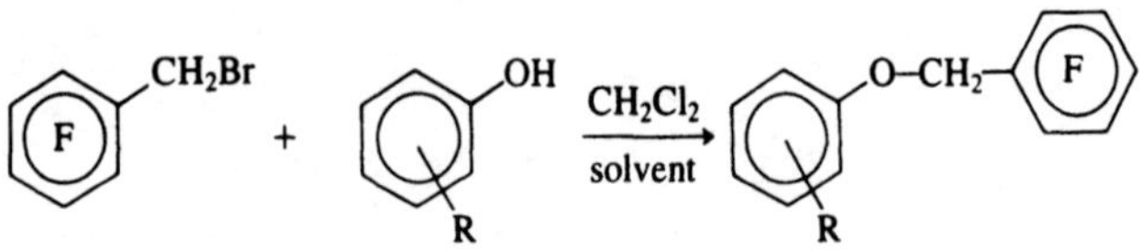

Dialkylacetals of DMF react instantaneously and quantitatively with acids, amines, amides, barbiturates and on-column derivatization is possible in some cases [5]. Methyl and butyl alkyls are available. No water, washing, extraction, etc. is necessary; the reaction mixture is injected immediately on to the gas chromatograph.

There is a considerable range of derivatization reagents available and the reader is referred to the literature and the reference texts quoted for further details [5]. In addition many suppliers of chromatography materials include details of reagents and methods of preparation in their catalogues [7].

5.3.2 Head space sampling

In this method of GC analysis the sample is contained in a sealed vial and maintained at a constant temperature for sufficient time to allow the vapour and liquid phases to equilibrate. Sampling is achieved by a predetermined volume of the vapour phase being swept on to the column by the inert carrier gas. This method avoids problems due to involatile materials being carried into the injector or on to the column (Fig. 5.7). The sampling process is in three stages;

1. insertion of the sample needle into the vial and pressurization of the container with carrier gas;
2. after equilibrium is established (approximately 20 minutes) the valve is rotated to allow the pressurized sample to pass into the injection port;
3. purging of the injector system;
4. the sample is changed whilst step 3 is in operation.

A more complete discussion of head space is given later in the chapter.

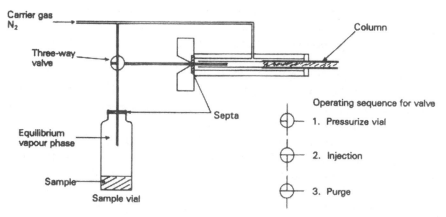

Fig. 5.7   Head space sample injection system (positioned in a heated oven).

5.3.3 Sample introduction by pyrolysis

Many solid materials have been qualitatively analysed by fingerprinting the products from controlled pyrolysis of a sample (e.g. polymeric materials, plastics, paint flakes). The sample is placed in a glass or platinum tube and inserted into a small heating element; alternatively a solution is used and the solvent evaporated leaving a film of sample on the element. The sample probe is inserted into a GC injection port and the temperature of the sample raised rapidly to a predetermined level, usually in the range 450–800° C, in about 1–5 s. The temperature is controlled accurately so that reasonable reproducibility is possible. Thorough method development is required to determine optimum pyrolysis conditions so that the characteristic volatiles, monomers, solvents, etc. are produced.

An alternative heating method uses curie point tubes or needles which attain the curie point temperature in 20–30 milliseconds by induction heating effected by a high frequency induction field. The ferromagnetic material heats up to the curie point for the particular alloy. At this point the energy absorption decreases rapidly as the ferromagnetism disappears, thus limiting the temperature. Different temperatures are obtained by choosing suitable alloys, e.g. iron–nickel (40:60 alloy) 590° C, pure iron 770° C, pure nickel 358° C.

The advantages of the curie point are two-fold, firstly, heating is extremely rapid and secondly very small samples can be handled.

5.3.4 Automation of sample introduction

Automatic sample introduction is regularly used in routine analyses. Automation of sample handling and sampling have enabled maximum use to be made of the data handling and control capabilities of microcomputer controlled instrumentation.

The entire process of sample transfer, sample injection, collection of chromatographic data and calculation of results is handled by microcomputer controlled instruments. All the sample introduction methods discussed above (with possibly the exception of pyrolysis) have been automated and most manufacturers have autosampler systems available for their instruments.

Automatic gas sampling valves for on-line monitoring of gases and vapours uses a pressurized or pumped sample introduced via a pneumatically operated or motorized multiport valve, the sample interval being predetermined and automatically controlled.

Head space analysis has been successfully automated and blood alcohol is measured in such a system. The samples are contained in a thermostatted oven and automatically move to the injection needle position, where they remain while the injection cycle shown in Fig. 5.7 is carried out. Problems due to blood residues remaining in the injection port and on the column are thus avoided.

Automatic liquid samplers also use sample vials which are transported to the sampling position. The sample may be taken up into a single, automatically activated syringe (the syringe is pumped several times to eliminate sample cross-contamination and air bubbles) and then transferred into the injection port. An alternative method is to flush the sample through a sample loop attached to a motorized multiport valve which functions in an analogous manner to a gas sampling valve.

Liquid and volatile solid samples can also be automatically injected by measuring, weighing and loading the samples into small aluminium capsules which are placed into a magazine. The capsules are pushed by a piston through a gas interlock into the special heated injection port, where they are pierced by a needle and the sample flushed out by carrier gas. Although there are problems these methods are frequently used in industrial laboratories for routine analyses of suitable samples.

5.3.5 Sampling of volatiles by adsorption

Sampling of compounds of environmental interest is now commonplace and is frequently a routine requirement. Sensitivity levels required are in the $\mu g\,m^{-3}$ range.

Volatile organic materials may be collected by drawing a known volume of air through a tube packed with an adsorbent. Small personal sampler pumps are available which have an adjustable flow rate of $1-200\,ml\,min^{-1}$ and can run for a typical working day of eight hours. A standard volume of $10\,l$, for example is sampled and the tube capped for return to the laboratory. The glass tubes are approximately $5-10\,cm$ in length with an OD of $3-5\,mm$ and an ID of $2-4\,mm$. The material collected on to the adsorbent can be analysed in three ways, involving thermal desorption of up to $300°$;

1. heating in a dry hydrogen or helium stream, the released compounds being carried into a cold-trap for subsequent GC analysis;
2. using a small glass tube which can be inserted into the injection port in place of the glass liner. After initial heating the components are flushed on to the column;
3. using a specially designed thermal desorption attachment, for example, the Perkin–Elmer ATD50.

Desorption can also be achieved using solvents such as carbon disulphide, hexane, trichlorethylene, and chloroform. An aliquot of the resulting solution is then analysed by GC [8].

Adsorbents

Perhaps the most commonly used adsorbents are activated charcoal and Tenax GC. Many applications using charcoal adsorbent tubes are reported in the literature [9]. Typically, 100–200 mg of 20–40 mesh charcoal is packed into a glass tube 2–4 mm ID with end plugs of glass wool or polyurethane foam.

Tenax GC is a recently introduced porous polymeric material based on 2,6-diphenyl-p-phenylene oxide, originally developed as a GCS column packing. It is hydrophobic and is excellent for adsorbing volatiles from the atmosphere at room temperature, yet is stable enough at high temperatures, up to 300°C and more, for efficient thermal desorption. Many evaluations and applications are described in the literature, including studies of the storage and stability of samples on Tenax, analysis of solvent vapours and pollutants in the atmosphere and

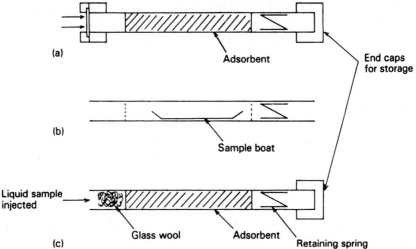

Fig. 5.8 Automatic thermal desorption sample tubes: (a) diffusive sampling; (b) solid sampling; (c) liquid sampling.

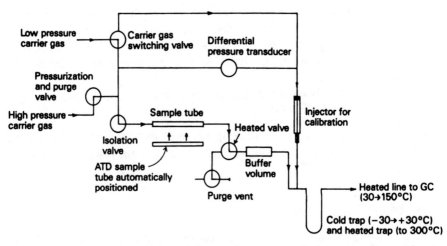

Fig. 5.9 Automatic thermal desorption system (schematic diagram).

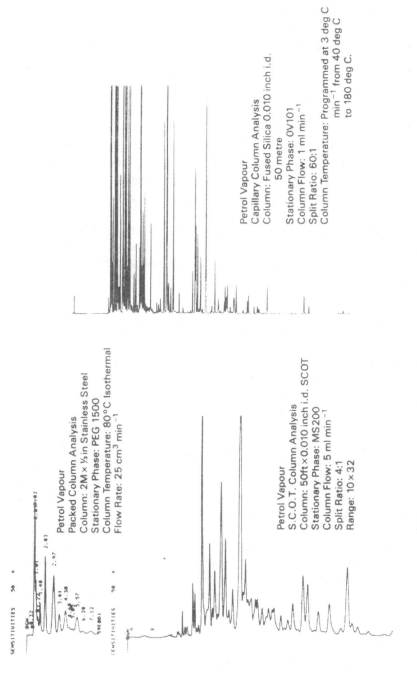

Fig. 5.10   Examples of automatic thermal desorption applications using packed, SCOT and WCOT columns. (Reproduced by permission of Perkin-Elmer Ltd)

volatiles from urine [10–13]. The importance of environmental and personal monitoring is demonstrated by the specialized equipment developed and marketed for this purpose. An example is the Perkin–Elmer automatic thermal desorption instrument the ATD50, which is capable of analysing up to 50 sample tubes in a run. Sampling may be carried out by pumped or diffusive sampling of vapours or volatiles from gaseous, liquid or solid samples, direct adsorption of liquid samples and direct analysis of solid samples placed in a sample tube (Fig. 5.8). Each tube is passed in turn into the desorption oven where thermal desorption takes place in either a single- or two-stage process. In the former method the desorbed vapours are swept directly on to the column, whereas in the two-stage process the desorbed material is collected in an electrically-cooled trap and is therefore concentrated. Rapid ohmic heating of the trap results in a narrow band of vaporized material being introduced on to the column (Fig. 5.9) Figure 5.10 illustrates the ATD analysis of petrol vapours using packed, SCOT and capillary columns and shows the increasing resolving power of the columns. SCOT columns produce a profile of the sample and capillary columns a fingerprint.

5.4 THE COLUMN AND COLUMN OVEN

The column is perhaps the most important feature of a GC instrument. It contains the stationary phase medium and thus effects the separation of the components in a mixture. The column may be made of glass or metal and is typically 2–6 mm ID and 1–3 m in length when packed with stationary phase material or 0.2–0.5 mm ID and 10–100 m long if in the form of a capillary column.

A packed column contains solid particles of uniform size generally coated with a stationary phase. Aluminium or copper tubing may be used for the columns; however, an active oxide film may form on the inner surface, which can catalyse reactions in some sensitive molecules and so are generally avoided. Stainless steel or glass tubing is therefore used for most columns.

Capillary or open tubular columns consist of long narrow tubing coated on the inner surface with about 1 μm of stationary phase and are known as wall-coated open tubular columns (WCOT). Columns may be of stainless steel but silane-treated glass (pyrex) and more recently silica columns are preferred due to their low catalytic activity. A more detailed discussion of capillary GC is given in Section 5.6.

5.4.1 Column oven and column temperature

The separation process occurring in the column involves an equilibrium established by the solute between the stationary and the mobile phases. The partition coefficient involved is dependant on solute vapour pressure and the thermodynamic properties of the bulk solute and is a function of temperature as related in the Clausius–Clapeyron equation;

$$\ln(p) = \Delta H/RT + C$$

where p is the solute vapour pressure, H the molar heat of solution and C a constant. Thus the relative retention α for an adjacent component pair (A and B) will be dependent on column temperature T and is given by:

$$\ln(\alpha) = -(\Delta H_A - \Delta H_B)/RT + C$$

The component with the longer retention time will have the higher heat of solution in the stationary phase. Relative retention of the two components will decrease as the stationary phase (column) temperature increases. Packed columns with larger amounts of stationary phase on the support material will require higher temperatures to obtain elution times equivalent to lower stationary phase loadings. However, decreasing the amount of stationary phase and reducing the column temperature results in the peaks first eluted having poorer separation. A balance of stationary phase loading is therefore required; 10–15% w/w loading is used for small molecules up to C_8 and up to 3–5% w/w for C_9–C_{20}. A compromise is required when selecting a column for a particular application. Once a column has been chosen, the two variables which can be modified to optimize the separation of components are temperature and carrier gas flow rate. The latter is often preset although the newer microcomputer-controlled instruments allow the flow rate and temperature to be changed between runs for automatic optimization. Control of column temperature is important in order to obtain reproducible chromatograms. A GC oven can be set to operate from about 10°C above ambient temperature, up to 450°C with a reproducibility of better than 0.1°C. The temperature of the heating element is carefully controlled by an electronic proportional controller and the oven designed so that temperature throughout the oven is uniform. Accurate control is important in isothermal analyses where retention times are being measured, and also in automatic GC systems for the separation of closely related components within a narrow boiling range. To avoid problems of the least volatile components in a mixture taking too long to elute and hence forming broad-tailing peaks, the column temperature can be progressively increased while the flow rate is kept constant. The rate of temperature increase is preset and typically involves an initial-hold stage when the starting temperature is held, perhaps long enough for the solvent to elute, a temperature ramp stage where the temperature is increased at a selected rate, e.g. 1–40°C min^{-1}, and a final stage where the upper temperature is held for a preselected time. At the end of the cycle the oven is cooled before a new analysis is carried out. Again, microcomputer control of instrument functions enables temperature increase profiles other than a linear increase to be programmed and also many more stages can be included in the overall cycle. An example of the effect of temperature programming is shown in Fig. 5.11.

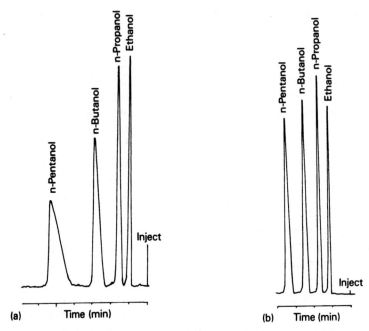

Fig. 5.11   Chromatograms to show the effect of temperature programming
1 μl injection of a 1:1:1:1 mixture containing ethanol, n-propanol, n-butanol, n-pentanol. 2m, Carbowax 1000 1/8 in. column, FID, response
factors; ethanol 1.0, n-propanol 1.41, n-butanol 1.63, n-pentanol 1.93, (a)
isothermal at 95° C; (b) temperature programmed 90–150° C at 10° min⁻¹,
initial hold 1 min.

5.4.2 Packed columns

The packed column consists of a glass or metal tube packed with either adsorbent
particles or stationary phase-coated particles, typically 60–80 or 80–100 mesh
size range. Both empty metal and glass columns can be obtained already formed
to the configuration required to fit various instruments, and packed as described
below. Straight metal tubing can be used and carefully coiled to shape before
packing. Alternatively prepacked columns can be purchased. A good packed
column would consist of 1000–2000 plates m⁻¹ in contrast to capillary
columns, where 2000–5000 plates are obtainable. Therefore a typical packed
column will contain 5000–10000 plates in which to achieve the separation while
a capillary column will have over 100000 plates.

The purpose of a support material is to provide a uniform, inert support for the
stationary phase with sufficient mechanical strength to avoid crushing of the
particles. Although many materials have been studied, only diatomaceous

materials and PTFE are commonly used. The former can be divided into two groups;

1. pink firebrick-derived materials, e.g. chromosorb P and Gas Chrom R, suitable for non-polar hydrocarbon compounds. Alcohols, acids and amines tail too much;
2. white diatomaceous materials derived from filter aids, e.g. chromosorb W, Gas Chrom Q.

The surface of these support materials contains mineral impurities and silanol (Si–OH) groups. The former can promote catalytic reaction and the latter are also reactive and polar, forming H-bonds with suitable components. This interferes with the equilibrium processes and results in tailing. The supports are therefore thoroughly treated with HCl to remove the minerals and silanized using dimethyldichlorosilane (DMDCS) or hexamethyldisilylazane (HMDS) to block the Si–OH groups with methylated siloxane bonds (Si–O–Si).

$$OH + Cl_2SiMe_2 / MeOH \longrightarrow O-SiMe_2(Cl) + MeOH \longrightarrow O-SiMe_3 + HCl$$

$$+ Me_3Si-N=N-SiMe_3 \longrightarrow O-SiMe_3 + N_2$$

The latter is useful for on-column silanization since the by-product of the reaction is nitrogen, which will not harm the metallic surfaces and the detectors. Several useful reviews of solid supports and properties have been published [14, 15].

In some applications it is necessary to prime the column before use by repeated injection of a substance with similar properties to the sample. For example, the analysis of barbiturates on an Apiezon column requires priming with barbitone. See experiment no. 20, Chapter 9. Another case where priming is required is when strongly polar materials such as acids and phenols or amines are being analysed. In the first case phosphoric acid may be used to prime the column and potassium hydroxide for the last. This process is sometimes referred to as 'tail reducing'.

PTFE supports, e.g. chromosorb T, are extremely inert and are used for corrosive materials, often with fluorocarbon oil, (e.g. KEL-F, Fluoropak-80), polyethylene glycol, and squalane stationary phase.

5.4.3 Stationary phases for packed columns

Separation of components occurs by partition between the mobile phase and a suitable stationary phase. The stationary phase therefore needs to be thermally stable, unreactive, have negligible volatility, and have a reasonable column life over the operating temperature range. The maximum practicable temperature for each stationary phase is therefore limited to minimize column or stationary phase bleed, which contributes to detector noise and baseline drift. The life of a stationary phase can be extended if its use is restricted to 20–50° C less than the recommended maximum. Although a large number of materials are available, few are necessary to achieve the separation of a wide range of chemical compounds. Many analytical laboratories achieve 90% of their analyses on as few as six different stationary phases, e.g. Apiezon, SE30, Carbowax20M, OV101, XE30 (Table 5.2). Recent developments in the preparation of bonded stationary phases for HPLC have resulted in such materials becoming available for GC columns. A

Table 5.2　Stationary phases

Stationary phase	Maximum temp. °C	McReynolds numbers					
		X	Y	Z	U	S	P/5
Squalane	150	000	000	000	000	000	000
Apiezon L	300	32	22	15	32	42	27
SE30 (methyl silicone)	300	15	53	44	64	41	43
SE54 (1% vinyl, 5% phenyl methyl silicone)	300	33	72	66	99	67	67
Dexil 300 GC (methyl silicone carborane)	400	47	80	103	148	96	95
OV-7 (20% phenyl methyl silicone)	350	69	113	111	171	128	118
Dinonyl phthalate	150	83	183	147	231	159	161
OV-17 (50% phenyl methyl silicone)	350	119	158	162	243	202	177
Tricresyl phosphate	125	176	321	250	374	299	284
OV-210 (50% tri-fluoropropyl silicone)	280	146	238	358	468	310	304
GE XE-60 (25% cyanoethyl methyl silicone)	250	204	381	340	493	367	357
OV-225 (25% phenyl methyl silicone)	250	228	369	338	492	386	363
Carbowax 20M	225	322	536	368	572	510	462
FFAP (Fatty acid free phase)	250	340	580	397	602	627	509
Carbowax 1000	150	347	607	418	626	589	517
Diethylene glycol succinate	180	496	746	590	837	835	701

P is a measure of polarity and is the sum of the other McReynolds terms.
X for benzene; Y, butanol; Z, 2-pentanone; U, nitropropane; S, pyridine.

detailed discussion is given in Chapter 6. Rather than coating the support with stationary phase, the latter is bonded on to the support through silyl ether linkages, prepared by reaction of the support silanol groups (Si–OH) with chlorosilanes.

$$\text{|-SiOH + Cl-SiR}_3 \longrightarrow \text{|-Si-O-SiR}_3 + \text{HCl}$$

R groups include octadecyl (C_8), Carbowax 1000 and $\beta\beta$-dioxypropionitrile. Column bleed is reduced but temperatures are limited to about 150° C when hydrolysis of the Si–O–Si bond occurs. Compounds with carborane structures included in the bonded group, modify the properties so that stability up to 400° C is possible.

5.4.4 Choice of stationary phase

The suitability of a stationary phase for a particular application depends on the selectivity and degree to which polar compounds are retarded relative to their elution on a non-polar stationary phase. Since the retention time is a function of temperature, flow rate, stationary phase type and loading, a practical method of indexing compounds can be developed.

Various retention index methods have been described; these involve evaluating the partition and separation properties of solute–stationary phase systems [16, 17].

Kovat's retention indices (KRI) are frequently used to indicate the chromatographic retention properties of a column with respect to the n-alkanes. The n-alkanes are used as reference materials since they are chemically inert, soluble in most common stationary phases, and are defined as having a KRI = $100 \times n$ (n being the no. of carbon atoms present in the molecule) e.g. n-hexane = 600 and n-octane = 800 regardless of the column used or the operating conditions, although these are recorded for a given column.

A graph of ln (RT) against retention index is constructed for several alkanes and the KRI of other compounds to be investigated are determined by recording their retention index (RI) and reading the RI off the graph. For example, propanol may have an RI of 650 on a Carbowax column, but only 500 on a OV101 column. This implies that the Carbowax is the more polar column by 150 RI units. Kovat's indices may also be calculated from the equation,

$$I = 100[(\log V^u - \log V^x)/(\log V^{x+1} - \log V^x)]$$

where V is the retention time of the compound denoted by the superscript, x is the carbon number of the alkane eluted before the unknown, ($x + 1$) is the carbon number of the alkane eluted after the unknown, u refers to the unknown. This formula is based on the linear relationship between log V (retention volume) and carbon number for a homologous series. A more general expression is given by

$$I = 100[n\{(\log V^n - \log V^x)/(\log V^{x+n} - \log V^x)\} + x]$$

The terms are as above with the addition that n refers to the difference in the number of carbon atoms for the n-alkanes used as reference.

Rohrschneider [16] and McReynolds [17] extended the RI system to a comparison of the RI for the n-alkanes on the given column compared to a squalane column. The difference in RI values gives the solute/stationary phase interactions due to hydrogen bonding, dipole moment, and acid-base properties since these will be over and above the squalane non-polar interaction. The method is useful for column selection where components have differing functional groups, and for identifying stationary phases with similar properties from the vast range available (Table 5.2).

A method to find an appropriate stationary phase for separation of a mixture, is to consider the polar properties of the solutes and stationary phase i.e. solute/solvent. If a solute is similar to the stationary phase (like dissolves like) then useful retention is likely to occur and conversely, if the solute is immiscible with the stationary phase then little or no retention difference will be obtained. A further useful indication is to analyse the sample with a dual column GC fitted with SE30/OV101 and carbowax 20M columns using a temperature control cycle, 50–220° C at 10° C min^{-1} with a final hold of 10 min. The chromatogram will indicate the polarity of stationary phase required for the components and the analysis can be repeated with columns of differing polarity, e.g. OV17, SE54.

5.4.5 Specialized stationary phases

Silver nitrate dissolved in polyethylene glycol forms loose adducts with olefins and is specific for such compounds, providing the temperature is not too high [18]. N-dodecylsalicylaldimines of nickel, palladium and platinum are able to retain selectively those molecules which can act as ligands to transition metals such as amines, ketones, alcohols, and $C = C$ and $C \equiv C$-containing compounds [19]. Tri-o-thymotide dissolved in tritolyl phosphate will selectively retard straight chain organic compounds relative to those with branched chains. Dicarboxylrhodium(II) trifluoroacetyl (+) camphorate has been used in squalane for purity determinations and separation of olefins [20]; dimeric rhodium(II) benzoate in squalane interacts reversibly with lone pair electrons, e.g. from ethers, ketones and esters, increasing their retention times. Other materials investigated include vanadium(II) and manganese chlorides.

5.5 DETECTORS FOR GC

The purpose of a detector is to monitor the GC column effluent, measuring variations in its composition which are due to eluted components. They do not identify the components except in the case of specific detectors. Most are of the differential type, i.e. they give a zero signal when the carrier gas alone is passing

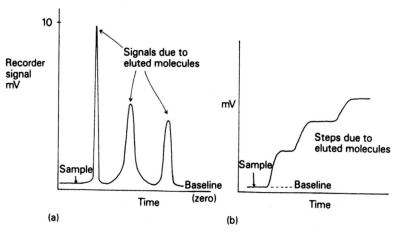

Fig. 5.12 Recording detector signals: (a) proportional (differential) signal; (b) integrated signal.

through. When a component is eluted and detected, the signal produced is proportional to the concentration or mass of that component (Fig. 5.12). Integrating detectors, on the other hand give a continuous signal which is proportional to the amount of substances which have been eluted, producing a stepped signal. Examples are absorption and gravimetric integral detectors [21–23]. Most commercial instruments today use proportional or differential detectors and the following types will be discussed:

1. flame ionization (FID);
2. nitrogen phosphorus (NPD);
3. flame photometric;
4. katherometer;
5. electron capture (ECD);
6. miscellaneous.

These detectors operate by measurement of concentration or mass flow rate.

5.5.1 Detector performance

The requirements of a detector for GC are exacting, and include adequate sensitivity to monitor the eluted sample components present in very low concentrations in the major eluting component, the carrier gas, and a rapid response to the changing concentration of the minor component.

5.5.2 Noise or signal/noise ratio

Noise present in the detector signal may have two components, long-term noise and short-term noise. The former causes a slow base line wander and may be

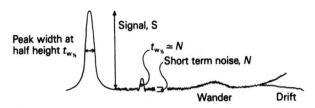

Fig. 5.13   Signal-to-noise ratio and determinable levels.

attributed to fluctuations in temperature, column stationary phase bleed, flow-rate variation, or pneumatic leaks. Short-term noise is generally observed as small, sharp spikes of shorter duration than component peaks and usually arises in the detector. It is important to establish the mean noise level in order to determine the limit of detection. The time period of a peak is most conveniently described by the peak width at half height and the noise is measured by the variation between maxima and minima of the noise peaks over that time period. The contribution of noise to the total component signal should be less than 1% (Fig. 5.13).

5.5.3 Minimum detection level

The minimal detectable level (MDL) is the level of sample being measured by the detector at peak maximum, i.e. maximum concentration, when the detector signal (S), is at least twice the mean noise signal level (N) (Fig. 5.13).

$$S/N \geqslant 2$$

MDL concentration is usually expressed in $\mu g\, ml^{-1}$ or $g\, ml^{-1}$. The MDL of the common detectors is given below.

Type of detector	$MDL(g\, ml^{-1})$
FID	10^{-12}
NPD	10^{-14}
Flame Photometric	10^{-11}
Katherometer	10^{-9}
ECD	10^{-14}

5.5.4 Linearity

Linearity or linear dynamic range is the sample concentration range over which the detector response is linear, from the MDL to the upper concentration which produces a deviation from linearity of about 5%. The FID can have a linear range of 10^7, i.e. it can be used over a concentration range of about 10^{-12} to $10^{-5}\,\mathrm{g\,cm^{-1}}$ of sample.

5.5.5 Response factors

Detectors produce an output signal in response to the sample passing through it. Different compounds can produce varying signals for the same concentration level. Thus the signal observed will need correcting to obtain accurate ratios of components in a mixture. The total amount of a component in a sample is given by the total or integrated signal it produces as it passes through the detector and is usually measured as peak area. In order to obtain the correct ratios the different response signals for a given detector to the compounds being determined have to be evaluated. The factors obtained are termed response factors (R_f). Typical response factors for n-alcohols to the FID detector of a Perkin Elmer F33 GC are given below;

n-Alcohol	R_f
Ethanol	1.00
Propanol	1.41
Butanol	1.63
Pentanol	1.97

The corrected peak area is given by area observed/response factor. Thus for butanol in a butanol/ethanol mixture the butanol peak area is given by:

$$A_{CORR} = A_{OBS}/1.63$$

See Experiment 19.

Response factors need to be accurately determined for good reproducible quantitative analyses by GC [24]. They may be conveniently obtained by the constant volume method; approximately 20 repeatable volumes of a sample are injected, peaks of interest measured and the response factors normalized to give the analytical data. The main disadvantage is the difficulty of achieving good reproducibility of sample volumes.

A second method uses an internal standard as a marker. A known amount of the standard is added to a standard mixture of all the components to be studied and the response factors relative to the internal standard calculated. The same amount of internal standard is added to each sample, the peak areas being corrected by the response factors. A more detailed account is given in Chapter 2.

5.5.6 Flame ionization detector (FID)

The flame ionization detector is almost the ideal GC detector and hence is used for routine and general purpose analyses. The outstanding features are:

1. high sensitivity to virtually all organic compounds;
2. has little or no response to water, carbon dioxide, the common carrier gas impurities, and hence gives a zero signal when no sample is present;
3. gives a stable base line as it is not significantly affected by fluctuations in temperature or carrier gas flow rate and pressure;
4. has good linearity over a wide sample concentration range (about 10^7).

The detector shown consists of a small hydrogen–air flame burning at a small metal jet (Fig. 5.14). The hydrogen is introduced into the column eluent and thoroughly mixes before emerging at the jet into the air stream, where the mixture burns. Organic compounds eluted from the column burn and form ions in the flame. The flame processes are complex and direct ionization only forms a small contribution [23, 25]. The organic molecules undergo a series of reactions including thermal fragmentation, chemi-ionization, ion molecule and free radical reactions, to produce charge-species. As organic compounds enter the flame the thermal energy available causes cracking and stripping of protons and terminal groups. A pure hydrogen–air flame contains $H^{\cdot}$, $O^{\cdot}$, $OH^{\cdot}$, $HO^{\cdot}$ radicals and excited species, but no ions. However, when organic molecules are present in the flame, ionization occurs, the amount being proportional to the number of carbon atoms present and hence the number of molecules. The main flame processes initially involve formation of $CH^{\cdot}$ from the organic molecules which immediately reacts with oxygen radicals:

$$CH^{\cdot} + O^{\cdot} \longrightarrow CHO^+ + e^-$$

The chemical nature of the organic molecule influences the effectiveness of the

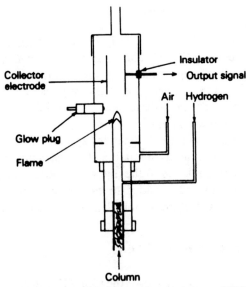

Fig. 5.14   Flame Ionization Detector (FID).

carbon atoms in producing the flame response and is corrected using the Effective Carbon Number Contribution (ECNC).

Atom	Molecule type	ECNC
C	Aliphatic	1.0
C	Aromatic	1.0
C	Olefinic	0.95
C	Carbonyl	0.0
O	Ether	−1.0
O	Primary alcohol	−0.6
O	Secondary alcohol	−0.75
N	Primary amines	−0.6
N	Secondary amines	−0.75
Cl	Aliphatic	−0.12

Small changes in carrier gas flow rate do not affect the response for a compound, since the FID is mass–flow sensitive. The sensitivity is usually measured in coulombs g^{-1} (carbon) and is generally in the region of 0.015 coulombs g^{-1} (C) with a linear dynamic range of 10^7. The ions travel to the collector electrode which is maintained at a negative potential (about − 150 V) with respect to the flame jet. Thus the current observed (about 10^{-14} A) is due to the concentration of the charged species present in the flame and the chemical structure of the molecules. The overall response therefore varies slightly for a given type of compound and carbon number. The signal is amplified and conditioned by an electrometer amplifier with a high input impedance to produce an output signal typically over a 0–10 mV or 0–1 V range, enabling a chart recorder, integrator or computer interface to be easily used as output for the results.

Inorganic materials not detected by the FID include H_2, O_2, N_2, $SiCl_4$, SiF_4, H_2S, SO_2, COS, CS_2, NH_3, NO, NO_2, N_2O, CO, CO_2, H_2O, Ar, Kr, Ne, Xe, HCHO, and HCOOH.

5.5.7 Thermionic–alkali bead nitrogen phosphorus detectors (NPD)

Since its introduction in 1964 the thermionic alkali flame detector has been successfully used for the specific detection of phosphorus compounds, particularly pesticides, and has been developed for the analysis of nitrogen-containing compounds [25]. The nitrogen-phosphorus (specific) detector (NPD) is a modified flame ionization detector (Fig. 5.15). To operate in the thermionic mode a source of alkali metal atoms is required. A bead of an alkali metal salt is mounted between the FID flame tip and the collector electrode with a flame temperature sufficient to volatilize the alkali metal salt and generate a stable population of alkali metal ions necessary for the thermionic process. The

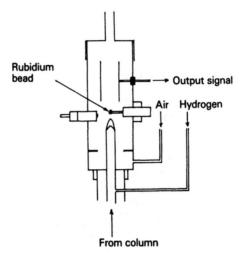

Fig. 5.15   Nitrogen phosphorus detector showing the position of the rubidium
bead (see FID given in Fig. 5.14 for further details).

combustion products of nitrogen and phosphorus compounds interact with the
alkali metal ions by a complex series of reactions, which produce thermionic
electrons. These are collected and give rise to the increase in current. The
sensitivity of the detector is dependent on the alkali ion concentration, and
therefore on the flame temperature. For good reproducible results, careful
control of the flame, carrier gas and oven temperature are required.

A number of alkali salts can be used; for optimum results for a range of
compound types a selection is required. For example, caesium bromide has the
best sensitivity and selectivity for organo-phosphorus compounds; rubidium
chloride or sulphate for organo-nitrogen compounds; and potassium chloride or
carbonate shows enhanced selectivity for halogenated compounds. For universal
applications, a rod of rubidium salt is used, the position of which can be readily
adjusted to account for vaporization of the salt.

A modified design of NPD has been developed to improve detector stability.
The alkali source consists of a glass bead which contains the alkali as an
essentially non-volatile rubidium silicate which is stable and results in a long
working life. The bead is electrically heated and its temperature is readily
controlled, so making the alkali source less sensitive to flame fluctuations than
other designs. By changing the electrical polarity of the jet and the carrier gas flow
rate the detector can be made specific either to phosphorus compounds only, or
to both nitrogen and phosphorus compounds. The bead is polarized at about
-150 V with respect to the collector while the jet polarity is switched for the P only
or N and P modes of operation.

In the P only mode a hot flame with a high (40–50 ml min^{-1}) of hydrogen is
used. Electrons from combustion of non-P-containing compounds are grounded
via the jet which has a positive potential relative to the bead. Combustion

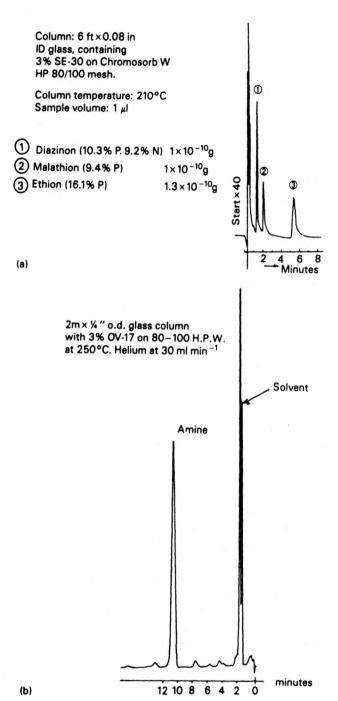

Column: 6 ft × 0.08 in
ID glass, containing
3% SE-30 on Chromosorb W
HP 80/100 mesh.

Column temperature: 210°C
Sample volume: 1 μl

(1) Diazinon (10.3% P. 9.2% N) 1×10^{-10}g
(2) Malathion (9.4% P) 1×10^{-10}g
(3) Ethion (16.1% P) 1.3×10^{-10}g

Start × 40

(a)

2 4 6 8
→ Minutes

2m × ¼ " o.d. glass column
with 3% OV-17 on 80–100 H.P.W.
at 250°C. Helium at 30 ml min^{-1}

Solvent

Amine

(b)

12 10 8 6 4 2 0   minutes

Fig. 5.16 Chromatograms obtained using an NPD detector: (a) analysis of pesticides in an aromatic solvent solution; (b) lubricating oil containing an amine antioxidant. (Reproduced by permission of Perkin-Elmer Ltd.)

products from P-containing compounds react on the surface of the bead to produce thermionic electrons which are captured by the collector electrode producing the P specific signal.

In the N-P mode the hydrogen flow rate is reduced ($1-5\,\mathrm{ml\,min}^{-1}$) and the jet polarized to the same potential as the bead. No flame is formed at the jet: the hydrogen burns on the surface of the bead to produce a plasma. N-containing compounds produce CN radicals probably as a result of pyrolysis, which react with the alkali atoms in the plasma to form an ion pair. The cyanide ion migrates to the collector electrode to form the detector signal. Alternatively the cyanide ion may be burnt in the oxidizing region of the flame producing electrons which travel to the collector. A similar process occurs for the formation of PO and PO intermediate radicals.

When compared with a standard flame ionization detector the NP detector is approximately 50 times more sensitive to nitrogen compounds and 500 times more sensitive to phosphorus compounds as shown in Fig. 5.16. The chromatograms were obtained by injection of $1 \times 10\,\mu\mathrm{g}$ of sample on to the column. The NPD detector has a linear range over 10^{-6} to $10^{-12}\,\mathrm{g}$ sample, and together with the selectivity enables identification of N and P-containing compounds without interference from large solvent peaks. Fig. 5.16 also shows the analysis of amine antioxidant in an engine lubricating oil where the major peak observed is that of the amine.

5.5.8 The Flame photometric detector (FPD)

The flame photometric detector is another type of flame dectector. It is compatible with the FID and offers specificity for phosphorus and sulphur with similar levels of sensitivity. Although first developed in 1966, the FPD has been progressively developed to take advantage of technological developments [26]. The principle of operation concerns the measurement of radiation emitted by excited species in the flame, the process observed in the simple flame tests familiar to all undergraduates. In a hydrogen flame, sulphur and phosphorus form excited species which emit radiation at 394 and 526 nm respectively and it has been reported that some nitrogen-containing compounds form emissions at 690 nm [27]. A narrow band-pass filter selects the wavelength to be observed and a photomultiplier detects and amplifies the emissions to form the detector signal (Fig. 5.17). Recent developments use fibre optics to transmit the radiation to a photomultiplier sited away from the heated detector block giving improved stability.

In contrast to the oxygen-rich flame of FIDs, the FPD uses a hydrogen-rich flame which is cooler. This enhances production of the two reactive species of interest, HPO^* and S_2^*, which give off the characteristic emissions at 526 and 394 nm respectively: the mechanisms for formation of HPO^* are not fully understood. However, the response is linear, in contrast to the square root

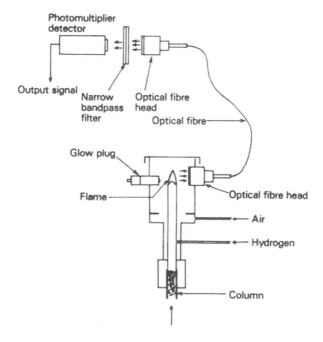

Fig. 5.17 Flame photometric detector (FPD).

response to concentration for sulphur compounds [28].

$$2RS + (x + 2)O_2 \longrightarrow xCO_2 + 2SO_2 \xrightarrow{4H_2} 4H_2O + S_2 \xrightarrow{\Delta E} S_2^*$$

The overall response is mass/flow rate sensitive and not concentration dependent. Selectivity of both modes over hydrocarbons is 10^4: 1, minimum detectable level is of the order of 10^{-12} g sec^{-1} and the linearity of response is over a 10^4 range for phosphorus and 10^3 for sulphur. Discrimination between S and P-containing compounds is only about 4:1 due to the spectral interference of HPO* and S_2^* emissions. It is therefore necessary to separate all the S-containing compounds from the P compounds.

The FPD has been used in a number of applications, particularly in environmental and food additive analyses. S and P-containing pesticides and their residues are of particular concern and the subnanogram sensitivity of the FPD over the FID and electron capture detector have enabled trace analyses to be readily carried out. Similar benefits have been utilized in the analyses of dyes and flavour additives in foods, soft drinks and organosulphur compounds in beer. Gaseous sulphur compounds such as thiophenes, mercaptans, disulphides, H_2S, SO_2 and the sulphurous content of fuel oils, petroleum and coal products, also of topical interest, have been analysed.

5.5.9 Electron capture detector (ECD)

The electron capture detector (ECD) is most frequently used for analysis of trace environmental pollutants. Its high sensitivity for halogenated compounds has enabled chlorinated pesticides and herbicides to be evaluated. The ECD utilizes the changes in electrical conductivity of gases in an ionization chamber caused by the presence of electron acceptor molecules [29]. Construction of the detector is usually one of two forms, the plane parallel or concentric cylindrical cell (Fig. 5.18). The latter design is preferred because of the ease of construction, greater sensitivity and smaller dead volume, typically $0.2 \rightarrow 0.5$ ml. The cell consists of two electrodes, an outer source electrode and a central collector electrode. The cylindrical source electrode consists of a β-ray emitter; the high energy electrons produced by the radioactive decay processes interact with the carrier gas (nitrogen or argon) to produce large quantities of thermal electrons which are collected by the positively polarized central electrode, producing the standing current or baseline signal.

$$N_2 + \beta^- \longleftrightarrow N_2^+ + e^-$$
$$Ar + \beta^- \longleftrightarrow Ar^* + Ar^+ + e^-$$

Molecules with high electron affinities capture the thermal electrons as they pass

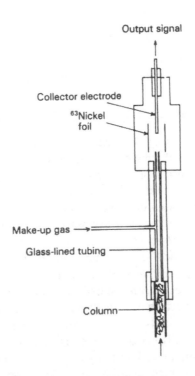

Fig. 5.18 Electron capture detector (ECD).

through the detector thus reducing the detector current and producing a decreased detector output signal, which is subsequently electronically processed to form the chromatogram. Any contaminants, stationary phase bleed, etc., may absorb electrons producing a background signal and decreased sensitivity [30].

In order to avoid space charge and other side effects a short duration positive potential is applied to the collector electrode (+ 50 V for 1.0 μs at 100 μs intervals) to collect the mobile electrons but not the slower negative ions. This allows maximum time for capture of the randomly moving thermal electrons by the sample molecules between the pulses, increasing sensitivity and enabling reproducible responses to be obtained.

The detector response follows a Beer's Law type of relationship:

$$I = I_o e^{(-ack)}$$

I = current when electron capturing material is present; I_0 = current when no electron capturing material is present; a = electron capture cross-section of material; c = concentration; k = proportionality constant related to the geometry of the cell and the operating conditions.

Although a number of radiation sources may be used, only tritium (^3H) and nickel (^{63}Ni) are commonly used. Tritium absorbed on a titanium foil is a weak β-emitter (18 KeV), but has a high flux of radiation, and therefore short distances (ca. 2.0 mm) are necessary for efficient ionization of the carrier gas. Nickel (^{63}Ni) on the other hand is more durable, its radiation (67 KeV) can penetrate at least 5.0 mm but the flux is lower. A ^{63}Ni source is therefore less efficient but this is offset by the longer active lifetime and higher maximum operating temperature of 450° C as opposed to that of ^3H (250° C). For safety reasons present-day instruments have sealed ECD detectors which can only be serviced by the manufacturers.

Although nitrogen or argon may be used as the carrier gas, metastable ions and cross-section effects can produce anomalous results. The addition of 5–10% v/v of an alkane, usually methane, overcomes these problems. Methane molecules undergo inelastic collisions with the slow β-electrons and metastable ions, which lose energy until thermal equilibrium is established. Thus the thermal electrons rather than the higher energy β-electrons are captured by the electrophilic molecules.

ECDs have high sensitivity to electrophilic molecules, in the order of 10^{-12} g s^{-1}, but have a rather small linear range of 10^4. Thus careful preparation of samples is required to ensure that the sample component concentrations fall within the operating range. At higher concentrations the detector may operate in an ionization mode. Relative response factors have been determined for a range of compound types [31]. These show enhanced responses of 10^2 to 10^4 for polyhalogenated, polynuclear aromatic and nitro compounds, anhydrides, conjugated carbonyls, and sulphur compounds. An approximate order of response for the halogens is F < Cl < Br < I.

Compound	ECD response relative to n-butyl chloride
Chloroalkane	1
Dichloroalkane	10^2
Bromoalkane	10^3
Dibromoalkane	10^5
Chloroform	10^5
Carbon tetrachloride	10^6
Benzene	10^{-1}
Bromobenzene	10^3
Polynuclear aromatics	$10–10^3$
Aliphatic alcohols, esters, ethers	1
Butan-2,3-dione	10^5

Applications include trace analysis of environmental samples for chlorinated pesticides and herbicides (DDT, γBHC/lindane, aldrin), SF_6 tracer in flue gases and mine atmospheres, organometallics (lead tetraalkyls), polynuclear aromatic carcinogens, NO_2 and SO_2 in chimney-stack gases.

5.5.10 Katherometer or thermal conductivity detector (TCD)

The katherometer or TCD is a bulk property detector i.e. it responds to some overall physical property of the sample molecules. The response of the carrier gas forms the baseline signal and any change in composition of the eluent will produce a change in the overall physical property being monitored by the detector, and hence a change in the detector signal. The detector will also be sensitive to variations in parameters that affect the specific property being measured, for example, temperature, flow rate, pressure, carrier-gas purity. The bulk property most commonly measured is the thermal conductivity of the gaseous eluent. Devices to measure thermal conductivity have been demonstrated since the 1920s, but it was in the 1950s that TCDs were developed as universal detectors for the newly emerging technique of GC. A study of the properties of carrier gases established helium as the preferred mobile phase, producing a suitable baseline signal and maximum signal differences for eluted organic materials and inorganic gases (Table 5.1). An excellent account of the principles and practice for the use of TCDs is given by Littlewood [32].

Thermal conductivity is the flow of heat from a body at a higher temperature than the accepting material. The flow of heat is dependent on the cross-sectional area, temperature, temperature coefficient and geometry of the donor body and the nature and cross-sectional area of the accepting material. A cylindrical cell geometry is used with a Pt, W or W/Re filament (0.02 mm in diameter) coiled along the axis of the cell. These filament materials have a high temperature

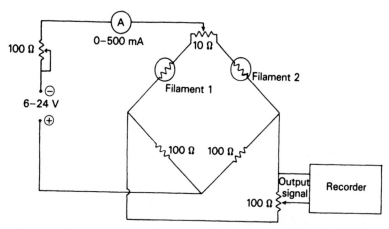

Fig. 5.19 Thermal conductivity detector, Wheatstone bridge network.

coefficient of resistance and are heated by a controlled constant mA current at a low voltage, e.g, 100 mA at 6–8 V. The response of the TCD depends on the thermal conductivity of the gas stream passing the filament. The temperature of the filament and hence its resistance is determined by the supply current and thermal conductivity of the ambient gas. Changes in composition of the gas cause a change in thermal conductivity and therefore a change in temperature of the filament. This results in a change in resistance of the hot filament which is one arm of a Wheatstone bridge network (Fig. 5.19). The out-of-balance current caused by a change in conductivity (resistance) of the filament may be amplified to form the recorder signal. The filament is housed in a detector block which acts as a thermal sink to minimize temperature fluctuations. In order to improve the stability and reduce base line drift due to flow and pressure fluctuations an identical reference cell is also housed in the detector block with pure carrier gas only passing through. This also forms an arm of the Wheatstone bridge network. It is extremely difficult to match the resistance of filaments and also the balancing resistances. A solution to this problem is to use four filament cells in a single detector block, each forming an arm of the Wheatstone bridge network. Two are reference cells and two are detector cells, each analysing half the GC effluent. Often the reference cells are used to monitor a second analytical column in a two-column oven. Both columns are fitted with injector blocks and either column may be used for analysis. Perfect matching is never achieved and degradation of the filaments during operation aggravates the problem. In practice the filaments are balanced using potentiometers or automatic electronic circuitry.

An alternative to filaments are thermistor metal oxide beads which have a negative temperature coefficient of resistance. They are efficient over a small temperature range (-20 to $+40°$ C), but are robust and therefore are used in portable ambient pollution monitoring systems.

The TCD responds to all types of organic and inorganic compounds including those not detected by the FID. It does not destroy the eluted components and therefore is suitable for use with fraction collectors for trapping of the separated components and for preparative work. Cell dead volume varies from about 1.5 ml for packed columns to 20 μl for capillary columns. The TCD is less sensitive than the FID, sensitivity being in the order of 1 ng cm^{-1} for a detector producing 8000 mV cm mg^{-1} with a linear range of 10^3.

Quantitative analyses can be readily carried out using a TCD and helium as carrier gas, the relative response factors being dependent on type of cell, detector temperature, filament temperature, sample concentration and flow rate. Relative response factors are similar for a homologous series and much data is available in the literature for helium, nitrogen and hydrogen carrier gases [33, 34]. The observations show that most compounds have a response similar to that of benzene ($\pm 20\%$) except for organometallic compounds and halocarbons which have lower response factors, and low molecular weight compounds, (MW < 40), which all have higher response factors.

A modified TCD with enhanced stability and sensitivity has recently been developed, particularly for use with capillary columns [35]. The design is based on a single, straight filament microcell with the housing made of ceramic material which has poor heat conduction. The analytical column effluent and the reference carrier gas are alternately directed through the cell at a switching frequency of 10 Hz. The amplitude of the modulated detector signal is proportional to the difference in the thermal conductivities of the two gases. The signal is then demodulated, amplified and processed to give the normal chromatogram signal.

5.5.11 Miscellaneous detectors

The use of spectroscopic techniques as detectors for GC is discussed in Chapter 7. The detectors already mentioned are those commonly used in present-day instruments; however there are a large number that have been developed over the years either for specialized applications or in the quest for the ideal universal detector. Some of these are outlined below. The reader is referred to specialized texts for further details of these and other detectors [23, 30].

Gas density balance

Designed by Martin and James, the gas density balance (GDB) is a universal detector and appears to be ideal for GC [36]. However, problems of sensitivity and stability compared to ionization detectors prevented its more widespread use. Interest has been maintained since direct determination of molecular weight is achieved and therefore recent studies and designs (Gow-Mac Instrument Co.) show improved performance and stability [37].

The operation depends on detecting minute gas flows in what amounts to a supersensitive anemometer (Fig. 5.20). The reference gas (pure carrier gas) enters the cell at A, divides and passes over both detector filaments. Column effluent enters at B with a flow rate (appox. 20 cm^3 min^{-1} slower) less than that of the

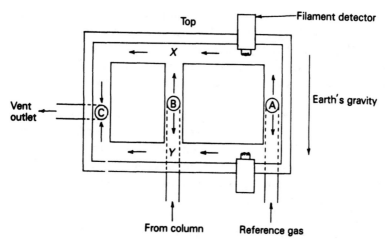

Fig. 5.20 Gas density balance detector, mounted as shown.

reference gas, thus preventing back diffusion to the detectors. If the overall density of the gas mixture at B is higher than the reference gas at A and hence at X and Y then the flow of gas from A is less on the lower arm since more of B moves downwards than proceeds to the upper arm. The resulting differing flow rates over the detector filaments cause imbalance in the Wheatstone bridge circuit, thus producing the detector signal and chromatogram. Negative responses are produced if less dense components are eluted. The response is a linear function of concentration and relative molar mass of the component.

$$A = Wk(M - m)/M$$

where A = peak area; W = weight component; k = constant; M = molecular weight of component; m = molecular weight of carrier gas.

Hydrogen and helium are not used as carrier gases because of their high diffusion rates. In order to determine molecular weights a standard of known molecular weight and the unknown component(s) are analysed using two different carrier gases. The equation below is solved for the molecular weight of the unknown.

$$A^{u_1}(M^s - m_1)/A^s_1(M^u - m_1) = A^u_2(M^s - m_2)/A^s_2(M^u - m_2)$$

Terms are as above with u = unknown, s = standard, 1 = carrier gas of lower MW, 2 = carrier gas of higher MW.

Conductivity detectors

Conductivity detectors convert the eluted components into ionic species in solution which are then monitored in a d.c. conductivity cell. The chemical reactions used in the conversion process determine the specificity of the detector. Trace amounts of nitrogen, chlorine and sulphur-containing compounds may be observed, as NH_3, Cl^-, S_2^-, which are readily determined [38]. Typically the effluent is mixed with hydrogen and hydrogenated over a nickel catalyst (800° C) forming NH_3, HCl, H_2S, H_2O and saturated low molecular weight hydrocarbons. Unwanted gases are removed in scrubbers, (such as $Ca(OH)_2$ or $Sr(OH)_2$, for acidic gases), and the remaining gases pass into a micro-electrolytic cell for measurement.

An alternative arrangement is to pass the oxygen-enriched effluent over a platinum catalyst where C, H, and O-containing compounds react. A constant amount of oxygen is continuously added to the effluent and after catalytic combustion any unreacted oxygen is determined in an oxygen-sensitive electrochemical cell. The resulting signal is therefore proportional to oxygen consumed and hence to the eluted components. A similar method using hydrogenation and a hydrogen-sensitive cell has also been reported.

Although capable of detecting nanogram samples and having a 10^4 linear range, the above detector systems suffer from a time lag in their operation which can cause problems unless suitable separation times can be achieved.

Helium and argon ionization detectors

These detectors operate by formation of excited carrier gas atoms (He or Ar) which collide with eluted component molecules in a small cylindrical cell of similar construction to that of the ECD [39]. The ionization energy of excited helium atoms (19.8 eV) is sufficient to ionize most other molecules in ion–molecule collision processes. The ions formed are collected on a central electrode under a polarized electrical field of up to 1 kV. Helium presents a number of problems, particularly the purity requirement of the carrier gas, and small linear range. Argon is less sensitive to sample saturation and due to the lower ionization energy of the excited atoms (11.6 eV) is less sensitive to contamination of the carrier gas by the permanent gases. Excitation of helium or argon is achieved using a high energy β-radiation source such as tritium on titanium foil. Both detectors are sensitive to contamination due to stationary phase bleed and therefore are frequently used with gas solid chromatography. Analysis of permanent gases (H_2, O_2, N_2, CO, CO_2, CH_4, NO, N_2O, H_2S, SO_2) has been achieved using a molecular sieve or cross-linked copolymer column with 10^{-13} g s^{-1} sensitivity over a 10^4 linear range [1].

Solid state detectors

Detectors for portable environmental monitoring equipment frequently use amorphous or thin film metal oxide detector elements, for example based on doped zinc or tin oxides. The elements operate at 200–350° C and involve a chemisorption/chemioxidation process [40]. The adsorption of the active compounds results in a change in the distribution of electrons and charge carriers on the solid surface which in turn produces a change in electrical conductivity. The oxides used are semiconductors because of the ability of the metal ion to exist in different oxidation states. All the oxides are non-stoichiometric and either contain an excess (n-type) or deficiency (p-type) of metal ions. It is these oxidation states and the electrical neutrality of the oxides which are ultimately modified by the complex chemisorption processes. Recent developments using mixed metal oxides have produced detectors with rapid response times and improved sensitivities ($10^{-8} g s^{-1}$) [41]. Metal oxide detectors can be fabricated to respond to a wide range of inorganic and low molecular weight organic compounds and therefore show promise as GC detectors for pollution monitoring.

Organic semiconductor detectors

Adsorbed gases also have a marked effect on the electrical conductivity of organic semiconductors such as metal complexes of phthalocyanine, merrocyanine and porphyrins [42]. The changes in electrical conductivity are due to the chemisorption of the gas onto the surface of a thin film (200 nm) of the organic semiconductor and subsequent electron transfer, the direction of transfer depending on the electronegativity of the gas and work function of the semiconductor. The change in conductivity can be several orders of magnitude with sensitivity of the order of $10^{-9} g s^{-1}$ and a linear range of 10^5. These detectors are inexpensive and easy to make and show potential in environmental pollution monitoring systems.

The silicon chip GC

The potential of the ubiquitous silicon chip has reached GC instrumentation. A recent paper describes the fabrication of a complete capillary GC system with TCD detector on a slice of silicon, 5 cm square [43]. The capillary column is a spiral 1.5 m long and 200 μm wide by 40 μm cross-section etched into the surface of the silicon. The seating for the inlet valve and mounting for the TCD detector, a thin film metal resistor, fabricated on a separate chip, are also etched on the chip. The silicon slice is bonded to a Pyrex glass wafer to form the final column. The small size has led to proposals for development of five parallel capillary columns lined with different materials and five detectors all on one chip. The different retention times for the different columns enable an instrument with multiple detector outputs and microcomputer decoding of the data to identify readily over one hundred polluted gases. The potential for such portable pocket GC monitors is indeed great.

5.6 CAPILLARY COLUMN GAS CHROMATOGRAPHY

The theory and application of capillary columns were first expounded by Golay [44]. The theory predicts a very high efficiency for a column which is simply a long length of tubing, 10 to 50 m long, 0.2 to 0.5 mm internal diameter, whose inner wall is coated with a thin layer of stationary phase. The early developments have been reviewed by Ettre and more recently by Jennings [45, 46]. Capillary columns have been constructed of copper, stainless steel and glass. Recent developments in vitreous silica materials have produced flexible inert columns and these are the preferred types today. Metal columns interact with the solute and can produce modifications to the chromatography.

One of the important differences between capillary and conventional columns is the liquid phase loading, the relative amount of liquid stationary phase present on the column packing. This is an important variable and is reflected in the overall column performance. Normal packed columns have about 5 to 30% stationary phase. The main reason for varying the amount is to optimize column efficiency and obtain the desired retention times. The latter is most important for high boiling compounds which typically are well retained; their residence time is reduced to produce a satisfactory chromatogram without degradation by reducing the liquid phase loading to 1 to 3%. Rapidly eluting peaks have a low capacity factor and hence require a higher efficiency than do peaks with greater retention for equivalent resolution. Thus the relative positions of peaks in a chromatogram can be modified by varying the amount of stationary phase. In capillary columns the amount of liquid phase is controlled by the film thickness of stationary phase on the inner wall. The overall performance in capillary columns is therefore a function of film thickness and column length. The high efficiencies are attributable to the thin films of stationary phase and short residence times of compounds coupled with the long columns. A summary of the main factors which contribute to the high performance of capillary columns when compared to normal columns is listed below;

1. very high number of theoretical plates, up to 500 000 plates per column for capillary columns (up to 20 000 plates for normal columns);
2. small sample loading due to the greatly decreased retention volume (samples injected are in the nanogram range);
3. time for elution is shorter for equivalent peak resolution and therefore analysis times are shorter by up to a factor of 10;
4. column temperatures are generally 20° C or more lower than required in packed columns because of the more favourable phase ratio in capillary columns;
5. there is greater flexibility of carrier gas flow rates due to the flatter curve obtained for the van Deemter plot of HETP (H) against flow rate of carrier gas ($\bar{u}$). (See Chapter 2);
6. recent developments in vitreous silica material technology have produced excellent chemically inert columns enabling separations of mixtures that would be impractical on packed columns due to the activity of the stationary phase support material;
7. generally only three or four columns are required to enable most sample mixtures to be analysed, especially if temperature programming is used. For example:

non-polar solutes	OV101, squalane, SE30
medium polarity solutes	OV17
polar solutes	Carbowax 20 M

8. the limit of detection is approximately the same as for packed columns, even though much less sample is used. This is due to the very narrow peaks obtained because of the narrow distribution of the sample in the carrier gas;

9. capillary column chromatography can be used for identification purposes, especially if a two-column system is used;

10. the flow path of the carrier gas is unrestricted in open tubular columns. Permeability is therefore very high so that long column lengths can be used and enormous separating power is obtained.

5.6.1 Types of capillary columns

Comparisons of capillary columns and conventional packed columns are shown in Table 5.3 and Fig. 5.21. Examples of chromatograms which illustrate the performance of the various types of columns are shown in Figs 5.22 and 5.10.

Table 5.3   Comparisons of the various types of capillary columns and packed columns

Column type	WCOT	SCOT	μSCOT	Conventional
Tubing OD (mm)	0.9	0.9	0.9	3.2–6.4
Tubing ID (mm)	0.2	0.5	0.3	1.6–5.0
Length (m)	20–80	20–80	20–50	2–5
Column efficiency				
$(N_{eff}\,m^{-1})$	2000–3000	800–1400	1500–2000	500–1500
(N_{eff})	40 000–200 000	20 000–80 000	40 000–100 000	1000–5000
Coating efficiency (%)	70–80	70–80	70–80	60–80
Sample size (μg)	10^{-3}–1.0	1.0–10.0	0.1–2.0	1.0–100
Inlet pressure (psi)	8–30	2–5	5–15	20–60

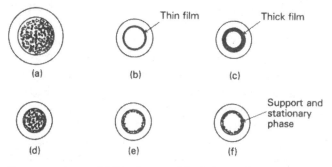

Fig. 5.21   Cross-sections of GC columns: (a) 1/8 in. packed column; (b) WCOT; (c) WSCOT; (d) 1/16 in. micropacked column; (e) PLOT; (f) SCOT.

Capillary columns can be classified into two groups:

1. Packed columns with solid particles coated with stationary phases filling the bore of the column, for example, micropacked columns. These have lower efficiencies than WCOT and SCOT columns described below and are not commonly used for routine analyses.

2. Open tubular columns with an open unrestricted flow through the bore of the column. This group can be further subdivided according to the method of supporting the stationary phase.

(a) WCOT, wall coated open tubular columns. These have a thin film (0.1 to 0.5 μm) of stationary phase coated on to the etched internal wall of the capillary tubing. They generally have greater separating power than SCOT columns (below). Selectivity is therefore less important than for conventional types of columns. It is even possible to separate polar compounds on suitably deactivated glass capillary columns with a non-polar stationary phase, e.g. silicone oil (SE30, OV101 or CP/SIL5). Glass WCOT columns often have a guaranteed performance expressed as the coating efficiency (60–80%). A high coating efficiency prevents rapid degradation of the column and lifetimes of six to 12 months can be expected if excessive amounts of solvents are not injected. Glass rather than stainless steel WCOT columns are most frequently used because of their relative inertness. Narrow bore WCOT columns (0.25 μm ID) have the greater efficiency or separating power (up to 6000 plates m^{-1}, N_{eff}) whilst wide bore WCOT columns (0.50 mm ID) have about half the efficiency (N_{eff} m^{-1}) and correspondingly lower resolution, by a factor of $\sqrt{2}$. Wide bore columns have the advantage that direct injection techniques without splitting may be used, and they are also generally more efficient than SCOT columns. A 25 m, 0.5 mm ID WCOT column will have the same performance as a 50–70 m SCOT column. The carrier gas flow rate is higher but less critical so that connections and injection techniques are correspondingly less of a problem. Wide bore WCOT columns also have elution times approximately twice as fast as narrow bore columns with an equal stationary phase film thickness because of the higher phase ratio (surface area per metre length) of the wide bore columns.

Stainless steel WCOT columns are readily available and are used where robust columns are required. The inner surface is generally specially treated to deactivate it but is still not to be recommended for polar or labile materials due to adsorption and catalytic activity. Adsorption results in peak tailing in the chromatogram and catalysis results in degradation and reactions which can lead to completely unrepresentative elution patterns and chromatograms. Nevertheless they are still used frequently in the petroleum industry and for analysing non-polar mixtures. Typical columns are 0.5 mm OD, 0.25 mm ID (narrow bore) to 0.8 mm OD and 0.5 mm ID (wide bore) and up to 100 m long.

(b) SCOT, support coated open tubular columns consist of 0.5 mm ID glass tubing with the inner wall coated with a layer of fine particular support material, for example, diatomaceous earth, which in turn is coated with a thin film of stationary phase [47]. SCOT columns have a larger surface area and a thicker effective film of stationary phase. This permits a higher sample capacity and retention volumes than WCOT columns but with less over-all efficiency. SCOT columns are prepared by a one-step process using a stationary phase coating solution containing a suspension of the support powder, which is passed down the column. Careful preparation techniques are necessary to produce good uniform columns. Recently 0.3 mm ID columns (μSCOT) with efficiencies approaching WCOT columns have become available.

(c) PLOT, porous layer open tubular columns are similar to SCOT columns and consist of a porous layer on the inner wall of the glass capillary tubing formed by a coating of a microcrystalline material or glass powder. This is then coated with stationary phase. There is really no clear distinction between PLOT and SCOT columns and between these and WCOT columns since surface porosity and support layer or etched support layers vary widely in their physical characteristics. PLOT columns are also used for gas-solid chromatography e.g. using KCl on an alumina support layer for the analysis of C_1–C_5 hydrocarbons [54(a)].

(d) Thick film WCOT columns. Liquid phase loading in capillary columns is a function of film thickness. The normal thickness of about 1 μm is a practical limit since column bleed is too great a problem with thicker films. These problems can be overcome by combining the features of WCOT and SCOT columns to produce thick film WCOT columns with film thickness of a similar order to SCOT columns [48]. This gives the higher sample capacity, higher stability and

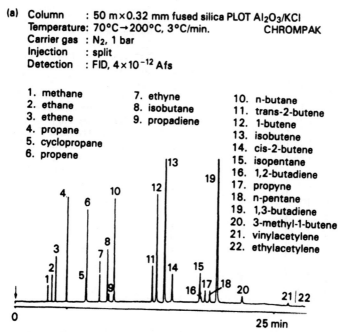

(a) Column   : 50 m × 0.32 mm fused silica PLOT Al$_2$O$_3$/KCl
Temperature: 70°C → 200°C, 3°C/min.   CHROMPAK
Carrier gas : N$_2$, 1 bar
Injection   : split
Detection   : FID, 4 × 10^{-12} Afs

1. methane
2. ethane
3. ethene
4. propane
5. cyclopropane
6. propene
7. ethyne
8. isobutane
9. propadiene
10. n-butane
11. trans-2-butene
12. 1-butene
13. isobutene
14. cis-2-butene
15. isopentane
16. 1,2-butadiene
17. propyne
18. n-pentane
19. 1,3-butadiene
20. 3-methyl-1-butene
21. vinylacetylene
22. ethylacetylene

Fig. 5.22 Examples of capillary GC analyses: (a) separation of C_1–C_5 hydrocarbons.

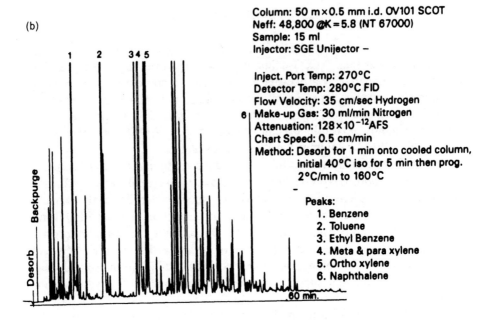

(b)

1 2 3 4 5

6

Column: 50 m×0.5 mm i.d. OV101 SCOT
Neff: 48,800 @K = 5.8 (NT 67000)
Sample: 15 ml
Injector: SGE Unijector –

Inject. Port Temp: 270°C
Detector Temp: 280°C FID
Flow Velocity: 35 cm/sec Hydrogen
Make-up Gas: 30 ml/min Nitrogen
Attenuation: 128×10^{-12} AFS
Chart Speed: 0.5 cm/min
Method: Desorb for 1 min onto cooled column,
initial 40°C iso for 5 min then prog.
2°C/min to 160°C

Peaks:
1. Benzene
2. Toluene
3. Ethyl Benzene
4. Meta & para xylene
5. Ortho xylene
6. Naphthalene

Backpurge

Desorb

60 min.

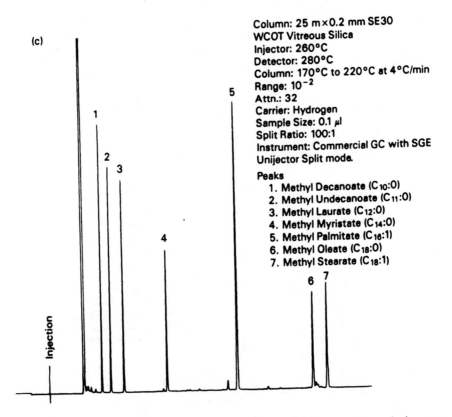

(c)

1
2
3
4
5
6 7

Injection

Column: 25 m×0.2 mm SE30
WCOT Vitreous Silica
Injector: 260°C
Detector: 280°C
Column: 170°C to 220°C at 4°C/min
Range: 10^{-2}
Attn.: 32
Carrier: Hydrogen
Sample Size: 0.1 μl
Split Ratio: 100:1
Instrument: Commercial GC with SGE
Unijector Split mode.

Peaks
1. Methyl Decanoate ($C_{10}:0$)
2. Methyl Undecanoate ($C_{11}:0$)
3. Methyl Laurate ($C_{12}:0$)
4. Methyl Myristate ($C_{14}:0$)
5. Methyl Palmitate ($C_{16}:1$)
6. Methyl Oleate ($C_{18}:0$)
7. Methyl Stearate ($C_{18}:1$)

Fig. 5.22 (Contd.) (b) Automative exhaust; (c) fatty acid methyl esters.

Injector SGE Unijector Splitless/Direct Mode
Injector Temperature: 240°C
Detector Temperature: 240°C
Column Temperature: 140°C Isothermal
Sample Size: 0.5 μl
Range: 10⁻¹⁰
Attn.: × 2

Order of Peaks
1. 2-Octanone
2. 1-Octanol
3. n-Dodecane
4. 2,6-Dimethylphenol
5. n-Tridecane
6. 2,4-Dimethylaniline
7. Naphthalene

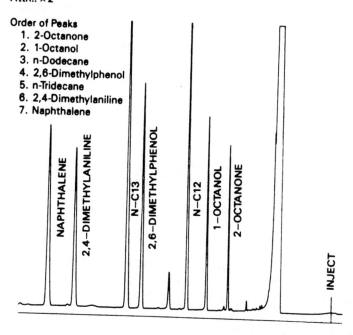

(e)

(i) *Column: 50 m×0.23 mm i.d. fused-silica capillary coated with immobilized methylsilicone phase. Liquid phase film thickness: 0.25 μm. Column temperature: programmed from 40 to 180°C at 4°C/min. Carrier gas: helium 1 ml/min. Sample size: 0.4 μl split 1/90 corresponding to 3.5 μg sample entering the column.*

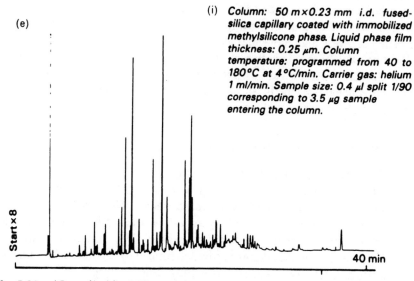

Fig. 5.22 (*Contd.*) (d) SGE activity test mix A; (e) analysis of coal tar fractions [48], (i) WCOT column, (ii) thick film WCOT (see p. 186). (Reproduced by permission of Scientific Glass Engineering Ltd.).

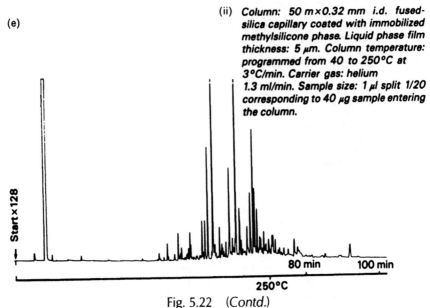

(e)

(ii) *Column: 50 m×0.32 mm i.d. fused-silica capillary coated with immobilized methylsilicone phase. Liquid phase film thickness: 5 μm. Column temperature: programmed from 40 to 250°C at 3°C/min. Carrier gas: helium 1.3 ml/min. Sample size: 1 μl split 1/20 corresponding to 40 μg sample entering the column.*

Fig. 5.22   (*Contd.*)

carrier gas flow rates and direct injection features of SCOT columns. Typical columns have a 0.3 mm ID and a 5 μm film of stationary phase on the inner wall giving an efficiency (N_{eff}) of about 2000 plates m^{-1}, 100 000 plates for a 50 m long column. Figure 5.22(e) shows comparative chromatograms for the WCOT and thick film WCOT column analysis of a coal tar extract. Note the different sample sizes, relative peak sizes and additional peaks.

The thick film is obtained using an immobilised liquid stationary phase consisting of a very high molecular weight polymer partially chemically bonded to the inner wall of the silica tubing. Examples of polymeric bonded stationary phases available include various polydimethylsilicones (equivalent to OV101, SE30), polyphenyl (5%) methylsilicone (SE54, OV17), polycyanopropyl silicone (OV1701), polyethyleneglycol (equivalent to Carbowax 20 M).

5.6.2 Performance of capillary columns

The performance of a capillary column (particularly a WCOT column) may be evaluated using methane. A needle sharp peak should be obtained at the recommended temperature and flow rates of carrier gas. The inertia and efficiency of a column may be easily assessed by analysing a test mixture that includes compounds with a variety of functional groups. The surface activity and separating properties of the column can be determined by carefully examining the peak shapes and relative retention times, [49]. (Fig. 5.22(d)).

Deactivation of a column to prevent tailing of polar compounds may be achieved by silylation, injecting a solution of a chloromethylsilane or hexamethyldisilazane. An alternative procedure is film deactivation using a polar stationary phase. This method uses a short packed precolumn of 5% Carbowax

20 M on an inert support which is placed into the heated injection port of the gas chromatograph and connected directly to the column. The precolumn is maintained at about 260° C and the column at 250° C for 12–15 hours [50].

5.6.3 Fused and vitreous silica capillary columns

The adsorption of even trace amounts of sample on to the walls of a capillary column can cause the loss of a significant proportion of any polar compound. Stainless steel columns are therefore unsatisfactory for many applications and although glass columns have surfaces which are much less active, problems still occur. The inertia and efficiency of a column can be determined using a test mixture as explained above. Pure vitreous silica columns overcome many of these problems [51]. Their main advantages are much higher tensile strength and flexibility and greater inertness due to the physical properties of the molecular structure of silica and the low metals content, particularly of the strong Lewis acids, boron, calcium and magnesium (Table 5.4). Inert fused silica columns also provide higher temperature stability of the stationary phase, lower bleed levels and longer lifetimes. They are also suitable for the preparation of chemically-bonded stationary phase WCOT columns, thus providing a range of tough, inert and versatile columns.

There are two methods for the manufacture of silica columns. The silica may be prepared from natural quartz crystals by melting at 1900° C under vacuum. The content of metals is typically 10–100 ppm. A second process uses purified silicon tetrachloride vapour which is introduced into a flame where it is hydrolyzed by the water formed in the flame from combustion of methane.

$$SiCl_4 + 2H_2O \longrightarrow SiO_2 + 4HCl$$

The silica is collected on a substrate as fused silica and is extremely pure (< 1 ppm other impurities) and has about 0.1% hydroxyl groups. These silanol groups are valuable sites for the preparation of bonded stationary phases and may also be reduced by heating, when water is eliminated and siloxane bridges formed. The final structure is a three-dimensional slightly distorted SiO tetrahedral lattice, giving great strength to capillary columns. Many silica columns are further strengthened by coating the external wall with a polymer such as a polyimide thermally stable up to 300° C.

Table 5.4   Analysis of glasses used for capillary columns showing the metal content (% w/w)

Glass	SiO_2	Al_2O_3	Na_2O	CaO	MgO	B_2O_3	BaO
Soda glass	68	3	15	6	4	2	2
Borosilicate glass	81	2	4	—	—	13	—
Synthetic fused silica	100			Total < 0.1 ppm			

5.6.4 Injection techniques

The ideal sample injection method is to introduce all the sample directly on to the first plate of the column. However, capillary columns have very low gas volumes, in the order of 10 μl per plate, which means that only equally small liquid samples are required. To overcome these problems special injection techniques have been developed which fall into two groups, splitless injectors and sample splitting injectors.

Splitless injectors

Splitless injectors are used for trace analysis and have the advantage that the injector is all glass lined, has good accuracy and reproducibility and injections can be carried out over a wide column temperature range without affecting the dynamics (Fig. 5.23). It is used with flow rates of 2 ml min^{-1} or higher and all the sample is carried very rapidly on to the column *via* a low volume transfer line. A variation of this type of injector is the GROB splitless injector. Injections of up to 10 μl can be made without the solvent obscuring the sample peaks. The whole of the sample is vaporized and then condensed in the first one or two turns of the capillary column by keeping the oven temperature at 20–30° C below the boiling point of the solvent. The injector is then flushed clean by high flows of carrier gas vented through an external valve. This removes the solvent which otherwise

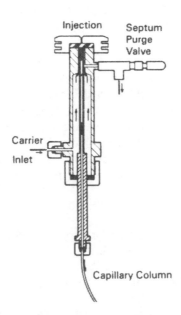

Fig. 5.23   Splitless/direct injector for SCOT and wide bore WCOT. (Reproduced by permission of SGE Ltd.).

would cause severe tailing in the chromatogram. The column temperature is then raised to start the chromatography of the sample.

Sample splitter injection method

The purpose of an inlet splitter is to reduce the size of the sample injected to a level within the capacity of the column [52], (Fig. 5.24). The split ratio is controlled by an infinitely variable microneedle valve. Silanized glass beads are placed in the vaporizer tube to reduce dead volume and band broadening. This also produces a homogeneous sample at the splitting point and serves as a clean-up trap for dirty samples. A stainless steel buffer volume delays entry of the rejected sample into the splitter valve so that the viscosity changes do not have any adverse effect on split ratios. Split ratios of 1:100 to 1:1000 are typical and can be varied within the linear range of the system. Thus if a 10^{-3} μg sample is required by a capillary column, it can be obtained by injecting 1 μl of sample with a split ratio of 1:1000.

The flow rate of carrier gas through a capillary column is very low, (0.5 ml min^{-1} upwards) and therefore the presence of dead or unswept volumes will cause band broadening, peak tailing and a drop in efficiency. It is important that the connections within the injector and between the column, injector and detector are of the correct type and match the diameters involved. A range of couplings, switching and sampling valves designed specifically for capillary column work are available. The ends of a column should fit right into the injector and detectors without any couplings disturbing the gas flow, couplings only being required to seal and interconnect the various components.

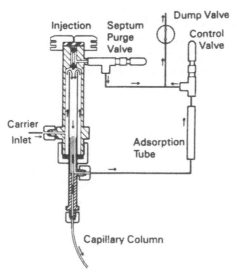

Fig. 5.24   Splitter injector for column sample size of 10^{-4} to 10^{-2} μl.

5.6.4 Supercritical gas chromatography

The greater selectivity of adsorption chromatography for compounds of different chemical types may be extended using supercritical fluids (SFs) as the mobile phase [53]. In normal gas chromatography the carrier gas does not interact significantly with the stationary phase, but when the mobile phase is above the critical temperature and pressure, strong interactions occur. This makes the solutes being analysed appear more volatile due to enhanced molecular interaction in the mobile phase and modified stationary phase surface properties due to the interaction of the mobile phase. Although the separating potential of SFs was demonstrated about 20 years ago, it is only recently that the practical difficulties have been overcome [54, 55] and a commercial instrument made available (Hewlett–Packard 1082B).

Supercritical fluids have liquid and gaseous states that are indistinguishable and are formed when both the critical temperature (T_c) and critical pressure (P_c) exceed the critical values for a given gas [56]. The critical values are high, requiring specialized equipment to withstand the temperatures and pressures involved (Table 5.5). Supercritical water behaves as a covalent material dissolving organic solvents, but not inorganic salts. It is no longer hydrogen bonded and is therefore miscible with many permanent gases, e.g. N_2, O_2 (air), a property with commercial potential [56]. Supercritical hydrocarbons have equally interesting properties and potential, but also present toxic and fire hazards.

The properties of supercritical carbon dioxide have been extensively studied since it is used commercially for extracting low molecular weight organic material from water and for decaffeinating coffee. It is inexpensive, not too hazardous and has therefore been developed for supercritical chromatography. It is a mobile non-polar solvent with properties similar to hexane and can be used from almost ambient temperatures ($> 31.1°C$). Increasing the temperature and decreasing the pressure decreases the density of CO_2 and the chromatograms produced change from LC-like to GC-like [53]. Ammonia has been used as the mobile phase for the analysis of C_1–C_4 hydrocarbons in synthetic fuel fractions [57]. One of the major

Table 5.5   Supercritical properties

Gas	T_c	P_c (BAR)
Carbon dioxide	31.1	72.7
Ammonia	132.5	112.5
Pentane	196.6	33.3
Diethyl ether	192.6	35.6
Propan-2-ol	235.3	47.0
n-hexane	234.2	29.9
Water	374.2	218.3

problems with packed columns is the pressure drop across the column; CO_2 is the only practical SF fluid for these systems. In contrast, a wider range of SFs can be used with open tubular capillary columns, e.g. ammonia and hydrocarbons. The technique, which is still in its infancy, requires equipment capable of generating mobile phase pressures of up to 10000 psi together with suitable detectors. UV detectors are used with carbon dioxide since it is transparent in this region of the spectrum.

5.7 APPLICATIONS OF GC

The range and variety of applications to which GC has been applied demonstrate the versatility and scope of the technique. The ever-changing complexity of present-day products, (e.g. drugs, foodstuffs, consumer products) the increased sensitivity and data collection and processing have all contributed to the steadily increasing use of GC. The aim of this section is to present an overview of the range of applications and where appropriate include references for further reading. Reviews frequently appear in the chromatography journals and the Chromatography Discussion Group publish an excellent quarterly, *Chromatography Abstracts* [58].

5.7.1 Headspace GC analysis

Headspace GC (HSGC) analysis employs a specialized sampling and sample introduction technique, making use of the equilibrium established between the volatile components of a liquid or solid phase and the gaseous/vapour phase in a sealed sample container [59, 60]. Aliquots of the gaseous phase are sampled for analysis. In many cases the detection limits for a particular component in a mixture are improved and the 'clean' nature of the sample makes HSGC ideal for automatic repetitive quantitative and qualitative analyses, at the same time prolonging the effective lifetime of a column.

An example of a quantitative application is the forensic analysis of blood and urine alcohol (ethanol) levels, particularly in connection with driving offences. The technique eliminates the need for a precolumn or regular repacking of the first section of the column, rendered ineffective by sample residues, since only volatile compounds are introduced on to the column. The blood sample is homogenized and an aliquot taken and diluted with an aqueous solution of an internal standard (*n*-propanol or isopropanol). Aqueous solutions of ethanol (80 mg/10 ml and 200 mg/100 ml) are used as standards to calibrate the internal standard. The sealed vials containing the diluted samples are loaded into an autosampler and are allowed to equilibrate at 40° C for 10 minutes. The vapour samples are then taken as described in the section on injection techniques and analysed on a polar column such as PEG400 or Porapak Q. See Practical Exercise No. 19, Chapter 9 for further details on the chromatography and calculations. In addition to ethanol, methanol, acetone, acetaldehyde and other volatiles which may be present in the blood can be observed. HSGC of volatile constituents in a sample can be extended to the detection of volatile solvents and materials such as white spirits (turpentine substitute), paraffin, petrol, diesel fuel and glue solvents in the blood to assist with determination of the circumstances or cause of death in arson, explosions, robberies and accident cases.

Quality and production control of beer constituents and other brewing products can be effectively carried out by HSGC to determine the ethanol content and the ratios and amounts of the fusil oils, higher alcohols (n-PrOH, i-PrOH, n-BuOH, 2-methyl and 3-methylbutan-1-ol), esters (ethyl acetate), acetaldehyde etc., using a Carbowax column [61], (Fig. 5.25). Aromatic flavours and trace volatiles in beer (26 have been observed), foods and soft drinks are also readily analysed [62, 63, 64]. Plastics packaging and consumer products have been analysed for residual monomer and other process residues such as O_2, CO_2, H_2O, solvents, acetates, aliphatic alcohols, printing inks and solvents [65]. These present problems of film stability, porosity and contamination of foods. A range of sampling techniques used include incubation of the materials in sealed vessels at 120°C.

HSGC has been used for monitoring atmosphere both of home and workplace,

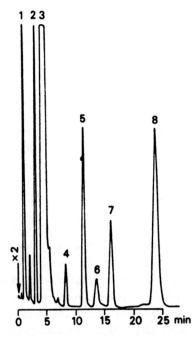

Fig. 5.25   Headspace analysis of beer with an FID; Carbowax 20M, 3m packed column (50–150° C): 1, acetaldehyde; 2, ethyl acetate; 3, ethanol; 4, n-propanol; 5, isobutanol; 6, isoamyl acetate; 7, n-butanol (internal standard); 8, amyl alcohols.

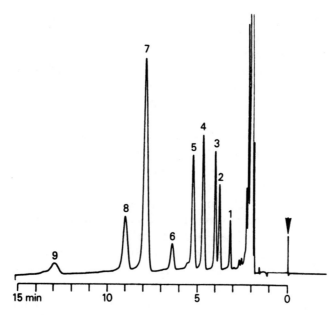

Fig. 5.26   Headspace analysis of the volatile free fatty acids from *Peptostrep-*
tococcus anaerobius grown in PYG culture: 2 m SP 1000/H$_3$PO$_4$ at 150° C,
FID: 1, acetic acid; 2, propionic acid; 3, isobutyric acid; 4, *n*-butyric acid;
5, isovaleric acid; 6, *n*-valeric acid; 7, isocaproic acid; 8, *n*-caproic acid;
9, heptanoic acid.

for hazardous trace pollutants such as formaldehyde, carbon monoxide,
trichloroethylene, benzene, and acrylonitrile [66]. Analysis of volatile free fatty
acids produced by bacteria, particularly anaerobic bacteria, enable a fingerprint
of the particular microorganism(s) to be obtained, which assists in the identification of the bacteria [67] (Fig. 5.26).

5.7.2 Food analysis

Analysis of foods involves the analysis of lipids, proteins, carbohydrates,
preservatives, flavours, colourants and texture modifiers, and also vitamins,
steroids, drugs and pesticide residues and trace elements. Most of the components
are non-volatile and although HPLC is now used routinely for much food
analysis, GC is still frequently used [68]. For example, derivatization of lipids to
fatty acid methyl esters, of proteins by acid hydrolysis followed by esterification
(*n*-propyl esters) and of carbohydrates by silylation produce volatile samples
suitable for GC analysis. Thus GC quality control analysis of food products can
confirm the presence and quantities of additives, etc. to ensure the product

complies with company and legislative requirements. For example, fruits, fruit-derived food-stuffs, vegetables and soft drinks and beverages (tea, coffee), are analysed for their polybasic and hydroxy acid content (citric, malic acids, etc.) as TMS derivatives using an OV17 column: the flavanols and caffeine are analysed on a SE30 column whilst the carbonyl-containing volatiles, e.g. vanillin, are analysed using a more polar Carbowax 20 M column [69].

Dairy products are analysed for volatile components (aldehydes, ketones) to determine age and rancidness, fatty acids (as methyl ester derivatives) and milk sugars (as TMS derivatives) [70]. The use of GC analysis in butter, cheese and yogurt is not only for the butter fat content but also for added colour and flavourings which are monitored to determine the quality and quantity of permitted additives and brand or type of product [71].

The composition of volatile components in a wide range of natural foods, fruits, vegetables, flavourings and beverages (tea, coffee, cocoa) which give them their characteristic flavours and odours has received considerable interest, particularly for the preparation of artificial flavourings and perfumes. The volatile nature of the flavours and essential oils are particularly suitable for GC analysis (particularly capillary column GC) since most of the above contain a complex mixture of a large number of these compounds, e.g. rose perfumes (more than 55), herb leaf oils such as juniper (more than 100), peaches and figs, (more than 40) [72].

5.7.3 Drugs

Analysis of drugs by GC is now complemented by HPLC. However, there are still numerous applications involving both quantitative and qualitative identification of the active components and possible contaminants, adulterants or characteristic features which may indicate the source of the particular sample [73]. Forensic analysis frequently uses GC to characterize drugs of abuse: in some cases the characteristic chromatographic fingerprint gives an indication of the source of manufacture of the sample or worldwide source of a vegetable material such as cannabis [74]. The drugs may be contained in commercial preparations, illicit drug samples or samples of blood, urine, stomach contents and therefore appropriate sample preparation and extraction are required. Schemes describing these processes are recorded in the literature.

Although some classes of drugs can be analysed directly after extraction or dissolution in a solvent, many require derivatization, usually silylation, acetylation or methylation. Retention data is available for over 600 drugs, poisons and metabolites for given sample preparation techniques, derivatization where applicable and chromatographic conditions [74]. Typical columns used are 2.5% SE30, 5% OV17, 1–10% Carbowax on inert supports. This data is extremely useful for forensic analysis to assist in identifying abused drugs [75]. Reviews and data are thus available to enable most drug samples to be successfully analysed [76].

5.7.4 Pyrolysis GC

PGC is used principally for the identification of involatile materials, such as plastics and natural and synthetic polymers, drugs and some microbiological materials [77]. The thermal dissociation and fragmentation of the sample produces a chromatogram which is a 'fingerprint' for that sample, consisting of small molecules that are frequently identified using a GC-MS system (see Chapter 7). The pyrogram can give information on molecular structure from identification of the fragments and also information on chemical composition of the sample. Thus for a plastic sample, information on the type of polymeric material, plasticizers, extenders and other additives would be obtained.

PGC, especially with capillary columns, has proved very useful in forensic analysis, particularly for characterizing plastics, rubbers and paint samples. Frequently only small fragments of sample are available from contact traces or debris at the scene of the crime. PGC requires only small samples and since in many forensic applications a comparison between test sample and reference samples is the main objective the pyrogram fingerprint can provide the comparative evidence required. [78]

5.7.5 Metal chelates and inorganic materials

Although inorganic compounds are generally non-volatile, GC analysis can be achieved by converting the metal species into volatile derivatives. Only some metal hydrides and chlorides have sufficient volatility for GC. Organometallics other than chelates, which can be analysed directly, include boranes, silanes, germanes, organotin and lead compounds. Several classes of derivatives, such as metal carbonyls and alkoxides, can be formed but only metal chelates have been used extensively in analytical applications. The chelating ligands contain oxygen, sulphur, selenium, phosphorus and nitrogen as donor atoms, but β-diketonates $R'-CO-CH_2-CO-R''$ have proved to be the most suitable, forming thermally stable, soluble, volatile metal chelates. The β-diketonates of di-, tri-, and tetravalent metals have proved the most suitable and the ligands acetylacetone, trifluoroacetylacetone and hexafluoroacetone the most used. In general, the more fluorinated the β-diketone the more volatile the chelate; also a greater sensitivity can be achieved with the ECD. During the past 20 years a large number of analyses involving metal chelates have been published [79].

5.7.6 Dual detector applications

A number of specific detectors or detectors with enhanced responses to certain classes of compounds are available and their specificity when compared to an FID for example, can be used for analysis of complex mixtures. Generally, the column effluent is split 50:50 between an FID and a second detector, such as, an NPD or ECD. Dual detector amplifiers and dual channel recording systems are required.

An example of this application is the identification and chemical classification of drugs based on the relative response of the nitrogen selective detector (NPD) and FID [80]. The drugs are analysed using caffeine as reference internal standard; in addition to characterizing the drug in terms of a retention time relative to caffeine, the drug is also characterized by the ratio of the NPD response to FID response determined by the caffeine standard. At least 70 drugs can be characterized by this system and with different columns other groups of drugs could be analysed.

Polychlorinated pesticides and herbicides produce larger responses from an ECD rather than an FID. This specificity can assist in the identification of polychlorinated components in a sample. A similar arrangement is used [81].

A TCD connected in parallel or in series (since the TCD is a non-destructive detector) with an FID enables samples containing permanent gases (which are not detected by an FID) and organic materials to be completely analysed with a single sample injection. An example of an application is the analysis of natural gases which invariably contain C_1–C_4 hydrocarbons, nitrogen, oxygen and carbon dioxide [82].

5.7.7 Dual column applications

Dual column analysis involves the simultaneous analysis of a sample using two columns in parallel having stationary phases with widely differing polarities such as Carbowax 20 M and SE30 or Apiezon L. The log/log plot of retention times on the two columns for the components to be identified are constructed, thus enabling complex mixtures to be analysed when there are problems of achieving good separations. Experiment 21, Chapter 9 illustrates this application.

5.7.8 Environmental analysis

Environmental pollution is an age-old trademark of man and in recent years as technology has progressed, populations have increased and standards of living have improved, so the demands on the environment have increased, with all the attendant problems for the earth's ecosystems. Combustion of fossil fuels, disposal of waste materials and products, treatment of crops with pesticides and herbicides have all contributed to the problem. Technological developments have enabled man to study these problems and realise that even trace quantities of pollutants can have detrimental effects on health and on the stability of the environment. There is a vast amount of literature on the use of GC for studying a wide variety of these problems and the reader is referred to the general review texts [83–85].

A variety of GC sampling techniques are used: for example, solvent vapour in the atmosphere may be analysed by adsorption on granular active charcoal followed by desorption with carbon disulphide and separation on a FFAP column. The sensitivity of the technique allows sub-TLV levels of a wide range of solvents to be monitored [83]. (TLV = Threshold Limit Value set by various Agencies. It is the maximum permitted in the environment, and is different for each compound.) Polycyclic aromatic hydrocarbons (PAH) in polluted waters have also received considerable attention due to the associated carcinogenic properties. PAH analysis is therefore important if water quality is to be assessed. Samples extracted with cyclohexane and concentrated, since their occurrence is in the ppb range, may be analysed by GC using an FID detector and OV1 or DEXIL columns [84]. Over 100 PAH compounds have been identified and their presence associated with combustion of wood and coal, biodegradation processes and crude oil.

Pesticides and related compounds also present a growing environmental problem. These include the polychlorinated biphenyls, chlorinated pesticides (DDT and BHC) and organophosphorus and sulphur compounds.

The Environmental Protection Agency (EPA) in the USA have produced a manual [85] of standard methods for analysis of pollutants in waters [85]. These include methods for multiclass analysis, for example, analysis of about 40 chlorinated, 40 organophosphorus and seven carbamate pollutant species. The method involves extraction into dichloromethane, concentration of the sample, separation into four fractions by column chromatography followed by GC of each fraction using OV210, OV17/OV210 columns at 180–200° C with an ECD detector for the chlorinated HC fraction and a flame photometric detector for the organophosphorus fraction. Carbamates are converted to their 2,4-diphenylether derivatives prior to GC.

GC is also valuable for fingerprinting oil spills or contamination of ground waters and for analysis of N-nitrosamines as their acetyl derivatives [86, 87]. Phenols, amines and organic acids form strong hydrogen bonds and therefore frequently produce broad or tailing peaks with long retention times. Various techniques have been reported to overcome these problems including derivatization [88].

Organometallic and inorganic pollutants are frequently encountered, some of which may be determined by GC, generally after extraction into $CHCl_3$, hexane or benzene. These include organotin biocides which are analysed as the methyl esters after extraction with $CHCl_3$ or as hydrides after treatment with $LiAlH_4$ using 3% OV17 or SE30 columns [88]. Tetraalkyl lead compounds have been analysed by extraction with hexane followed by GC using a 3% OV1 column and an atomic absorption spectrometric detector [89]. Organomercury compounds have been chromatographed on 5% PEGS after extraction and a sequence of pretreatment steps. Selenium in natural waters may be analysed as the 4,6-benzodiazo-dibromopiazselenol formed from Se(IV) and 1,2-diamino-3,5-dibromobenzene. Se(II) and Se(0) can be analysed similarly [90, 91]. Chromium and other heavy metals may be determined as their β-diketonates as described earlier.

5.8 GAS–SOLID CHROMATOGRAPHY

The apparatus and techniques for gas–solid elution chromatography are the same as those for gas–liquid chromatography. The only differences are the nature of the stationary phase – the column packing – and the length of column required: hence, this account will deal almost exclusively with the column packing. Before this, however, it will be useful to look at the advantages and disadvantages of gas–solid as compared with gas–liquid chromatography. Active solids which will be described will include: carbon, alumina, silica gel, molecular sieves and porous polymers.

Solids are usually more thermally stable than liquids and possess lower vapour pressures; hence columns packed with active solids are not subject to bleeding at high temperatures, which upsets the detection system, quite apart from producing variations in retention volumes. Prolonged high temperature treatment of some active solids may result in variations in their suface properties, perhaps by loss of chemisorbed species, or by sintering (the reduction of the surface area at temperatures below the melting point), but such changes are unusual at the temperatures used in chromatography, or may be prevented by appropriate pretreatment.

A column packed with an active solid may produce retention times greatly in excess of those obtained with a column of equal volume in gas–liquid chromatography, and hence more volatile substances can be separated conveniently. GSG is used mainly for separations of permanent gases and low boiling materials, up to about 150 molecular mass. The most obvious disadvantage of solid adsorbents is that they frequently give rise at low concentrations of adsorbate, to strongly curved isotherms, of the Langmuir type (see Curve IV, Fig. 5.27). The isotherms are formed by plotting the weight of vapour sorbed per gram of stationary phase–solid or liquid against the relative pressure. This is to enable comparisons to be made between solid and liquid stationary phases. Normally when discussing solutions of gases in liquids the Raoult Law plot of relative pressure (p/p') against mole fraction is employed.

Langmuir-type isotherms result from two properties of the adsorbent; microporosity and polarity. Polarity will give rise to such effects as hydrogen bonding in extreme cases, and under normal circumstances will enhance the normal van der Waal's attraction between the adsorbent and adsorbate, particularly if the latter is itself polar. Microporosity describes the presence of pores with diameters up to about 5 nm (50 Å).

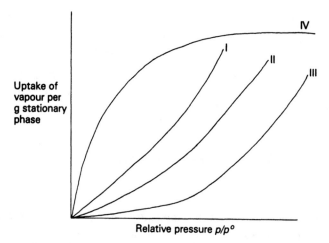

Fig. 5.27   Isotherms: I, II, III partition isotherms: IV adsorption isotherm.

Many active solids are also efficient catalysts and may result in the irreversible adsorption of a substance on the column, or complete or partial conversion of substances giving rise to artefacts which will show in the chromatogram.

5.8.1 Linear gas–solid chromatography

In order to use the elution technique successfully in gas–solid chromatography it is necessary to work with concentrations of adsorbates that correspond to the linear parts of their appropriate isotherms, or to straighten the isotherm. Complete linearity is unobtainable, but it is possible to get sufficiently close for symmetrical elution peaks to be obtained, which is the principal objective. It is also worth remembering that an anti-Langmuir isotherm is usually preferable to a Langmuir isotherm; surface treatment of an active solid (silanization, for example) will often change the isotherm for a particular adsorbate from Langmuir to anti-Langmuir.

There are three main methods for producing linearity in an isotherm, or for working on the most nearly linear portion of a curved isotherm:

1. separation is effected at temperatures which are high relative to the boiling point of the sample being separated. As already mentioned, many separations by gas–solid chromatography are carried out on low-boiling materials;
2. adsorbents with suitable surface characteristics are prepared. Examples are aluminas modified with inorganic salts; silicas modified by hydro-thermal treatment and silanization; graphitized carbon black; porous polymers;
3. the surface is pre-loaded with liquids to reduce surface inhomogeneity, for

example, squalane on carbon black. Alternatively a carrier gas which interacts with the surface is used, such as water vapour with alumina or silica columns. Supercritical fluids are also used.

Further examples of the application of these methods are given in the more detailed accounts of selected adsorbents which follow. A separate section (5.6.4) deals with the application of supercritical fluids.

5.8.2 Adsorbents for gas–solid chromatography

Alumina

Alumina has found quite wide application in gas–solid chromatography, although it does have some disadvantages. In the first place it is highly polar and therefore interacts strongly with polar molecules such as water. Secondly it possesses high catalytic activity and hence should be used with caution; for example, it may convert acetone to diacetone alcohol. Thirdly it is not readily prepared to yield a highly consistent product from the surface-chemical point of view. Much of the early work on alumina was carried out by Scott who concentrated on surface modified materials [92]. He first worked with water deactivated samples, and found that polarity was at a minimum with approximately a monolayer of adsorbed water. Mixtures of hydrocarbons up to C_5 could then be separated effectively at room temperature without significant tailing, but a disadvantage was the need to pre-saturate the carrier gas to prevent water being stripped from the column.

Scott measured polarity as a function of the retention of ethylene relative to non-polar ethane and propane. Activation by heating at temperatures up to $500°\,C$ increased the polarity, presumably by loss of water. Conversely, adsorption of water reduced the polarity until a minimum was reached when the amount of water required to fill a monolayer had been adsorbed. Further water continued to reduce the activity (presumably by reducing the surface area) but increased the polarity [94]. Scott later extended his work on alumina to substances modified with sodium hydroxide and obtained results similar to those given by the water-modified aluminas without, however, the need to pre-saturate the carrier gas. Static experiments showed that the isotherms for cyclohexane and benzene were substantially linear, but that for benzene was slightly Langmuir in type while that for cyclohexane was slightly anti-Langmuir. This also reflected the tendency to tailing and to fronting with these compounds. Aluminas were also modified with sodium chloride, bromide and iodide, and it was found that the retention of benzene relative to heptane increased markedly in the order.

$$OH^- > Cl^- > Br^- > I^-$$

Other interesting modifiers were CuCl, $AgNO_3$ and CdI. Aluminas and magnesium silicates modified with various salts, for example, alumina coated with 10% Na_2SO_4, Na_2MoO_4, NaCl, or $Al_2(SO_4)_3$, were found to be useful for the separation of *cis-trans*-isomers, chlorobenzene and the various dichlorobenzenes. For olefins the *cis*-isomer is retained more strongly than the *trans*- [93].

A recent advance in gas–solid chromatography is the application of capillary columns consisting of alumina/KCl porous layer open tubular (PLOT) columns. These are excellent for separating C_1–C_{10} hydrocarbons. Further details are given in the capillary GC section of this chapter (p. 186) [54a].

Silica gel

Silica gel is somewhat easier to prepare in a reproducible form than is alumina, and this may account for its more extensive use in gas–solid chromatography. Porasil (Pecheney–Saint–Gobain) is a porous spherical bead form of silica which can be supplied with pores that vary from 100 nm to about 150 nm in diameter. Because of the uniformity of the beads both from the point of view of the particle size and the porosity, they clearly offer advantages. Zipax (du Pont) is a related material in which the beads have impervious silica cores surrounded by a porous layer. As would be expected, silica gel resembles alumina in its surface properties, i.e. it is polar and catalytically active. Much work has been carried out to modify silica surfaces and render them suitable for gas–solid chromatography, not only by salts but also by chemical bonding of materials such as silanes and by hydrothermal treatment.

As with most active solids silica gel tends to contain micropores and it is these pores, along with the polar surface, that give rise to strongly curved Langmuir isotherms. In particular the micropores are solely responsible for this behaviour with non-polar, non-polarizable adsorbates. Geometrical modification simply means the removal of the micropores by hydrothermal treatment involving contact with steam at 850° C for about 24 h. The pore enlargement that results can be controlled by varying the time and temperature of treatment. Pores as large as 5000 nm can be generated. As expected, non-polar molecules, which give rise to symmetrical peaks, can be separated on such gels. Polar and polarizable molecules such as benzene, on the other hand, still give rise to tailing, mainly on account of surface hydroxyl groups. Tailing can be reduced by chemical modification.

Chemical modification means silanization of the surface hydroxyl groups with chlorotrimethyl- or dichlorodimethylsilane. Static measurements with benzene show a progressive change in the isotherm from Langmuir to anti-Langmuir as the degree of silanization is increased. It is probably wise to carry out silanization at an elevated temperature since there appears to be evidence that chlorosilanes will react with water at room temperature but not with surface hydroxyl groups until a temperature of about 200° C has been reached. Silanization renders the surface non-polar or non-specific. Substances such as ether and acetone which are normally very strongly adsorbed by silica gel are quickly eluted from a silanized column. An alternative surface treatment is esterification and both methanol and ethanol have been successfully bonded to the surface.

There have been two main approaches to the problem; first the formation of a chemically bonded stationary phase in proportions comparable with those in gas–liquid systems, and second, the formation of a monolayer of chemically bonded material as in silanization. For example, Porasil has also been modified by chemically bonding various materials to the surface, some of which are familiar as liquid stationary phases, such as Carbowax 400. Such modified beads go under the trade name *Durapak* stationary phases, the surface layer of modifier being limited to a monolayer. The polarity appears to increase with increasing chain length of Carbowax, for example, from Carbowax 200 to Carbowax 2000, whereas the reverse appears to happen when these materials are conventionally supported. Carbowax 400 bleeds at 40° C normally, but the Durapak material is stable up to 150° C [94].

XAD amberlite resins are agglomerated microspheres, beads of nearly continuous solid phase and pore phase, and hence a large surface area of adsorbent is exposed to the solute molecules. This highly macroreticular structure allows rapid diffusion of solvents and solutes through the resin. XAD resins are widely used for sampling and trapping organics. Typical applications include air and stack emission sampling, water analysis and clinical assays. The U.S. Environmental Protection Agency has published procedures for using these resins (EPA 600/7-78-201 October 1978), and (EPA 600/7-78-054 March 1978).

Advantages claimed for such modified materials, apart from the enhanced thermal stability for the liquid phase and the improved surface properties for the solid, are that the HETP is independent of the nature of the sample, the temperature of the analysis and the sample size, and that mass transfer problems are minimized.

Carbon

Active carbons are, perhaps, the most difficult solids to prepare in a reproducible form. They often have very high (nominal) surface areas and are usually microporous. One advantage they do possess, however, is that they are not very polar and often produce fronting peaks with water, indicative of an anti-Langmuir isotherm. The surface of normal active carbon black may sometimes by slightly polar owing to the presence of chemisorbed oxygen, sulphur or nitrogen. The largely non-polar nature of the carbon surface is useful, although the microporosity of active carbons can still lead to strongly curved isotherms and hence tailing. Graphitization overcomes both polarity and microporosity problems and gives carbon with a high homogeneity of surface.

The surface of the carbon can be modified with phthalocyanins to reduce the elution time, since the carbon atomic density is reduced compared with the graphite itself; hence as adsorption energies are smaller, compounds can be eluted at temperatures up to 100° C lower, although the temperature limit of such a column is about 350° C [95]. The inner walls of capillaries have been coated with graphite by a technique similar to that used for gas–liquid capillary columns, that is, by evaporation of the solvent from a graphite suspension [95].

Graphitized carbon blacks have been used in packed capillaries. The thickness of the carbon layer varies between 0.0045 and 0.0100 mm [96]. It is claimed that such columns are non-specific, have high permeability, small pressure drop across them and high selectivity for certain systems e.g. geometrical and structural isomers such as *ortho-*, *meta-*, and *para-*cresols and xylenes and polar compounds such as alcohols and isotopic systems e.g. deuteroacetone and acetone.

Molecular sieves

Most molecular sieves are of the zeolite type and consist of an aluminosilicate skeleton with pores of regular size and shape formed by the stacking of polyhedra made up from SiO_4 and AlO_4 tetrahedra. Since the large internal surfaces of these solids derive from the nature of the crystal lattice rather than from random cracks and holes as in other active solids, their behaviour is much more predictable and consistent. The effective pore diameter may be varied by ion exchange. They have a very high affinity for water, and in fact, water will be adsorbed in preference to practically any other molecule, which is why molecular sieves are used for drying carrier gases. For gas–solid chromatography pelletized material of, for example, 60–80 mesh is used.

Molecular sieves are probably the most popular stationary phases for the separation of permanent gases, although, like water, carbon dioxide is irreversibly adsorbed at room temperature. Hydrogen, nitrogen and oxygen are easily separated on 5 Å sieve at temperatures up to 100° C. Argon may be separated from oxygen at − 78° C, or at room temperature if the column is long enough. *Ortho-* and *para-*hydrogen can be separated on 13 X at − 195° C but there is partial conversion of *ortho-* to *para-*. In spite of the considerable microporosity of these solids, even at the lowest temperatures just mentioned, separations are still being carried out at relatively high temperatures compared with the boiling points of the gases, and hence the isotherms are still effectively linear.

Other separations depend on the complete or nearly complete exclusion of some molecules but not others; for example, ethane (0.4 nm. diameter) is adsorbed by 4 Å sieve but butane (0.5 nm) is not. Type 5 Å sieve will take up butane and unbranched alkanes but not branched chain compounds or cyclic compounds such as benzene (0.63 nm diameter). On the other hand, on 10 X and 13 X, benzene is adsorbed in preference to unbranched alkanes because of π-electron interaction. Analyses are therefore possible in which a small molecule such as methane may be extracted from a mixture in a small pre-column of sieve before passing the rest of the mixture on to another column. The amount of material extracted may

Table 5.6   Porapak/relative retentions to hexane. (Reproduced by permission of Phase Separations Ltd.).

Sample	P-S	P	Q	Q-S	R	S	N	T
Water	0.408	0.467	0.056	0.082	0.131	0.109	0.135	0.188
Methanol	0.475	0.542	0.127	0.134	0.180	0.168	0.193	0.244
Formaldehyde	0.475	0.517	0.134	0.127	0.190	0.172	0.195	0.172
Acetaldehyde	0.475	0.542	0.169	0.170	0.190	0.187	0.222	0.259
Ethanol	0.592	0.666	0.218	0.230	0.307	0.291	0.367	0.462
Formic acid	0.717	0.717	0.225	0.189	0.368	0.386	0.819	0.187
Acetonitrile	0.792	0.934	0.287	0.286	0.358	0.348	0.497	0.670
Propylene oxide	0.666	0.784	0.314	0.327	0.336	0.329	0.406	0.444
Propionaldehyde	0.750	0.808	0.338	0.343	0.376	0.383	0.476	0.543
Acetone	0.758	0.850	0.343	0.349	0.390	0.391	0.544	0.666
Isopropanol			0.351					
Methylene chloride	0.960	0.950	0.373	0.403	0.407	0.438	0.510	0.545
Acrylonitrile	0.892	1.00	0.388	0.404	0.474	0.475	0.660	0.853
Acetic acid	0.926	1.03	0.419	0.379	1.31	1.91	1.34	1.90
Methyl acetate	0.800	0.883	0.419	0.434	0.445	0.438	0.598	0.735
Propanol	0.883	0.984	0.479	0.478	0.660	0.641	0.862	1.06
Pentane	0.666	0.684	0.501	0.536	0.481	0.469	0.490	0.467
Isobutyraldehyde	0.934	1.05	0.598	0.623	0.670	0.676	0.905	1.04
Butyraldehyde	1.10	1.22	0.711	0.710	0.776	0.802	1.09	1.28
2-Butanone	1.18	1.26	0.734	0.730	0.820	0.846	1.20	1.41
Chloroform	1.28	1.35	0.753	0.718	0.854	0.791	0.966	1.24
Ethyl acetate	1.13	1.22	0.812	0.852	0.864	0.862	1.20	1.44
Isobutanol	1.26	1.36	0.902	0.900	1.24	1.21	1.76	2.07
Propionic acid	1.53	1.67	0.909	0.843				4.27

Hexane	1.00 (0.944 min)	1.00 (0.945 min)	1.00 (4.93 min)	1.00 (5.50 min)	1.00 (4.67 min)	1.00 (4.97 min)	1.00 (6.94 min)	1.00 (4.84 min)
Butanol	1.48	1.58	1.07	1.07	1.47	1.46	2.08	2.50
Benzene	1.69	1.86	1.16	1.16	1.24	1.25	1.42	1.67
Carbon tetrachloride	1.53	1.53	1.16	1.14	1.07	1.07	1.17	1.34
Isopropyl acetate	1.47	1.46	1.33	1.43	3.48	1.44	2.04	2.38
Propyl acetate	1.85	1.83	1.72	1.83	4.20	1.83	2.64	3.19
Isopentanol	2.29	2.27	2.10	2.09	2.91	2.85	4.25	5.10
Heptane	1.64	1.58	2.28	2.28	2.18	2.05	2.18	2.20
Pentanol	2.61	2.63	2.46	2.46	3.38	3.35	4.93	5.86
Toluene	2.92	3.18	2.71	2.69	2.43	2.85	3.24	3.65

There are eight types of Porapak, basically porous polymer beads, modified to give varying retention characteristics.
1 metre × 2.3 mm ID column
Temperature: 175° C
Flow Rate: 25 ml min^{-1}
Detector: FID (except TC for water)

be estimated from the areas of the chromatograms obtained before and after using the pre-column.

Like other adsorbents, molecular sieves require higher temperatures than does gas–liquid chromatography for a given separation, and this is frequently a disadvantage particularly with high boiling materials because the decomposition temperature may be approached.

Microporous polymers

Copolymerization of styrene with divinylbenzene yields a porous polymer, the pore size depending, in part at least, on the proportion of divinylbenzene which also produces the cross-linking. Such a system is, in fact, the basic polymer of many ion-exchange resins, which have ionizable or polar groups grafted on to the aromatic nuclei. Ion-exchangers are about 10% cross-linked, and microporous polymers about 30–40%. Surface areas of these materials are about $50 \, m^2 \, g^{-1}$, and average pore diameter 7.5 nm. Chromosorb 102, a styrene-divinylbenzene copolymer has a nominal area of $300–400 \, m^2 \, g^{-1}$ and pores 8.5–9.5 nm. It is claimed for these beads that partitioning occurs with the polymer itself, that is, they behave like 'solid' liquid stationary phases, but they can be modified with genuine liquid stationary phases in the same way as any other solid support. Various workers recommend conditioning of porous polymers before use, for example, at 200° C 12 h for normal use and 10 days for trace analysis. Rapid oxidation occurs in air at 200° C. As with most adsorbents for gas–solid chromatography, porous polymers can only be used in the analysis of substances of relatively low molecular mass. Heavier substances produce long retention times and tailing.

Microporous polymers are produced by the copolymerization of, for example, styrene-divinylbenzene mixtures or ethyldivinylbenzene and divinylbenzene [97]. The divinylbenzene content is used to control pore size and also the cross-linking. Although the surface areas of these materials is about $50 \, m^2 \, g^{-1}$, little adsorption of polar compounds occurs. Water, amines and glycols are rapidly eluted with symmetrical peaks. Maximum temperatures are around 250° C and no column bleed occurs thus giving good baseline stability. One readily available GSC column packing material is Porapak, and a second range of materials is the Chromosorb Century Series of rigid copolymer beads. A wider range of polymers are used to prepare the copolymers resulting in materials with varying polar characteristics, pore size and hence general areas of application as shown in Tables 5.6 and 5.7.

Tenax–GC is a new porous polymer packing material based on 2,6-diphenyl-p-phenylene oxide and is suitable for the separation of high boiling polar compounds such as alcohols, polyethylene glycols, diols, phenols, mono- and di-amines, ethanolamines, amides, aldehydes and ketones [98]. A rather unusual application of Tenax–GC was experimental molecular analysis of the Martian Soil by the Viking Mars Lander to detect the presence of organic compounds and

Table 5.7 Typical physical properties of the various chromosorb polymers. (Reproduced by permission of Phase Separations Ltd.)

Physical properties	101	102	103	104	105	106	107	108	T
Type	STY-DVB	STY-DVB	Cross-Linked Polystyrene	ACN-DVB	Poly-aromatic	Cross-Linked Polystyrene	Cross-Linked Acrylic Ester	Cross-Linked Acrylic	Tetrafluor-ethylene TFE Fluoro-carbon
Polarity	Non-Polar	Slightly Polar	Non-Polar**	Very Polar	Moderately Polar	Non-Polar	Polar	Polar	Non-Polar
Free fall density (g/cc)	0.30	0.29	0.32	0.32	0.34	0.28	0.30	0.30	0.42
Surface area (m²/g)	Less than 50	300–400	15–25	100–200	600–700	700–800	400–500	100–200	7–8
Average pore diameter (μ)	0.3–0.4	0.0085	0.3–0.4	0.06–0.08	0.04–0.06	0.0050	0.0080	0.0250	0.5
Water affinity	Hydro-phobic	Hydro-phobic	Hydro-phobic	Hydro-phobic	Hydro-phobic	Hydro-phobic	Hydro-philic	Hydro-phobic	Hydro-phobic
Colour	White	White	White	White*	White	White	White	White	White
Temperature limit (Isothermal) °C	275	250	275	250	250	225	225	225	250
Temperature limit (Programmed) °C	325	300	300	275	275	250	250	250	250

*Turns yellow after column conditioning and brown after extended use. This in no way affects column performance. **The surface is Basic.

thus provide evidence for the existence of life forms [99]. The column consisted of 60–80 mesh Tenax–GC coated with poly-MPE (methyl phenyl ether) and was selected for effective separation of water and carbon dioxide and elution of most compound classes at ng levels.

REFERENCES

1. Bourke, P. L. J., Dawson, R. W. and Denton, W. H. (1965) *J. Chromatogr.*, **19**, 425.
2. Knox, J. H. (1959) *Chem. Ind.*, 1085.
3. Schomberg, G. *et al.* (1976) *J. Chromatogr.*, **122**, 55; Muller, F. and Oreans, M. (1977) *Chromatographia*, **10**, 473.
4. Muller, F. (1983) *International Laboratory*, **July**, p. 56.
5. Knopp, D. R. (1979) *Handbook of Analytical Derivatisation Reactions*, Wiley, New York; Blau, K. and King, G. (1977) *Handbook of Derivatives for Chromatography*, Heyden, London; Pierce, A. E. (1968) *Silylation of Organic Compounds*, Pierce Chemical Company, Rockford Illinois.
6. Kanahara, F. K. (1971) *Environ. Sci. and Tech.*, **5**, 235; (1976) **10**, 761.
7. Phase Separations Ltd., Queensferry, Clwyd CH5 2LR, UK, and River Street Norwalk Connecticut 06850, USA; Chrompack Ltd., Shrubbery Road, London SW16, Middleburg, Netherlands and Bridgewater, New Jersey USA; Fierce Chemicals, Chester CH14 4EF, UK and Rockford Illinois, USA.
8. Taylor, D. G. and White, L. D. (1970) *Amer. Ind. Hyg. Assn.*, **31**, 225.
9. Joint Committee Report on Adsorbants, (1971) *Amer. Ind. Hyg. Assn.*, **32**, 404.
10. Zlatkis, A., Lichtenstein, H. A. and Tishbee, A. (1973) *Chromatographia*, **6**, 67.
11. Novotny, M., Lee, M. L. and Bartle, K. D. (1974) *Chromatographia*, **7**, 333.
12. Bellar, T. A. and Lichenberg, J. J. (1974) *Amer. Water Works Assn.*, **66**, 739.
13. US Environmental Protection Agency (EPA) (1978) 600/7-78-054 and 201.
14. Ottenstein, D. M. (1973) *J. Chromatogr. Sci.*, **11**, 136.
15. Supina, W. R. (1974) *The Packed Column in Gas Chromatography*, Supelco Ltd., Bellefonte, Pa.
16. Rohrschneider, L. (1966) *J. Chromatogr.*, **22**, 6.
17. McReynolds, W. (1970) *J. Chromatogr. Sci.*, **8**. 685.
18. Bradford, B. W. and Harvey, D. (1955) *J. Inst. Petrol*, **41**, 80.
19. Scott, R. P. W. (ed) (1960) *Gas Chromatography* 1960, Butterworth, London, p. 284.
20. Zlatkis, A., Chang, R. C. and Schurig, V. (1973) *Chromatographia* **6**, 223.
21. Bevan, S. C. and Thorburn, S. (1965) *J. Chromatogr.*, **11**, 301.
22. Janak, J. (1953) *Chem. Listy*, **47**, 464.
23. David, D. J. (1974) *Gas Chromatographic Detectors*, Wiley, New York.
24. Deans, D. R. (1968) *Chromatographia*, **1**, 187.
25. Bocek, P. and Janak, J. (1971) *Chromatogr. Revs.*, **15**, 111.
26. Brody, S. S. and Chaney, J. E. (1966) *J. Gas Chromatogr.*, **4**, 42.
27. Krost, K. J., Hodgeson, J. A. and Stevens, R. K. (1973) *Anal. Chem.*, **45**, 1800.
28. Adlard, E. R. (1975) *CRC Critical Reviews in Anal. Chem.*, **5**, 1, 13; Patterson, P. L., Howe, R. L. and Abu-Shumeys, A. (1978) *Anal. Chem.*, **59**, 339.
29. Lovelock, J. E. (1958) *J. Chromatogr.* **1**, 35; (1963) *ibid.* **35**, 474; Deveaux, P. and Guichon, G. (1970) *J. Chromatogr. Sci.*, **8**, 502.
30. Littlewood, A. B. (1970) *Gas Chromatography*, Academic Press, London, p. 315.
31. Deveaux, P. and Guichon, G. (1967) *J. Gas Chromatogr.*, **5**, 314.
32. Littlewood, A. B. (1970) *Gas Chromatography*, 2nd edn, Academic Press, London, Chapter 10, p. 339.
33. Rosie, D. M. and Barry, E. F. (1973) *J. Chromatogr. Sci.*, **11**, 237.

34. Jentzsch, D. and Otte, E. (1970) *Detectors in Gas Chromatography*, Akademische Verlag, Frankfurt. (German); Jameson, G. R. (1960) *J. Chromatogr.*, **3**, 464, 494; (1963) **8**, 544; (1964) **15**, 260.

35. Craven, J. S. and Clauser, D. E. (1979) *Paper 408, Pittsburgh Conference on Analytical Chemistry and Applied Spectroscopy*, Cleveland.

36. Martin, A. J. P. and James, A. T. (1956) *Biochem. J.*, **63**, 138.

37. Kiran, E. and Gillham, J. K. (1975) *Anal. Chem.*, **47**, 983; Phillips, C. S. G. and Timms, P. L. (1961) *J. Chromatogr.*, **5**, 131.

38. Coulson, D. M. (1965) *J. Gas Chromatogr.*, **3**, 134.

39. Lovelock, J. E. (1958) *J. Chromatogr.*, **1**, 35.

40. Frith, J. G., Jones, A. and Jones, T. A. (1975) *Ann. Occup. Hyg.*, **18**, 63; Eur. Pat. 0 030 112 A1 (1981).

41. Braithwaite, A. and Gibson, S. (1984) Trent Polytechnic, unpublished results and National Coal Board internal report.

42. Jones, T. A. (1984) *Technical Information Leaflet No. 8, Organic Semiconductor Gas Sensors*, Health and Safety Labs, Sheffield S3 7HQ, UK; Van Ewyck, R. L., Chadwick, A. V. and Wright, J. D. (1980) *J. Chem. Soc. Faraday 1*, **76**, 2194.

43. Angell, J. B., Terry, S. C. and Barth, P. W. (1983) *Scientific American*, **June**, 36–47.

44. Golay, M. J. E. (1958) *Gas Chromatography 1958* (ed. R. P. W. Scott) Butterworths, London, p. 36.

45. Ettre, L. S. (1965) *Open Tubular Columns in Gas Chromatography*, Plenum Press, New York.

46. Jennings, W. (1980) *Gas Chromatography with Glass Capillary Columns*, Academic Press, London.

47. Horvath, C., Ettre, L. S. and Purcell, J. E. (1974) *American Lab.*, **6**(8), 75–86.

48. Ettre, L. S., McClure, G. L. and Walters, J. D. (1983) *Chromatographia*, **17**, 560–69; Ettre, L. S. and DiCesare, J. L. (1984) *Int. Laboratory*, **June**, 44–49.

49. Grob, K. J. R., Grob, G. and Grob, K. (1978) *J. Chromatogr.*, **156**, 1.

50. de Nijs, R. C. M., Franken, J. J., Dooper, R. P. M. and Rijks, J. A. (1978) *J. Chromatogr.*, **167**, 231.

51. Jennings, W. G. (1981) *Comparisons of Fused Silica and Other Glass Columns in Gas Chromatography*, Huthig, Heidelburg.

52. Jennings, W. G. (1977) *J. Food Chem.*, **2**, 185.

53. Rawdon, M. G. and Norris, T. A. (1984) *International Laboratory*, **June**, 12–23.

54(a) de Nijs, R. C. M. (1984) *Chrompack News*, **11**(3E), 6. Published by Chrompack, Middleburg, Netherlands.

54(b) Sie, S. T. and Bleumer, J. P. A. (1969) *Gas Chromatography 1968* (ed. C. L. A. Harbourn), Institute of Petroleum, London, p. 235; Novotny, M. *et al.* (1981) *Anal. Chem.*, **53**, 407A.

55. Peaden, D. A. and Lea, M. L. (1982) *J. Liquid Chromatogr.*, **5** 119–221.

56. Josephson, J. (1982) *Environ. Sci. Technology*, **16**, 548A–551A.

57. Borman, S. A. (1983) *Anal. Chem.*, **55**, 22–35; (1983) *Chem. Eng. News.*, **Jan. 10**, 22–35.

58. Chromatography Journals; *Chromatography Newsletter; Chromatographia; Journal of Chromatography; Journal of Chromatographic Science; Analytical Chemistry; Chromatography Discussion Group*, Secretariat, Department of Physical Sciences, Trent Polytechnic Nottingham NG11 8NS, UK.

59. Drozd, J. and Novak, J. (1971) *J. Chromatogr.*, **165**, 141.

60. Kolb, B. (ed) (1980) *Applied Headspace Analysis*, Heyden and Son, London; Hachenberg, H. and Schmidt, A. P. (1977) *Gas Chromatography Headspace Analysis*, Heyden and Son, London.

61. Mandl, B. *et al.* (1969) *Brauwissenschaft*, **22**, 477; (1974) **27**, 57.

62. Jansen, V. J. and Horn, G. B. (1965) *Am. Soc. Brew. Chem.*, 194; Rumani, R. J. and Ku, L. (1966) *J. Food Sci.*, **31**, 558.

63. Basselle, R., Ozeris, S. and Whitney, C. H. (1962) *J. Food Sci.*, **28**, 84; Hurst, R. E. (1975) *Anal. Chem.*, **47**, 1221.
64. Jennings, W. and Shibamoto, T. (1980) *Qualitative Analysis of Flavours and Fragrances by Glass Capillary GC*, Academic Press, London; Klimes, I. and Lamparsky, D. (1978) *Analysis of Foods and Beverages by Head Space Techniques*, Academic Press, London, p. 95.
65. Jeffs, A. R. (1980) *Applied Headspace Analysis* (ed B. Kolb), Heyden and Son, London, Chapter 12.
66. Hachenberg, H. (1973) *Industrial GC Trace Analysis*, Heyden and Son, London; Rohrschneider, L. (1971) *Z. Anal. Chem.*, **255**, 345; Crompton, T. R. and Myers, L. (1968) *Plastics and Polymers*, 205.
67. Taylor, A. J. (1978) *J. Med. Microbiol.*, **11**, 9; Larson, L., Mardh, P. A. and Odham, G. (1978) *J. Clin. Microbiol.*, **7**, 23.
68. Baltes, W. (ed) (1982) *Recent Developments in Food Analysis*, Verlag Chemie Basel, pp. 120–189; Rothbart, H. L. (1977) *Modern Practice of Gas Chromatography*, Wiley Interscience, London, Chapter 9, pp. 449–493.
69. Fernandez, E. *et al.* (1970) *J. Ass. Off. Anal. Chem.*, **53**, 17; Pierce, A. R. *et al.* (1969) *Anal. Chem.*, **41**, 298.
70. Reineccius, G. A. *et al.* (1970) *J. Dairy Sci.*, **53**, 1018.
71. Withington, D. F. (1967) *Analyst*, **92**, 705; Langer, J. E., Libby, L. M. and Day, E. (1967) *J. Agric. Food Chem.*, **15**, 386.
72. Kugler, E. and Langlais, R. (1975) *Chromatographics*, **8**, 468; Jennings, W. G. and Filsoof, M. (1977) *J. Agrifood Chem.*, **25**, 440; Jennings, W. G. (1977) *J. Food Chem.*, **2**, 185.
73. Berman, E. (1977) *Analysis of Drugs of Abuse*, Heyden, London, Chapter 6, p. 34; Gudzinowicz, B. J. (1968) *Gas Chromatographic Analysis of Drugs and Pesticides*, Vol. 2, *Chromatographic Science Series*, Dekker, New York; McGonigle, E. J. (1977) *Modern Practice of Gas Chromatography*, Wiley Interscience, New York, Chapter 12, p. 591.
74. Kazyak, L. and Knoblock, E. (1963) *Anal. Chem.*, **35**, 1448; Finkle, B. Cherry, E. and Taylor, D. (1971) *J. Chromatogr. Sci.*, **9**, 393.
75. Moffat, A. (1975) *J. Chromatogr.*, **113**, 69.
76. Kern, H. *et al.* (1978) *Pharmaceuticals and Drugs*, Monograph on GC applications by Varian Aerograph, UK.
77. Berezkin, V. G. *et al.* (1977) *Gas Chromatography of Polymers*, J. of Chromatogr. Library, Elsevier, Amsterdam, Vol. 10; May, R. W., Pearson, E. F. and Scothern, D. (1977) *Pyrolysis–Gas Chromatography*, Analytical Sciences Monograph 3, Royal Society of Chemistry, London; Irwin, W. J. (ed) (1981) *Analytical Pyrolysis*, Vol. 22, Chromatographic Science Series, Dekker, New York; Coupe, N. B., Jones, C. E. and Perry, S. (1970) *J. Chromatogr.*, **47**, 291; Jones, C. E. (1973) *Chromatographia*, **6**, 483.
78. Raaschoo Nelsen, H. K. (1984) *J. Coatings Tech.*, **56**, 21; Noble, W. and Wheals, B. B. (1974) *J. Forensic Science Society*, **14**, 23.
79. Moshier, R. W and Sievers, R. E. (1965) *Gas Chromatography of Metal Chelates*, Pergamon Press, London; Guichon, G. and Pommier, C. (1973) *Gas Chromatography in Inorganics and Organometallics*, Ann Arbor Science, Ann Arbor, Michigan.
80. Baker, J. K. (1977) *Anal. Chem.*, **49**, 906; Meola, J. M. (1977) *Chromatogr. Newsletter*, **5**, 1; Menyharth, P., Levy, A. L. and Lehane, D. P. (1976) *Chromatogr. Newsletter*, **4**, 15.
81. Colenutt, B. A. and Thorburn, S. (1980) *Int. J. Env. Studies*, **15**, 25.
82. Grob, R. L. (1977) *Modern Practice of Gas Chromatography*, Wiley Interscience, New York, p. 347.
83. White, L. D. *et al.* (1970) *Am. Ind. Hyg. Assoc. J.*, **31**, 225.

84. Caddy, D. E. and Meek, D. M. (1976) *Water Research Centre (UK) Technical Report*, TR36; Grob, R. L. and Kaiser, M. A. (1982) *Environmental Problem Solving Using Gas and Liquid Chromatography*, Elsevier, Amsterdam; Grob, R. L. (ed) (1983) *Chromatographic Analysis of the Environment*, Marcel Dekker, New York; Albaiges, J. (ed) (1980) *Analytical Techniques in Environmental Chemistry*, Pergamon Press, London; Harrison, R. M. (ed) (1983) *Pollution, Causes, Effects and Control*, Royal Society of Chemistry, London.

85. Franson, M. A. *et al.* (1975) *Standard Methods for the Examination of Water and Waste Water*, American Public Health Association, Washington.

86. Frame, G. M., Flanigan, G. A. and Carmody, D. C. (1979) *J. Chromatogr.*, **168**, 365; Thompson, J. F. (1980) *Analysis of Pesticide Residues in Human and Environmental Samples*, US Environmental Protection Agency, Washington DC.

87. Oshima, H., Matsui, M. and Kawabata, T. (1979) *J. Chromatogr.*, **169**, 279; Kuwata, K., Yamazaki, Y. and Uebori, M. (1980) *Anal. Chem.*, **52**, 1980; Matsumoto, G, *et al* (1977) *Water Research*, **11**, 693.

88. Meinema, H. A. *et al* (1978) *Environ. Science Technology*, **12**, 288; Soderquist, C. J. and Drosby, D. G. (1978) *Anal. Chem.*, **50**, 1435.

89. Radzuik, B., Thomassen, Y., Butler, L. R. P. *et al* (1979) *Anal. Chem. Acta*, **108**, 31; Chau, Y. A. *et al.* (1979) *Anal. Chem.*, **51**, 186 and (1976) *Anal. Chem. Acta*, **85**, 421.

90. Nishi, S., Horimoto, Y. *et al.* (1970) *Bonseki Kagaku*, **19**, 1646 and (1971) **20**, 16.

91. Shimoishi, U. and Toei, K. (1978) *Anal. Chem. Acta*, **100**, 65; Uchida, U. and Shimoishi, Y. (1980) *Environ. Science Technology*, **14**, 541.

92. Scott, C. G. (1959) *J. Inst. Petrol*, **45**, 118; Scott, R. P. W. (ed) (1960) *Gas Chromatography 1960*, Butterworth, London, p. 137.

93. McCreery, R. L. and Sawyer, D. T. (1970) *J. Chromatogr. Science*, **8**, 122 and (1968) *Anal. Chem.*, **40**, 106.

94. Little, J. N. (1970) *J. Chromatogr. Sci.*, **8**, 647.

95. Vidal-Madjar, C., Ganansia, J. and Guichon, G. (1970) *Gas Chromatography 1970* (ed R. Stock) Institute of Petroleum, London, p. 20.

96. Goretti, G., Liberti, A. and Nota, G. (1969) *Gas Chromatography 1968* (ed C. L. A. Harbourn), Institute of Petroleum, London, p. 22.

97. Dave, S. (1969) *J. Chromatogr. Sci.*, **7**, 389.

98. Russel, L. W. (1981) *J. Forensic Science Society*, **21**, 317.

99. Novotny, M. and Hayes, J. M. (1975) *Science*, **189**, 215 and (1976) *Science*, **194**, 72.

6 HIGH PERFORMANCE LIQUID CHROMATOGRAPHY (HPLC)

Liquid chromatography (LC) is the generic name used to describe any chromatographic procedure in which the mobile phase is a liquid. Techniques already discussed which belong to this general classification are paper chromatography, thin-layer chromatography (TLC) and variants of traditional column chromatography.

In the last, solvent is gravity fed on to a column of large (~ 150–$250\,\mu$m) particles, and the components of the mixture are then carried through the packed column with the passage of the eluant; separation being achieved by differential distribution of the sample components between the stationary and mobile phases. However, classical liquid chromatography suffers from a number of disadvantages:

(i) the column packing procedures are tedious and the column is usually only used once, which makes the technique expensive;

(ii) the efficiency achieved by these large particle columns is relatively low and the analysis time lengthy, even for fairly simple mixtures; the practice of the technique is operator sensitive, e.g. sample application;

(iii) detection of the solute in the eluant is achieved by the manual analysis of the individual fractions, which in itself is labour intensive and time consuming.

Thin-layer chromatography offered an improvement in some of the above aspects, though it suffers from several limitations, especially in the areas of automation, reproducibility, quantitation and preparative studies.

The pioneering work of Martin and Synge [1] led to the development of gas–liquid chromatography, an elegant chromatographic method, which overcame many of the problems associated with classical LC and TLC; column efficiencies achieved were high and the technique could be used with equal facility for both analytical and preparative studies. The essential prerequisite for the analysis of a mixture by GC is that each of the sample components has an appreciable vapour pressure at the operating temperature of the column. The limitations imposed by volatility can in many cases be overcome by the conversion of the less tractable compounds to suitable volatile derivatives. Nevertheless, there still remains a large number of compounds, such as pharmaceuticals, polymers, proteins and dyestuffs, which cannot be volatilized, or even heated, without decomposition, and which therefore cannot be analysed by GC. Thus the established techniques of TLC and LC, despite the limitations mentioned above, provided a valued means for the analysis of mixtures of such compound classes.

The principal factor limiting column performance in classical open-bed liquid chromatography was the decreased rate of diffusion of solute molecules between the phases due to the use of a liquid eluant. The key to achieving improved column efficiencies in LC lay in increasing the rate of mass transfer and equilibration of solute molecules between the mobile and stationary phases. The classic theoretical treatise of van Deemter [2] and Giddings [3] acknowledged the need for improved inter-particle diffusion rates and suggested that the above objectives could be attained by using packing with a small particle size. Concomitant with the use of small particle size were large pressure drops across the columns, and consequently equipment for HPLC, such as pumps, columns and fittings, had to be capable of delivering and withstanding the required high inlet pressures. A further consequence of the reduction in column and particle size was that the volume of the detector cell had to be modified accordingly as the peak volumes expected would be much smaller.

Though the theoretical principles of modern liquid chromatography were firmly established by Martin and Synge in the same paper as they laid the foundation for GLC, it is unclear why the development and evolution of LC was so protracted. It may be that, as the establishment of modern LC depended upon advances and innovations in several areas such as the preparation of packing material and the design of pumps and detectors, available resources were preferentially expended on the development of gas chromatography.

Whatever the reason, it was not until the late '60s, when active and intensive research and development culminated in the availability of commercial apparatus for modern LC, that the potential of the technique was realised. Horvath et al. [4] constructed one of the first practical HPLC systems for use in their work on nucleotides. About the same time successful procedures for packing microparticulate materials were being developed [5]. Modern high resolution liquid chromatography, variously known as high pressure, high performance and high speed liquid chromatography, and universally referred to as HPLC, has become firmly established at the fore of chromatographic techniques in the past decade. For instance HPLC has found substantial application and in many instances offered significant advantages in the analysis of pharmaceutical formulations, biological fluids, synthetic polymers, environmental residues and trace-element contaminants.

The developing stature and importance of HPLC is evidenced by the vast growth in published scientific papers which cite the technique as the chosen method of analysis. In comparison with GC, HPLC is not limited in applicability by component volatility or thermal stability, which makes it the method of choice for polymers, polar, ionic and thermally unstable materials. Furthermore, comparable, if not greater, separation and column efficiency can be achieved due to the greater control and choice of both stationary and mobile phases. An added advantage is that many detectors used in HPLC are non-destructive, thus facilitating sample recovery and providing the opportunity for subsequent spectroanalytical studies.

To summarize, modern liquid chromatography has the advantages that the columns are reusable, that sample introduction can be automated and detection and quantitation can be achieved by the use of continuous flow detectors; these features lead to improved accuracy and precision of analysis. Thus it would seem that the stature of the technique is assured and it may be that it will supplant gas chromatography as the most useful and expedient of chromatographic methods in the coming decade.

6.1 MODES OF CHROMATOGRAPHY

HPLC can be carried out in any of the classical modes, of which the most important are:

1. liquid–solid adsorption;
2. partition: (liquid–liquid and organo-bonded)
3. ion-exchange;
4. ion-pair;
5. size-exclusion;
6. affinity.

The exact mode of chromatography operating in a given application is determined principally by the nature of the packing, though it must be appreciated that, while there may be one dominant mechanism, the modes are not mutually exclusive. For completeness at this stage brief synopses of the above techniques are included.

6.1.1 Adsorption

The lattice of the common porous adsorbents, e.g. alumina and silica, is terminated at the surface with polar hydroxyl groups, and it is these groups which provide the means for the surface interactions with solute molecules.

The eluant systems used in adsorption chromatography are based on non-polar solvents, commonly hexane, containing a small amount of a polar additive, such as 2-propanol. When the sample is applied to the column, sample molecules with polar functional groups will be attracted to the active sites on the column packing; they will subsequently be displaced by the polar modifier molecules of the eluant, as the chromatogram is developed, and will pass down the column to be re-adsorbed on fresh sites. The ease of displacement of solute molecules will depend on their relative polarities: more polar molecules will be adsorbed more strongly and hence will elute more slowly from the column.

6.1.2 Partition

In both the following modes of partition chromatography, separation is achieved by differences in the distribution coefficients of the sample components between the mobile and stationary phases. The techniques differ, however, in the manner by which the stationary phase is bonded to the support.

Liquid–liquid partition

In liquid–liquid partition chromatography, the column packing material can be prepared in an analogous manner to gas chromatography, i.e. by adding a solution of the stationary phase to the support and then slowly removing the solvent, thus leaving an even loading of the stationary phase distributed over the support material. However, due to the problems of solvent stripping and limited hydrolytic stability, these classical partition systems, though developed for a few specialized applications, have been displaced largely by organo-bonded station-ary phase packings.

Organo-bonded partition

The limitations of classical liquid–liquid partition chromatography systems led to the development of packing material where the stationary phase is chemically bonded or organo-bonded to an insoluble matrix. The most common stationary phase is octadecylsilane (ODS), which is bonded to a silica support via a silyl ether (siloxane) linkage (Fig. 6.1). Such a packing material is used with a polar eluant, e.g. methanol or methanol–water, an elution technique commonly referred to as reverse-phase chromatography. Other reverse-phase packings in common use have bonded to the support one of the following: C_8 hydrocarbon chains, C_8 groupings containing aromatic moieties, phenyl groups and polar materials such as cyanopropyl and nitropropyl. The range of stationary phases, though extremely varied in character, is small in number due to the extensive

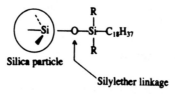

Fig. 6.1   Octadecylsilane (ODS) chemically-bonded stationary phase.

control that can be exerted over selectivity by variation in the eluant composition, a feature in marked contrast to GC. These packing materials, with some restrictions on the pH of the eluant used, provide for good hydrolytic stability and are resistant to solvent stripping within normal column operating pressures.

6.1.3 Ion-exchange

Ion-exchange chromatographic techniques utilize the differing affinities of ions in solution for oppositely charged ionic groupings located on the packing. While the nature of the functional groups providing the sites for exchange, quaternary ammonium ($-NR_3$) for anions, and sulphonic acid ($-SO_3H$) for cations, are the same in HPLC as in classical ion-exchange chromatography, a variety of substrates ranging from cross-linked polystyrene, cross-linked polydextrans, cellulose and silica have been utilized. However, due to the problems of swelling, compressibility and mass transfer encountered with polymeric supports and the limited pH stability of silica-based packings, the efficiencies achieved in IE-HPLC applications have been moderate.

6.1.4 Ion-pair partition

Due to the limitations and problems encountered with conventional ion-exchange chromatography (see above) the analysis of ionic materials is being increasingly tackled using a technique known as ion-pair partition. This mode utilizes an eluant system which contains a counter-ion with the opposite charge to that of the ion(s) to be analysed, and which will form an ion-pair with the ionic sample components:

$$A^+ \; + \; B^- \rightleftharpoons AB$$

| ion | counter- | ion- |
| sample | ion | pair |

While there are different exposés of the technique, the essential prerequisite is that the counter-ion contains bulky organic substituents so that the ion-pair subsequently formed will be hydrophobic in character. This enables conventional reverse-phase packings and methanol–water based solvent systems to be used for ionic samples. The great utility of this technique is in its efficiency in the analysis of mixtures which contain ionic and non-ionic analytes.

6.1.5 Gel permeation-exclusion

Exclusion chromatography, one of the newer of the LC methods, is variously known as gel chromatography, gel filtration and gel permeation chromatography

(GPC). Exclusion chromatography utilizes the selective diffusion of solute molecules within the solvent filled pores of a three-dimensional lattice. Small molecules will permeate the pores while large bulky molecules will be excluded. Thus separation is achieved principally on the basis of molecular weight and size, with the larger molecules being eluted from the column more quickly.

A number of types of packing are available for GPC analysis. Semi-rigid organic gels based on cross-linked polystyrenes are the choice for the analysis of organic polymers, though their application is limited as they cannot be used with aqueous mobile phases since water cannot penetrate the pores due to its high surface tension. Other organic gels, such as polyacrylamides, are available for the HPGPC analysis of water-soluble materials, though their limited mechanical strength restricts the applied pressure to less than 200 psi. Rigid packings, based on silica, with in some instances chemically modified surfaces, have proved of increasing interest and utility. The main advantages associated with these packings is in the increased stability to pressure and temperature and in the fact that they are compatible with both aqueous and organic eluants.

6.1.6 Affinity

The chromatographic modes described so far depend for their effectiveness on differences (often small) in adsorption, partition, ionic charge or size, between analyte components of similar chemical character. A modified gel technique which exploits the unique biological specificity of the protein–ligand interaction is affinity chromatography. The ligand is covalently bonded to the gel to form the packing material. The sample is applied to the column in a suitable buffered eluant so that the substrate becomes specifically, though not irreversibly bound to the ligand (see Chapter 4. Fig. 4.15). The composition or pH of the eluant is then altered in such a manner as to weaken the ligand–substrate bonding, thus promoting dissociation and facilitating elution of the retained compounds. Due to the nature of the technique packings are synthesized for particular applications. Thus affinity chromatography, while outside the mainstream of HPLC, has considerable potential and utility in biochemical and clinical applications, such as the purification of antigens, enzymes, proteins, viruses and hormones.

6.2 OVERVIEW OF HPLC INSTRUMENTATION

The following is intended as no more than a brief overview of HPLC instrumentation at this stage; the individual components will be discussed in detail later in the chapter.

In HPLC filtered eluant is drawn from the solvent reservoirs, the eluant composition being determined by the proportion of each solvent delivered to the column *via* a high pressure pump and a solvent mixing system. The sample

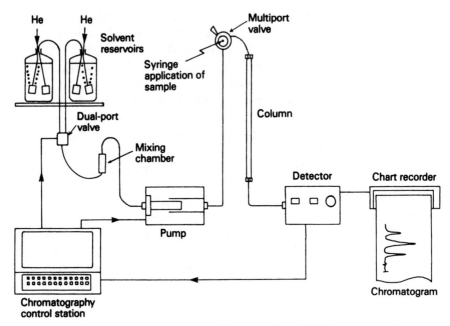

Fig. 6.2   Low-pressure mixing gradient HPLC system.

mixture is applied to the top of the column and the components of the mixture are then carried down through the column by the eluant at a rate which is inversely proportional to their attraction for the packing material. The passage of the solutes from the column is monitored by the detector and the response displayed on either a chart recorder or an integrator.

Though resolution of sample mixtures can often be effected using a solvent of constant composition (isocratic elution) gradient elution techniques, which involve changing the eluant composition during the development of the chromatogram, provide a powerful tool for the optimization of difficult separations. This has led to the development of LC systems which incorporate gradient forming and solvent mixing capability. The system illustrated (Fig. 6.2) uses a low pressure mixing procedure (i.e. solvents A and B are mixed on the low pressure side of the pump; an alternative configuration of the system components would provide for solvent mixing on the high pressure side of the pump. Equipment for both approaches is modular in design and though described more fully in later sections a brief description of the essential common components follows.

6.2.1 Packings

The fundamental problem in achieving high resolution liquid chromatography was in attaining rapid mass transfer of solute molecules between the packing material and the mobile phase, and thus considerable effort was committed to the development of suitable support materials. These efforts culminated in the provision of microporous particles of $10\,\mu m$ diameter or less, with large unit surface areas permitting high loadings of stationary phase if required. This development allowed the theories of van Deemter and Giddings, which had postulated the potential of liquid chromatography using microparticulate packings, to be applied which, more than anything else, engendered the rapid advancement in HPLC techniques. The nature of the stationary phases required for the different modes of HPLC has previously been indicated.

6.2.2 Pumps

As a consequence of the large back pressures encountered, due to the small particle size of packing used in HPLC, pumps must be employed to achieve acceptable eluant flow rates. The pumps may be classified as either those which provide constant inlet pressure or those which provide constant outlet flow and should be capable of delivering up to 7000 psi. They are constructed from materials which are resistant to the organic solvents and aqueous buffer solutions commonly used as eluants. The system may also have provision for microprocessor control of the pumps to provide for complex gradient elution with high pressure mixing.

6.2.3 Detectors

It is convenient to use continuous monitoring detectors located at the column exit. Various detector designs have been used and may be classified either as those which monitor a specific property of the solute or those which detect changes in a bulk property of the column effluent.

An example of the former is the UV spectrophotometer which may be of fixed wavelength (usually 254 or 280 nm) or variable wavelength design. The detector functions by monitoring the change in absorbance as the solute passes through the detector flow cell, i.e. it utilizes the specific property of the solute to absorb UV radiation.

An example of the second type of detector is the refractive index monitor which functions by recording the refractive changes in the eluant as the solute passes through the detector cell. Bulk property detectors, though more versatile, are generally several orders of magnitude less sensitive than specific property detectors and the choice for a particular application is often dictated by solute characteristics.

6.2.4 Solvents

The eluants employed for HPLC separations may comprise water, aqueous buffer solutions, organic solvents such as methanol and acetonitrile or a mixture of the above. All solvents should be of high spectroscopic purity, dust free, and should be degassed (i.e. have dissolved gases displaced) before use. They should also, if UV detection is being employed, be transparent to the detector wavelength employed.

6.2.5 Columns

Columns for analytical HPLC are typically 10–25 cm long and 4–6 mm internal diameter. The columns are constructed of stainless steel to cope with the high back pressure and are glass lined to prevent metal catalysis of solvent–solute reactions at the high column pressures experienced.

As mentioned previously, optimum packing size is $\leqslant 5 \mu m$ and columns with such packing would yield > 10000 theoretical plates m^{-1}. An important consequence of the small size of packing materials and columns is that the volumes of detectors and column couplings (known collectively as extra-column volumes) must be minimized to avoid excessive distortion of the chromatographic peaks on passage of the solute bands to the detection system. The volume of detector flow cells is commonly $\leqslant 10 \mu l$.

6.2.6 Injection

Application of the sample to the column can be achieved by one of the following techniques: (a), syringe and septum; (b) multiport valve.

In the former the syringe needle passes through an elastomer septum as in GC and the sample is injected on to a layer of ballotini glass beads, thus preventing disturbance at the top of the packing in the column which would seriously impair column performance, while dispersing the sample over a small portion of the column cross-sectional area. Though syringe injection is economical in sample usage, and sample loading can be varied as required, the technique is operator sensitive and cannot be used at pressures much above 750 psi.

The most common injection technique is *via* 6-port valves of the Valco and Rheodyne design. These valves afford precise, accurate sample loading with minimal interruption to solvent flow. They can be used up to column pressures of 7000 psi and the sample loading can be varied either by part-filling the loop or by changing the loop.

6.3 THEORY

The following section is intended as no more than an overview of the theoretical principles considered relevant to a basic understanding of the factors which influence chromatographic performance in liquid column chromatography. The reader is directed to Chapter 2 and references therein for a fuller account of the principles and theories of chromatographic processes. Up to this point the discussion of the chromatographic processes in HPLC has been largely qualitative; however, many of the foregoing principles and concepts can be expressed in precise mathematical relationships.

6.3.1 Retention

In order to achieve separation in chromatography, one must first have retention. The fundamental relationship between the retention volume (V_r), the quantity of stationary phase (V_s) and the partition coefficient (K) is expressed in the following equation:

$$V_r = V_m + KV_s \qquad (6.1)$$

where V_m is the volume of mobile phase within the column. The retention volume can be determined directly from the chromatogram as $V_r = f \times t_r$, where $f =$ the flow rate of solvent and $t_r =$ the retention time of the component; similarly $V_m = f \times t_m$ where t_m is the time taken for an unretained compound to traverse the column; however, in order for K, which measures the extent of the retention, to be evaluated, V_r must be known.

A more practical expression of solute retention is given by K' the capacity factor.

$$K' = n_s/n_m \qquad (6.2)$$

Here, n_s is the total number of moles of solute component in the stationary phase and n_m is the total number of moles of solute component in the mobile phase. It can subsequently be shown that

$$V_r = V_m(1 + K') \qquad (6.3)$$

and that $$K' = (t_r - t_m)/t_m \qquad (6.4)$$

Thus the capacity factor, K', is a measure of the sample retention by the column and can be determined from the chromatogram directly.

6.3.2 Column efficiency

The concept of plate number and plate height in chromatography was developed by Martin and Synge who used an analogous model and theory of mass distribution to that adapted for the elucidation of processes occurring in a distillation column.

The empirical expressions derived are generally applicable to all types of column chromatography and are used universally, first as a measure of column performance and efficiency, expressed in terms of the number of theoretical plates

(N) and the height equivalent of a theoretical plate (HETP) denoted by H, and secondly, to measure the resolution (R_s) attained in the chromatogram. For a fuller discussion the reader is directed to Chapter 2, though a brief resumé of the expressions for these parameters is presented below.

A measure of the separating efficiency is given by the number of theoretical plates the column is equivalent to, which is defined in terms of the retention time (t_r) and the base width of the peak (t_w):

$$N = 16(t_r/t_w)^2 \qquad (6.5)$$

The efficiency of any column is best measured by the height equivalent to a theoretical plate which is expressed as:

$$H = L/N \qquad (6.6)$$

where L is the length of the column. The resolution, R_s, of two compounds is defined as being equal to the peak separation divided by the mean base width of the peaks:

$$R_s = 2(t_{rb} - t_{ra})/(t_{wb} + t_{wa}) \qquad (6.7)$$

A more practical expression for R_s in terms of the experimental factors α, K'_2 and N, can be arrived at by substitution for t_r and t_w in terms of N. Thus R_s as a function of α, K'_2 and N is given by:

$$R_s = 1/4[(\alpha - 1)/\alpha][K'_2/(K'_2 + 1)](N)^{1/2} \qquad (6.8)$$
$$\text{(i)} \qquad\qquad \text{(ii)} \qquad\quad \text{(iii)}$$

where the selectivity factor $\alpha = K'_2/K'_1$ for component bands 1 and 2 in the chromatogram. The three terms are broadly independent and thus can be individually optimized.

The selectivity of the column as measured by α may be varied by changing the temperature, or the stationary or mobile phases. However, if $\alpha \Rightarrow 1$ then no matter how long the components stay on the column, or how many theoretical plates the column is equivalent to, there will be no separation. Thus, the greater the difference between K'_1 and K'_2, the better the resolution as term (i) becomes more significant.

The expression in term (ii) of equation (6.8) is a measure of the retention times of the peaks being considered and is only significant at small values of the capacity factor ($K' < 2$). The value of the capacity factor is most readily adjusted by varying the solvent strength.

The third term is a measure of the column efficiency, and N can be varied by changing the column length, the particle size of the packing or the optimum mobile-phase velocity.

In practice, the following stepwise procedure is often adopted:

1. the column of highest efficiency is selected;
2. the capacity factor is optimized by adjusting the solvent strength so that

the capacity factor lies within the range $5 < K' < 10$. Values outside this range lead to poor chromatograms (due to reduced peak height) and overlong analysis time. To increase K' values a weaker solvent is used and *vice versa*;

3. if however, the resolution is still inadequate due to $\alpha \Rightarrow 1$, then the selectivity ratio may be modified by altering the nature of the mobile and/or stationary phases.

Plate theory, though useful in monitoring and comparing column performance and in giving a measure of the resolution achieved in the chromatogram, has a number of shortcomings. Some of these deficiencies arise from the simplicity of the model adopted. The main criticism, however, is that the treatment does not consider the influence of important chromatographic variables such as particle size, stationary phase loading, eluant viscosity and flow rate on column performance, and how these factors might be adjusted to optimize chromatographic efficiency.

6.3.3 Rate theory

The rate theory of chromatography avoids the assumptions of plate theory such as instantaneous equilibrium and isolated chromatographic contact units, and examines column efficiency with reference to the kinetic effects which operate during development of the chromatogram and which give rise to band broadening. The kinetic effects giving rise to band broadening in HPLC are similar to those considered in other modes of chromatography, though their relative contributions may be different.

Each of the rate factors contributing to the band broadening is considered in isolation and a mathematical expression evaluated for the plate height contribution in terms of the variables governing the kinetic effect under examination. These contributions are then combined to give a general expression for the overall plate height, commonly referred to as the van Deemter equation. The following terms are considered to contribute to the broadening of the solute band during development of the chromatogram:-

Multipath term (H_p)

Broadening of a chromatographic zone as it passes through the column arises from the variable channels which the solute molecules may follow through the packing. This effect is known variously as the multipath, the eddy-diffusion or non-uniform flow term. However, in practice the solute molecules are not fixed in single channels but can diffuse laterally into other paths. These composite motions result in a decreased contribution to band broadening from this term. The contribution of this effect to the overall plate height (H) is proportional to the particle size (dp) of the packing material within the column and is expressed as

$$H_f \sim \lambda(dp) \tag{6.9}$$

where λ is a measure of how uniformly the column is packed.

Longitudinal diffusion (H_{dm})

Whenever a concentration gradient exists in the column then spreading, i.e. diffusion of the molecules from a region of high concentration to a region of low concentration, will occur due to random thermal processes. This interdiffusion of the two molecular species, which occurs in all directions independent of whether solvent is flowing or not, is dependent upon two factors: first, the diffusion coefficient (D_m) for interdiffusion of solute and solvent molecules; and second, the time over which this diffusion occurred, i.e. the time spent in the mobile phase (t_m). However, as t_m is inversely proportional to the mobile phase flow rate (u), the longitudinal diffusion contribution to the effective plate height of the column may be expressed as

$$H_{dm} \propto D_m/u \tag{6.10}$$

Furthermore, as diffusion can also take place radially, migration of solute molecules towards the column walls can occur. This could lead to appreciable band broadening because of the slower flow at the walls of the column, and solute molecule interaction with the walls, causing retardation of the zone. However, provided the sample is applied as a narrow concentrated band and the solvent has suitable viscosity, the rate of radial diffusion is not sufficient to become a problem, and under these conditions the column is described as operating in the infinite diameter mode.

There is also an analogous contribution to the overall plate height due to diffusive spreading in the stationary phase. Using similar reasoning as above this may be expressed as

$$H_{ds} \propto D_s/u \tag{6.11}$$

where D_s is the interdiffusion coefficient of the solute and stationary phase molecules.

Slow equilibration (H_{em})

The assumption in the plate theory that the transfer of solute molecules between the mobile and stationary phases was instantaneous is invalid due to the finite rates of mass transfer within the mobile and stationary phase. This contribution to the effective plate height may itself be regarded as arising from two separate effects.

First, the system deviates from ideality since there is a finite rate of mass transfer of solute molecules across the chromatographic interface. The contribution to the overall HETP arising from this kinetic control of the sorption–desorption process increases with increasing mobile phase flow rate.

The second effect, commonly labelled diffusion controlled kinetics, arises from the finite rate at which molecules can diffuse to the interface and become available for transfer, and itself has two contributions. In the mobile phase there exist velocity gradients across the channels in the packing material so that solute molecules closer to the packing will, in addition to having a shorter distance to diffuse, also flow more slowly than those in mid-channel and thus the latter will have less opportunity to reach the interface and transfer.

The above effects, collectively referred to as mobile phase–mass transfer effects, may be expressed as:

$$H_{em} \propto dp^2 u/D_m \qquad (6.12)$$

Analogous arguments can be developed to take account of stationary phase–mass transfer effects which can similarly be expressed as

$$H_{es} \propto d^2 u/D_s \qquad (6.13)$$

where d is the thickness of the conceptual stationary phase and D_s is the diffusion coefficient of solute molecules within it.

Stagnant mobile phase ($H_{em'}$)

Finally, the presence of substantial amounts of immobile solvent, which is either trapped in the interstices between the packing material or in the deep pores within the particles, is a further cause of band broadening; solute molecules entering these stagnant pools may quickly diffuse out or conversely diffuse further in, thus becoming effectively trapped.

The factors affecting the contribution of this effect to the overall plate height are as those experienced for H_{em}, the mobile phase–mass transfer term. Thus the mobile phase–mass transfer term may be expressed as

$$H_{em'} \propto dp^2 u/D_m \qquad (6.14)$$

Giddings [3] has shown that the overall plate height arising from these kinetic factors can be expressed mathematically as

$$H = 1/((1/H_f) + (1/H_{em})) + (H_{dm} + H_{ds}) + H_{em'} + H_{es} \qquad (6.15)$$

where
$$H_f = C_f \lambda dp \qquad \text{(Multipath term)}$$
$$H_{em} = C_{em} dp^2 u/D_m \qquad \text{(Mobile phase–mass transfer)}$$
$$H_{dm} = C_{dm} D_m/u \qquad \text{(Diffusion mobile phase)}$$
$$H_{ds} = C_{ds} D_s/u \qquad \text{(Diffusion stationary phase)}$$
$$H_{em'} = C_{em'} dp^2 u/D_m \qquad \text{(Stagnant mobile phase–mass transfer)}$$
$$H_{es} = C_{es} d^2 u/D_s \qquad \text{(Stationary phase–mass transfer)}$$

and C_f, C_{em}, C_{dm}, C_{ds}, C_{es} and $C_{em'}$ are plate height coefficients. The equation is commonly represented in its simplified form:

$$H = Au^{0.33} + B/u + Cu + Du \qquad (6.16)$$

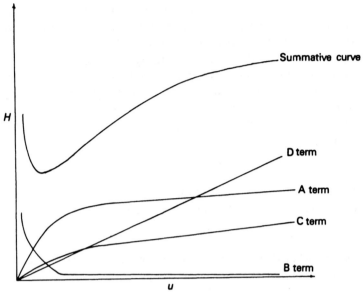

Fig. 6.3   Plot of plate height (*H*) versus linear velocity (*u*), showing contributions from the four terms in equation (6.16).

The equation, though complex, shows the importance of particle size, mobile phase flow rate and diffusion coefficients and indicates that the deleterious effects on *H* and thus on the column performance can be minimized by reducing the packing particle size, the stationary phase thickness and the solvent viscosity (thus decreasing D_m and D_s). The latter can be achieved by using elevated column temperatures.

A representation of the variation with flow rate of the individual contributions to *H* is shown in Fig. 6.3. The main differences between the GC and LC plots of *H* vs. *u* arise from the reduced rates of sample diffusion in liquids compared to gases.

D_m is 10^4–10^6 times greater in gases than in liquids. For LC columns containing large particles ($> 10\,\mu m$) H_{dm} is insignificant compared with those terms which are a function of *dp* or dp^2. However, as *dp* decreases then the contribution to the overall plate height *H*, from H_{dm}, will become dominant at low flow velocities.

In consequence the *H* vs. *u* plot shows a minimum at flow velocities which are of importance for routine analytical analysis with the arrival of $3\,\mu m$ packings.

The other main difference between GC and LC is that the gradient of the curve is shallower for the latter and thus mobile phase velocities substantially greater than u_{opt} can be used without seriously impairing column performance.

6.3.4 Extra-column band broadening

The discussion of band broadening so far has been concerned with effects occurring in the column. The resolution attained can be further reduced if connecting tubing is of too large a volume or column connections contain unswept volumes. These extra-column and dead volumes are present in any chromatographic system; there is a finite volume between the point of injection and the column, between the column end and the detector, and in the detector flow cell itself. The peak dispersion produced at different regions of the chromatogram is additive.

As the sample, dissolved in the mobile phase, passes through the extra-column volume, broadening takes place simply as a result of the velocity gradient across the diameter of the connecting tubing. The solvent and the solute in it nearest the walls will move more slowly than that in mid-stream with a resultant dilution of the sample and broadening of the peak.

This effect is more noticeable in LC than GC due to the lower rates of interdiffusion in liquids.

To minimize these effects the following procedures should be adhered to:

1. connecting tubing should be < 0.025 mm bore and less than 20 cm in length;
2. detection cells should be not larger than 10 μl and if possible smaller, especially where high efficiency, short or small particle size columns are being used;
3. there should be no voids in the system between the injector and the detector.

6.3.5 Temperature effects and diffusion

The distribution coefficients of solutes and the resolution obtained in a chromatogram are temperature dependent. In general, increasing the temperature gives sharper peaks, improved resolution and lower values of H. Temperature, though, has much less effect on the degree of retention in LC than GC, since the heat of transfer of solute between mobile and stationary phase is much smaller in liquids.

In GC retention and selectivity are controlled by adjusting the column temperature and stationary phase characteristics. In liquid chromatography change in the composition of the eluant serves both purposes and thus solvent programming (otherwise known as gradient elution) is used in HPLC where temperature programming would be employed in GC.

An important feature in the control of interdiffusion of solute and solvent molecules is the solvent viscosity. An increase in temperature would reduce solvent viscosity, thus improving mass transfer and lead to improved peak shape and resolution. However, due to problems of thermostatting the column, the solvent and the detector, the great majority of LC applications are carried out at ambient temperature.

Solvent viscosities, however differ markedly and thus, wherever a choice is possible the solvent with the lower viscosity should be chosen, e.g. methanol in preference to ethanol.

6.4 DETAILED DISCUSSION OF HPLC INSTRUMENTATION

6.4.1 Solvent delivery system

The main criteria for a suitable pump can be summarized as follows:

(i)   the materials of construction should be inert towards the solvents used;
(ii) the pump should be capable of delivering high volumes of solvent;
(iii) it should be capable of delivering a precise and accurate flow;
(iv) the pump-head should have a small volume to facilitate rapid change of solvent composition;
(v)   it should be capable of delivering high pressures up to around 7000 psi;
(vi) it should deliver a pulse-free flow and hence not contribute to detector noise.

There are three main designs of solvent delivery system: (a) the constant pressure type; (b) the syringe design which delivers a constant non-pulsating flow; (c) the reciprocating piston pump which may be of the single, dual or triple head design.

Constant pressure pumps

Constant pressure pumps (Fig. 6.4) deliver solvent *via* a small headed piston which is driven by a pneumatic amplifier. A gas acts on the relatively large piston area of the pneumatic actuator. This is coupled directly to a small piston which pushes the eluant through the column. Pressure amplification is achieved in direct ratio to the piston areas and thus for low inlet pressures (approximately 100 psi) it is possible to obtain large column pressures (10 000 psi). The main

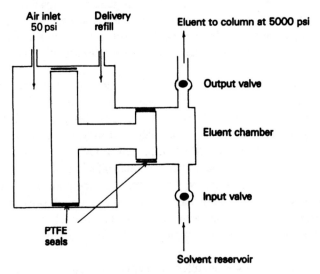

Fig. 6.4   Constant pressure pump.

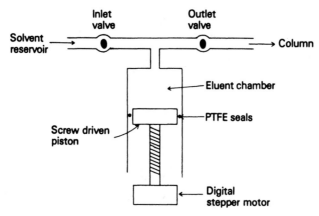

Fig. 6.5 Syringe pump.

advantages of these pumps are: (1) low cost; (2) ability to deliver high pressure; (3) stability of flow during the delivery stroke of the pump.

However, due to their mode of operation, pneumatic amplifier pumps have certain disadvantages. They deliver constant pressure rather than constant flow and therefore, as the elution volume is proportional to flow, fluctuations in the latter – from, for example, partial column blockage or temperature change – can lead to poor precision and accuracy of analysis. In addition, the chamber has to be refilled periodically with solvent, thus resulting in an interruption of the analysis. The design of such pumps also makes it difficult to change solvent compositions. However, although they are not ideally suited for analytical LC, constant pressure pumps are still commonly used for slurry packing of columns because of their ability to deliver high flows and pressures.

Syringe pumps

The construction of this pump (Fig. 6.5) is similar to the constant pressure pump, except in this instance the piston delivering the solvent is driven by a digital stepping motor. As the flow delivered is determined by the incremental rotational rate of the motor, the piston is driven at constant speed during the delivery stroke, and hence delivers a constant flow rate to the column. This overcomes the major disadvantage of pneumatic amplifier type pumps, and makes syringe pumps ideal for reproducibility of retention time data. However, the major problem encountered with the syringe pump is the design of a suitable refill mechanism. Whilst several systems have been developed, none is totally successful and the modifications are expensive.

Reciprocating pumps

Reciprocating pumps of the single piston design (Fig. 6.6) function by having a slow solvent delivery cycle compared to rapid refilling of the piston chamber. The

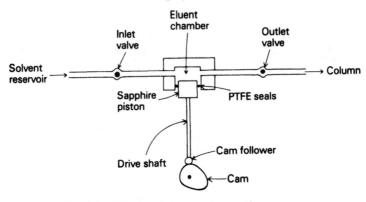

Fig. 6.6   Single piston reciprocating pump.

flow rate to the column is modified by changing the length or rate of the piston stroke. There is, however, associated with this type of solvent delivery module, some pulsing of the flow because of the finite time taken to fill the piston reservoir and also the fact that the initial part of the delivery stroke is concerned with compression of the solvent prior to pumping. Precise uniform flow is achieved by suitable design of the cam system (so that the compression portion of the delivery cycle is very small compared to the displacement segment) and by the use of microstep controlled direct drive motors. Such drive systems largely eliminate flow rate instabilities and are capable of providing precise flow rates to 0.01 ml min^{-1}. Further smoothing of fluctuations in flow delivered from the pump can be achieved using pulse dampeners, i.e. Bourdon coils, which are essentially coiled tubing inserted between the piston and the column. The disadvantages of using pulse dampening coils are the attendant problems of dead volumes and unswept dead volumes introduced prior to the column, which makes change of solvent composition rather difficult and inefficient.

Improved precision and smoothing of flow is provided by twin-piston reciprocating pumps. Here, the pistons are driven, either via a single cam (Fig. 6.7) or more commonly by individual cams on a single rotating drive shaft and a variable speed motor, approximately 180° out of phase (Fig. 6.8). As piston A completes its compression stroke, piston B begins its refill cycle. These pumps provide a constant solvent flow which is easy to control, almost entirely pulse free, and with a small pump-head delivery volume, afford rapid change of solvent composition. This makes them readily adaptable for gradient elution chromatography. A recent advance has been the design of triple-headed pumps, where two heads are in different stages of filling as the third is pumping thus smoothing the flow considerably.

The advantages of reciprocating pumps over other designs can be summarized as follows: (1) they can be used continuously, as theoretically they have infinite solvent reservoirs; (2) they can readily be made pulse-free; (3) the low piston chamber volume facilitates rapid change in solvent composition.

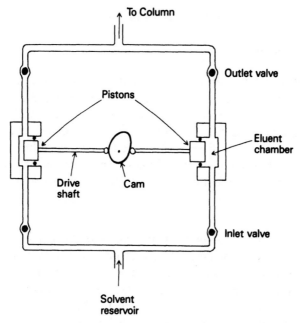

Fig. 6.7   Single cam dual piston reciprocating pump.

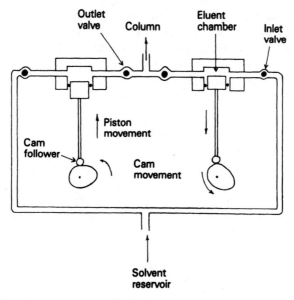

Fig. 6.8   Twin-cam dual piston reciprocating pump.

6.4.2 Gradient elution

The quality of an HPLC analysis is often equated with the resolution of the peaks achieved and, as previously discussed, this may be optimized by adjusting the solvent composition to obtain appropriate capacity factors for the solutes. For difficult separations, isocratic elution may be inadequate and the desired resolution may only be achieved using gradient elution techniques. Gradient elution involves changing the composition of the eluant during development of the chromatogram. There are two types of system commercially available.

Low pressure mixing

In this system the solvent is drawn from the reservoirs at a ratio determined by the switching valve rate and then passed through a mixing chamber prior to delivery to the piston head. The switching valve is microcomputer controlled and gradient-profile data is entered *via* the keyboard for construction of the desired gradient. These systems are adequate down to 5% of one or other solvent. However, lower solvent compositions are difficult to obtain due to the finite actuation time of the solenoid valve as the opening time becomes comparable with the flow time in the low composition position. Also, since even with dual piston reciprocating pumps, there is a short time when no solvent is being drawn by the pump (due to the fill-cycle of the pump being shorter than the compression cycle), further inaccuracies in gradient profile can arise at low switching rates. These problems can be overcome by using a mixed solvent in one of the reservoirs. For example, in the system shown (Fig. 6.9) 99% B can be achieved with a 9:1 switching rate. An incidental advantage of this technique is the degassing which occurs during premixing. The main advantage of low pressure mixing systems is in cost, since only one pump is required. A disadvantage is the greater dead volumes prior to the pump which delay the effect of solvent change at the switching valve acting on the column.

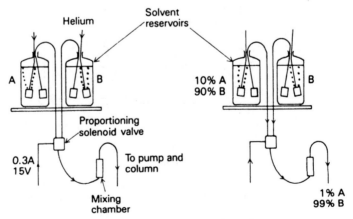

Fig. 6.9   Low pressure gradient former.

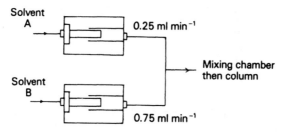

Fig. 6.10   High pressure gradient former.

High-pressure mixing

High-pressure mixing uses two pumps (Fig. 6.10) whose flows are controlled *via* a microcomputer. The total flow required for the application is selected and the composition of A and B entered, e.g. for 75% A at $1\,\mathrm{ml\,min^{-1}}$, pump A is programmed to deliver $0.75\,\mathrm{ml\,min^{-1}}$ and pump B $0.25\,\mathrm{ml\,min^{-1}}$. The solvent streams are then mixed between the pumps and the column, i.e. on the high pressure side of the pumps. This system can be used at low compositions (1%) of A or B (except at low flow rates). The main disadvantage is cost and inconvenience, as two pumps are required, and the system is generally limited to two-solvent gradients.

Quaternary gradient systems

A recent development has been the introduction of four-solvent delivery modules. Initial studies have indicated the importance of quaternary solvent systems in the optimization of resolution and in method development [6]. Commercially available systems such as marketed by Perkin–Elmer and Du Pont use low pressure solvent mixing *via* a 4-way solenoid valve. The principal instrumental innovation is in pump design which allows considerably extended solvent proportioning times; for example, at a flow rate of $1\,\mathrm{ml\,min^{-1}}$, the proportioning time is 6 s; this advance provides for good accuracy and reproducibility of the complex solvent mixtures required.

The pump consists of two pistons, but solvent is delivered to the column only from one piston, the other piston chamber serving as a reservoir. As illustrated the pistons are 180° out of phase so that when piston A is delivering solvent to the column, the piston reservoir B is being replenished. The piston volumes are $100\,\mu l$ and thus at a flow rate of $1\,\mathrm{ml\,min^{-1}}$ the delivery–fill cycle is 6 s. As the fill cycle takes the same time as the delivery cycle the proportioning valves on the low pressure side have 6 s to actuate. Mixing of the component solvents occurs inside the pump and connecting tubing during the transfer of the solvent from the reservoir piston to the delivery piston.

The routines developed for determining the optimum four-solvent eluent composition are designed to yield a pre-chosen level of resolution for all pairs of

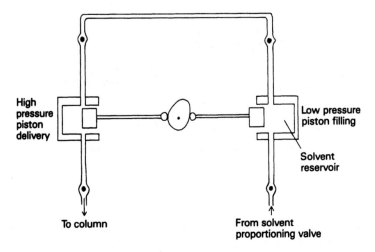

High
pressure
piston
delivery

Low pressure
piston filling

Solvent
reservoir

To column

From solvent
proportioning valve

(a)

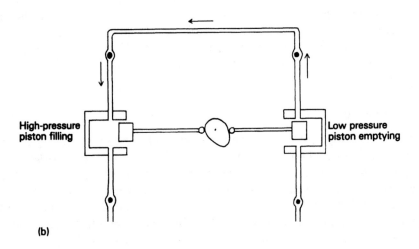

High-pressure
piston filling

Low pressure
piston emptying

(b)

components in a mixture by carrying out no more than seven analyses with various solvent compositions. Evaluation of these chromatograms allows selection of a set of standard conditions for the given application. The technique has a sound basis in theory, appears to have general applicability and has been used with both normal and reverse phase systems. The routines associated with the optimization process have been reviewed by Glajch *et al.* [7] and Poile [8].

A detailed discussion is outside the scope of this text: however an appraisal of recent work leads to the conclusion that the use of four solvents actually simplifies HPLC method development compared with binary and tertiary solvent systems.

6.4.3 Sample introduction

Sample application techniques can be broadly classified as either syringe or valve injections.

Syringe injection

The first type of sample application system developed closely resembled those of GC and involved syringe injection of the sample through a self-sealing septum. The greatest column efficiency is achieved by application of the sample *via* a syringe directly on to the column bed, because of: (a) minimal back-diffusion of sample; and (b) application of the sample to the chromatographic bed as a small point source results in the transport of the component bands through the core of the column, well away from the walls, thus preserving the infinite diameter effect [9, 10].

Two types of septum injector are commercially available: single septum suitable for inlet pressures of ~ 1500 psi; and double septa for inlet pressures of ~ 3000 psi. The septa are coated with PTFE to prevent attack by organic solvents. The principal merits of such systems are: the ability to vary sample size; the efficiency of sample usage; and cost is relatively small. However, on-column injection has a number of disadvantages. For instance, debris from the septum can be carried on to the column; blockage of the needle by microparticulate material and distortion of chromatographic peaks due to disturbance of the bed can also occur. The latter problem can be overcome by topping the column with ballotini beads (30–40 μm) [11]. Further disadvantages are that septa lifetimes are short due to their pressurization with mobile phase and finally that syringe malfunction or lack of technique can make it difficult to achieve the desired reproducibility of sample size which thus demands the use of an internal standard.

One on-column sample application method involves stop-flow techniques. In this instance, the pump is stopped and isolated by a three-way valve from the column; the sample is then loaded *via* a syringe through an injection port which does not contain a septum. The pump is then restarted, the flow restored by switching the valve, when the sample is rapidly flushed on to the column. There is no apparent loss in efficiency but inaccuracies in retention measurement occur due to the finite time required for flow to be established.

Valve injection

Valve injection of the sample is now the preferred and accepted technique. Six-port valves are commonly used, either fitted with an internal or an external sample loop.

For the former, the volume of the internal loop is formed from a machined groove in the surface of the rotor. When in the load position this channel is isolated from the solvent flow through the column and can be filled with sample as shown (Fig. 6.12(a)). On turning the rotor to the injection position the channel containing the sample is relocated at the solvent outlet ports and the sample is flushed into the column. This system is simple and reliable to use and has the advantage that the pump does not need to be stopped. The disadvantage of internal loops is that they are fixed and can only be altered by changing the rotor. This has led to the development of external interchangeable loop valves of the type marketed by Valco and Rheodyne. Here dead volumes are minimized and the loop can readily be exchanged for other desired sample sizes, e.g. $10 \mu l$, $20 \mu l$ and $50 \mu l$. Operation of the valve is similar to those with internal loops i.e. a load position and an inject position (Fig. 6.13).

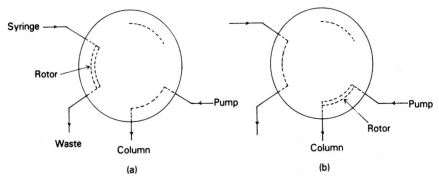

Fig. 6.12   Internal loop valve: (a) rotor fill; (b) sample inject.

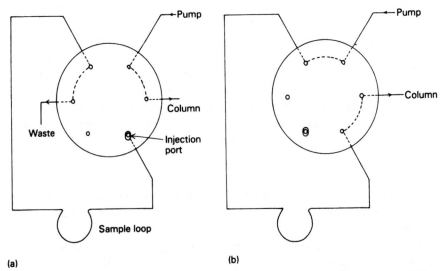

Fig. 6.13   External loop injection valves: (a) load position; (b) inject position.

6.4.4 Detectors

Various approaches to solute detection have been pursued and have led to the development of a range of detectors which may be classified as follows:

1. Detectors which monitor a specific property of the solute not shared with the solvent e.g. UV absorbance and fluorescence. Possession of such a property by the solute affords its detection in the effluent.
2. Detection systems which monitor a bulk property of the eluant e.g. refractive index; in this instance the solute modifies the base value of the property associated with the solvent.
3. Detectors which function by separating the solvent from the eluant, thus allowing subsequent detection by techniques such as flame ionization (FID) [12, 13] or mass spectrometry (MS) [14].

The choice of detector is often dictated by the properties of the solutes and/or the sensitivity required from the analysis. The more important detector parameters governing the choice are:

(a) the noise level (n) of the detector. This may be present as long-term or short-term noise and is caused by changes in mobile phase composition, incomplete mixing, temperature variation, voltage fluctuations in the electronics, etc;
(b) lower limit of detection, i.e. that concentration which produces a signal having twice the background noise level;
(c) linearity, the concentration range over which the detector response is linear. If the concentration of sample is outside this range, the sample should be diluted or an extended calibration curve constructed.

Ultraviolet detectors

Ultraviolet detectors function by monitoring the light absorbed by the solute molecules from the incident beam. The first source in common use was a mercury lamp which emits intense radiation at 254 nm which is easily isolated using simple narrow band-pass filters. The addition of phosphor convertors can be used to provide a line at 280 nm of adequate intensity for absorption measurements.

Many organic compounds, such as those containing conjugated chromophores, aromatic or heteroaromatic rings, can be adequately detected using the Hg lamp as a source. In addition, due to the intensity of the Hg 254 nm line, very narrow band-pass filters can be used giving essentially a monochromatic source; thus the absorbance obeys the Beer–Lambert Law which is defined as follows:

$$\text{Absorbance} = \log I_0/I_t = \varepsilon c l$$

where ε is the absorptivity coefficient, c is the solute concentration and l is the pathlength.

However, there are many classes of compound which do not absorb significantly at the above wavelengths, e.g. barbiturates and pesticides, and consequently sensitivity is very poor. To increase sensitivity and specificity the Hg lamp has been replaced by the deuterium (190–400 nm) and the tungsten (400–700 nm) lamps coupled with manually adjustable diffraction grating monochromators. These are referred to as variable wavelength detectors and allow the wavelength for optimum sensitivity in a given application to be chosen.

A consequence of the high sensitivities demanded by LC (down to 0.001 absorbance units) full scale deflection (AUFSD) is the need to use greater band widths with variable wavelength detectors (+ 5 nm being typical), otherwise the resulting noise would render the detector unusable. However, as deviations from Beer's Law can arise with the use of non-monochromatic radiation, it is important to check the linearity of response of the sample components over the concentration range of interest; with photometric sensitivity of this order it is possible to monitor solutes having only moderate absorptivity.

A schematic diagram of the optical layout of a typical LC spectrophotometer is shown in Fig. 6.14. The instrument is described as a double-beam photometer, although the reference beam in fact passes directly on to a reference photocell.

Reference cells filled with the eluant being used for analysis were incorporated into early instrumentation. However, this served no useful purpose and in fact caused additional noise due to the difficulty in exactly matching the solvent flows, a problem especially in gradient work.

Detectors are now commercially available which allow programmable wavelength switching during analysis, thus optimizing sensitivity and selectivity. As many as 12 wavelengths can be selected. The systems use reversed-optics geometry, i.e, the light from the source is dispersed after passing through the sample by a holographic grating on to an array of photodiode detectors. One system uses a Xenon strobe lamp, thus giving a wavelength range of 190–800 nm. Deuterium lamps have also been used.

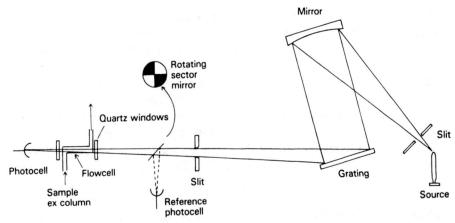

Fig. 6.14   Schematic diagram of a variable wavelength UV detector for HPLC.

(a) Absorbance ratioing techniques

Spectrophotometers are available for the simultaneous monitoring of light at two wavelengths; for example, suitable orientation of a mercury lamp and phosphor allows light of 254 and 280 nm to be directed through the flow cell and to subsequently impinge on individual detector cells. This is a technique which provides for direct absorbance ratioing, an accurate method for determining the homogeneity of a chromatographic zone [15]. In general the ratio of two absorbances at any two wavelengths is a constant, (the ratio of the absorptivity coefficients at wavelength 1 and wavelength 2 respectively) and is diagnostic for a pure compound. If the ratio of absorbances across the chromatographic zone is not constant this is indicative of peak overlap and incomplete resolution.

Variable wavelength detectors extend the scope of the technique. Using programmable multiwavelength detectors, wavelengths for ratio absorbance monitoring can be pre-selected to maximize the ratio discrepancy due to peak overlap. Sophisticated microprocessor control allows the ratiogram to be evaluated and plotted in real time whilst monitoring the effluent at additional pre-programmed wavelengths, to maximize detectability and selectivity and plotting the chromatogram.

Whilst single wavelength detection using variable wavelength UV monitors give adequate sensitivity and selectivity for quantitative and qualitative analysis further spectroanalytical data can be obtained by stopped-flow scanning [16]. Computerised data collection and processing systems have enabled spectra to be collected, added, subtracted and scaled. Thus when the eluant flow is stopped, the solution in the detector cell can be scanned and a background subtraction of the solvent spectrum, which has been previously recorded and stored in the data system, performed; the resultant spectra can then be displayed.

(b) Photodiode array spectrophotometers

Photodiode array technology allows continuous scanning of the absorbance spectrum of the chromatographic eluent, thus eliminating the need to stop the flow of the mobile phase [17, 18]. Diode array spectrophotometers employ reversed-optic geometry, in which all of the light from the source is focused on to the sample, rather than dispersing the light in a monochromator and passing single wavelengths through the detector cell (Fig. 6.15). The full spectrum of light emerging from the flow cell is dispersed by a holographic diffraction grating into single wavelengths which are focused simultaneously on to a linear array of photodiode detectors. The photodiode array is a row of detectors (up to 400) mounted on a 1 cm silicon chip, each diode receiving a different wavelength. When transmitted radiation falls on the photodiodes photocurrents are generated. The electronic signal from each photodiode detector is processed to give absorbance data, which is then displayed as a spectrum across the complete spectral range of the array is as little as 1 s; thus several spectra can be evaluated and displayed for even the fastest eluting peak. The absorbance data can be displayed as a function of wavelength and time (Fig. 6.16).

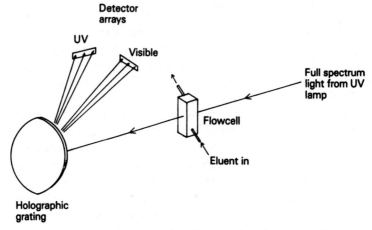

Fig. 6.15   Photodiode array spectrophotometer.

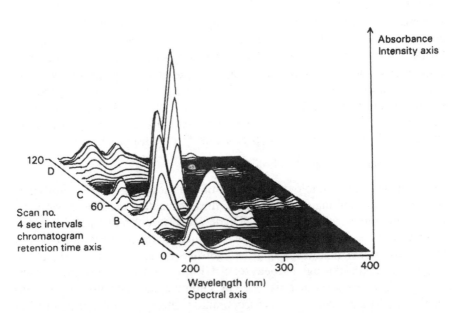

Fig. 6.16   UV diode array spectral map of an HPLC separation.

The full spectra obtained from diode array spectrophotometers are a useful aid to component identification. The examination of the many spectra taken during the elution of a peak gives information on the peak homogeneity thus aiding accurate quantitation. It is possible to optimize detectability for an analysis by averaging absorbance data either in the time axis or the wavelength axis, as

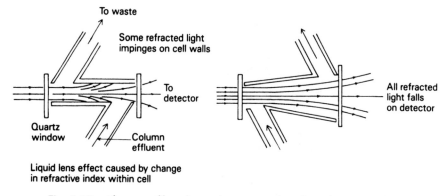

Fig. 6.17   Flow profiles through conventional and taper cells.

random noise decreases by the square root of the number of readings taken. Furthermore the detection wavelength can be changed during the analysis as many times as necessary so that every peak is detected at its optimum wavelength.

Typically the flow cells for spectrophotometric detection have a pathlength of 10 mm and a bore of 1 mm. Common flow cells in use are shown in Fig. 6.17. The various flow cell designs have been developed to minimize flow disturbances within the cell. These fluctuations arise from changes in the refractive index of the eluate which distorts the incident beam and causes variance in the intensity of the light falling on the detector. These effects are referred to as the liquid lens phenomena [19].

Fluorescence Detectors

A smaller number of compounds possess the ability to fluoresce, i.e. to absorb radiation of one wavelength and subsequently to emit radiation of longer wavelength. Fluorescing compounds typically contain highly conjugated cyclic systems, for instance, polynuclear aromatics, quinolines, steroids and alkaloids. Many compound classes which do not fluoresce can be reacted with fluorogenic reagents [20], for instance, amino acids react with *o*-phthalaldehyde or ninhydrin to give fluorescent derivatives [21]. The fundamental properties of fluorescence make this a particularly attractive basis for an HPLC detection system, for, whereas photometers depend upon the measurement of fairly small differences between the intensity of a full and slightly attenuated beam, the measurement of fluorescence starts in principle from zero intensity. At sufficiently low values of concentration (< 0.05 absorbance) the intensity of fluorescence is directly proportional to concentration. Consequently, fluorescence detectors are more selective and sensitive than UV detectors in LC by a factor of 10^2 giving sensitivities of $1\,\text{ng ml}^{-1}$.

The optical layout (Fig. 6.18) is similar to the conventional fluorimeter in that the detector is placed at right angles to the primary incident beam. However, because of the flow cell dimensions and orientation only a small amount of the

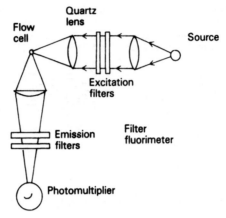

Fig. 6.18   Schematic diagram of a Filter fluorimeter.

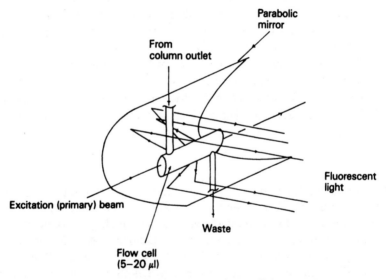

Fig. 6.19   Filter fluorimeter flowcell for HPLC.

fluorescent energy will fall on the photodetector. Increased sensitivity is provided by the use of parabolic collecting mirrors which focus the fluorescent radiation on to a photomultiplier tube (Fig. 6.19). Notwithstanding this, larger flowcells (10–30 μl) are used to give improved resolution at the expense of reduced sensitivity. As in conventional fluorimetry, scatter of the primary beam in the direction of the detector occurs and must be removed either by filters or monochromators. Likewise, narrow band-pass or cut-off filters or monochromators are used to select the wavelength of the exciting beam.

Spectrofluorimeters are available in which both excitation and fluorescent wavelengths can be chosen using variable monochromators. The excitation energy may be provided either with a deuterium lamp (190–400 nm) or a tungsten lamp (250–600 nm). Fluorescence measurements in LC are susceptible to the usual limitations such as quenching and turbidity. They are, however, relatively insensitive to fluctuations in solvent pulsing and temperature and are suitable for use with gradient systems [20].

Infrared detectors

The eluant can be monitored by observing its absorbance of infrared radiation. Variable wavelength detectors, fitted with low volume flow cells (5–200 μl, pathlength 1.5 mm), are commercially available which cover the spectral range 2.5–14.5 μm (4000–690 cm^{-1}). The detection wavelength can be chosen to respond to a particular compound class for instance, alkenes ($\sim 6 \mu$m), thus making it highly specific. Alternatively a wavelength can be chosen at which many compound classes will absorb, for instance, all compounds with aliphatic C–H bonds absorb at $\sim 3.4 \mu$m. Quantitative studies can be readily carried out since as with UV photometers, absorbance is proportional to concentration.

The major limitation of the IR detector in LC is that the mobile phase must have adequate light transmission at the wavelength of interest. Many of the common HPLC solvents absorb in the infrared and one must be chosen which has a suitable spectral window ($> 30\%$ transmittance) for the application. Solvent opacity is reduced and more spectral windows provided by using flow cells with short pathlengths.

The sensitivity of the IR detector is comparable with the refractive index detectors (5–15 μg ml^{-1}, $\sim 1 \mu$g using CH band), though it has the advantage of being relatively insensitive to fluctuations in temperature or flow; it can also be used in gradient elution work.

Fourier transform infrared spectrophotometers for use with HPLC are now commercially available (Nicolet) and, as with UV photodiode array spectrophotometers, enable the absorbance data to be displayed as a function of wavelength and time.

Electrochemical detectors

Whilst polarography and voltametry are recognised as well established techniques for metal ion estimation, the technique is not specific to metals, but can be readily applied to the detection of organic compounds which are electroactive [22].

Electrochemical detection coupled to LC (ECLC) is now used for the selective monitoring of a wide range of trace organic components (Table 6.1) in a variety of matrices, such as are encountered in environmental, pharmaceutical and clinical studies. The technique is most suitable for the detection of electrooxidizable compounds; monitoring of electroreducible compounds is complicated by the high background currents generated by dissolved oxygen and other reducible

Table 6.1 Compound types sensed by electrochemical detectors

Reduction	Oxidation
Aromatic amines	Ketones
Phenols	Conjugated acids, esters
Oximes	Nitriles and alkenes
Mercaptans	Activated halogens
Peroxides	Nitrates
Carbohydrates	Catecholamines
Alcohols	Aldehydes

trace impurities in the eluent such as metal ions. The development of ECLC continues and has recently been reviewed by Bratin [23].

EC detector cells can be made which contain only two electrodes, a working electrode and a reference electrode. A pre-selected potential equal to or greater than the half-wave potential of interest is applied constantly across the electrodes. As an electrochemically active species passes through the cell it is oxidized or reduced and the current generated in the flow cell continually monitored.

However, two electrode systems give a non-linear response as the voltage drops across the eluent with current flow changes. Thus electrochemical detectors typically employ a three electrode cell. The additional electrode known as the auxiliary or counter electrode, serves to carry any current generated in the flow cell thus enabling the reference electrode to ensure a fixed potential.

EC flow cells are relatively simple in construction. The electrodes are mounted in a suitable matrix (PTFE). The reference electrode is either of Ag/AgCl or a standard calomel type; the auxiliary electrode is made from either glassy carbon or platinum. Successful working electrodes have been formed from a variety of materials, for instance, carbon paste and gold. The former is most commonly used; it has good conductivity, low chemical reactivity, is inexpensive and has a wide range of working potentials (-1.3 to 1.5 V, versus the calomel electrode) [24]. A pulsed amperiometric detector for CHOH bearing species such as carbohydrates and alcohols using a gold working electrode has recently been developed [25]. In addition the potential of a static mercury drop as working electrode has been examined. It has little application in detecting electrooxidizable compounds and its value for monitoring electroreducible compounds depends on the elimination of the background currents, as previously discussed.

A typical electrochemical detector is depicted in Fig. 6.20. Regardless of the electrodes chosen the cells have a number of common design features. The working electrode is located directly opposite the column inlet with the auxiliary electrode located directly opposite and the reference electrode located downstream. This geometric arrangement produces flow cells of very low working or effective or internal volume, typically $1 \mu l$ or less. As electrochemical reaction

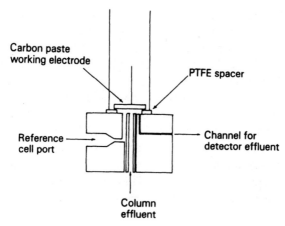

Fig. 6.20 Schematic diagram of a typical electrochemical detector using a glassy carbon working electrode.

occurs decomposition products can be deposited on the electrode surfaces, altering the surface characteristics and causing noise drift and reduced response. Carbon paste electrodes are particularly susceptible, and thus must be frequently recalibrated and may need periodic replenishing. Alternatively the contaminants can be removed by pulsing or stepping the potential to a more positive or negative value as required.

The selectivity and sensitivity of EC detectors can be further enhanced by using pulsed amperiometric techniques where multiple potentials are applied in a repeating sequence. In the pulsed mode, the detector measures current during a short sample interval and thus sensitivity is reduced [26].

As with other polarographic systems ECLC is limited by the fact that the test solution must be electrically conducting and thus ECLC is restricted to reverse-phase systems and to ion-exchange systems where the aqueous phase contains an electrolyte. The detectors are flow sensitive and thus pulse-free constant flow reciprocating pumps must be used. In addition the solvent must be thoroughly degassed as dissolved oxygen interferes with redox reactions occurring in the cell.

Conductivity detectors

Many HPLC applications involve the separation of mixtures of ionic compounds. Consequently a continuous record of the electrical conductivity of the effluent can be used to detect the eluting species. Commercial conductivity meters with flow cells of approximately 1 μl are available for the monitoring of inorganic ions, e.g, Na^+, NH_4^+ and K^+; also anions such as halides, NO_3^- and SO_4^{2-}. The HPLC cell is a scaled-down version of the normal laboratory conductivity cell and consists of a pair of electrodes mounted in a low volume PTFE flow cell. The cell is mounted in an a.c. Wheatstone bridge and thus small changes in the electrical conductivity of the eluant can be detected. For most inorganic and organic species in aqueous media the conductivity is proportional to concentration.

However, the separation of ionic species is usually achieved using aqueous-based eluants containing electrolytes. The high ionic strength of the eluant thus reduces the sensitivity of the conductivity detector and makes it very susceptible to fluctuations in solvent flow and solvent composition and also prevents gradient elution work. This restriction has been overcome by using stripper columns for removal of the background electrolyte (re p. 268) [27]. Alternative systems are being developed and marketed which use only a single column [28], thus avoiding any broadening due to dead volumes, though the reproducibility of these chromatographic units is unclear. The detectors are sensitive to temperature fluctuation and require rigorous thermostatic control.

Radioactivity detectors

Radioactivity detectors are based on standard Geiger counting and scintillation systems, and specifically monitor radio-labelled compounds as they elute from the LC column. Unfortunately the common labels, ^{14}C, ^{3}H, ^{32}P and ^{35}S are low energy β-emitters and hence the sensitivity of these detectors is low. Improvement in detector sensitivity can be achieved either by increasing the volume of the flow cell or by reducing the flow rate to give a longer residence time of the sample in the flow cell. This improvement is at the cost of chromatographic performance and speed of analysis. Stopped-flow monitoring has also been used. Separation and detection of compounds labelled with stronger β-emitters (e.g. ^{131}I, ^{210}Po and ^{125}Sb) has been reported. Radiochemical detection has been used most successfully with large columns and with strongly-retained solutes. Useful discussion of the procedures for optimizing sensitivity and chromatographic efficiency in radiochemical LC monitors has been presented [29].

Refractive index detectors

(a) Principles

For dilute solutions the additivity law of refractive index is applicable. Thus the composite refractive index (N_c) of a solution in the flow cell can be expressed in terms of the refractive index of pure solvent and solute, N_1 and N_2 respectively and the volume of each present, V_1 and V_2 respectively, where the sum of V_1 and V_2 equals the flow cell volume:

$$N_c = N_1 V_1/(V_1 + V_2) + N_2 V_2/(V_1 + V_2) \qquad (6.17)$$

that is:

$$N_c = (N_1 V_1 + N_2 V_2)/(V_1 + V_2) \qquad (6.18)$$

If solvent only is present in the flow cell then from examination of equation (6.18) it can be seen that the refractive index is equal to N_1.

Refractometers, irrespective of design, are differential monitors and hence the signal (S) resulting from presence of solute in the flow cell may be expressed as:

$$S = N_c - N_1 \tag{6.19}$$

N_1 may be expressed as follows:

$$N_1 = N_1(V_1 + V_2)/(V_1 + V_2) \tag{6.20}$$

Substituting for N_c and N_1 in equation (6.19):

$$S = [V_2/(V_1 + V_2)](N_2 - N_1) \tag{6.21}$$

Therefore:

$$S \sim c(N_2 - N_1) \tag{6.22}$$

where c is the concentration of solute. Thus for a given solvent the detector signal is proportional to concentration.

A consequence of using a bulk property for detection is that this property of the solvent must be controlled very closely; the refractive index of the eluent is sensitive to fluctuations in pressure, temperature and composition. Whilst the pressure and composition can be controlled using pulse dampeners and reciprocating pumps, the limits of sensitivity and stability of the RI detector are determined by temperature. For accepted noise levels the temperature must be controlled to ± 0.0001 K. Fluctuations in the RI caused by temperature and noise changes are compensated for by use of a reference cell.

However, refractometers, despite the above disadvantages, most closely approach the ideal of a universal detector in that most compounds modify the refractive index to some extent. Both negative and positive changes in the solvent RI can be detected and recorded using integrators capable of processing positive and negative signals.

(b) Fresnel refractometer

The refractometer shown (Fig. 6.21) is based on Fresnel's Law, which states that the fraction of light reflected at a glass-liquid interface varies with the angle of incidence and the refractive index of the liquid. The beams produced by the source and collimating lens are focused on to the reference and sample prism/liquid interfaces. The light is then refracted through the liquid in the cell, reflected off the backing surface and passed through the liquid/prism interface on to the detection system. With mobile phase in both cells the beams are refracted equally and light beams of equal energy fall on the dual element photodetector. With analyte in the sample cell the light beams are refracted to differing extents and different amounts of radiation fall on the photodetector.

The disadvantages of this system are: (a) two prisms are required to cover the range of RI of solvent encountered (1.31–1.55); (b) small volume cells (5 μl) help enhance sensitivity; however the limited sensitivity ($\times$ 1000 less than UV) and stability are the principal limits to the universal application of this technique.

(c) Deflection refractometer

In the deflection refractometer light from the source is collimated by the lens and

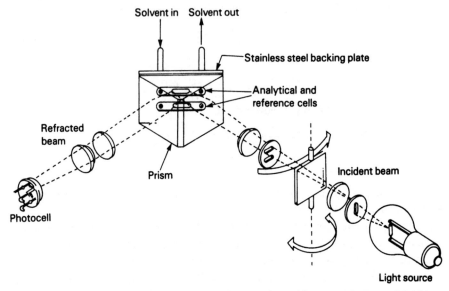

Fig. 6.21   A Fresnel prism RI detector. (Reproduced by permission of Perkin-Elmer Ltd.).

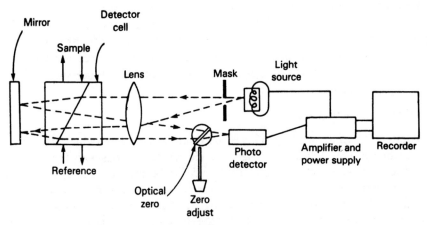

Fig. 6.22   Deflection refractometer detector (Reproduced by permission of Waters).

falls on the detector cell, which consists of sample and reference sections separated by a dividing plate (Fig. 6.22). As the incident light passes through the cell it is refracted, reflected and refracted again before passing through the lens and on to the photodetector. The signal produced is proportional to the position at which the beam strikes the detector which itself is dependent upon the refractive index within the sample compartment. Though larger flow cells are used a single flow cell is adequate for the normal range of applications.

(d) Shearing interferometer

In a shearing interferometer radiation of known wavelength (546 nm) is split into two beams of equal intensity by the beam splitter. These beams are then focused by the lenses and pass through the reference and sample cells (Fig. 6.23). (Typical sample flow cell volume is $5 \mu l$ with a 3.2 nm pathlength.) The beams are then focused on to a second beam splitter, which corrects the wavefronts so that the beams are in phase and interfere. When solvent is present in both sample and reference cells constructive interference occurs. However, if solute is present in the sample compartment, the sample beam has a different optical pathlength, which can lead to destructive interference when the sample and reference beams interact after the second beam splitter, since the beams are then out of phase. A relatively long wavelength is chosen as this provides a greater linear working range.

The advantages and disadvantages of refractive index detectors can be summed up as follows:

1. excellent versatility and detector of choice for a wide range of sample types, for instance carbohydrates, sugars and gel permeation work;
2. moderate sensitivity – to optimize the sensitivity, the refractive index increment between solute and solvent should be maximized. However, even under the optimum conditions, the sensitivity of RI detectors, defined as being equal to the noise level, is 10^{-7} riu, equivalent to ~ 1 ppm of sample in the eluent, approximately a factor of 10^3 less than UV photometers;
3. generally not useful for trace analysis;
4. sensitive to small temperature fluctuations – the temperature coefficient of the refractive index is 1×10^{-4} riu/$^\circ$C;
5. accurate temperature control is required; however, inclusion of heat exchangers increases the dead volume which causes band broadening and limits column efficiency;
6. difficult to use with gradient elution because of the inability to match the refractive indexes of the sample and reference streams;
7. the detectors are non-destructive.

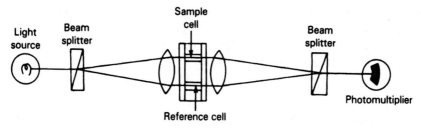

Fig. 6.23 Shearing interferometric refractometer detector (Reproduced by permission of Optilab).

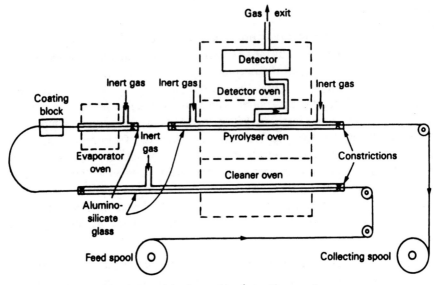

Fig. 6.24   Moving wire detection system.

Desolvation/transport detectors

The principle of transport detectors, typified by the moving wire detector (Fig. 6.24), is based on the concept of physically separating the solvent, which is necessarily volatile, from the involatile solute. The transport wire is passed through a coating block where eluant from the column is applied. The solvent is then evaporated, and the wire plus solute then passes to a pyrolysis or combustion unit. The pyrolysis unit, at approximately 800° C, is purged with nitrogen gas and the gaseous products from the unit passed directly to a flame ionization detector (FID). In the alternative combustion system, oxygen was used as the auxiliary purge gas. The sample is oxidized to carbon dioxide in the combustion chamber. The resultant gases are then passed to an auxiliary reactor, mixed with H_2 and passed over a nickel catalyst. The carbon dioxide is thus converted to methane, which is then passed to the FID (Fig. 6.24) for detection and quantitation. The transport detector is ideal for most gradient elution applications, the major limitation being those systems which use involatile buffers. The full potential of the FID cannot be realised due to the deficiencies of the transport system. The overall detector response is dependent on temperature stability and on the coating procedure which is related to both viscosity and surface tension of the solvent and sample.

Electron capture detector (ECD)

The specificity of the ECD detector has been exploited by coupling to HPLC *via a* transport wire system [30], for instance in the analysis of pesticide residues [31]. Improved sensitivity, stability and performance has been achieved by vaporizing the eluent and passing it directly into the ECD [32]. Though not as sensitive as the GC–ECD system, it is nevertheless for specific applications, considerably more sensitive than other available LC detectors. While gradient elution techniques have been reported, the system is restricted to solvents which are non-electron-capturing. The solvents must be thoroughly degassed prior to use by purging with high purity gas (argon or nitrogen) to remove oxygen.

Mass spectrometric detection

The success of coupling GC with mass spectometry detection provided the impetus for extending this combination technique to liquid chromatography. The attractions of such a system are: (a) aids identification of compounds; (b) single ion monitoring can improve overall sensitivity and selectivity; (c) use of different ionizing processes may provide additional information on the molecular structure of the compounds.

For LC/MS to become a reality an interface had to be designed which was capable of providing a vapour sample feed consistent with the vacuum requirements of the mass spectrometer ion source and of volatilizing the sample without decomposition. Various enrichment interfaces have been developed such as the molecular jet, vacuum nebulizing and the direct liquid introduction inlet systems. The latter, also referred to as the continuous-belt interface, has been the most successful at the time of writing. A diagram of a typical commercial moving belt interface is shown in Fig. 6.25, and was first developed by McFadden [33]. In this system the column effluent is introduced directly on to a polyimide or stainless steel belt (which minimizes peak distortion) and is then passed under an infrared heater to evaporate the solvent. The infrared reflector is especially effective for polar solvents such as methanol and acetonitrile. Residual solvent is

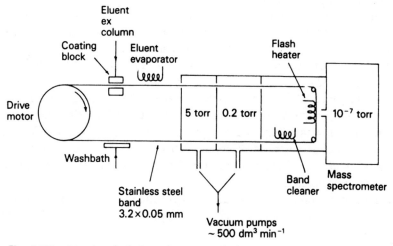

Fig. 6.25   Moving-belt interface coupled to mass spectrometer.

removed by passage through two vacuum lock chambers which also serve to protect the high vacuum of the mass spectrometer. The sample is then flash vaporized at the source of inlet, to minimize decomposition and the volatilized sample is drawn into the ion chamber. Problems are still encountered in this system with aqueous-rich eluants due to the formation of beads of solvent on the belt; also, in reversed-phase systems only a portion of the eluant can be handled by the interface, which reduces the sensitivity.

Recent studies linking microbore columns to mass spectrometry detection indicate considerable potential. Microbore columns require eluant delivery rates of only $10 \mu l \, min^{-1}$, thus enabling direct feed of the eluant to the mass spectrometer without interfacing. Such a design has the additional advantages that extra-column dead volume and peak dispersion are minimized, hence ensuring good retention of chromatographic efficiency and resolution. The utility of microbore LC/MS has been demonstrated with both isocratic and gradient elution techniques though the remaining restraint is that inorganic salts must be absent from the eluant.

In practice the system illustrated achieves an enrichment of 10^5 of solute over solvent and can detect solute concentration of $10^{-9} \, gs^{-1}$ by monitoring production of a single ion peak at a fixed m/e ratio. The data are capable of qualitative as well as quantitative interpretation.

Flame detectors

Various studies have explored the possibilities of interfacing HPLC to a range of selective detectors routinely used in GC, for instance, electron capture, flame photometric, thermionic and microwave induced plasma detectors. These detectors offer extreme selectivity since only those compounds containing the requisite heteroatom or functional group, will be detected; co-eluting solutes without the appropriate structural property do not respond.

With conventional HPLC direct introduction of the eluent into the flame proved impractical since the flow rates typically encountered (1 ml min^{-1}) cause severe disturbance of the flame/plasma chemistry. Coupling of these detectors with transport devices for solvent removal was not entirely successful and had severe limitations [34–36].

However, interest in coupling these detectors with HPLC has revived and gained a fesh impetus with the establishment of microcolumn (low dispersive) LC. The reduced flow rates required by these systems (10 μl) makes possible the direct introduction of nebulized microcolumn effluent into the detector. Flow rates in excess of $10 \mu l \, min^{-1}$ have been reported which have no detrimental effect on the detector performance.

Flame ionization [12], flame emission [37] and thermionic emission detectors [38] have been developed which are compatible with microcolumn HPLC systems.

Other detectors

The above discussion has been concerned with those detectors most commonly employed in routine HPLC analysis. Many other detectors have been developed to monitor specific solute properties in column effluents and new detection systems continue to be reported in the literature. The interested reader is directed to the reviews of Hein [39] and McKinley [40] for a more detailed discussion of detector types employed in HPLC.

Some of these less-used systems have limited applications in specific areas and combine HPLC with, for instance chemiluminescence techniques [41], viscometry [42] and optical activity measurement [43], piezoelectric crystals for mass scanning [44], inductively coupled organic plasma [45, 46], photoacoustic monitors [47], nuclear magnetic resonance [48] and photoconductivity measurement [49].

Sample Derivatization

Derivatization of a sample is undertaken principally for two reasons. First, there is no detector for HPLC that has universally high sensitivity for all solutes; hence, the use of a suitable chemical transformation of the solute can greatly extend the sensitivity and versatility of a selective detector. Second, sample derivatization may be undertaken to enhance the detector response to sample bands relative to overlapping bands of no analytical interest. These reactions can be carried out either before or after the passage of solute through the column.

An example of pre-column derivatization, in order to enhance the spectrophotometric response of the sample is the reaction between naphthacyl bromide, the derivatizing agent, and carboxylic acids (Fig. 6.26). The ester product contains a chromophore unit and the sample derivatives are now able to absorb ultraviolet radiation.

An example of post-column derivatization is the reaction of amino acids with ninhydrin; again a chromophoric unit is present in the sample derivatives. The replacement of ninhydrin by *o*-phthalaldehyde [50] as the derivatizing agent introduces a fluorescent group into the molecule and thus enables the highly sensitive fluorescent detector to be employed.

There are several factors to consider before choosing either pre- or post-column derivatization. The former can be carried out manually, off-line from the

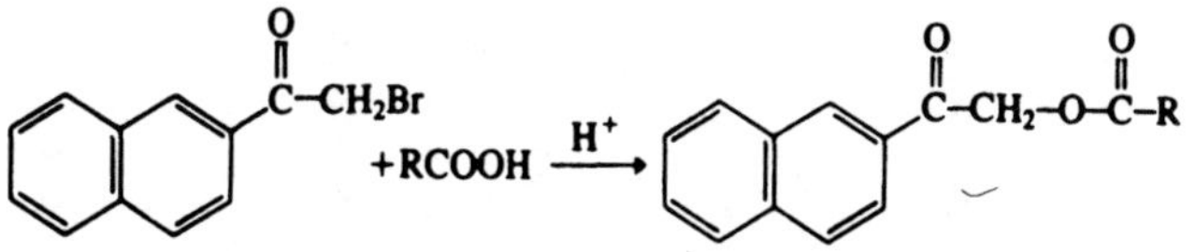

Fig. 6.26 Derivatization of carboxylic acids with naphthacyl bromide.

Table 6.2 Characteristics of chromatographic detectors

	Response	Detection limit for sample	Flow sensitive	Temperature sensitive	Useful with gradient	Favourable samples	Reference
UV (Absorbance)	S	2×10^{-10} g cm^{-3}	No	Low	Yes	Conjugated aromatics and heterocyclic compounds	54
Photo-Diode (Absorbance)	S	$> 2 \times 10^{-10}$	No	Low	Yes		17
Fluorescence	S	$\sim 10^{-12}$	No	Low	Yes	Vitamins and steroids	55
Infrared (Absorbance)	S	10^{-6}	No	Low	Yes	Carbonyl and aliphatic	56
FTIR (Absorbance)	S		No	Low	Yes		57
Reflactive Index (RIU)	G	5×10^{-7}	No	$\pm 10^{-4}\,^\circ$C	No	Universal	58
Conductometric (μmho)	S	10^{-8}	Yes	$\pm 1\,^\circ$C	No	Ionic substances	59
Electrochemical (μamps)	S	10^{-12}	Yes	$\pm 1\,^\circ$C	No	Catecholamines electroactive	25
Radioactivity	S	50 cpm ^{14}C cm^{-3}	No	Negligible	Yes	Labelled compounds	29
Transport FID (amp)	G	5×10^{-7}	No	No	Yes	Oxidizable hydrocarbons	60
Transport ECD (amp)	S	10^{-11}	No	No	Yes	Chlorinated insecticides	36
Transport MS (amps)	S	1×10^{-9} g s^{-1}	No	No	Yes	Universal	61

Adapted from Snyder, L. R. and Kirkland, J. J. (1979) *Intro to Modern Liquid Chromatography*, 2nd edn, Wiley-Science, New York.

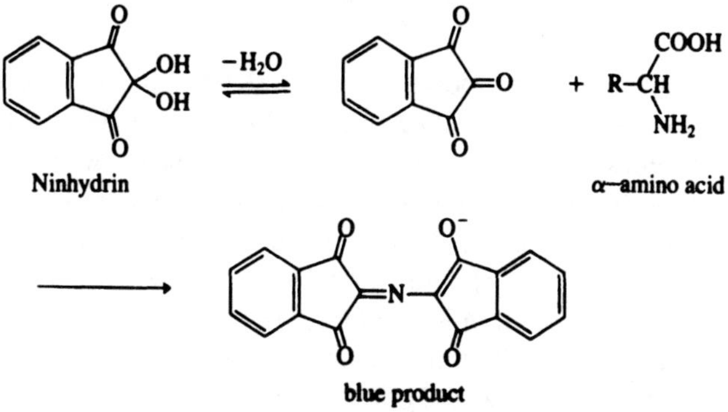

Fig. 6.27   Derivatization of amino acids with ninhydrin.

system and places little restriction on the choice of reagents, solvents, length of reaction time, etc., all of which are important restrictions in post-column applications. The reaction, however, may give rise to more than one product which can subsequently complicate the chromatogram. For quantitative work, the extent of the reaction must be precise and reproducible for different sample concentrations.

Post-column derivatization techniques, though imposing restrictions on the reagents and solvents which can be used have the advantages that it may be readily incorporated as part of a fully automated system and thus will not complicate the chromatography even if the reaction yields more than one product. However a major consideration is the extra-column effects which can impair the overall resolution of the LC system. For post-column reactors it is not essential that the derivatization is carried out to completion, only that the extent of reaction is reproducible.

Non-chemical derivatization has been employed for the detection of photo-ionizable species. The effluent is passed through a quartz tube where it is irradiated with UV and the photoionized products passed to the conductivity detector [51, 52]. Krull has reported the detection of the active components, (typically organonitro-derivatives) in a large number of explosives and drugs by in situ LC photolytic decomposition [53].

In conclusion, it must be emphasised that each reactor must be tailored to its particular application. For every post-column reaction there will be a set of optimum operating parameters such as temperature, concentration of reagent, flow rate of reagent, reaction time, etc. These variables have to be studied in detail in order to optimize the configuration and operating conditions of the reactor. Thus each final reactor design will tend to be specific for a particular application, and it may well be limited to a small range of eluent flow rates and compositions.

6.5 COLUMN PACKINGS AND STATIONARY PHASES FOR LC

The majority of packings for modern LC are based on microporous particles of varying size, shape and porosity. The surface of these particles can be modified subsequently by either physical or chemical means to afford access to any of the classical modes of chromatography. The most common material used is silica, as it can withstand the relatively high pressures in use and is available with large surface area $(200–300 \, \text{m}^2 \, \text{g}^{-1})$ and small particle size. Other microporous packing materials based on alumina and ion-exchange materials are also in use.

Microporous particles $(5–10 \, \mu\text{m})$ give columns that are ten times as efficient as porous layer bead or pellicular $(40 \, \mu\text{m})$ packings. Whilst modern LC is based almost exclusively on microporous packing materials it is of interest to relate the advances in particle design to the attempts to eliminate the deleterious effects on column performance since the latter as expressed by H is related to experimental variables, such as the particle size (dp), the nominal stationary phase thickness (d) and the mobile phase velocity (u) (see equation (6.16)).

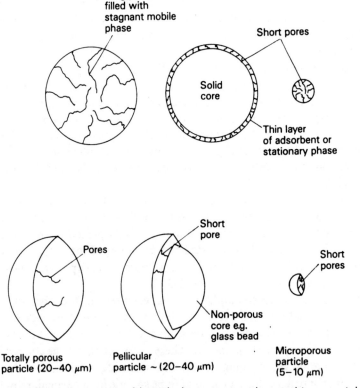

Fig. 6.28   Characteristics of liquid chromatography packing particles.

Totally porous beads

Initially packing materials were based on porous beads, usually silica or alumina, of 20–40 μm particle size; they gave poor column efficiencies as the particles were totally porous and had large volumes of associated stagnant mobile phase. This led to the A and C terms being substantial and dominant in the expression for H which effectively reduced to:

$$H \sim Au^{0.33} + Cu \qquad (6.23)$$

thus illustrating the importance of good column packing procedures on chromatographic performance.

Pellicular packings

Pellicular packings, also known as porous-layer beads or controlled surface porosity supports (that is, solid impervious beads of high mechanical strength), have the impervious core constructed from materials such as stainless steel, glass, silica, alumina or ion-exchange materials. The chromatographically active layer on the surface is commonly silica, alumina, an ion-exchange material or a cellulose derivative. An important advantage of the solid impervious core was that it did not swell when wetted and could withstand high inlet pressures without deformation. The shallow pore structure led to a marked improvement in the column performance due principally to the virtual elimination of the stagnant mobile phase and the associated increased rate of mass transfer between the mobile phase and porous layer; hence the van Deemter equation reduces to:

$$H \sim Au^{0.33} + B/u + Du \qquad (6.24)$$

The large particle size allows H to be further approximated to:

$$H \sim Au^{0.33} \qquad (6.25)$$

A major disadvantage of pellicular packings is the low surface area associated with the shallow pores which limits sample capacity.

Microporous particles

The use of microporous particles of 5–10 μm ushered in the era of genuine high performance liquid chromatography. Because of the small particle size stagnant mobile phase mass transfer effects are minimized as with pellicular packings whilst multipath (H_f) and mobile phase–mass transfer effects ($H_{em'}$) being due to dp and dp^2 respectively are substantially reduced.

A further advantage of these columns is afforded by the large surface area with concomitant increase in sample capacity. The totally porous microparticle is generally a high surface area, small porosity silica gel or alumina.

Angular silicas such as Partisil and Lichrosorb are prepared by the reaction of sodium silicate with hydrochloric acid. Spherical particles e.g. Spherisorb are synthesized by the hydrolytic polycondensation of polyethoxysilane. These synthetic procedures can be tailored to the production of microporous particles of size (3–10 μm), of controlled porosity (6–10 nm) and specific surface area (200–400 m^2 g^{-1}). Packings based on these particles give a tenfold increase in column performance thus allowing shorter columns to be used, giving faster separations and requiring smaller operating pressures.

6.6 ADSORPTION CHROMATOGRAPHY

Silica gel has a highly active surface layer of randomly distributed silanol groups. The mechanism of adsorption is thus the interaction of the surface silanol groups with any polar functions which may be present in the solute molecules, e.g. alcohols, amines, ketones and carboxylic acids.

As in classical LC, the method of preparation and activation of the packing material must be consistent in order to obtain reproducible separations for a given application. The main method of activation involves dehydration. Associated with the silanol surface groups is water of hydration which may be classified as belonging to one of three types:

1. loosely bound water easily removed by heating or by solvent extraction;
2. strongly held water;
3. water present as OH in adjacent silanol groups, which can be removed by strong heating.

Removal of water in the first two cases is reversible; in the last irreversible.

The surfaces of narrow-pore silicas are covered mainly by hydrogen-bonded hydroxyl groups, while the surfaces of wide-pore silicas are covered mainly with isolated hydroxyl groups. In wide-pore silicas, heating at 110°C produces siloxane groups from adjacent silanols (Fig. 6.29). The siloxanes are weak absorbent sites and are not important chromatographically. The reaction is

Fig. 6.29   Wide pore silicas.

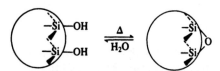

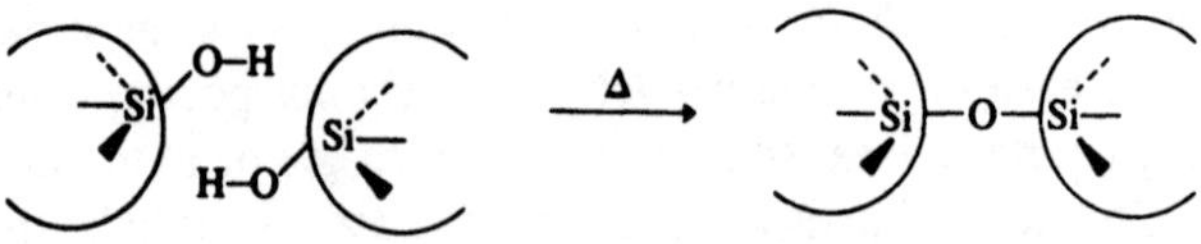

Fig. 6.30   Narrow pore silicas.

reversible by heating in the presence of water. In narrow-pore silicas water is eliminated by reaction between hydroxyl groups on adjacent sites (Fig. 6.30). No reverse reaction is possible and there is an effective loss of surface area due to the cross-linking effect.

The vast majority of silicas used in HPLC applications today are of the totally porous spherical and irregular type, with surface areas of the order of 200–500 $m^2 g^{-1}$ and a range of pore sizes of 4–400 nm. For analytical scale work 5 μm or 10 μm particle size is used: preparative separations, operated in the overload mode, use larger particle size, 40–60 μm, with larger surface areas 500–800 $m^2 g^{-1}$.

The eluant pH is restricted to between 3 and 8 pH units to avoid damage to the silica matrix. This deleterious effect can be minimized by passing the eluant through a pre-column inserted between pump and injector, thus pre-saturating the eluant with silica.

Almost all the available silicas whether spherical or irregular are very similar in terms of separation efficiency and retentive properties.

Solvent systems

A variety of solvent systems can be used for adsorption chromatography, ranging from non-polar to polar. When a mixed solvent system is used the polar component will be adsorbed on to the surface and will modify the adsorptive capacity of the packing material. Examples of polar modifiers are butyl chloride, dioxane and ethyl acetate. During the chromatographic process, solute molecules may displace the polar modifier and then subsequently be displaced themselves, or they may not interact with the silanol layer as such, but with the adsorbed layer. In the situation where the adsorbed layer is strongly held it is difficult to distinguish between adsorption and partition chromatography. Adsorption chromatography functions best for the separation of non-polar or moderately polar compounds using moderately polar eluants. It does not function well with high polarity eluants.

Compounds with polar substituents can interact with the active surface silanol groups. The strength of the adsorption is proportional to the polarity of the compound and so liquid–solid chromatography (LSC) is best used for the separation of mixtures into functional group classes. In addition, because of the sterically controlled interactions between adsorbent surface layer and the sample molecules LSC can also provide for the separation of structural isomers, including polyfunctional isomeric compounds. LSC is not suitable for the separation of compounds only sparingly soluble in the eluant, such as polyaromatics, fats and oils, nor for the separation of the members of a homologous series. It is the preferred mode for preparative scale analysis because of the higher sample capacity and greater pH stability. Due to the difficulty in achieving rapid equilibration with solvents containing polar modifiers, gradient elution work is to be avoided with adsorption chromatography.

6.7 LIQUID–LIQUID PARTITION CHROMATOGRAPHY (LLC)

Classical liquid-liquid chromatography (LLC) differs little from the traditional column methods. LLC systems consist of a mobile phase and a stationary phase which is held on the support by adsorption. The column materials are commonly prepared using the solvent evaporation technique developed for GC. In order to avoid solvent stripping of the stationary phase, it is necessary for the eluent to be saturated with the stationary phase component. Though many of the applications of LLC are now carried out more conveniently using bonded phase techniques (BPC) the method has several advantages which make it an important adjunct to the other modes of column chromatography. The major benefits derive from the ease of renewal of the stationary phase, the degree of selectivity which can be achieved (as a wide range of liquids can be selected for the stationary phase) and the reproducibility of the chromatography.

LLC systems can be classified as either normal or reverse-phase. The latter are more stable because of the strong bonding that exists between the stationary phase and the support material. However, immiscible pair systems, such as isopropanol/hexane, suffer the disadvantage that sample components tend to have partition coefficients which are either very small or very large with little differentiation.

Normal phase systems, such as squalane/water/alcohol, require the eluent to be saturated with the squalane stationary phase to avoid solvent stripping; however the binding forces are so weak that shearing occurs at high pressures. The other main disadvantages associated with LLC are that as the eluent must be saturated with the stationary phase, gradient elution techniques cannot be used and to maintain the required stationary phase loading the temperature must be controlled to $\pm 0.5\,K$.

Stationary phase	Mobile phase	Sample	Ref.
Cyanoethylsilicone	Water	Coumarins	62
Squalane	Water/Acetonitrile	Hydrocarbons	62
$\beta\beta'$-Oxydipropanitrile	Hexane	Phenols	63

6.8 CHEMICALLY-BONDED STATIONARY PHASES (BP) FOR HPLC

The severe restrictions on classical liquid-liquid partition chromatography with regard to solvent stripping of the stationary phase from the analytical column and the incompatibility with gradient elution techniques, led to the development of a range of chemically-bonded stationary phases. Bonded-phase chromatography as practised in its various forms is the most widely used technique for the following reasons:

1. polar, nonionic, ionic and ionizable molecules can be effectively chromatographed using a single column and mobile phase;
2. it permits a wider choice of eluent;
3. the predominant eluent is water-based with organic modifiers such as methanol and acetonitrile which are all readily available and inexpensive;
4. gradient elution techniques can be used without fear of stripping the stationary phase;
5. no restriction on solvent inlet pressure.

The principal limitation is in the range of pH of the eluent used as cleavage or hydrolysis of the stationary phase can occur; similar restrictions apply to certain oxidizing solutions. Almost all commercially available bonded materials use silica gel as the support. The preparation of the bonded materials involves the derivatization of the surface silanol groups. The bonded phases available may be classified as follows:

1. hydrocarbon groups, such as octadecyl ($C_{18}H_{37}$), but also groups with shorter chain lengths such as C_1, C_2, C_8;
2. polar groups such as amino and cyanopropyl, ethers and glycols;
3. ion-exchange groups such as sulphonic acid, amino and quaternary ammonium.

6.8.1 Synthesis of bonded phase materials

The synthetic methods used for the preparation of bonded phase materials are illustrated in Fig. 6.31. One of the first reported bonded phases [64], the alkoxy silanes (1) also referred to as silicate esters, was prepared by the direct esterification of silanol groups with alcohols. The major disadvantage of this packing material was its limited hydrolytic stability, as it is readily hydrolyzed by aqueous alcohol eluents.

Other syntheses were developed leading to the linkage of stationary phases via Si–C and Si–N bonds. The common step in these reaction sequences was the chlorination of the silanol groups using thionyl chloride (2). Organic groups can then be bonded directly to the surface on reaction with Grignard or organolithium derivatives (3). Alternatively, reaction of the chlorosilane with amines gives alkylaminosilane-linked bonded phases (4). While Si–C bonds have good hydrolytic stability, the reaction and handling of organometallic reagents with silica gel is difficult and leads to incomplete coverage and deposition of hydrolyzed reagent. The Si–N bonds have limited hydrolytic stability and are restricted to aqueous eluants in the pH 4–8 range.

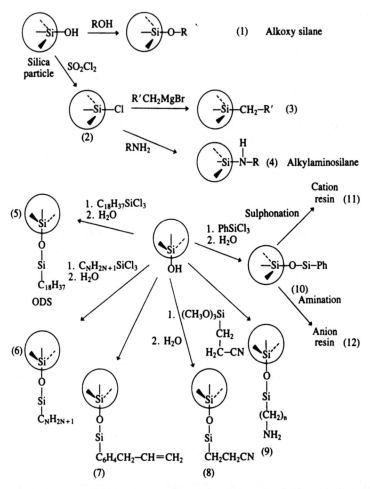

Fig. 6.31   Reaction schemes for preparation of chemically-bonded stationary phases.

The most widely used bonded-phase materials are those derived from the reaction of the surface silanol groups with organochlorosilanes, which leads to linkage of the stationary phase to the support *via* a siloxane (Si–O–Si) bond. For octadecylsilane (ODS, $C_{18}H_{37}Si–$) bonded phases the reagent used is octade-cyltrichlorosilane. This reaction is followed by hydrolysis of the residual chlorines and the resulting material is a silica base with a coating of ODS groups on the surface (5). Residual silanol groups cause tailing and these groups can be blocked or 'capped' using trimethylsilyl chloride. There is a trend towards using dense monolayers of monofunctional dimethylsilanes.

A typically commercial material will have 50–70% of the available sites derivatized. The advantage of these supports is the stability of the siloxane

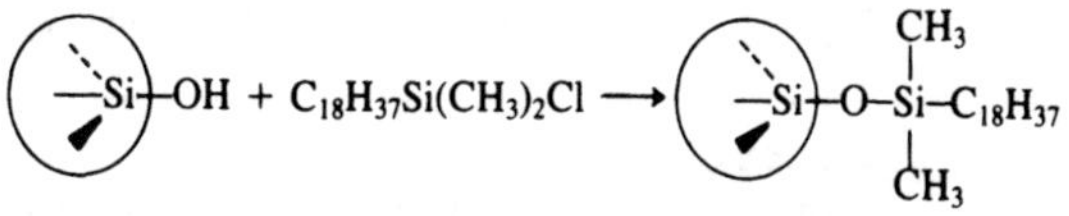

Fig. 6.32   Reaction of silica with monofunctional dimethylsilanes.

Table 6.3   Commercially available reverse-phase materials

Commercial name	Chain length	Particle size (microns)	Percentage loading
μ-Bondapak	C_{18}	10	10
Hypersil ODS	C_{18}	5	10
Lichrosorb	C_{18}	10	18.5
Lichrosphere	C_{18}	5	20
Nucleosil	C_{18}	5, 7, 10, 30	16
Partisil ODS I	C_{18}	10	5
II		10	15
III		5, 10	10
Spherisorb ODS	C_{18}	5, 10	7
ODS2		5	12
Techsil	C_{18}	5, 10	4
Hypersil MOS	C_8	5	6.5
Lichrosorb	C_8	7	11.5
Lichrosphere	C_8	5	12
Nucleosil	C_8	5, 7, 10	10.5
Spherisorb	C_8	5	6
Techsil	C_8	5, 10	6
Spherisorb	C_6	5	5
Spherisorb	C_2	5	2.2
Hypersil SAS	C_1	5	2.6

(Adapted with permission of HPLC Technology Ltd.)

linkages to column inlet pressures and hydrolysis, thus allowing use of solvents at 6000 psi in the pH range 2.0–8.5.

Using other trichlorosilane derivatives as reactants, a variety of functional groups can be bonded to the silica support, for instance alkyl C_8 ($-O-Si-C_7H_{14}CH_3$), C_2 and C_1 (6), alkenephenyl($-O-Si-C_6H_4CH_2-CH=CH_2$) (7), cyanoethyl ($-O-Si-CH_2-CH_2-CN$) (8), aminoalkyl ($-O-Si-(CH_2)_n NH_2$) (9) and phenyl ($-O-Si-Ph$) (10). Sulphonation and amination of phenylalkyl groups can be carried out, giving materials with ion-exchange capability. Ionogenic groups can also be introduced into the alkenephenyl BP by suitable chemical modification. The above are the common chemically-bonded stationary phases, which are marketed under a variety of trade names. The phases commercially available and their differences in alkyl chain length, percentage carbon loading and particle shape are indicated in Tables 6.3 and 6.4.

Table 6.4   Commercially available packing materials

Commercial name	Functional group	Particle size (microns)	Comment
μ-Bondapak	Phenyl	10	
Hypersil		5	5% loading (C)
Nucleosil		7	
Spherisorb		5	2.5% loading (C)
μ-Bondapak	Amino	10	
Hypersil		5	2.2% loading (C)
Lichrosorb		5, 7, 10	250 m^2 g^{-1} surface area
Nucleosil	Amino	5, 10	
	Diamino	5, 10	Dimethylamino groups
Spherisorb	Animo	5	
Techsil		5, 10	500 m^2 g^{-1} surface area
μ-Bondapak	Nitrile	10	9% CN loading
Hypersil CPS		5	4% C loading
Lichrosorb		5, 7, 10	
Nucleosil		5, 10	
Spherisorb		5	
Vydac		10	
Nucleosil	Nitro	5, 10	
Techsil	Nitro	5, 10	
Lichrosorb	Diol	5, 7, 10	250 m^2 g^{-1} surface area
Nucleosil	Diol	7	Alcoholic OH group

(Adapted with permission of HPLC Technology Ltd.)

In reverse-phase chromatography retention times increase with increase in chain length of the bonded phase. Longer solute retention generally provides for enhanced resolution and thus varying the chain lengths of the bonded phase is a further aid to optimizing the resolution.

The percentage carbon loading is not as important a consideration as is the percentage coverage of the silica. Residual silanol groups and their adsorption effects can cause tailing of the peak. It is thus preferable to use a reverse phase packing with a high percentage coverage, or one in which the residual silanol groups have been treated with TMS, a procedure referred to as end-capping.

As to the choice of long or short alkyl chain, generally polar solutes are better separated on short-chain alkyl phases, and non-polar on long-chain alkyl phases. Variation in selectivity between the same packings of different manufacturers is generally due to differences in percentage carbon loading and the degree of end-capping. Of the other stationary phases the amino phases have been used extensively to separate sugars and peptides; the nitrile phase has found application in the separation of porphyrins. An important consideration in the use of polar BP materials is an awareness of the reactivity of the terminal functional group; for example aminoalkyl BP should not be used for the chromatography of carbonyl compounds because of possible condensation reactions and formation of Schiff's bases.

The number of stationary phases encountered in HPLC is small as the selectivity can be readily adjusted by variation in the nature and strength of the eluent. This contrasts with the situation in GC, where the selectivity can only be adjusted either by altering the stationary phase, the support or the column temperature. The plate efficiency of bonded-phase materials is at least equal to that of the support materials, while there is evidence to suggest that they have substantially higher load capacities. The mechanism of solute retention on bonded-phase materials is not fully understood; however, it is satisfactory to consider the organobonded layer as a thin liquid film since this allows reasonable prediction of retention behaviour. The solvent commonly employed in normal phase BPC, i.e with polar-bonded stationary phases, such as cyanopropyl, are hydrocarbons containing small amounts of a polar solvent. Typical polar eluents in order of decreasing solvent strength are methanol, chloroform, methylene chloride and isopropylether. The resolution is systematically investigated by varying the solvent strength.

In reverse phase BPC, water is used as the base solvent; the eluent strength is adjusted by using organic modifiers most commonly methanol and acetonitrile. The resolution is optimized as before by modifying the capacity factors through changes in the solvent strength. Because of the similarities in the proton donor and acceptor properties between methanol and water, substantial quantities of the former are required before it modifies the behaviour of water. Acetonitrile, on the other hand, has a much more pronounced effect at lower concentrations due to the marked difference in solvent properties, so that a change in organic modifier from methanol to acetonitrile can lead to a variation in the order of elution of sample components.

Highly polar and ionizable molecules such as acids have such a high affinity for aqueous eluents that they wash through the column without being retained at all by the packing material. Modifications, however, can be made to the technique so that even highly dissociated molecules can be successfully chromatographed by BPC. This has been achieved by using ODS-silica materials with aqueous buffer solutions containing no organic modifier. Solute retention is influenced by eluent pH, which controls the degree of dissociation of the solute and hence its partition between the bonded organo-phase and the aqueous mobile phase. For effective chromatography the eluent pH should be greater than the pK_a of the ionizable component. Non-ionizable compounds show little change in retention with variation of pH.

The ion suppression technique can be used to great effect for the analysis of weak acids or bases. For the analysis of acidic compounds the technique consists of the addition of a small amount of acetic or phosphoric acid to the mobile phase. By reducing the eluent pH dissociation of the sample molecules is suppressed. They thus have decreased affinity for the eluent and are retained to a greater extent by the ODS phase. The range of BPC is considerably extended using techniques such as ionic suppression and this mode of LC using ODS bonded phases finds wide application.

6.9 CHIRAL STATIONARY PHASES

The resolution of optically active compounds is of increasing importance, as in many instances it is only a particular stereoisomer of a compound which is pharmacologically active. The resolution of racemates can be achieved by chemical reaction to form a pair of diastereoisomers which can then be separated by chromatographic or other physical techniques. However, this procedure relies on high purity of the derivatizing agents and is further complicated by the fact that the rates of reaction of the enantiomers are often different which results in formation of diastereoisomers in differing proportions to the enantiomers present in the racemate.

An alternative approach for the direct resolution of enantiomers by HPLC is to use a chiral stationary phase. This technique relies on the formation of transient/temporary diastereoisomers between the sample enantiomers and the chiral stationary phase. Differences in stability between the diastereoisomers is reflected in differences in retention times, the enantiomer forming the less stable complex being eluted first.

A difficulty is that each new class of enantiomeric compound would appear to require a different stationary phase. However, chiral stationary phases have recently been developed which have a number of possible sites for interaction, and which are not limited to a single compound class. For instance, a chiral phase developed by Pirkle [65] $(R)-N-(3,5-dinitrobenzoyl)phenylglycine$ bound to an aminopropyl packing (Fig. 6.33) has been successfully employed to separate alkylcarbonyls, arylacetamides, methylarylacetic acids, phenyl ethylamines and binaphthols. An interesting example of the application of this stationary phase was the separation of the anti-inflammatory drug, ibuprofren after derivatization to its amide (Fig. 6.34).

The growing need to resolve enantiomers in both biological and pharmaceutical studies provides a continuing impetus for the design of chiral stationary phases, a number of which are now commercially available [66].

A number of review articles have been presented [67, 68] most recently by McKerrell [69].

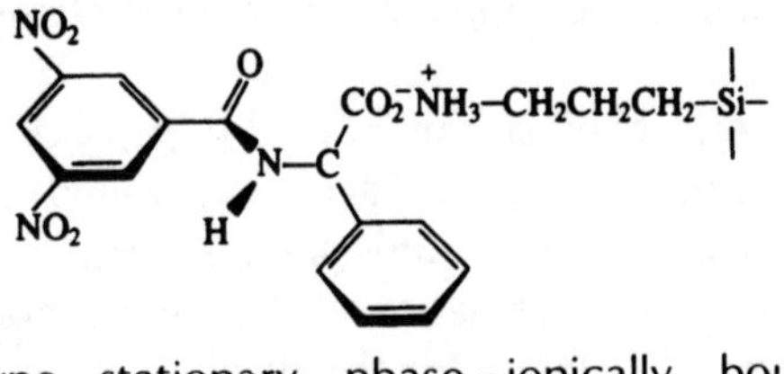

Fig. 6.33   'Pirkle'-type stationary phase—ionically bound (R)-N-(dinitrobenzoyl)-phenylglycine.

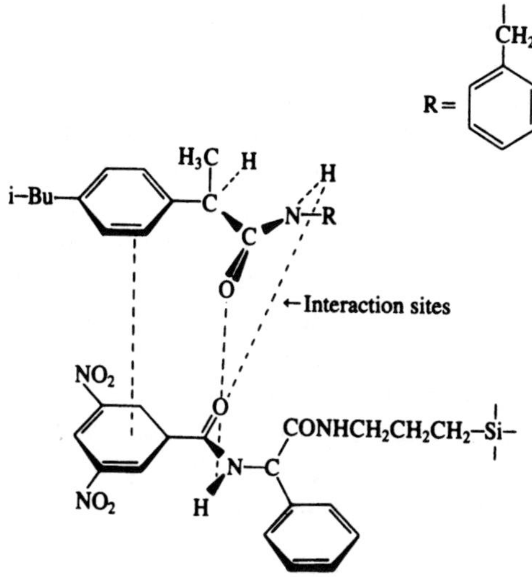

Fig. 6.34 Reaction between chiral stationary phase and amide derivative of (R)-ibuprofen.

6.10 ION-EXCHANGE CHROMATOGRAPHY (IEC)

The primary process of ion-exchange chromatography (IEC) involves adsorption and desorption of ionic species from ionogenic groups located in the packing. IEC was the first of the traditional column techniques to be exploited for modern LC, due principally to the need for the fast routine analysis of amino acids and protein mixtures.

Modern IEC may be used with one of three types of resin/packing:

1. polymeric porous particles;
2. pellicular and superficially porous particles;
3. totally porous particles.

Polymeric porous particles, also referred to as macroporous or macroreticular, are formed from the co-polymerization of styrene–divinylbenzene. The porosity can be modified by altering the degree of cross-linkage though this has an adverse effect on the mechanical strength, the degree of wetting (and hence swelling) and the resin capacity (see Chapter 4). A compromise packing is used which has an intermediate degree of cross-linkage and has small particle size ($\sim 5\,\mu$m). However, these are the least efficient of the ion-exchange materials available due to the slow diffusion of sample species into the lattice. They have limited capacity and are restricted to use with small ions.

Pellicular packings are formed by coating the ion-exchange resin ($\sim 2\,\mu$m) onto an impervious, inert core (30–40 μm). Also falling within this classification are superficially porous particles. These are constructed by first coating the core material with a thin layer of silica microspheres (0.2 μm) and this layer is then coated with the ion-exchanger. The principle disadvantage with these materials is the low exchange capacity. Other polymeric materials used to coat the core material and support the ionogenic groups are cellulose and polydextrans.

Finally, ion-exchange capability can be conferred on packing materials by chemical modification of the existing BP. This involves using in the initial silization reaction a monofunctional organochlorosilane where one of the hydrocarbon moieties contains an alkene functional group (Fig. 6.31). The vinylated silica then undergoes an addition reaction with styrene. Ionogenic groups, quaternary ammonium for anion exchange and sulphonic acid for cation exchange, may then be introduced as discussed previously. These packings are available as 5–10 μm spherical particles. They have good mass transfer properties, can be used at high flow rates and have much improved ion-exchange capacity (0.5–2 meq g^{-1}).

Selectivity and retention in ion-exchange analysis is affected by a number of parameters:

1. the size and charge of the solvated sample ion;
2. the pH of the mobile phase;
3. the total concentration and type of ionic species in the mobile phase;
4. the addition of the organic solvents to the eluent;
5. the column temperature.

These features are similar in nature to those affecting separation in traditional open column ion-exchange and have been discussed in detail elsewhere.

Initial application of ion-exchange to modern LC depends on the analyte having a specific property such as ultraviolet absorbance, fluorescence or radioactivity. As many ion-exchange methods required the presence of complexing agents (EDTA, citrate) and various electrolyte additions to achieve the required resolution, conductivity detectors could not be used without modification of the technique, since this parameter is a universal property of ionic species in solution.

This restriction was overcome through the work of Small et al. [70], who developed a general technique for the removal of background electrolytes. The technique developed utilizes a scrubber column also referred to as a stripper or suppressor column (Fig. 6.35). This secondary column effectively removes ions due to the background electrolyte leaving only the species of analytical interest as the major conducting species in deionized water. For the separation of a mixture of cations the eluent commonly used is a dilute solution of HCl. The analytical column achieves the required separation while the scrubber column, in this instance a quaternary ammonium hydroxide resin, combines with the H$^+$ ions in the eluent and at the same time converts analyte ions to their hydroxides. The eluent then passes directly to a conductivity cell, where the analyte ions can be monitored in a background of deionized water, thus allowing quantitative

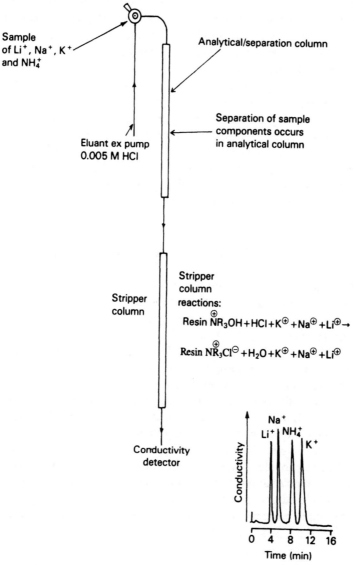

Fig. 6.35 Ion chromatography analysis system.

determination from measurement of peak height or area. This system forms the basis for commerical systems marketed by Dionex.

The scrubber column is continuously regenerated by passing a dilute solution of hydroxide ion over the external wall of the resin, in the opposite direction to the eluent flow. Counter ions are replaced with a common ion e.g. cations are replaced with H^+ ions. This improvement in signal/noise ratio increases the sensitivity of the system. Anion suppression proceeds in an analogous manner with appropriate changes in suppressor column and regenerant used.

The loss in efficiency arising from the dead-volumes introduced by the inclusion of a suppressor column (approximate volume $100 \mu l$) is more than compensated for by the use of a small flow cell and the improved sensitivity and noise reduction achieved by the removal of the background electrolyte.

The column packings used by Dionex are pellicular in nature and are composed of a highly rigid inert divinylbenzene–styrene copolymer core to which is bonded the exchanger which is in the form of a porous latex particle. The core material has a high degree of cross linkage and forms a very rigid substrate. It is very resistant to change in the eluant strength and/or flowrate and shows little swelling or shrinkage of the column bed with change in ionic strength of the eluant. The selectivity of the resin material can be readily changed by modifying the latex in terms of the degree of cross linkage, particle size or functional group. No change is required in the core material.

6.11 ION PAIRING

The utility of ion suppression techniques in the analysis of ionizable molecules by reverse-phase chromatography is limited to samples of weakly basic or acidic compounds. The analysis of stronger acids ($pK_a < 3$) or stronger bases ($pK_b > 8$) would require eluent of pH < 2 or > 8 respectively. Reverse-phase chromatography with chemically bonded stationary phases is, however, restricted to eluent pH > 2 and < 8 for reasons previously discussed.

An attractive alternative to ion-exchange and ion-suppression analysis of ionic samples is the technique commonly referred to as ion-pair chromatography. The pH of the eluent is adjusted in order to encourage ionization of the sample; for acids 7.5 is used and for bases 3.5. The chromatographic retention is altered by including in the mobile phase an ion of opposite charge – the counter-ion. The reagents used to provide counter-ions are similar to those exploited in liquid–liquid extraction procedures. For example, tetrabutylammonium phosphate for acids, and octane sulphonate for bases.

There are three basic models proposed to describe the ion-pair mechanism: ion-pair, ion-exchange and ion-interaction.

Ion-pair

This hypothesis postulates formation of a tightly bound ion-pair of zero charge. The eluant pH is adjusted as previously described and then a counter-ion, which has the opposite charge to that of the compounds to be determined, is added to the sample and forms an ion-pair.

$$HA \rightleftharpoons H^+ + A^- + B^+ \rightleftharpoons A\text{--}B$$
$$\text{ion-pair}$$

The ion-pair is formed in aqueous phase and the retention can be altered by varying the alkyl chain length of the counter-ion [71].

Ion-exchange

This postulates that the lipophilic tail of the counter-ions locates on to the bonded stationary phase, effectively causing the column to behave as an ion-exchanger.

Ion-interaction

This suggestion is based neither on ion-pair nor ion-exchange phenomena, though the lipophilic ions are adsorbed onto the surface but are associated with a primary ion giving an electrical double layer. The analyte then interacts dynamically with this double layer by both electrostatic and van der Waals type forces.

Whatever the model used to describe the ion-pair phenomenon, the technique has gained wide acceptance and application because of the inability of ion-exchange to separate samples containing both ionic and neutral materials and also because of the limitation of ion suppression to the analysis of weak bases and acids and the inability of the latter to cope with ionic materials.

6.12 SIZE EXCLUSION CHROMATOGRAPHY

Size exclusion chromatography (SEC), though an established technique for the separation of macromolecules using open-column systems, met with limited success when applied to modern LC, as many of the commercially available packings did not meet the constraints and instrumental demands of HPLC. Recently (from 1982) a variety of packings have been developed which have led to a spectacular growth in the HPLC analysis of macromolecular samples, such as polydisperse polymer samples and biological materials, such as proteins and carbohydrates.

Column packings

Support materials may be subdivided into two classes: (a) semi-rigid cross-linked polymer gels and (b) inorganic materials with controlled pore size, such as microporous silica.

(a) Semi-rigid gels

A number of polymers of this general classification are available, though many are restricted in use due to solvent incompatibility and pressure restriction. Polyacrylamide gels are compatible with aqueous systems and can be used for the analysis of water-soluble compounds. Such gels are available with a molecular weight exclusion limit of 5×10^5, though it is only the smaller pore size material which has the required mechanical strength for modern LC (even here the upper pressure limit is 200 psi).

Cross-linked polydextrans have also been used for the analysis of aqueous samples in the molecular weight range $100-10^8$. The utility of these materials has been extended by the synthesis of hydroxypropylated derivatives which allows use with polar organic solvents. These packings suffer the restrictions incumbent upon large particle size (30 μm) and low mechanical strength. Cross-linked polymers of styrene and divinylbenzene are the most popular packings of the above class. Extensive development has led to the synthesis of 10 μm spherical packings of controlled pore size and pore volume. A high degree of cross-linkage confers excellent stability allowing the packings to be used at elevated temperature, flow and pressure (6000 psi). They are available in a range of pore sizes, 50–10^6 Å as well as mixed pore size corresponding to a fractionation range of 100–(5×10^8) daltons, and find application in the analysis of both polymer and low molecular weight materials. Swelling and shrinkage is minimal and the packings are compatible with most organic solvents although not acetone or methanol.

Suspension co-polymerization of 2-hydroxyethylmethacrylate and ethylene dimethylacrylate gives hydrophilic porous packings which can be used with aqueous and polar organic eluents. The packings can be used at elevated pressures (3000 psi), although they have a restricted molecular weight operating range.

(b) Rigid packings

Glasses and silica-based particles have found increasing application in SEC. Some of these materials have chemically modified surfaces in order to reduce the adsorptive properties of the packing. The 10 μm packings are available in a range of pore size diameter (40–2500 Å) corresponding to a mass range of 10^2–(5×10^7) daltons, are stable at pH < 10 and can be used with aqueous and polar solvents.

The packings are stable at elevated temperatures, and have high mechanical strength with good 'mass transfer' properties allowing rapid equilibration with fresh solvent. As the volume remains constant and there is no possibility of biodegradation the columns, especially those silylized, can be used routinely and indefinitely after calibration.

SEC differs from other LC modes in that separation takes place exclusively because of differences in molecular size; consequently solvent selection is simpler, as the requirements of the solvent are simply that of sample solubility and packing compatibility. Bearing in mind the rationale of the separation process, all the sample components should elute between the interparticulate volume and the pore volume.

The principles causing retention behaviour, separation variables, molecular weight calibration and associated terminology such as interparticle and intraparticle volume, selective permeation, fractionation range and molecular hydrodynamic radius are as for open-column size exclusion (Chapter 4).

The techniques of polymer characterization and of the application of SEC to biological studies is a broad and detailed subject and consequently this section can only provide a brief overview of the subject material. The interested reader is referred to the text by Snyder and Kirkland [73] and references therein.

6.13 LC METHOD DEVELOPMENT

The development of an LC procedure begins with the choice of the chromatographic mode and solvent system. A column and solvent selection guide (Fig. 6.36) based on molecular weight, solubility and ionic characteristics of the sample can be used as an empirical aid in this procedure. A decision is made at each branch in the flow chart and the appropriate channel followed. The procedure outlined is merely a guide to choice and is in no way a substitute for experience.

Following a choice of the LC method a column and column packing appropriate to the analysis must be selected. Established packing materials are available in 5 and 10 μm particle size; the former give greater resolution ($\times$ 3), though the 10 μm packings are adequate for all but the most demanding of separations. The relationship between column back pressure (Δp) and particle size (dp) is defined by

$$\Delta p \propto 1/dp^2$$

and will rise by a factor of ~ 4 on moving from 10 μm to 5 μm packings. It is advised therefore that lower flow rates (~ 1 ml min^{-1}) are used with the latter; flow rates for the former are commonly 2 ml min^{-1}. Column dimensions vary, diameters range from 2 to 8 mm and length from 5 to 50 cm. For analytical scale separations 4 mm diamter is adequate while the length of the column required is dictated by the complexity of the sample but is typically 10–25 cm.

The experimental factors influencing chromatographic resolution have previously been discussed as has the generalized stepwise procedure for establishing optimum conditions, using isocratic (equal strength) elution techniques for a given application. However, for difficult separations isocratic elution may not afford adequate resolution as the capacity factors (K') for some bands may be small while others may be large. Thus, for samples where K' values differ widely it is not possible to adjust the solvent strength so that all bands elute in the optimum range $1 < K' < 10$, using a constant strength eluent. For difficult separations the desired resolution may be achieved using gradient elution techniques. This involves changing (in a controlled manner) the solvent strength during the development of the chromatogram, thus enabling optimization of the capacity factors for the individual bands.

A general approach to the elution problem described above is to use the technique of gradient elution. For example, a reverse-phase gradient elution would use a linear profile from 10–100% of organic modifier in water, thus allowing a measure of the range of the capacity factors of the sample components. If the retention times of the sample components are close, this indicates a relatively narrow band of capacity factors. Therefore in this instance isocratic elution using a solvent system slightly less rich in the organic modifier at the elution of the bands of interest, should provide adequate resolution. The stepwise procedure for optimization can then be used. If the selectivity proves inadequate

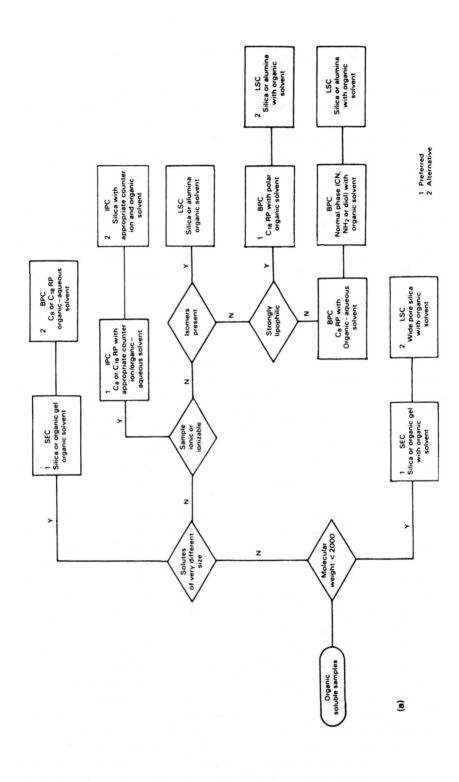

(a)

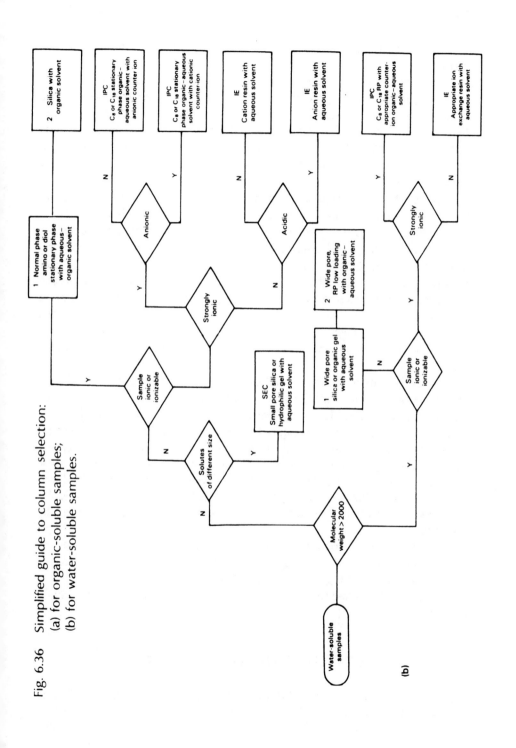

Fig. 6.36 Simplified guide to column selection:
(a) for organic-soluble samples;
(b) for water-soluble samples.

then it may be that either an alternative solvent or alternative LC mode should be investigated.

If the initial evaluation run indicates the sample components to vary markedly in capacity factor value, a gradient elution system may prove more effective. The design of a gradient separation and program requires consideration of not only the solvent components, but also the gradient range, shape and steepness. A guide to suitable solvent gradient programs, for various combinations of LC mode and instrumentation, and detailed discussions of the technique have been presented elsewhere [72, 73].

Gradient elution is effective in dealing with the general elution problem and has other advantages, such as improved resolution of early bands and increased sensitivity for components which elute at higher solvent strength. There are, however, associated disadvantages both in terms of the instrumental requirements and in the practice of the technique. The technique requires higher performance pumps and additional instrumentation, such as solvent degassing modules and mixing chambers and solvent programmes. These requirements add considerably to the cost of a LC system. A practical drawback is that the initial solvent composition must be re-established at the end of a chromatogram before the next analysis can commence, thus effectively increasing the sample analysis time.

A detailed discussion of the theoretical principles underlying gradient elution and the design of such separations is outside the scope of this text. The interested reader is directed towards an excellent exposé of the topic by Snyder [72].

A number of alternative techniques have been developed to tackle the general elution problem, such as flow and temperature programming, and especially column switching techniques. Coupled column chromatography involves the use of three and sometimes four different stationary phases. The sample is introduced to the primary column for a preliminary separation before the various polar fractions are switched to the appropriate secondary columns and then to the detector.

Coupled-column chromatography provides enhanced resolution, and as isocratic elution is used the technique is particularly useful for the routine assay of samples with a wide range of capacity factor values.

Further details of these various techniques may be found in a review by Snyder and Kirkland [73].

6.14 QUANTITATIVE ANALYSIS

The methods of quantitation for LC are similar to those used in GC, though there are a number of important differences. External standard calibration i.e. where the detector response to a solution of known concentration is measured and a calibration curve constructed, is the recommended method for quantitation in LC. The increased precision obtained compared with GC is attributable to the high degree of accuracy and reproducibility of sample loading afforded by microvalve injection.

The internal standardization technique actually increases the analytical error due to the measurement of two peak areas and should be reserved for samples undergoing pre-treatment or pre- or post-column derivatization to account for variable sample recovery or conversion. Quantitative analysis when applied to gradient elution systems affords reduced accuracy and precision due to the practical disadvantages of constancy of flow, reproducibility of gradient formation and solvent demixing.

6.15 PREPARATIVE LIQUID CHROMATOGRAPHY (PLC)

In addition to the analytical-scale assay of trace impurities modern LC can be employed in the preparative mode for the isolation of appreciable amounts of pure component. Where only a few milligrams ($\leqslant 5$ mg) of a compound is required a few repetitive injections on an analytical scale column (~ 4.6 mm ID) will provide the requisite amount. The analytical scale equipment required has been described in detail earlier in the chapter. However, there are many other instances when larger quantities (50 mg–50 g) of pure material may be required. Separations of this scale are normally accomplished using larger bore columns which are designed for use with proprietary LC analytical scale equipment. The principal features of the methods are as follows.

1. High resolution preparative procedures use a large bore column ($\leqslant 10$ mm) packed with analytical grade packing material ($\leqslant 10\ \mu$m particle size), thus giving a comparable degree of resolution and speed of separation to the parent analytical procedure. The flow rate required (u) for the preparative procedure is given by:

$$u = u_1(d_1/d_2)^2$$

where u_1 is the solvent flow rate in the analytical procedure, d_1 is the ID of the preparative column and d_2 is the ID of the analytical column. The maximum sample size is obviously dictated by the separation factor, α, but should be no more than ~ 10 mg of compound [74].

2. The second mode is referred to as the 'sample overload' technique and sacrifices column efficiency and resolution in favour of sample throughput. The use of wide diameter columns ($\geqslant 10$ mm) packed with large microporous particles ($\sim 50\ \mu$m) allows isolation of gram quantities of material in relatively short elution times as the column can be operated at high flow rates without seriously degrading resolution. By its nature this technique is best used with samples containing one principal component or sample mixtures where the solutes are well resolved. The techniques of peak shaving and heart-cutting i.e. collecting a portion of a chromatographic zone, followed by recycling can give a sample of the desired purity.

A recent advance has been the development of radial compression column technology by Waters, both for preparative and analytical procedures. In the preparative mode the packing material is constrained in a flexible plastic tube which in turn is housed in a metal cylinder. The tube is pressurized with nitrogen, which causes the flexible walls to be compressed against the packing, thus eliminating column voids and wall effects. The efficiencies obtained are noticeably improved and the large columns used (up to 300 mm in length by 50 mm diameter) have excellent sample capacity and allow the separation of ∼ 10 g quantities of component [75].

Regardless of the procedure employed preparative HPLC has most commonly been used in the adsorption mode with silica packings because of their sample versatility and loading capacity; however large bore preparative columns are now commercially available, packed with any of the proprietary reverse-phase and ion-exchange media.

6.15.1 Practical aspects

An essential preliminary to preparative scale HPLC is to establish the solvent system for the separation. This can be determined either on an analytical scale HPLC system or through TLC studies. The solvent system determined by the former method may be applied directly to the preparative HPLC. However, while TLC provides an inexpensive alternative and allows many solvent systems to be examined at little cost and effort, it gives results which must be treated with caution, especially when the chromatographic layer is silica. First, samples are more strongly retained in TLC due to the greater surface area of TLC silica compared with column materials and hence a solvent system should be chosen so that $R_f \leqslant 0.3$. Second, where the components of mixed solvent systems have widely different affinities for silica, for instance, ethanol and chloroform, then an effective solvent gradient exists on a TLC plate, the solvent front being richer in the less polar component. On an HPLC column fully conditioned with the mixed solvent this effect is not present and to take account, an eluant of lower solvent strength should be used. If the solvents are of similar strength then the mixed solvent system may be transferred directly from TLC to HPLC.

In order to obtain reproducible chromatography whether in analytical or preparative scale work the column must be conditioned before use. As a guide, the amount of solvent required for equilibration is approximately 15–20 column volumes. If equilibration is incomplete this can lead to poor reproducibility and separation.

Ideally the sample should be dissolved in the mobile phase and applied to the column in as small a volume as possible. Solvents of greater eluting power should not be used to dissolve the sample as this disturbs the system equilibrium. The sample solution can be applied via a six-port valve of the Rheodyne type fitted with an appropriate sized loop. Loops up to 10 ml are commercially available.

Alternatively the sample can be applied to the column *via* a small volume secondary pump, though this has the disadvantages associated with stopped-flow techniques (discussed previously in Chapter 6). This complex subject has been reviewed by Hupe [76].

In preparative LC it is advisable to use both protector and guard columns [77, 78, 79]. Where any polar, ionic or basic mobile phase which could dissolve the column packing is being used as eluent, a precolumn of $\sim 40\,\mu m$ silica should be fitted between the injector and the pump. The column should be of similar length but approximately half the diameter of the preparative column. This ensures that the eluent is saturated with silica. As in analytical work a guard column should be inserted after the injector to catch undesirable sample impurities and to act as a final filter. The dimensions are somewhat smaller than the protector column both in length and ID in order to maintain efficiency. The instrumental modifications required are minimal. Commercially available analytical reciprocating pumps can be readily modified (at cost) with preparative head assemblies which provide solvent delivery capacity of up to $100\,ml\,min^{-1}$. A stream splitter is located at the column outlet, normally with a 5–10% split ratio. The detector flow can be recombined with the major flow stream before passage to the fraction collector. Pure samples can be obtained by collection of suitable fraction cuts, which can be checked by analytical LC before bulking.

6.16 MICROCOLUMNS IN LIQUID CHROMATOGRAPHY

Thoughout the development of HPLC workers have striven to improve chromatographic performance by either increasing the efficiency of separation, reducing the analysis time, or a combination of both.

One approach, using the conventional 4–5 mm ID columns, is the reduction of the packing material particle size and further improvement of the packing technique. This increases efficiency and facilitates the shortening of columns to reduce analysis time. Columns are now commercially available with $3\,\mu m$ packings and Stout [80] has demonstrated high speed separations with these. Efficiencies are being achieved which approach the theoretical limit where $dp = 2$ (i.e. the height equivalent to a theoretical plate, HETP, is equal to twice the particle diameter). Siemion [81] has described an improved slurry packing technique and obtained efficiencies of 70 000 plates per metre. However, due to the high pressure gradients encountered with decrease in particle size, it is unlikely that further advances can be achieved at the moment with particles below $3\,\mu m$.

The continuing quest for improved efficiency has given fresh impetus to the study of reduced diameter columns, and though still in their initial stages of development, it is likely these new column technologies will have considerable influence on the practice of HPLC. The incentive for the

Table 6.5   Microbore column types [99]

Column type	Material	Column ID μm	Particle size μm	Column length m	Flow rate μl/min
Open tubular column	Soft glass Fused-silica glass	10–300	—	0.5–35	0.01–1
Microbore packed column					
Microcapillary packed column	Soft glass Pyrex glass	50–200	10–100	10–60	0.01–5
Small-bore packed column	Stainless steel Teflon	500–1000	5–20	0.1–1	30–100
Narrow-bore packed column	Pyrex glass PTFE Fused-silica glass Stainless steel	100–500	3–10	0.1–2	0.1–20

development of microcolumns for HPLC lies in the various practical advantages they have over standard analytical columns. For instance:

1. due to the narrow bore, high linear flow rates can be achieved with substantially lower total solvent volumes and thus solvent flow rates of $50 \mu l \, min^{-1}$ or less are used (cf. $1 \, ml \, min^{-1}$ with conventional columns). This provides for substantial savings in solvent consumption and is of importance where solvent costs are a consideration (for instance, use of ion-pairing reagents and deuterated solvents.);

2. the increased linear velocity of eluent allows in theory high speed separations; furthermore, the reduced flow rates and the concomitant reduction in the column backpressure allow columns to be readily connected in series, enabling efficiencies of 10^5 theoretical plates to be realised. The small peak volumes result in increased mass sensitivity and can provide a 20-fold enhancement in detector response;

3. the reduced solvent flow provides the potential for direct interfacing to mass spectrometers [82, 83] and flame-based detectors [84, 85].

Four main categories of microcolumn types can be distinguished: open tubular [86, 87]; packed microcapillaries [88]; microbore [89] and narrow bore [90]. The principal features of these column types are outlined below and in Table 6.5.

6.16.1 Open tubular columns (OTC)

As in capillary GC these are columns made of narrow tubing on the inside of which is coated or bonded the stationary phase. They have been developed mainly by Ishii, Tsuda and co-workers . Theory developed by Knox and Gilbert [91], Hibi et al. [92] and Yang [93] shows that for capillary columns to rival packed columns then:

$$(hv)dc^2 = (hv)dp^2$$

where h = reduced plate height, v = reduced velocity, dc = capillary diameter, dp = particle diameter. This means that for an open tubular column the bore must lie in the $1-10 \, \mu m$ range. However this suffers from a concomitant reduction in sample capacity. Tijssen has shown that this performance may be achieved by larger bores of $10-30 \, \mu m$ if very tightly coiled columns, and high flow velocities are used. The practical limitation of capillary columns is caused by dispersion in the detector/injector systems producing peak broadening. If detector volumes can be reduced to around $0.001 \, mm^3$ [94] capillary HPLC would become a highly efficient and faster technique than packed columns, when the number of theoretical plates is above 30 000. Knox [91] states that capillary columns would be 27 times faster than packed columns with plate numbers greater than 100 000. Difficulties arising from their low sample capacity may be overcome by stream splitting of the sample and etching of the interior walls to give higher stationary phase loadings.

6.16.2 Small bore packed columns

These are similar to conventional HPLC columns but have IDs of about 0.5–1.0 mm. They are packed with materials in the range 5–30 μm using established high pressure ($\sim 25\,000$ psi) slurry packing techniques [95, 96]. Theoretical plate counts of $30\,000$ m^{-1} using 10 μm particles in 1 mm ID columns have been reported [97]. Higher resolution can be achieved by butting columns together, so avoiding introduction of any dead volume; for 5 μm silica columns 50 000 plates m^{-1} and total efficiencies of 650 000 plates have been reported [98]. A drawback of small-bore columns packed with large particles ($\sim 10 \mu$m) is that the column efficiency/unit length is low and increased efficiency has to be paid for at the cost of long analysis times. High speed, high efficiency small-bore column separations can only be achieved with efficient packing of small particles ($\sim 3 \mu$m). Efficiencies of 10^5 plates m^{-1} have been reported for 5 μm 1 mm ID columns [99].

6.16.3 Packed microcapillary columns

These have mainly been developed by Novotny [84, 85] and co-workers and are characterized by low column-diameter to particle size ratios of 2 to 5. This is much less than small-bore packed columns (50–200) or conventional columns (500–2000). Below ratios of ~ 2, it has been reported [100] that the packing structure collapses under the viscous flow and causes clogging of the column.

The microcapillary columns are prepared by extruding a heavy walled glass tube, 0.5–2 mm ID, packed with 10–100 μm particle size high temperature resistant silica or alumina. Microcapillary dimensions are in the range of 50–100 μm ID and 60 m length. For reverse phase work the stationary phases have then to be bonded *in situ*. Chromatographic performance in terms of speed of analysis and resolving power has been found to be poor relative to conventional small particle packed columns. Although packed capillary columns have a low flow resistance enabling longer columns to be used to increase total plate numbers, long analysis times are needed and sensitivity is reduced.

6.16.4 Narrow-bore packed columns

A recent innovation has been the introduction of narrow-bore packed columns, characterized by having IDs in the range 0.25–0.5 mm and particle size of 3–30 μm. Ishii and co-workers [101, 102] evaluated several types of column materials, for instance stainless steel, Pyrex glass, PTFE and fused silica glass, and concluded that the last gave the best column efficiency.

Using proprietary packing techniques detailed by Yang [103] microparticulate columns of up to 2 m can be prepared. For columns of $\sim 300 \mu$m ID packed with $3 \mu m$ packings typical efficiencies are of the order of 10^5 plates m^{-1} [104]. Narrow-bore packed columns have a number of advantages in addition to those mentioned for other microcolumns; for instance, fused silica has extremely high mechanical strength allowing the use of inlet pressures up to 12 000 psi. Thus long length columns can be used; silica glass has good optical transparency and thus on-column UV and fluorescence detection can be employed; finally good flexibility allows easy coupling of column to detector and pump, and also allows columns to be coiled thus saving space and simplifying oven design.

In conclusion Knox and Gilbert [104] and Halasz [105, 106] have considered the theoretical limits on the separation performance of OTCs. They conclude that in order to match the performance and speed of analysis of conventional HPLC systems, ultra low flow rates and dead volumes are required, and that it is unlikely that OTCs will offer any significant advantage. However, until the very stringent instrumental requirements are satisfied the theoretical potential of open tubular columns cannot be satisfactorily examined. Many workers, on the other hand, have already demonstrated the advantages of microbore and narrow bore columns in terms of low solvent consumption, increased sensitivity and in the latter, dramatically increased performance.

6.16.5 Instrumentation

Despite the numerous advantages the instrumental demands of microcolumn LC are considerable, and these demands are further accentuated as the requirements vary from one column type to another. A consequence of the reduced flow rates is that the detector flow cell volume should be reduced to ~ 10 nl for OTCs, $0.1 \mu l$ for packed microcapillaries and $1 \mu l$ for microbore columns. An additional demand of the detector is that it should have a rapid response (< 0.5 s). Study of detector systems has focused on two areas; firstly, the miniaturization of UV, fluorescence and electrochemical systems, using in the first two systems lasers as excitation sources to increase sensitivity [107]: secondly the direct interfacing with systems which previously required transport and/or concentration of the eluent. Interfacing of HPLC with mass-spectroscopy has been undertaken by Hennion [82] and Takeuchi [108], with FTIR by Jinno et al. [109, 110] and flame systems (FPD and TSD) as demonstrated by McGuffin and Novotny [84, 85]. The phosphorus flame detector could accept in excess of $20 \mu l$ min^{-1} of 10–25% aqueous methanol and had a limit of detection for phosphorus of 2 pg [111].

6.16.6 Solvent delivery

The reduced column diameters necessitate accurate and precise flow rates in the region of $1–100 \mu l$ min^{-1}. A number of pumps are commercially available which meet these requirements under isocratic conditions. In HPLC, solvent gradients are normally generated by controlling the flow of the component solvents; with microcolumns this requires control at sub μl flow rates. A number of systems have been developed for both linear and exponential gradient generation based on reciprocating pumps. These systems give comparable accuracy and precision of retention time and peak area as obtained in conventional HPLC, and have been reviewed by Yang [99].

6.16.7 Injection systems

Extra column dispersion, such as would result from large injection volumes $> 1 \mu l$ and dead volumes introduced by frits and fittings must be reduced to obtain optimum performance. A variety of injection systems have been reported,

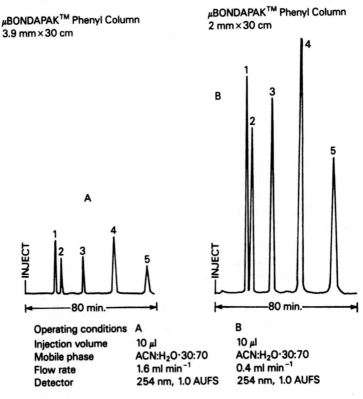

Operating conditions	A	B
Injection volume	10 μl	10 μl
Mobile phase	ACN:H$_2$O·30:70	ACN:H$_2$O·30:70
Flow rate	1.6 ml min^{-1}	0.4 ml min^{-1}
Detector	254 nm, 1.0 AUFS	254 nm, 1.0 AUFS

Fig. 6.37   Steroid analysis using a 2 mm ID microbore column provides a fourfold increase in sensitivity over the 3.9 mm ID column. In addition the microbore column consumed only 32 ml of solvent compared with 128 ml for the 3.9 mm ID column. (Reproduced with permission from *Water Product Bulletin 1982*).

including those of split injection, internal loop-rotary valve and 'microfeeder'. Considerable advances have been made in quantitative reproducibility. Dead volumes have been minimized by locating the columns directly into the injection and detector systems.

6.16.8 Microcolumn applications

Higher column efficiencies are required in order to investigate the complex mixtures encountered in petrochemical studies, biochemical and clinical studies, fermentation processes and pollution monitoring.

At present only microbore (0.5–2 mm ID) packed columns are commercially available and considerable literature on applications is available from manufacturers and suppliers. For applications where amounts of analyte may be limited, e.g. environmental, food analysis, biological applications and forensic science, the use of microbore columns could be extremely advantageous. Figure 6.37 demonstrates the increased sensitivity achieved using a column of smaller diameter.

Where solvent costs are an important consideration the reduced solvent consumption of microbore columns will allow the use of more exotic solvents.

For the other column technologies there is no substantial literature on

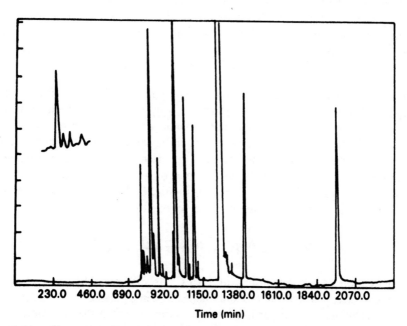

230.0 460.0 690.0 920.0 1150.0 1380.0 1610.0 1840.0 2070.0

Time (min)

Fig. 6.38   Chromatogram of an essential oil obtained with a 14 m × 1 mm ID microbore silica column (510 000 theoretical plates); n-hexane/ethyl acetate 95:5 solvent.

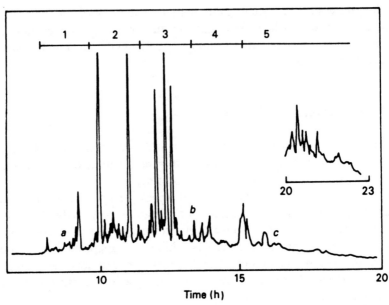

Fig. 6.39   Chromatogram of the aromatic fraction of coal tar. Mobile phase, stepwise gradient: (1) methanol-water (80:20); (2) methanol-water (90:10); (3) methanol; (4) 1% methylene chloride in methanol; (5) 3% methylene chloride in methanol. Column: 55 m × 70 μm ID, basic alumina (30 μm)/octadecylsilane. After 20 h (inset), inlet pressure and temperature were increased. Solute   a = fluorene,   b = dibenzo [gh,i] perylene,   and   c = coronene. (Reproduced from reference 110 by permission of the Elsevier Publishing Company).

applications as the investigative work has been carried out on individually prepared columns. The chromatograms in Figs 6.38 and 6.39 illustrate the potential of small bore packed and microcapillary packed columns respectively. Figure 6.38 is an example of a highly efficient separation of a complex natural sample using a small bore packed column 14 m in length coupled in 1 m segments. An example of the separation obtained of an aromatic fraction of coal tar using a microcapillary packed column is shown in Fig. 6.39; the chromatogram was obtained using a stepwise gradient in the reversed-phase mode.

6.17 APPLICATIONS OF HPLC

An indication of the versatility of HPLC, as evidenced by the variety of compound classes which can be examined, has been indicated in Fig. 6.36(a) and (b) The technique is of major importance to the analyst in the pharmaceutical, food and fine chemical industries and has also played a significant role in forensic, environmental, chemical and biochemical studies. In the latter field it has been used by molecular biologists to isolate gene probes, i.e. short lengths of DNA (~ 30 bases), from synthetic mixtures [112].

For the practising chromatographer, often a search of the relevant literature will identify a similar application which with some minor modification will prove suitable for the particular need. The applications literature available is formidable; a number of technical abstracts are published [113], technical information published by instrument manufacturers and suppliers is also a valuable source of reference and there are a number of excellent monographs [114, 115]. Available space does not allow a fuller discussion of the various application areas and readers requiring more detailed information are directed to the references cited above.

REFERENCES

1. Martin, A. J. P. and Synge, R. L. M. (1950) *J. Biochem.*, **50**, 679.
2. van Deemter, J. J., Zinderweg, F. J. and Klinkenberg, A. (1956) *Chem. Eng. Sci.*, **5**, 271.
3. Giddings, J. C. (1965) *Anal. Chem.*, **35**, 2215; and (1965) *Dynamics of Chromatography*, Dekker, New York.
4. Horvath, C., Priess, B. and Lipsky, S. R. (1967) *Anal. Chim. Acta*, **38**, 305.
5. Majors, R. E. (1972) *Anal. Chem.*, **44**, 1722.
6. Conlon, R. D., Ettre, L. S., Schmid, C. E. and Schwartz, A., (1982) *Int. Lab.* October, 52–62.
7. Glajch, J. L., Kirkland, J. J., Squire, K. M. and Minor, J. M., (1980) *J. Chromatogr.* **199**, 57.
8. Poile, A. F. (1982) *33rd Pittsburg Conference on Anal. Chem. and Applied Spectroscopy.*
9. Kirkland, J. J. (1969) *J. Chromatogr. Sci.*, **7**, 7.
10. Kirkland, J. J. (1971) *J. Chromatogr. Sci.*, **9**, 206.
11. Karger, B. L., Conroe, K. and Englehardt, H. (1970) *J. Chromatogr. Sci.*, **8**, 242.
12. Kreji, M., Tesarik, K., Rusek, M. and Pajurek, J. (1981) *J. Chromatogr.* **218**, 167.
13. McGuffin, V. L. and Novotny, M. (1981) *Anal. Chem.* **53**, 946.
14. Young, T. E. and Maggs, R. J. (1967) *Anal. Chim. Acta*, **38**, 105.
15. White, P. C. (1980) *J. Chromatogr.*, **200**, 271.
16. Readman, J. W., Brown, L. and Rhead, M. M. (1981) *Analyst* **106**, 122.
17. Klatt, L. N. (1979) *J. Chromatogr. Sci.*, **17**, 225.
18. James, G. E. (1981) *Can Res* **13**, 39.
19. Little, J. N. and Fallik, G. J. (1975) *J. Chromatogr.* **112**, 389.
20. Lawrence, J. H. and Frei, R. W. (1976) *Chemical Derivatization in LC*, Elsevier, Oxford.
21. Simons, S. S. and Johnson, D. F. (1977) *Anal. Biochem.*, **82**, 250.
22. Kissinger, P. I. (1977) *Anal Chem.* **49**, 477.
23. Bratin, K., Blank, C. L., Lunte, C. E. and Shoup, R. E. (1984) *Int. Lab.* June, 24.
24. Bullet, C., Oliva, P. and Caude, M. (1977) *J. Chromatogr.* **149**, 625.
25. Edwards, P. and Haak, K. (1983) *Int. Lab.*, June, 38.
26. Swatzfager, D. G. (1976) *Anal. Chem.*, **48**, 2189.
27. Pohl, C. A. and Johnson, E. L., (1980) *J. Chromatogr. Sci.* **18**. 442.
28. Gjerde, D. T., Schmuckler, G. and Fritz, J. S. (1980) *J. Chromatogr.* **187**, 35.

29. Reeve, D. A. and Crozier, A. (1977) *J. Chromatogr.* **137**, 271.
30. Compton, B. J. and Purdy, W. C. (1979). *J. Chromatogr.*, **169**, 39–50.
31. Willmott, F. W. and Dolphin, R. J. (1974) *J. Chromatogr. Sci*, **12**, 695.
32. Willmott, F. W. and Dolphin, R. J. (1976) *Spectrophot. Chromatogr. Anal. News*, 7, 6.
33. McFadden, W. H. (1980) *J. Chromatogr. Sci.*, **18**, 97.
34. Julin, B. G., Vandenborn, H. W. and Kirkland, J. J. (1975) *J. Chromatogr.*, **112**, 443–453.
35. Locke, D. C., Dhingra, B. S. and Baker, A. D. (1982) *Anal. Chem.*, **54**, 447–450.
36. Willmott, F. W. and Dolphin, R. J., (1974) *J. Chromatogr. Sci*, **12**, 695–700.
37. McGuffin, V. L. and Novotny, M., (1981) *Anal. Chem.*, **53**, 946–951.
38. McGuffin, V. L. and Novotny, M., (1983) *Anal. Chem.*, **55**, 2296–2302.
39. Hein, H. (1980) *Chem. Lab. Betr.*, **31**, 559.
40. McKinley, W. A., Popovich, D. J. and Layne, T. (1980) *Amer. Lab.*, **12**, 37.
41. Veazey, R. L. and Nieman, T. A. (1980) *J. Chromatogr.*, **200**, 153.
42. Onano, A. C., Horne, D. L. and Greggs, A. R. (1974) *J. Polym. Sci. Polym. Chem. Ed.*, **12**, 307.
43. Westwood, S. A., Games, D. E. and Sheen, L. (1981) *J. Chromatogr.* **204**, 103: Boehme, W., Stenz, H. and Bonisignori, O. (1983) *Int. Lab.* **6**, 28.
44. Konash, P. L. and Bastanus, G. J. (1980) *Anal. Chem.* **52**, 1929.
45. Gast, C. H., Kraak, J. C., Poppe, H. and Maesson, F. J. M. (1979) *J. Chromatogr.*, **185**, 549.
46. Krull, I. S. and Jordan, S. (1980) *Int. Lab.*, **129**(Nov).
47. Shohei, O. and Tsugo, S. (1981) *Anal. Chem.*, **53**, 471.
48. Buddrus, V., Herzog, H. and Cooper, J. W. (1981) *J. Magn. Reson.*, **42**, 453.
49. Popovich, D. J., Dizon, J. B. and Ehrlich, B. J. (1980) *J. Chromatogr. Sci.*, **18**, 442.
50. Griffin, M., Price, S. J., Palmer, T. (1982) *Clinica Chem. Acta*, **125**, 89–95.
51. Popovich, D. J., Dixon, J. B. and Ehrlich, B. T. (1979) *J. Chromatogr. Sci.*, **17**, 643.
52. Krull, I. S. and Ding, X. D. (1984) *J. Agric. Food Chem.*, **32**(3), 622–8.
53. Krull, I. S., Ding, X. D., Selavka, C., Bratin, K. and Forcier, G. (1984) *J. Forensic Sci.*, **2**, 29.
54. Knox, J. H., (1978) *High Performance Liquid Chromatography*, University Press, Edinburgh.
55. West, M. A. (1975) *Int. Lab.*, **45**, (Jan/Feb).
56. Parris, N. A. (1979) *J. Chromatogr. Sci.*, **17**, 541.
57. Hirshfield, T. (1984) *European Spect. News.* **55**, 15: and (1983) **51**, 77.
58. Simpson, C. F. (1976) *Practical High Performance Liquid Chromatography*, Heyden and Sons, London.
59. Svoboda, V. and Marsel, J. (1978) *J. Chromatogr.*, **148**, 111.
60. Pretorius, V. and Rensburg, J. F. J. (1973) *J. Chromatogr. Sci.*, **11**, 355.
61. McFadden, W. H., Schwartz, H. L. and Evans, S. (1976) *J. Chromatogr.*, **122**, 389.
62. Schmidt, J. A. (1971) *Modern Practice of Liquid Chromatography*, Wiley Inter-science, New York.
63. Done, J. N., Knox J. H. and Lobeac, J. (1974) *Applications of High Speed Liquid Chromatography*, John Wiley, London.
64. Halasz, I. and Sebastian, I. (1969) *Angew. Chem. Int. Edn.*, **8**, 453.
65. Pirkle, W. H. and House, D. W. (1979) *J. Org. Chem.*, **44**, 1957.
66. Chrompack UK Ltd, Unit 4, Indescon Court, Millharbour, London E14 9TN; J. T. Baker Chemicals, Phillipsburg. USA, UK Agent Linton Instrumentation, Hysol, Harlow CM 18 6QZ; Phase Separations, Deeside Industrial Estate, Queensfery, Deeside, Clwyd CH5 2LR.
67. Lochmuller, C. H., Souter, R. W. (1975) *J. Chromatogr.*, **113**, 283.
68. Krull, I. S. (1978) *Adv. Chromatogr.*, **16**, 175.
69. McKerrell, E. (1984) *European Spect. News*, **55**, 10.

70. Small, H., Stevens, T. S. and Bauman, W. C. (1975) *Anal. Chem.*, **47**, 1801.
71. Bidlingmeyer, B. A. (1980) *J. Chromatogr. Sci.*, **18**, 525.
72. Snyder, L. R., (1980) *High Performance Liquid Chromatography, Advances and Perspectives*, Vol. 1 (ed. C. Horvath), Academic Press, London, Chapter 4.
73. Snyder, L. R. and Kirkland, J. J. (1979) *Introduction to Modern Liquid Chromatography*, 2nd edn, John Wiley & Sons, New York.
74. Verzele, M. and Geeraert, E. (1980) *J. Chromatogr. Sci.*, **18**, 559.
75. Bundle, D. R., Iversen, T. and Josephson S. (1982) *Int. Lab.*, 27.
76. Hupe, K. P. and Lauer, H. H. (1981) *J. Chromatogr.* **203**, 41.
77. Rabel, F. M. (1980) *Amer. Lab.*, **12**(1), 81.
78. Atwood, J. G., Schmidt, G. J. and Slavin, W. (1979) *J. Chromatogr.* **171**, 109.
79. Wehrli, A., Hildebrand, J. C., Keller, H. P., Stampfi, R. and Frei, R. W. (1978) *J. Chromatogr.* **149**, 199.
80. Stout, R. W., De Stefano, J. J. and Snyder, L. R. (1983) *J. Chromatogr.* **261** (2), 189.
81. Siemion, C. C. (1983) *J. Liq. Chromatogr.*, **6**(4), 765.
82. Hennion, J. D. (1981) *J. Chromatogr. Sci.* **19**, 57.
83. Takeuchi, T., Ishii, D., Saito, A. and Otiki, T. (1982) *J. High Res. Chromatogr and Chromatogr Commun.* **5**, 91.
84. McGuffin, V. L. and Novotny, M., (1981) *Anal. Chem.*, **53**, 946.
85. McGuffin, V. L. and Novotny, M., (1981) *J. Chromatogr.* **218**, 179.
86. Tsuda, T., Novotny, M., (1978) *Anal. Chem.*, **50**, 632.
87. Tsuda, T., Hibi, K., Nakanishi, T., Takeuchi, T. and Ishii, D. (1978) *J. Chromatogr.* **158**, 227.
88. Tsuda, T. and Novotny, M. (1978) *Anal. Chem.*, **50**, 271.
89. Scott, R. P. W. (1978) *Analyst*, **103**, 37.
90. Ishii, D., Asai, K., Hibi, K., Jonokuchi, T. and Nagaya, M. (1977) *J. Chromatogr.* **144**, 157.
91. Knox, J. H. and Gilbert, M. T. (1979) *J. Chromatogr.* **186**, 405.
92. Hibi, K., Ishii, D., Fujishima, I., Takeuchi, T. and Nakamishi, T. (1980) *J. High Res. Chromatogr. and Chromatogr. Commun.* **1**, 21.
93. Yang, F. J. (1982) *J. Chromatogr Sci.* **29**, 241.
94. Scott, R. P. W. and Kucera, P. (1979) *J. Chromatogr.* **185**, 27.
95. Majors, R. E., (1972) *Anal. Chem.*, **44**, 1722.
96. Kirkland, J. J. (1971) *J. Chromatogr. Sci.*, **9**, 206.
97. Scott, R. P. W. and Kucera, P., (1979) *J. Chromatogr.* **185**, 27.
98. Scott, R. P. W. and Kucera, P., (1979) *J. Chromatogr.* **169**, 51.
99. Yang, F. J. (1983) *J. High Res. Chromatogr. and Chromatogr. Comm.*, **3**, 348.
100. Guichon, G. (1981) *Anal. Chem.*, **53**, 1318.
101. Takeuchi, T. and Ishii, D. (1982) *J. Chromatogr.* **238**, 409.
102. Takeuchi, T. and Ishii, D. (1981) *J. Chromatogr.* **213**, 25.
103. Yang, F. J. (1982) *J. Chromatogr.* **236**. 265.
104. Knox, J. H. and Gilbert, M. T. (1979) *J. Chromatogr.* **186**, 405.
105. Halasz, I. (1979) *J. Chromatogr.* **173**, 229.
106. Hoffman, K. and Halasz, I. (1979) *J. Chromatogr.* **173**, 211.
107. Folestad, S., Johnson, L. and Josefsson, B. (1981) *J. Chromatogr.* **218**, 15.
108. Takeuchi, T., Ishii, D., Saito, A. and Ohki, T. (1982) *J. High Res. Chromatogr. and Chromatogr. Commun.*, **5**, 91.
109. Jinno, K., Fujimoto, C., and Hirata, Y. (1982) *App. Spectrosc.* **36**, 67.
110. Jinno, K., Fujimoto, C., and Ishii, D. (1982) *J. Chromatogr.* **239**, 625.
111. Hirata, Y. and Novotny, M. (1979) *J. Chromatogr.* **186**, 521.
112. Gait, M. J., Popov, S. G., Singh, M. and Titmas, R. C. (1980) *Nucleic Acids Symp. Ser.*, **7**, 243.

113.   (i) *Gas and Liquid Chromatography Abstracts*; (ii) *Liquid Chromatography Litera-ture*; (iii) *Liquid Chromatography Abstracts*; (iv) *C. A. Selects.–High Performance Liquid Chromatography* (v) *Journal of Chromatography* (vi) *Chromatographia*.

114.   Parris, N. A. (1984) *J. Chromatogr. Lib.*, Vol. 27, *Instrumental Liquid Chroma-tography*, Elsevier, Oxford.

115.   Hamilton, R. J. and Sewell, P. A. (1982) *Introduction to High Performance Liquid Chromatography*, 2nd edn, Chapman and Hall, London.

7 SPECTROSCOPIC TECHNIQUES AND CHROMATOGRAPHY

Chromatography is primarily a separation technique, the observed detector response being a record of the quantity of solute molecules eluted from the chromatographic system. Although procedures have been developed for identifying separated components in a mixture, for example the two column GC method (see Experiment 21, Chapter 9), and a system of reference indices has been collated, they are limited either to a specific application or to a group of compounds. Identification of the component or components in an eluted band (peak) is only possible if we can ascertain that one type of molecule alone is present and can obtain sufficient unique information on the structure and physical properties of the compound. The latter may be achieved by obtaining spectroscopic data on the eluted molecules; if a peak is sampled several times during elution then the number of components contained in the peak can be established. In order to obtain the spectral data the spectrometer must be capable of performing a scan very rapidly and certainly several times during the elution time for the first peak of a chromatogram. Developments in microelectronics, instrument design and microcomputers have enabled mass spectrometers, infrared and UV–visible spectrophotometers and atomic absorption instruments to be successfully used as chromatography detectors.

The chromatographic methods most suitable for spectroscopic identification techniques are GC and HPLC although TLC methods have received some attention. GC was the first technique to be interfaced since it proved relatively easy to handle the gaseous effluent and mass spectrometers were capable of sufficiently fast scan times even in the 1960s. Hence GC–MS was the first chromatographic–spectroscopic technique to be developed [1]. Interfacing to HPLC proved more difficult but after considerable effort reliable interfaces have been developed and commercial systems are available. A mass spectrometer scans sufficiently rapidly for 'on the fly' analysis, i.e. the spectrum is obtained in a few seconds as the eluent emerges from the chromatograph.

Recent development in Fourier transform infrared instruments and UV–

visible diode array detectors have enabled a range of spectroscopic detectors to be developed which provide the analytical chemist with a powerful, sensitive, and almost ideal range of analytical techniques. The power of such systems is given by the amount of data obtained. This amounts to the detail or number of data points in a single spectrum recorded up to 1000 times during a chromatographic run:

UV – number of data points per spectrum 2–10
IR – number of data points per spectrum 10–50
MS – number of data points per spectrum 10–500

Such large amounts of data can only be sensibly and rapidly analysed and compared with reference spectra using computers. The availability of fast 16 bit microcomputer systems has resulted in affordable GC/HPLC spectroscopic systems. The main systems in use today are discussed below, including the above mentioned techniques and also the Microwave Plasma Detector (MPD). The MPD is used as a GC detector and employs a helium microwave plasma emission source coupled to an optical emission spectrometer.

7.1 CHROMATOGRAPHIC REQUIREMENTS

The essential requirements of a GC or HPLC chromatographic system linked to a spectrometer follow normal practice. However, great care needs to be exercised to ensure that good separations and reproducible chromatograms are obtained. The main requirements may be summarized as follows:

1. reproducible chromatograms:
   stable mobile phase flow rate and pressure, achieved by using accurate control systems;
2. stable stationary phase, with virtually no column bleed (GC) or dissolution (HPLC), achieved by using bonded stationary phases or operating the column at temperatures well below the operating limits;
3. obtaining sharp chromatographic peaks with minimal tailing (sharp narrow peaks produce the greatest concentrations of solute in the mobile phase);
4. peak widths as uniform as possible throughout the chromatogram, using column temperature programming (GC) or solvent programming (HPLC) if possible;
5. using a mobile phase that can, if necessary, be efficiently removed from the eluent in an interface, has minimal spectral interference with the spectra of the eluted components, is thermally stable and does not react with the components at the elevated temperatures of an interface.

No modifications are required to the conventional sample introduction techniques used in GC and HPLC. The normal mobile phase flow and pressure control systems are usually suitable providing their specification meets the stability requirements of the interfaces. Normal GC and HPLC detectors can still be used to follow the progress of the chromatography and a stream splitter employed to divert most of the eluent to the spectroscopy interface. Split ratios are typically in the range 1:100 to 1:1000. In instruments specifically designed as an integrated GC/HPLC-spectroscopic system a chromatography detector is not usually included (Fig. 7.1). The chromatogram is constructed from the total spectrum signal or current. This is the total signal obtained for one spectral scan and since a scan rate of at least 1 per second is used, a plot of total spectrum signal against

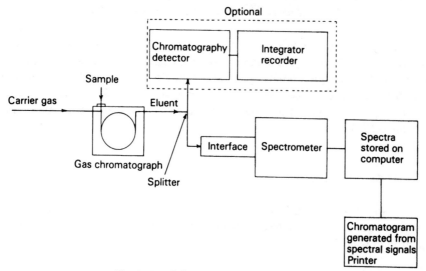

Fig. 7.1   GC–spectrometer system.

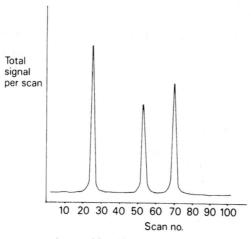

Fig. 7.2   Chromatogram formed by plotting total signal for each scan *vs* scan number.

time produces the chromatogram. For example, in GC–MS systems, the total ion current for each scan is plotted against scan number as shown in Fig. 7.2 (the scan number being representative of the retention volume). All the spectral data is stored in the computer and it is easy therefore to recall the data and reconstruct the chromatogram for inspection or for printing out after each scan has been completed.

7.2 MASS SPECTROSCOPY–CHROMATOGRAPHIC TECHNIQUES (GC–MS, HPLC–MS)

Technological developments over the past decade have enabled manufactures to construct sophisticated, yet reliable instruments, having overcome the problems of interfacing a high volume gaseous or liquid effluent with the vacuum requirements of the mass spectrometer ion source. Before discussing the interfacing requirements a brief outline of mass spectrometer instrumentation is presented [2, 3].

7.2.1 Mass spectrometers

A mass spectrometer can be divided into four sections, the sample inlet system and ion source, mass analyser, detector, and control and signal processing electronics (Fig. 7.3).

Ion source and inlet system

The mass spectrometer ion source is maintained at a pressure of $10^{-3}\tau$ or less. The inlet system is designed to release the sample into the centre of the source at a carefully controlled rate. This is dependent on the concentration of the sample and its physical properties. In chromatography interfaces the inlet consists of a short length of heated stainless steel capillary tubing or an orifice linking the ion source inlet with the effluent after removal of most of the mobile phase.

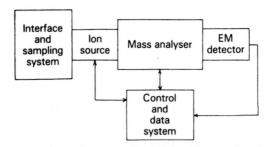

Fig. 7.3   Schematic diagram of a mass spectrometer system

Ion source

There are many methods used to produce ions in a mass spectrometer, with the electron impact (EI) process being the most widely used, although chemical ionization and field ionization have attracted specialized interest. The electron impact ion source is efficient, simple to construct, stable and produces ions with a narrow kinetic energy spread. The spectra obtained are specific and characteristic of the molecular structure of the sample. Some groups of compounds give similar spectra but generally, since the fragmentation of the molecule into constituent ions is characteristic, the spectrum provides a fingerprint. Numerous designs are used to construct an EI source but the overall principle is the same (Fig. 7.4). Electrons emitted at a hot filament are accelerated and the resulting electron beam traverses the ion chamber to the collector anode. Interaction between the electron beam and the organic molecules (M) results in an energy transfer of 10–20 eV which is sufficient to ionize most molecules; in many cases smaller fragment ions are also formed. The resulting positive ions move out of the ionization area

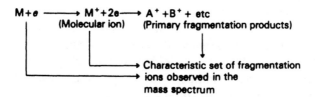

through the slits and an ion lens system into the mass analyser, under the influence of a small positive repelling potential in the source. The degree of fragmentation and hence the spectral fingerprint or pattern, depends on the energy of the bombarding electron beam. The energy range 60–80 eV is most frequently used and is the range within which most reference spectra are obtained.

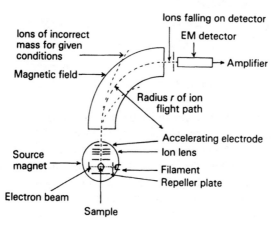

Fig. 7.4 Single focusing magnetic analyser with an electron impact source.

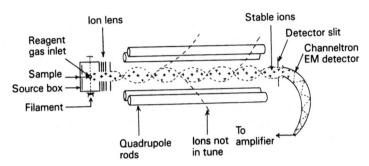

Fig. 7.5 Quadrupole mass analyser with a chemical ionization source.

An EI source requires a pressure of less than $10^{-3}\tau$ and a pumping system with vacuum conductance of 30–$100\,\mathrm{l\,s}^{-1}$.

Chemical ionization (CI) is a variation on the electron impact source (Fig. 7.5). EI spectra frequently contain weak molecular ions or none at all due to the molecules gaining energy in excess of their ionization potential. In the chemical ionization process a much lower transfer of energy occurs and a quasi-molecular ion formed by the loss $(M - 1)^+$ or addition $(M + 1)^+$ of hydrogen ions is formed with little attendant fragmentation. Thus CI spectra provide molecular weight information and frequently structural features not revealed by EI spectra. The ionization chamber in a CI source is of a 'tight' design allowing pressures in the order of 1 torr to be maintained. The sample molecules and a reagent gas (usually methane or isobutane) up to 10^6 times in excess are introduced into the ionization region where the methane is ionized by the electrons. A secondary process (an ion–molecule reaction) then occurs between the sample molecules in low abundance and the primary ions $(CH_5^+, C_2H_5^+)$. The resulting secondary ions proceed to the mass analyser.

$$CH_4 + e \longrightarrow CH_5^+ + C_2H_5^+ + M \longrightarrow (M + H)^+$$
$$\text{or} \quad (M - H)^+ + \text{fragment ions}$$

Because large volumes of reagent gases are used, it is essential to have a source vacuum system with a high pumping speed in addition to the analyser vacuum pump.

Field ionization (FI) sources have been used in GC–MS work. Ions are produced in the FI source by the high positive electric field (typically $10^8\,\mathrm{v\,cm}^{-1}$) produced between a wire and a knife edge. The energy available is generally 12–13 eV which is sufficient to ionize most organic molecules (ionization potential typically 7–13 eV) but since there is less excess energy than with the EI source, less fragmentation occurs and the parent ion can usually be observed. The main disadvantage concerns sensitivity which is of the order of 100 times lower than the EI process.

Mass analysers

The mass analyser produces the separation of the ion beam according to the mass of the ions. There are numerous types and designs but few are relevant to GC–MS; these can be divided into two groups, magnetic and non-magnetic analysers. The most important parameter determined by the analyser is the mass resolution (*R*) which is defined as

$$R = M/\Delta M$$

where *M* is the mass of the first peak of an adjacent pair and ΔM the difference in the masses of two peaks of approximately equal intensity which are separated by a valley between them of 10% peak height. A second parameter which influences GC–MS performances is the length of the ion flight path. A good vacuum must be maintained in the analyser region to ensure that the mean free path of the ions will be significantly greater than the analyser flight path. To avoid vacuum problems, particularly in GC–MS, differential pumping between the source housing and analyser section is used so that a pressure greater by 10^2 may occur in the source whilst the mean free path of the ions in the analyser is not affected.

Magnetic analysers

Single focusing magnetic analysers with a resolution of 500–3000 are commonly used in organic analysis (Fig. 7.4). The ions formed are accelerated through the source slit into a homogeneous magnetic field and then follow a curved path, the radius (*r*) of which is determined by the accelerating potential (*V*) and magnetic field strength (*B*). The mass/charge ratio (*m/e*) of an ion is given by:

$$m/e = B^2 r^2/2V$$

Since the radius is fixed in the design of the instrument, varying either *B* or *V* will result in ions of varying *m/e* values falling on the detector. Varying *B* at a fixed accelerating potential is commonly used to scan through the mass range. However, GC–MS requires a fast reproducible scan which may be readily controlled electronically for reliable interfacing to data acquisition systems. The resolution of magnetic analysers is principally determined by the radius of curvature and also by the width of the source and detector slits, which can be controlled by the operator. Other parameters are built into the design.

(a) Double focusing instruments

To achieve resolution of > 10 000, double focusing analysers are employed. These use an additional ion focusing system, an electrostatic analyser, which generates a radial electric field to counteract the velocity dispersion and hence peak broadening that occurs in a magnetic field (Fig. 7.6). The limitations imposed by this system on scan speed, etc. require special designs and interfacing require-ments, particularly to data systems, the discussion of which is beyond the scope of this text. Double beam techniques, in which the sample and a reference (e.g.

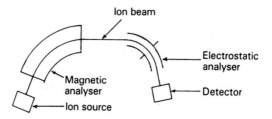

Fig. 7.6   Double focusing mass analyser, Nier–Jordan geometry.

perfluorokerosene, PFK) are run together in a tandem system through the same magnetic and electric fields, are used to calibrate accurately the mass of the ions, the reference ions acting as mass markers. Double focusing instruments are used where separation of ions with a mass that varies in the second or third decimal place is required, for instance in metabolic studies. Since high resolution spectra are complex it is preferable in GC–MS or HPLC–MS work to precede any attempt to obtain accurate data by a low resolution run. Thus the relevant peaks and mass range may be determined and the problem of handling excessive amounts of data is avoided.

(b) The quadrupole mass analyser

The quadrupole mass analyser is the most commonly encountered non-magnetic analyser (Fig. 7.5). It consists of a set of four round or hyperbolic rods in a quadrant formation. Opposite rods are electrically connected together and a voltage applied which consists of a d.c. and r.f. (1–2 MHz) component. Thus an oscillating field is set up between the rods and when an ion moves into this quadrupole field it will oscillate between the electrodes. If the mass of the ion is such that these oscillations are stable then the ion will move through the analyser to the electron multiplier. Ions of other m/e value will undergo unstable oscillations of increasing amplitude until they move out of the quadrupole field. Since there is no force along the axis of the rods an ion accelerating potential of 20–30 V only is required. Scanning is achieved by varying the magnitudes of the d.c. and r.f. voltages; however, by keeping the ratio constant, a linear mass spectrum is produced. A wide range of practical quadrupole spectrometers are manufactured with resolution varying from 100 for analysis of gaseous mixtures to organic quadrupoles with a resolution of 2000 and mass range to 1000. The ability to produce very fast scan times, down to 1 ms, linear spectra and easy interfacing for electronic control have contributed to the popularity of these analysers for GC–MS systems, particularly when microcomputer control is used.

Gas chromatograph interfacing techniques

It is essential to optimize the gas chromatographic procedure for good GC–MS results. The various parameters need to be evaluated and optimized so that a uniform, reproducible chromatogram with good resolution and a narrow spread of the eluted fractions may be obtained. The choice of carrier gas is important; it must be chemically inert, must not interfere with the mass spectral pattern, should permit enrichment of the eluent and should not contribute to the total ion monitor signal. Of the common GC carrier gases, only helium meets these four requirements; it is an unreactive small inorganic molecule and has a high ionization potential (24.6 eV). Gases such as CO_2, N_2, argon and methane have been used in specialized applications, particularly in conjunction with a chemical ionization source as an alternative to a reactant gas introduced directly into the ionization chamber.

No special design of GC sample injector is required and normal practice may be followed. Generally the common 0.125 in. OD column gives a good performance over a wide sample range, typically from nanograms up to 50 mg. Flow rates of these columns vary from 15–100 ml min^{-1} and in order to maintain a good uniform peak shape with minimum sample distribution in the carrier gas, a temperature programming unit is necessary to increase progressively the column temperatures. Capillary columns can also be used, although the sample size is much reduced, as modified interfaces have overcome the problem of sensitivity. The greater resolution of capillary columns is a distinct advantage. Although the choice of stationary phase and support is determined by the chromatographic separation, there are a number of additional points to consider. The stationary phase must have minimum volatility otherwise any column bleed will be transferred through the interface into the mass spectrometer to give a continuous background spectrum, sometimes leaving a coating on the walls of the interface. It is also advantageous to be able to obtain or prepare reproducible columns, so that future analyses may be accurately referenced.

The quantity of effluent gas that may be accepted by the mass spectrometer depends primarily on the pumping rate of the vacuum system and may be in the order of 1–5 ml min^{-1}. Thus a high percentage of the carrier gas must be removed in the interface. An alternative is to use a capillary open tubular column directly connected to the ion source. The flow rate of such columns must be stable and optimized not only for the separation but also to be compatible with the mass spectrometer pumping system and source characteristics. Columns with flow rates of 1–5 ml min^{-1} are regularly used and if carefully interfaced give good results that illustrate the excellent resolution of capillary columns.

(a) Interfacing a gas chromatograph

As mentioned above the ion source pressure is typically less than 10^{-3} τ and since this has to be maintained with the given pumping capacity or conductance of the vacuum system, various types of interface are used to reduce the carrier gas component in the GC effluent. The main reasons for maintaining these pressures are to prevent the filament burning out, reduce background spectra, prevent ion–molecule reactions occurring, and thus altering the fragmentation pattern, maintaining the mean free path of the ions and avoiding high voltage discharges. Although the pumping speed of the vacuum system may be known, the effect of

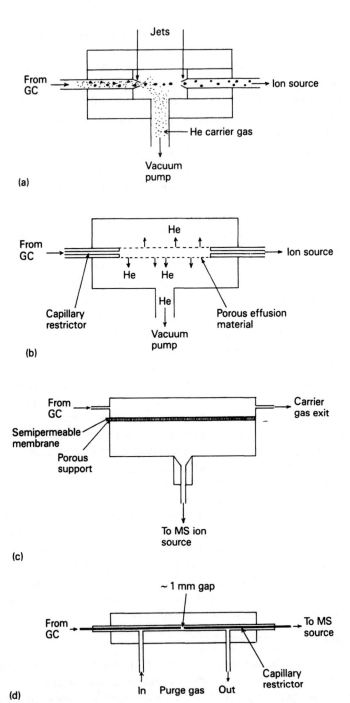

Fig. 7.7 GC–MS interface systems: (a) molecular jet separator; (b) effusion separator; (c) semipermeable membrane diffusion separator; (d) open split interface.

the various restrictions on the conductance must be obtained so that the acceptance rate of the source is known and the performance of the interface may be defined. In order to prevent condensation and cross-contamination the interfaces are heated to at least the column temperature.

The most commonly used interface is the jet separator (Fig. 7.7(a)). The GC effluent passes through a jet and expands into a partial vacuum; only the heavier sample molecules pass through into the collecting jet, the lighter helium being pumped away. Frequently two stages are used to give the desired performance, and the overall assembly requires careful design to obtain an efficient separation. A separate additional pumping system is required.

Alternative separators are mainly based on effusion or diffusion principles. The effusion separator generally consists of a tube through which the GC effluent flows at slightly reduced pressure (Fig. 7.7(b)). A range of porous materials are used, for example glass, stainless steel, silver, or PTFE. The rate at which molecules diffuse through to the lower pressure side is inversely proportional to the square root of the molecular weight. Thus the carrier gas will be preferentially removed from the effluent. Again additional pumping is required.

Semi-permeable membrane separators use a variety of polymeric materials, the most popular being a silicone rubber membrane (Fig. 7.7(c)). In operation the GC exit gas passes over a thin silicone membrane supported on a fine metal mesh or glass sinter. The inorganic carrier gas is insoluble in the silicone polymer and most of it passes on to the exit. However, the organic material, which has a considerable attraction towards the silicone polymer, diffuses through the film to the other side and flows on to the ion source. The rate of conductance of the molecules through a polymer membrane is a function of specific solubility, the diffusion characteristics of the molecules and the physical dimensions of the membrane. In practice, one or two stage membrane separators may be used. The main advantage of these separators is that no additional pumping system is required. The interface uses the low pressure of the ion source to conduct the solute molecules from the membrane to the active region of the source. Many integrated GC–MS systems employ semi-permeable membrane separators because of their simplicity which results in a compact efficient instrument.

The popularity of vitreous silica capillary columns and the good pumping capacity of modern mass spectrometers enable a simple interconnection between the end of the column and ion source to be made without the need for an additional pumping system. Direct connection would present problems due to pressure differentials and lack of control of effluent entering the source. These problems are overcome using an Open Split interface (Fig. 7.7(d)) [4]. The flow into the mass spectrometer is governed by the ion source pressure and hence by flow into the source, the column flow rate, the flow of the purge gas and the predetermined length of the restrictor. The only variable is the purge gas flow rate which is readily adjusted via a needle valve to give the desired flow of column effluent into the ion source. By increasing the purge flow rate, solvent dumping and splitting of selected peaks can be achieved.

(b) Interfacing HPLC ststems

The problems of interfacing HPLC to mass spectrometers are considerably greater than for GC. It is only in recent years that efficient reliable interfaces have been developed and are now commercially available. Early interfaces used cryogenic methods to remove the solvent, but were not too successful. Considerable volumes of solvent have to be removed to concentrate the solute for analysis in the ion source. Two methods are used, one based on a moving belt transport system that includes a flash vaporizer, and a second based on a thermospray injection method which also uses a novel ionization method.

The moving belt LC–MS interface overcomes two major problems; that of removing the solvent yet maintaining a high solute yield, and vaporizing the solute without decomposition. Eluent from the HPLC system is introduced directly on to a continuously moving polyimide or stainless steel belt (Fig. 7.8(a)). An infrared evaporator removes much of the mobile phase (aqueous or polar

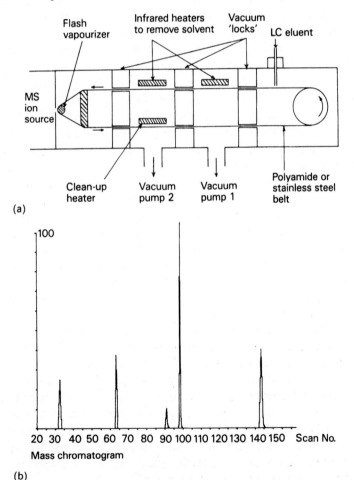

Fig. 7.8   (a) HPLC moving belt interface.

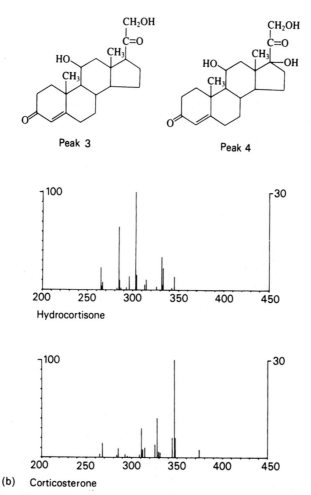

Peak 3

Peak 4

Hydrocortisone

(b)   Corticosterone

Fig. 7.8 (*Contd.*)   (b) LC–MS of steroids, mass chromatogram and mass
spectra of scans 91 (peak 3), 97 (peak 4).

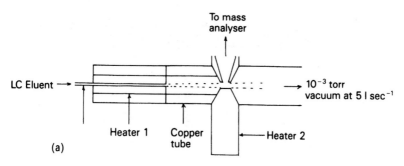

To mass
analyser

LC Eluent →

10^{-3} torr
vacuum at 5 l sec^{-1}

Heater 1   Copper
tube

Heater 2

(a)

Fig. 7.9   (a) HPLC thermospray interface.

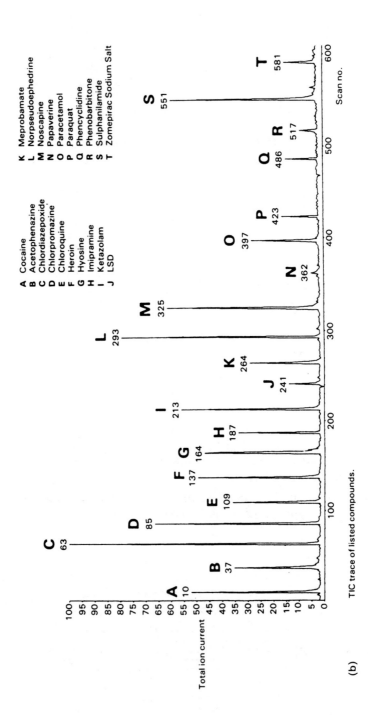

A Cocaine
B Acetophenazine
C Chlordiazepoxide
D Chlorpromazine
E Chloroquine
F Heroin
G Hyosine
H Imipramine
I Ketazolam
J LSD
K Meprobamate
L Norpseudoephedrine
M Noscapine
N Papaverine
O Paracetamol
P Paraquat
Q Phencyclidine
R Phenobarbitone
S Sulphanilamide
T Zomepirac Sodium Salt

TIC trace of listed compounds.

(b)

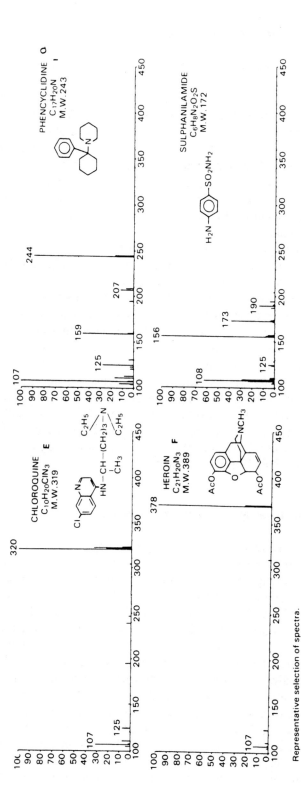

(c)

Representative selection of spectra.

Fig. 7.9 (Contd.)   (b) Mass chromatogram; (c) spectra from HPLC thermospray system. (Reproduced by permission of VG Analytical).

solvents) and removal is completed as the sample moves through two differenti-ally pumped vacuum locks; less than $10^{-7}\,\mathrm{g\,sec^{-1}}$ of solvent enters the mass spectrometer. Inside the mass spectrometer the belt passes through a flash vaporization chamber attached directly to the ion source. The sample is vaporized so quickly that little decomposition occurs and the molecules pass immediately into the ion source. The belt then passes over a clean-up heater to remove any residual sample that might cause interference with the next belt cycle. Up to $2.0\,\mathrm{ml\,min^{-1}}$ of volatile non-polar solvents or up to $1.0\,\mathrm{ml\,min^{-1}}$ of polar solvents can be introduced and subnanogram sensitivity can be obtained. Figure 7.8(b) shows a mass chromatogram of a mixture of steroids and mass spectra of two of the components.

Thermospray interfacing technique permits the continuous introduction of liquid eluent directly into the ion source of a mass spectrometer (Fig. 7.9). The method was developed by Vestal and also incorporates a novel ionization technique [5]. LC effluents are vaporized as they pass through an electrically heated block, the resulting thermospray mist contains desolvated ions which pass straight into the ion source with the excess vapour being pumped away by an added vacuum pump. The system provides stable vaporization and ionization at flow rates up to $2\,\mathrm{ml\,min^{-1}}$ of a polar mobile phase. When ions are present in the mobile phase (ca. 10^{-4} to 1.0 molar concentration) no external ionizing source is required to achieve CI type spectra at sub-nanogram detection levels for a wide range of non-volatile solutes. A conventional electron beam is required for weakly ionized mobile phases to provide gas phase reagent ions for the chemical ionization of solute molecules. Figure 7.9(b) shows a mass chromatogram and typical mass spectra for three of the components [6].

7.2.2 Chromatography–mass spectrometry data systems

A chromatogram usually consists of a number of peaks and since mass spectral data on most of the components may be required a large number of spectra are recorded for analysis. Although it is quite feasible to interpret the mass spectra manually it is rather tedious and indeed would be impracticable for complex mass chromatograms [Figs. 7.8, 7.9] where up to 1000 spectra may be recorded and up to 50 require inspection and interpretation. Computerized data systems are therefore used for data collection and processing. These range from systems which record the spectra and produce conventional relative abundance bar charts for subsequent analysis to systems which analyse the spectra and compare the information with reference data stored on the computer disc memory. An additional feature is the use of the computer for overall control of an integrated GC–MS or LC–MS system. This gives the required stability and optimized operating parameters essential for producing accurate data and interpretations. A high resolution video display and x–y plotter complete the system.

The complex software programs have been developed over many years and

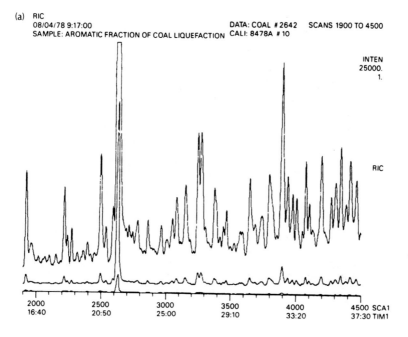

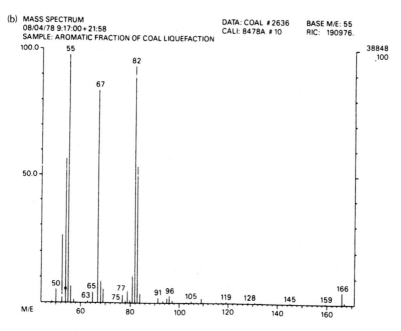

Fig. 7.10   Example of GC–MS data system. (a) A partial reconstructed ion current (RIC) plot for the automatic fraction of a coal liquefaction sample; (b) mass spectrum of the major component, scan 2636.

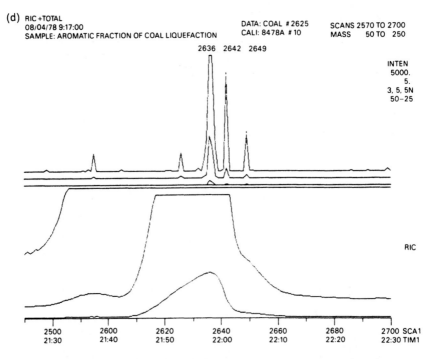

(c) LIBRARY SEARCH   DATA: COAL #2636   BASE M/E: 55
    08/04/78 9:17:00+21:58   CALI: 8478A #10   RIC: 189695
    SAMPLE: AROMATIC FRACTION OF COAL LIQUEFACTION

    31331 SPECTRA IN LIBRARY NB SEARCHED FOR MAXIMUM PURITY
      262 MATCHED AT LEAST 6 OF THE 16 LARGEST PEAKS IN THE UNKNOWN

    RANK IN NAME
    1   8361 1,1'-BICYCLOHEXYL
    2   12080 CYCLOHEXANE, 1,1'-(1,2-ETHANEDIYL)BIS-
    3   18079 HEXANE, 1,6-DICYCLOHEXYL-
    4   2806 CYCLOPENTANE, 1-METHYL-2-(2-PROPENYL)-, TRANS-
    5   13842 CYCLOHEXANE, 1,1'-(1,3-PROPANEDIYL)BIS-

    RANK FORMULA   M.WT   B.PK   PURITY   FIT   RFIT
    1   C12.H22   166   82   873   953   889
    2   C14.H26   194   83   782   852   803
    3   C18.H34   250   83   771   835   778
    4   C9. H16   124   55   763   876   787
    5   C15.H28   208   83   745   842   756

(d) RIC +TOTAL
    08/04/78 9:17:00   DATA: COAL #2625   SCANS 2570 TO 2700
    SAMPLE: AROMATIC FRACTION OF COAL LIQUEFACTION   CALI: 8478A #10   MASS   50 TO 250

                         2636   2642   2649

                                                    INTEN
                                                    5000.
                                                    5.
                                                    3, 5, 5N
                                                    50-25

                                                    RIC

    2500   2600   2620   2640   2660   2680   2700 SCA1
    21:30   21:40   21:50   22:00   22:10   22:20   22:30 TIM1

Fig. 7.10 (*Contd.*) (c) Library search report for the mass spectrum of the major component of the mixture, scan 2636; (d) Biller–Biemann type ion maximization analysis of the region from scan 2570 to scan 2700.

(e)   LIBRARY SEARCH   DATA: USER DEFINED   BASE M/E: 56
31331 SPECTRA IN LIBRARY NB SEARCHED FOR MAXIMUM PURITY
 229 MATCHED AT LEAST 5 OF THE 16 LARGEST PEAKS IN THE UNKNOWN
RANK IN NAME
1   7509 BENZENE, 4-(2-BUTENYL)-1,2-DIMETHYL-, (E)-
2   7508 BENZENE, 1-(2-BUTENYL)-2,3-DIMETHYL-
3   7486 STYRENE, O-ISOPROPYL-. ALPHA.-METHYL-
4   7499 NAPHTHALENE, 1,2,3,4-TETRAHYDRO-1,8-DIMETHYL-
5   7495 NAPHTHALENE, 1,2,3,4-TETRAHYDRO-1,5-DIMETHYL-

RANK	FORMULA	M.WT	B.PK	PURITY	FIT	RFIT
1	C12.H16	160	145	581	857	590
2	C12.H16	160	145	531	807	540
3	C12.H16	160	145	529	823	547
4	C12.H16	160	145	519	790	540
5	C12.H16	160	145	504	782	515

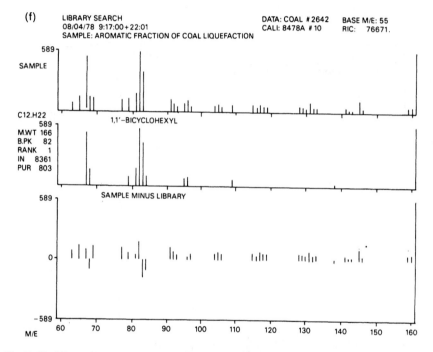

(f) LIBRARY SEARCH   DATA: COAL #2642   BASE M/E: 55
     08/04/78 9:17:00+22:01   CALI: 8478A #10   RIC: 76671.
     SAMPLE: AROMATIC FRACTION OF COAL LIQUEFACTION

Fig. 7.10 (*Contd.*) (e) Library search report for the difference mass spectrum between scan 2642 and 1, 1'-bicyclohexyl; (f) plots of the mixed mass spectrum at scan 2642 with the library spectrum of 1, 1'-bicyclohexyl and the difference between the two spectra, to find minor component.

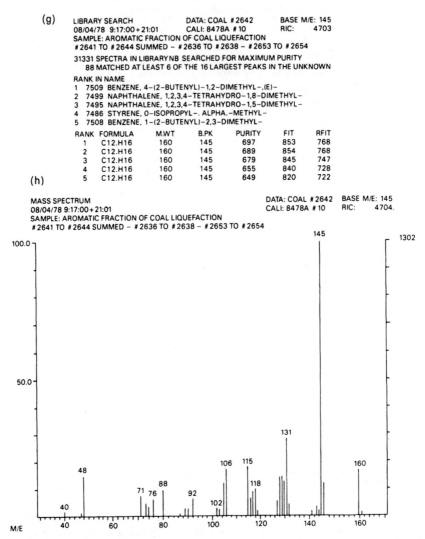

(g)

LIBRARY SEARCH   DATA: COAL #2642   BASE M/E: 145
08/04/78 9:17:00+21:01   CALI: 8478A #10   RIC: 4703
SAMPLE: AROMATIC FRACTION OF COAL LIQUEFACTION
#2641 TO #2644 SUMMED – #2636 TO #2638 – #2653 TO #2654

31331 SPECTRA IN LIBRARY NB SEARCHED FOR MAXIMUM PURITY
    88 MATCHED AT LEAST 6 OF THE 16 LARGEST PEAKS IN THE UNKNOWN

RANK IN NAME
1   7509   BENZENE, 4–(2–BUTENYL)–1,2–DIMETHYL–,(E)–
2   7499   NAPHTHALENE, 1,2,3,4–TETRAHYDRO–1,8–DIMETHYL–
3   7495   NAPHTHALENE, 1,2,3,4–TETRAHYDRO–1,5–DIMETHYL–
4   7486   STYRENE, O–ISOPROPYL–. ALPHA.–METHYL–
5   7508   BENZENE, 1–(2–BUTENYL)–2,3–DIMETHYL–

RANK	FORMULA	M.WT	B.PK	PURITY	FIT	RFIT
1	C12.H16	160	145	697	853	768
2	C12.H16	160	145	689	854	768
3	C12.H16	160	145	679	845	747
4	C12.H16	160	145	655	840	728
5	C12.H16	160	145	649	820	722

(h)

MASS SPECTRUM   DATA: COAL #2642   BASE M/E: 145
08/04/78 9:17:00+21:01   CALI: 8478A #10   RIC: 4704.
SAMPLE: AROMATIC FRACTION OF COAL LIQUEFACTION
#2641 TO #2644 SUMMED – #2636 TO #2638 – #2653 TO #2654

Fig. 7.10 (*Contd.*)   (g) Library search report for the reconstructed minor component spectrum from (d) at scan 2642; (h) reconstructed minor component spectrum by selective subtraction of spectra. (Reproduced by permission of Finnegan Instruments).

have now reached the level where automatic sample analysis and sample identification can be carried out. Calibration of the mass spectrometer is straightforward and automatic using standard reference compounds such as PFK (perfluorokerosene), or FC43 (perfluorotributylamine). On quadrupole instruments the calibration may be retained for several weeks due to their inherent stability, although for highly accurate work calibration is carried out prior to sample analysis. The calibration routine memorizes the spectrum position and instrument parameters for the reference peaks of the calibration material and then calibrates the m/e scale over the whole mass range. Accuracies of ± 10 mmμ with quadrupoles and ± 60 ppm with magnetic instruments can be achieved. All calibration data and spectra obtained during sample analyses are stored on disc for further data processing as required, some examples of which are given in Fig. 7.10.

The software is able to reconstruct the mass chromatogram using the total ion current for each scan, enhance the resolution and reduce the background to produce a clearer chromatographic trace. This is important in the analysis of complex mixtures where minor peaks may be of interest. Selected component peaks can also be 'flagged' or marked on the chromatogram. Peaks of interest can be selected for further analysis by printing out the mass spectrum and comparison of the spectrum with a library of spectra for possible identification [Fig. 7.10]. Routines for specific applications may be written and a library file built up so that routine analysis and quality control may be carried out. An isometric map reconstructed from the ion current shows how the intensities of a chosen mass volume or mass range varies with time and further illustrates the overall flexibility and power of MS data systems in processing data to provide molecular structural information.

7.3 INFRARED SPECTROPHOTOMETRY

Infrared spectrophotometry is a familiar established analytical technique which provides identification of compounds by fingerprint spectra, of which a vast library is available. Both liquid and gaseous samples may be easily analysed and therefore modifications of established sample handling techniques have enabled both GC and HPLC instruments to be readily interfaced. The main problem has been the scan time of several minutes which made it difficult to scan each chromatography peak in real time. Stop-flow techniques stopping the mobile phase flow whilst a spectrum is recorded have been used but introduced additional problems with the chromatography. Ideally scan times of 1 s or less are required to be able to record each peak and peak shoulders for a sensitivity of less than 100 ppm of sample. Fourier transform infrared (FT–IR) spectroscopy is able to meet these criteria but until recently the instrumentation and computer system have been too expensive for routine use. The new generation of FT–IR instruments are controlled by microcomputers and incorporate data handling facilities. A schematic diagram of a typical instrument is shown in Fig. 7.11. Conventional spectrophotometers achieve the spectral dispersion using a diffraction grating. FT–IR instruments operate on a completely different principle. In Fourier transform optics, the source radiation passes into a Michaelson interferometer consisting of a beam splitter and moving mirror [7,8]. The beam splitter passes approximately half the radiation to a moving mirror, where it is reflected back again. The rest of the radiation passes through the beam splitter to a stationary mirror whereupon it too is reflected back. The

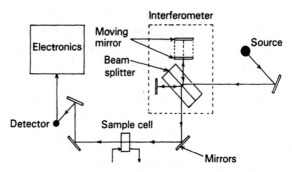

Fig. 7.11   Infrared interferometer Fourier transform instrument.

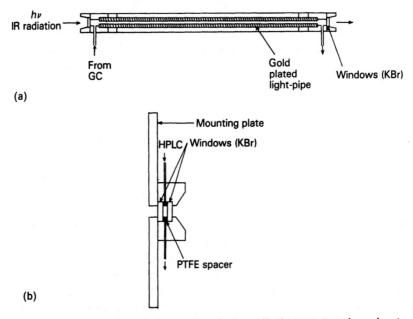

Fig. 7.12   (a) GC–infrared light-pipe sample cell; (b) HPLC–infrared micro-
liquid sample cell.

relative path lengths of the two beams are varied by the moving mirror,
thus introducing a phase difference between the two beams. After recombination
interference occurs between the beams and the resulting encoded beam passes on
to the sample compartment and detector. The latter requires a rapid response
and is usually a doped triglyceryl sulphate detector. The spectral range is covered
by the range of path difference achieved by translating the moving mirror. The
resulting detector signal is an interferogram consisting of the complex Fourier
transform of the spectrum. The spectrum is obtained by carrying out an inverse
Fourier transform using a specially written computer program. The resolution

and scan speed of FT–IR instruments is sufficient for on-line interfacing to GC and HPLC instruments. Recent developments in this area and in applications are now frequently reported [9, 10].

Interfacing consists mainly of transferring the GC or HPLC column eluent *via* a heated capillary line to a flow-through sample cell. The volume of the cell must be less than the volume between the half-height points of the narrowest chromatographic peak so that peaks that are only just resolved do not merge in the sample cell.

The sample cell system for GC–IR consists of a micro light-pipe cell. This is typically a 42 cm internally gold plated Pyrex tube with an internal diameter of 3 mm, giving a sample volume of 3 ml, and fitted with spring-loaded KBr disc windows on the ends (Fig. 7.12(a)). The light-pipe cell may be operated up to 350° C. HPLC sample flow cells have internal volumes of less than 30 μl, and therefore to present a suitable window area to the spectrophotometer a 1 mm to 3 mm pathlength is used with a 3 × 5 mm beam area. Standard NaCl or KBr window materials may be used with many organic solvents and PTFE or polyethylene windows are also available (Fig. 7.12(b)). Micro HPLC is a rapidly developing variation of LC particularly for applications requiring organic solvents. Micro HPLC–FTIR techniques may employ a direct flow cell or solvent elimination techniques [9, 10]. Considerable care is required to match the chromatographic system with the sample cell to avoid loss of resolution.

7.3.1 Data collection and processing

The spectrophotometer monitors the infrared absorbance in the sample cell by carrying out repetitive scans of the predetermined wavelength or frequency range at a scan rate of approximately 5 s. The number of consecutive scans can be co-added prior to the Fourier transformation. When this is performed in real time typically 1024 points corresponding to a resolution of 16 cm are used. The integrated absorbance for each scan is then calculated and used to construct a 'chemigram', the chromatogram obtained by plotting absorbance data. The chemigram may also be plotted as a series of windows covering a specified spectral range (Fig. 7.13). This is useful for distinguishing compound types and assists the identification of separated components. At the end of the chromatographic analysis a series of spectra are present as stored data points which may be processed in a number of ways.

If a solvent is present in the sample, as in HPLC, the solvent spectrum (previously recorded) can be subtracted from the recorded spectrum to produce a solute spectrum (Fig. 7.14). Due to the variation in infrared molar absorptivity coefficients between substances (up to 50:1 between a small polar molecule and a medium-sized hydrocarbon), a fixed sensitivity figure is difficult to assign. Therefore, a minimum weight of sample for analysis is usually specified. Sensitivities down to μg s^{-1} levels can be achieved.

The chemigram is inspected to identify the spectra of components of interest, these spectra are then transformed and stored as disc files (e.g. spectra 18–22 for peak 2 toluene, Fig. 7.13). A series of data manipulation routines are available to process and evaluate the spectra. These include noise filtering techniques to improve the signal to noise ratio and baseline correction, windowing to select a wavelength range for scale expansion, measuring exact peak positions and intensities, interconversion of frequency and wavelength scales and production of transmittance or absorbance spectra. Spectral subtraction routines enables non-chemical separations to be carried out, for example, subtraction of a major

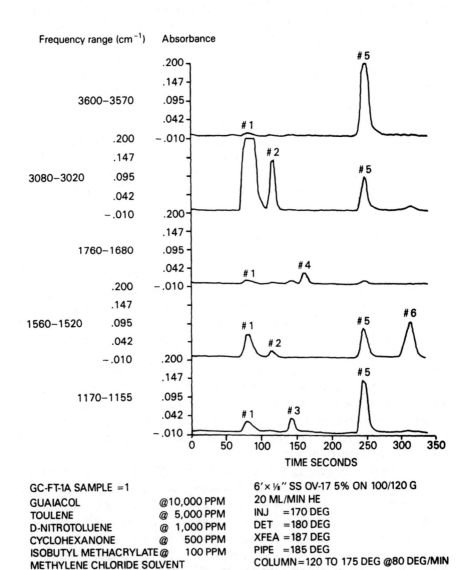

GC-FT-1A SAMPLE =1
GUAIACOL   @10,000 PPM
TOULENE   @ 5,000 PPM
D-NITROTOLUENE   @ 1,000 PPM
CYCLOHEXANONE   @   500 PPM
ISOBUTYL METHACRYLATE@   100 PPM
METHYLENE CHLORIDE SOLVENT
6 MICAOLITER INJECTION

6′ × ⅛″ SS OV-17 5% ON 100/120 G
20 ML/MIN HE
INJ   =170 DEG
DET   =180 DEG
XFEA =187 DEG
PIPE =185 DEG
COLUMN=120 TO 175 DEG @80 DEG/MIN
ATTN.=0.5 MV×16

(Contd.)

(a)

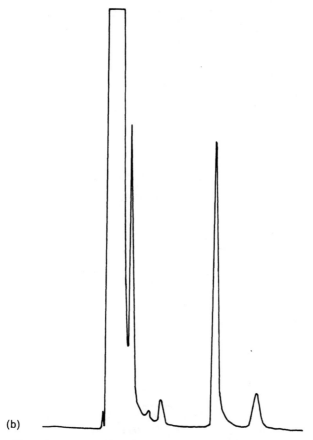

(b)

Fig. 7.13   Chemigram   and   chromatogram   from   GC–FT–IR   analysis:
(a) Chemigram; (b) chromatogram.

component in a mixture to identify a minor component. Integration techniques are generally more useful than peak height calculations for automatic quantitation procedures. The pre-programmed facilities usually include integration and peak height routines which can be extended for calculation of quantitative results specific to a particular application using the command language (BASIC or a similar language syntax) to prepare pre-programmed procedures. A library of spectra may be used to identify components by comparing spectral character-istics with the library. Data bases such as the Aldrich, Sadtler, EPA and Nicolet libraries are available and provide a new dimension in component identification in the analysis of mixtures.

7.4 UV–VISIBLE SPECTROPHOTOMETRY

Chromatography–UV–Visible spectrophotometry techniques are mostly used with LC. The UV-Visible detector is the most widely used HPLC detector but the

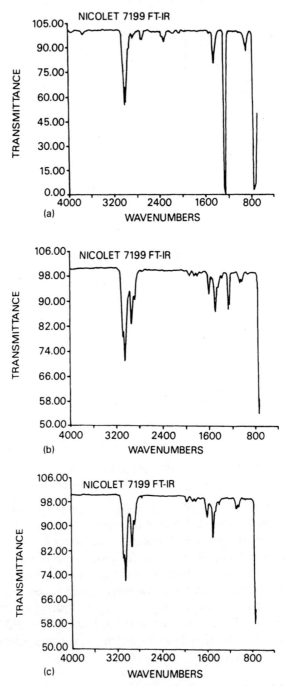

Fig. 7.14 IR spectra from Fig. 7.13 after data processing: (a) spectrum of methylene chloride; (b) spectrum of toluene before solvent subtraction; (c) spectrum of toluene after solvent subtraction. (Reproduced by permission of Nicolet Inc.)

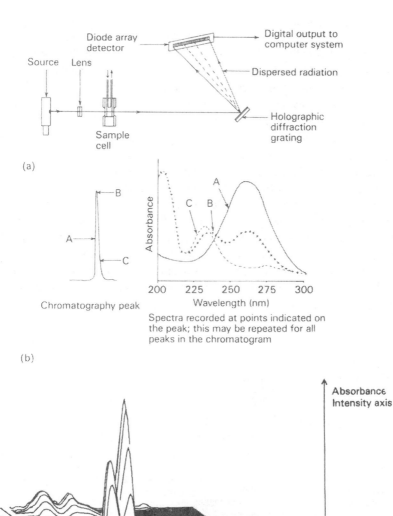

Fig. 7.15 (a) HPLC diode array UV detector system; (b) UV spectra recorded at three points on an HPLC peak to enable peak purity to be determined; (c) isometric map obtained by plotting successive spectra from an HPLC separation of polynuclear aromatics using a diode array detector; A, naphthalene; B, fluorene; C, anthracene; D, chrysene.

scan times of conventional instruments which use a rotating diffraction grating to direct the dispersed spectrum over a single detector element are too slow to record the spectra of rapidly eluting peaks in real time. Stopped flow techniques do overcome some of the problems but also adversely affect the chromatography. Thus most chromatograms are recorded at predetermined wavelengths. Recent developments in detector technology have produced a range of instruments which can record a complete spectrum in as little as 0.01 s. We can therefore obtain multiple spectra of a single rapidly eluting peak. Multi-element diode array spectrophotometers use a detector consisting of 256 or 512 photodiode detector elements. The dispersed spectrum falls on to the array and each element records a small band within the required wavelength range thus recording all the spectrum at the same instant. Resolution of better than 1 nm is possible depending on the wavelength range scanned (Fig. 7.15(a)). As with IR the spectral intensities can be used to construct a chromatogram or chemigram and selected spectra processed and evaluated. Characteristic reference data from each spectrum may be referenced to a library of data files for identification purposes or used for quantitation calculations. Conventional HPLC flow through sample cells are used and the extremely rapid response enables the cell contents to be

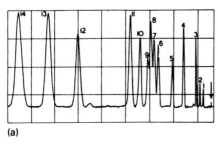

(a)

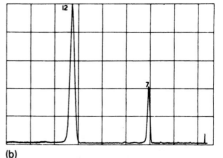

(b)

1 Deuteroacetone
2 Nitroethane
3 Fluorobenzene
4 Toluene
5 n-Butyliodide
6 n-Nonane
7 Chlorocyclohexane

8 Anisole
9 Diethyl disulphide
10 Octanone – 2
11 Bromobenzene
12 o-Dichlorobenzene
13 o-Bromotoluene
14 n-Undecane

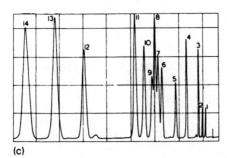

(c)

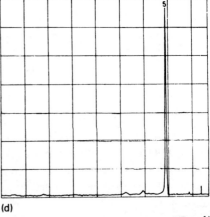

(d)

(Contd.)

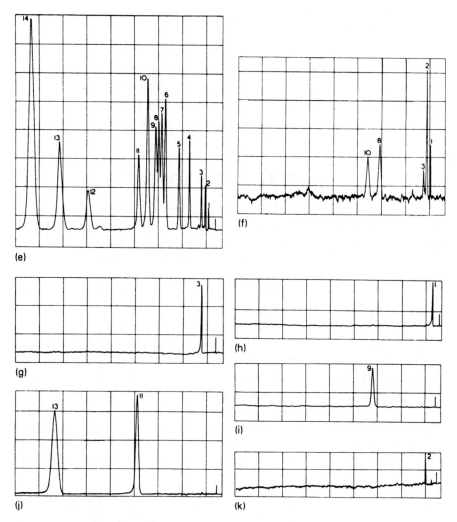

Fig. 7.16 Elemental chromatogram from GC–MPD850 system: (a) FID channel; (b) chlorine channel; (c) carbon channel; (d) iodine channel; (e) hydrogen channel; (f) oxygen channel; (g) fluorine channel; (h) deuterium channel; (i) sulphur channel; (j) bromine channel; (k) nitrogen channel.
(Reproduced by permission of Applied Chromatography Systems).

scanned in less than 0.1 s. Sensitivities are similar to conventional HPLC systems [11].

Chromatography is a separation technique and therefore it is often important to check the purity of a peak. Peak shape, shoulders, etc. are an unreliable indication. At least three scans on each peak are obtained and the spectra compared (Fig. 7.15(b)). This can indicate that at least two components are present. In some cases when it is difficult to compare spectra due to varying quantities of eluted sample in the sample cell, the problem is overcome by automatic normalization. It is not entirely satisfactory to identify a peak by retention time only. Repetitive scans of the detector cell contents are stored in memory. Scans mode can be selected and may be on a sequential time basis, at peak maxima, inflection points, baseline and at peak half height. When this is combined with multiple peak recording a spectral map of a complete chromatogram can be obtained, (Fig. 7.15(c)). Further capabilities include signal to noise optimization, parallel detection of up to eight wavelengths, creation of library data bases and adding specific processing requirements for report formatting and print-out, error checking and validation procedures.

7.5 ATOMIC SPECTROSCOPY

Trace element analyses are often required for monitoring impurities and for analysis of environmental samples. Conventional methods requiring extraction and separation procedures are time-consuming. However, recent developments in GC and HPLC interfaced to atomic absorption and plasma emission spectrometers have enabled on-line analyses to be carried out.

Gas chromatography may be interfaced to an atomic absorption spectrometer *via* a heated stainless steel tube (2 mm outside diameter). The column effluent is introduced into the fuel mixture of an air–acetylene flame just below the burner rail [12]. Alternatively an electrically heated silica tube furnace (7 mm ID, 6 cm long) may be used. GC–AAS has been used to study the tetraalkyl lead residues in environmental samples [13]. Plasma emission spectroscopy has a distinct advantage over atomic absorption, since many elements may be monitored simultaneously. This permits on-line trace elemental analyses to be rapidly carried out on a variety of samples [14, 15]. GC interfacing is relatively straightforward. The column effluent is transferred by a heated line to the plasma source unit of the spectrometer at a carefully controlled flow rate to maintain a

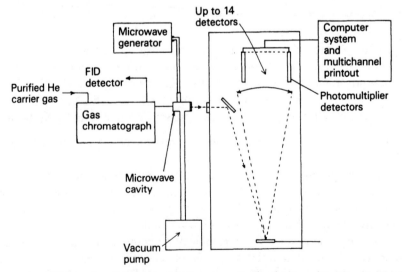

Fig. 7.17 Schematic diagram of GC–microwave plasma detector system.

stable plasma. The plasma source may be one of three distinct types, microwave induced plasma (MIP), direct coupled plasma (DCP) and inductively coupled plasma (ICP), all of which are commercially available [16]. To illustrate the versatility of MIP systems Fig. 7.16 shows the chromatogram of a test mixture and the corresponding 'elemental chromatograms' produced by parallel monitoring of pre-selected atomic lines. This system uses helium as the GC carrier gas and a microwave powered helium plasma [17] (Fig. 7.17).

HPLC is virtually incompatible with a MIP and only ICP has received much attention. The development of a suitable interface has proved a challenge with a neubulization design finding most favour [18]. Initial problems with hydrocarbon or halocarbon solvents have now been overcome by modifications to the nebulizer design. Reverse-phase solvents present fewer problems. Sensitivity and linearity of response vary from element to element as one would expect but is generally within the range 10 ng to 10 mg, the lower detection limits being comparable with flameless atomic absorption analysis. The potential and usefulness of the technique can be extended by using derivatization reagents containing an organometallic or inorganic derivatizing species [19].

REFERENCES

1. McFadden, W. H. (1973) *Techniques of Combined Gas Chromatography/Mass Spectrometry*, Wiley Interscience, London.
2. Hill, H. C. (1974) *Introduction to Mass Spectrometry*, Heyden, London.
3. Dawson, P. H. (ed) (1976) *Quadrupole Mass Spectrometry*, Elsevier, Amsterdam.
4. Henneberg, G. *et al.* (1978) *Chromatography 78*, Elsevier, Amsterdam, p. 111.
5. Blakely, C. R. and Vestal, M. L. (1983) *Anal. Chem.*, **55**, 750–754.
6. Lewis, I. A. S. (December 1983) *Insight, No. 13*, V. G. Analytical Ltd., Wythenshawe, Manchester M23 9LE.
7. Griffiths, P. R. (1978) *Transform Techniques in Chemistry*, Heyden, London, Chapter 5, p. 109.
8. Griffiths, P. R. (1975) *Chemical Infrared Fourier Transform Spectroscopy*, Wiley, New York.
9. Vidrine, D. W. (1979) *Fourier Transform Spectroscopy* Vol. 2, Academic Press, New York, Chapter 4, pp. 129–163: Brown, R. S., Hauster, D. W., Taylor, L. T. and Carter, R. C. (1981) *Anal. Chem.* **53**, 197.
10. Kuehl, D. T. and Griffiths, P. R. (1979) *J. Chromatogr. Sci.* **17**, 471: (1980) *Anal. Chem.* **52**, 1394.
11. Miller, J. C., George, S. A. and Willis, B. G. (1982) *Science*, **218**, 241–246.
12. Chau, Y. K., Radziuk, B., Thomassen, Y., Butler, L. R. P. and Van Loon, J. C. (1979) *Anal. Chim. Acta.*, **108**, 31–38.
13. Chau, Y. K., Wong, P. T. S., Bengert, G. A. and Kramer, O. (1979) *Anal. Chem.*, **51**, 186–188.
14. Krull, I. S. and Jordan, S. (1980) *Int. Lab.* November, 13–25.
15. Barnes, R. M. (1978) *CRC Critical Reviews, Anal. Chem.*, September, 203.
16. Fraley, D. M., Yates, D. and Manahan, S. E. (1979) *Anal. Chem.*, **51**, 2225.
17. McLean, W. R., Stanton, D. L. and Penketh, G. E. (1973) *Analyst*, **98**, 432.
18. Gast, C. H., Kraak, J. C., Poppe H. and Maessen, F. J. (1979) *J. Chromatogr.* **185**, 549.
19. Blau, K. and King, G. (1980) *Handbook of Derivatives for Chromatography*, Heyden, London.

8 PROCESSING OF CHROMATO- GRAPHIC DATA

Chromatograms are produced by plotting the continuously varying signal from the instrument against time. The time (x axis) is representative of the retention time or retention volume. The y axis plot is a direct representation of the detector signal after suitable electronic processing to produce an appropriate output voltage for use with chart recorders, integrators or computers (Fig. 8.1).

The detector signal is produced in response to the measurement of some property of the sample molecules. The magnitude of the signal at any given time is proportional to the concentration of sample molecules present in the detector. In addition to separating the components of a sample mixture, the chromatographic process causes band broadening. Therefore the detector records a broad signal in the form of a Gaussian peak since the solute molecules will be more numerous at the centre of the band (Fig. 8.2). The area under the peaks is a measure of the relative amounts of each component in a sample mixture.

8.1 METHODS OF RECORDING THE CHROMATOGRAPHIC SIGNAL

8.1.1 Chart recorder

Chart recorders used in chromatography are y/t recorders where the y axis is driven by the output of the instrument and therefore records detector signal intensity. The t or time axis is driven at constant speed by the chart paper drive motor; it is calibrated in seconds (time) or volume of mobile phase (Fig. 8.2). The y axis is calibrated to respond to signals over a preset range, which is set to match the output signal range of the instrument amplifier (Fig. 8.1). The true detector signal is measured from the detector base-line background signal. The main disadvantage of a chart recorder is that if the detector signal goes above the preset output voltage range it cannot record the true signal level

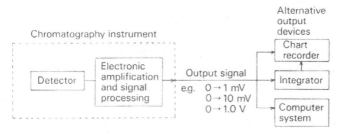

Fig. 8.1 Signal processing in chromatography systems.

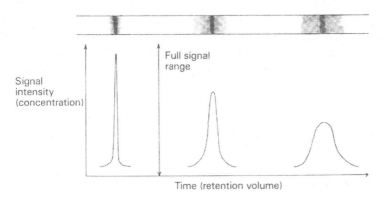

Fig. 8.2 Detector response for various solute bands from chromatogram plotted on a chart recorder.

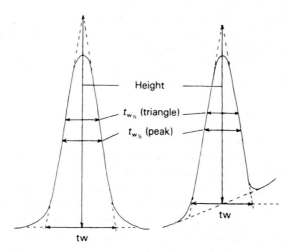

Fig. 8.3 Measurement of peak areas.

unless the sensitivity of the instrument amplifier is adjusted using the attenuator control. This is rather inconvenient and produces untidy chromatograms. A further problem of using only a chart recorder is the procedure used to obtain the area under the chromatographic peaks in order to calculate the ratio of the components in a mixture. There are two main methods.

1. Carefully cutting out the peaks and weighing each one: this produces reasonable results providing the chart paper is of uniform thickness and moisture content. Relative precision is better than 15%.

2. Calculating peak areas by triangulation. This is feasible since Gaussian peaks approximate to an isosceles triangle. The relative precision is better than 13%. An approximate value for the peak area may therefore be obtained by multiplying the peak height (h) with half the base width. Base width is difficult to determine and width at half height ($t_{W_{1/2}}$) is used instead. If baseline drift has occurred then the peak height is measured from the mid point on the line joining start and end points of the peak. The apex is found by extending the sides of the peak (Fig. 8.3).

$$\text{Area} = h \times t_{W_{1/2}}$$

This method is unreliable for narrow and unsymmetrical peaks.

8.1.2 Integrators

Various integration devices have been developed over the years. However present integrators are based on digital electronics and microprocessor systems. The analog detector signal is converted into digital signals using an analog to digital converter (ADC) and the resulting digital data is summed for the duration of the peak and stored. The total count is then printed out for each peak, together with retention times. Electronic integrators have a wide linear range enabling them to cope with wide variations in signal magnitude, for instance solvent and solute peaks. Many can also automatically correct for baseline drift and overlapping peaks. The relative precision is better than $\pm 0.5\%$.

Computing integrators

Computing integrators may be based on specially designed microprocessor systems or readily available personal computers. In all cases an interface containing an ADC is required to monitor the detector signal and produce digital data for the microcomputer system (Fig. 8.4). Once the chromatographic data is stored in memory a wide range of data processing procedures can be carried out, limited only by the ingenuity of the programmer. All the present generation of chromatographic instruments also use a microprocessor system for control and therefore digital control and data signals (e.g. RS232 and IEEE488) are available for linking into computers and integrated laboratory networks (Fig. 8.5). It is

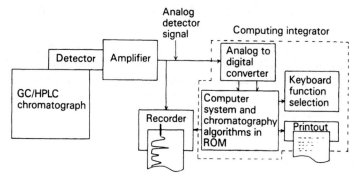

Fig. 8.4 Computing integrator.

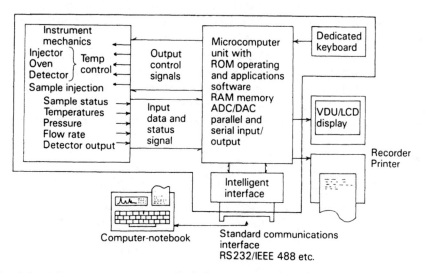

Fig. 8.5 Microcomputer controlled chromatograph with standard communications interface.

thus quite feasible for a personal or a hand-held 'laboratory notebook' computer to communicate with the instruments and download sample and parameter information setting up the chromatograph for a particular application and analysis. When this is completed the data can be transferred from the instrument back to the computer or laboratory network for reporting. It is beyond the scope of this book to explain computer systems; there are however some excellent reviews and text books on the subject [1].

8.2 DATA COLLECTION AND PROCESSING

There are two main features required for processing chromatographic data; accurate digitization of the analog detector signal and software for detection of peaks, correction for baseline drift, calculation of peak areas, retention times, concentrations of components using stored detector factors and production of the final analytical report.

8.2.1 Signal digitization

The analog detector signal is converted into digital binary data required by computers *via* an interface unit which includes signal buffering, amplification and attenuation and an analog to digital converter (ADC) (Fig. 8.6). It is important to use an ADC with adequate resolution since the resulting digital signals must accurately describe the analog signal, including such details as shoulders and overlapping peaks which may be reflected in small differences in signal intensity or rapidly changing signals. An ADC samples the analog signal at a fixed rate, the time interval having been previously established. At least 10 points are generally required to describe a peak accurately and more if a shoulder is present, otherwise detail will be lost (Fig. 8.7). A sampling rate of at least 10 readings per peak width at half height or about 10 readings/second is acceptable for most chromatography. Resolution is determined by the number of binary bits (BInary

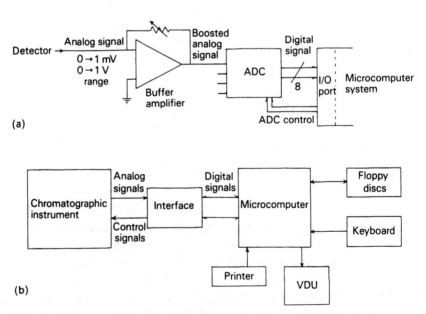

Fig. 8.6 (a) Interface for a chromatograph detector signal; (b) microcomputer system interfaced to a chromatograph.

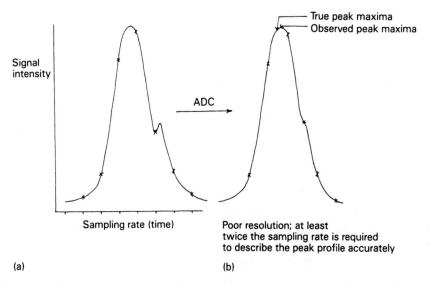

Fig. 8.7   Effect of ADC sampling rate on resolution: (a) analog plot; (b) digital
representation.

digIT) used to describe the full signal range. Thus an 8-bit ADC uses 256 (2^8)
incremental steps to represent the range of an analog signal. A 12-bit ADC uses
4096 (2^{12}) steps and therefore has a 16-fold increase in resolution (see Fig. 8.8).
Chromatography data systems often use a 14-bit ADC with a resolution of 16 384
(2^{14}) steps. This is sufficient to resolve very small solute base line peaks and
solvent peaks with sufficient accuracy for quantitative calculations using one
attenuation range. Autoattenuation procedures are also used, implemented in
software or hardware using a multichannel ADC [2, 3].

8.2.2 Data processing

The digital data for each ADC reading is stored in memory, two bytes generally
being required, together with the corresponding elapsed time value. At the end of
the analysis the chromatogram is present in memory as a sequential file of ADC
readings representing the y axis intensity values. Since the ADC readings are
usually taken at fixed time intervals then it is not necessary to hold a separate
elapsed time file for retention data. This is obtained from the number of the ADC
reading (N) multiplied by the time interval (t_1) between readings. Thus when
the ADC reading corresponding to a peak maxima is found the retention time
(t_R) for that component is calculated by:

$$t_R = N \times t_1 \text{ seconds}$$

With a time interval of 0.1 seconds, a peak maxima at the 1600 ADC reading would have a retention time of:

$$t_R = 1600 \times 0.1 \text{ seconds}$$
$$= 160 \text{s}, 2.6 \text{ mins}$$

The advantage of this method is that an accurate reconstruction of the whole chromatogram can be produced and subsequent inspection carried out. When all the required checks have been performed and data processing completed, the chromatogram can be dumped to floppy disc for storage and a reduced data report produced or a print-out of the chromatogram and required data produced. The computer is then ready for a new analysis. Personal computers now have sufficient memory for the above method of data collection and processing, and are fast enough for a real-time display on VDU or dot matrix printer of the chromatogram and peak areas and retentions. However, if memory limitations are a problem then only the ADC readings which constitute a peak are stored, together with the reading number. The disadvantage of this method is that only peak information is collected and therefore the complete chromatogram cannot be recalled after the analysis unless a chart recorder is used in parallel with the computer.

8.2.3 Computer hardware

A typical personal or home computer is capable of being used as a chromatographic data system, preferably including floppy discs and a VDU screen (resolution of at least 256×200 pixels) together with a dot matrix printer. For example, Apple II, BBC B, CBM 64, IBM PC, SIRIUS, APRICOT, all have

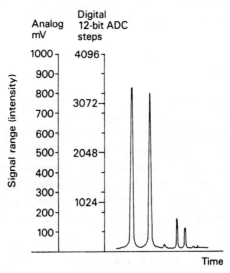

Fig. 8.8   Resolution of a 12-bit analog-to-digital converter (ADC).

sufficient RAM memory and screen resolution and have suitable I/O expansion facilities for interfacing. They are also fast enough for real-time display of the developing chromatogram and limited real-time calculations.

To obtain optimum real-time performance it is necessary to write the routines for screen display and calculations such as retention times and peak areas in machine code for speed rather than high level languages such as BASIC and PASCAL. Newer commercial data systems use 16-bit processors such as the MC 68000 or 8086, with at least 128K bytes of RAM; 320 × 200 pixel graphics, two floppy disc units and interface sensitivity of 100 μv at 10 counts s^{-1}. They also have communication facilities for local area networking (LAN). Many also store up to 16 sets of method details and have the capability to control a completely automated gas or liquid chromatograph.

8.2.4 Chromatography software

Preprogrammed software for standard chromatography calculations is included in most commercially available chromatography integrators and data station packages. Additional routines can generally be added as BASIC-like pro-grammes for specific applications and for producing the final analytical report [4].

A brief description of the main chromatography data processing routines is given below.

Calculation of peak area

The fundamental calculation performed is the determination of the area under a peak. Although peak shapes and the base line may vary the procedure for calculation of the area, once the limits have been found, is similar. The area between the limits is integrated using a summation algorithm which can be based on Simpson's Rule, simple summation of ADC readings or trapezoidal

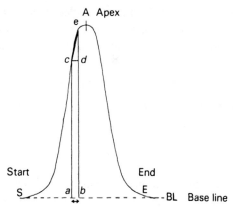

Fig. 8.9   Trapezoidal integration.

integration, the latter being the most accurate (Fig. 8.9). In the trapezoidal method an area slice or integral of the peak is determined by using successive ADC readings, *ac* and *eb*, and the slope *ce* of triangle *ced* to calculate the area of the trapezium *aceb*. Note the base line signal BL is subtracted from the readings to obtain *ac*, *eb*. Area percentage is calculated using the raw peak area data. The total of all peak areas is found and the percentage contribution of each peak is calculated.

$$A_{TOTAL} = \sum_i^n A_n, \quad A_n\% = (A_n)/(A_{TCTAL}) \times 100$$

Normalized area percentage

The area of each peak is first corrected ($A_{CORRECT}$) using the relative response factor (R) for that particular component. The area percentage is then calculated as above.

$$A_{nCORRECT} = A_n \times R_n$$

Internal standard

The results derived from the peak areas are calculated relative to a standard added to each sample. Accuracy is therefore not dependent on repeatable sample size or other peaks. The internal standard is first standardized against known concentrations of one or more components to obtain the relative response factors (see Chapter 2 page 22):

$$C_n = (A_n \times C_{IS})/(A_{IS} \times R_n)$$

where C = concentration, A = peak area, R = response factor, n = nth component, IS = internal standard.

Standard addition

When an internal standard cannot be added to a sample the method of standard addition may be used to calculate the concentration of a component in a mixture. The sample is first analysed as normal, and the analysis is then repeated with a known amount of the component of interest added to the sample. The increase in peak area is due to the amount of added component and this factor is used to calculate the concentration of the component in the sample mixture (see Chapter 2 page 23):

$$C_n = (x \times A_1)/(A_2 - A_1)$$

where $(A_2 - A_1)$ is the difference in peak area due to standard addition of weight x mg of added component.

Peak detection

Peak detection algorithms use a predetermined signal threshold level above the baseline. Once the threshold is exceeded peak monitoring occurs. There are two main methods (Fig. 8.10).

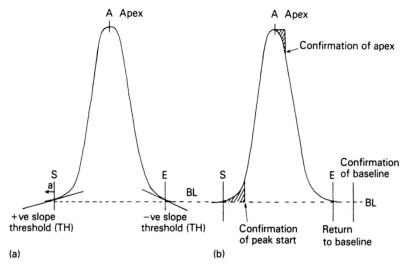

Fig. 8.10   Peak detection based on: (a) slope monitoring; (b) area integration.

(i) Peak detection based on slope monitors the slope of the changing signal. If this is positive and equal to or greater than the threshold value integration begins. Peak termination may also be based on a negative slope equal to or less than the threshold. During integration the change in slope of the signal or zero slope can be used to detect peak apex.

(ii) The test integral area method calculates an integral area every time the signal increases and if this exceeds the preset threshold value then integration begins. The test integral method may also be used to detect the peak maximum by looking for a negative change in integral area.

Baseline correction and overlapping peaks

During many chromatographic separations the baseline drifts in a linear or non-linear manner in either a positive or negative direction. Correcting algorithms are used so that peak areas can be accurately calculated. If the baseline has moved upwards more than the threshold during elution of a peak then peak termination occurs when the current baseline value is equalled. A more common occurrence is when the baseline moves down and has a lower value than the original baseline. Integration is therefore continued until the slope or integral area is equal to or less than the threshold (Fig. 8.11). When peak termination occurs the triangle *abc* is added to the peak area.

The area of individual peaks in a set of merged peaks is most commonly calculated by detection of the valleys between peaks (zero slope between negative and positive going slopes) and dropping a perpendicular down to the baseline. A linear baseline is assumed between the start and end of the set (Fig. 8.12). This free-running algorithm can also be applied to a peak on the tail of a larger peak or

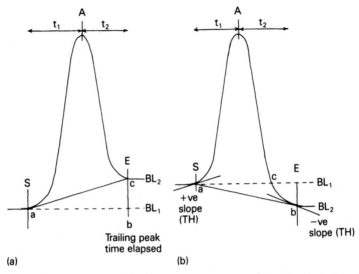

Fig. 8.11   Detection of end of peak after: (a) upward baseline drift; (b) negative baseline drift.

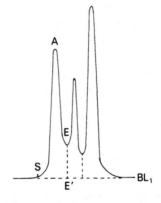

Fig. 8.12   Analysis of merged peaks.

alternatively a tangent skimming routine may be used (Fig. 8.13). The baseline is followed when it is within the threshold. Peak integration begins when the valley is detected, (a) this provides the first baseline point, BL1. Integration ends when the slope threshold is reached, (b) and forms the new baseline, BL2. The area of the triangle *abc* is added to the integrated peak area *adc*. An alternative is to predict the change in baseline during the elution of a peak. This is only possible if sufficient pre-peak baseline is available for a matrix algorithm to calculate the rate of change in baseline signal and extrapolate it to forward-project the baseline (Fig. 8.14).

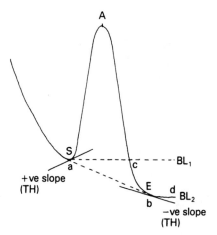

Fig. 8.13   Baseline followed in free-running mode.

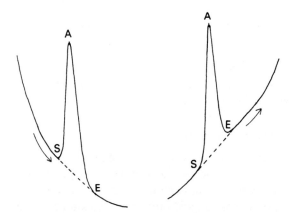

Fig. 8.14   Tracking of the baseline by predicting baseline slope.

Where the chromatogram shows a cluster of peaks on a non-linear baseline a valley-to-valley algorithm can be used to calculate the areas of the individual peaks by starting and ending integration at the valleys between peaks. A new baseline value is established at each valley and a corrected peak area calculated (Fig. 8.15). A routine to detect negative-going peaks is also used to avoid confusion with an altering baseline. Alternatively response to all negative-going peaks can be inhibited.

Most computing integrators allow selection of the sampling rate slope sensitivity and signal smoothing or filtering factors. All chromatographic peaks should give a positive slope value visibly greater than the baseline variation. Facilities to reject peaks with a width at half height below a selected value and termination of tailing peaks after a selected time are generally included in the software.

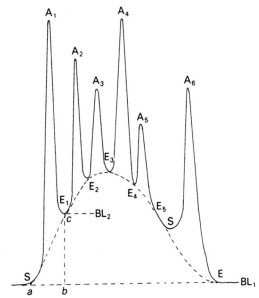

Fig. 8.15   Peak cluster analysis by valley-to-valley baseline correction.

Reference files of chromatographic data can be accumulated either for a specific analysis or group of applications. Data from a run may then be compared with the files for checking and identification purposes. Examples of typical printouts are shown in Fig. 8.16.

Optimization in chromatography

Microcomputer data processing systems can be programmed to analyse features in a chromatogram and to determine whether the separation of the individual components is satisfactory. If the computer is also used to control the instrument variables, (particularly column and mobile phase parameters) these can be reset according to the evaluated data and the analysis repeated until the optimum or satisfactory separation is achieved. A fully automated system including autosampling is required as outlined in Fig. 8.4. Optimization procedures simplify the rather lengthy process of developing a new method, particularly in HPLC, and replace the rather empirical approach based on experience, guess-work and some theory [5]. Most attention has centred on HPLC, optimization being achieved by adjusting the mobile phase composition of a binary mixture until the desired selectivity, analysis time or other criteria are met [6]. A flow diagram of a typical optimization procedure is shown in Fig. 8.17. There are a number of optimization methods available which are based on linear techniques employing theoretical and semi-empirical models or on a sequential or statistical search technique [7]. The most popular method uses the Simplex optimization algorithm, an efficient multidimensional sequential search technique which has been applied to a variety of analytical problems and has been adapted for HPLC [6, 8, 9]. In order to use any optimization routine it is necessary to have a quantitative assessment of the separations achieved in a chromatogram. The chromatographic work function (CRF) provides a numerical description of the quality of a separation and may be used as the response input into the optimization routine [6, 10]:

$$CRF = \sum_i^n R + f_1(N) + f_2(t_A - t_n) + f_3(t_1 - t_0)$$

where R = the resolution between adjacent peaks, N = number of peaks, t_A = specified analysis time, t_n = retention time of the last eluted peak, t_1 = retention time of the first eluted peak, t_0 = specified minimum elution time.

A number of sequential analyses are carried out automatically with the mobile phase composition being adjusted between analyses as determined by the optimization procedure. Typically 5 to 10 analyses are required for optimization.

Poorly resolved chromatographic peaks can be deconvoluted using a second differential method [11]. The first differential plot of a Gaussian peak gives a

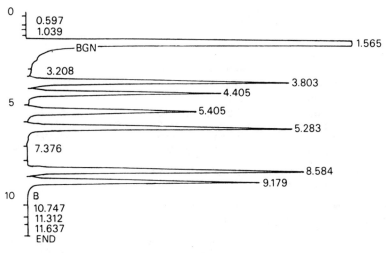

(a)   RUN 42   10:33 83/06/19
       METHOD 4   AROMATICS

RUN 42   10:33 83/06/19
METHOD 4   AROMATICS   CALCULATION: %

RT	AREA	BC	AREA %
3.208	3.37	T	0.6357
3.803	97.68	T	18.4125
4.405	68.78	T	12.9756
5.405	69.14	T	13.0436
6.283	102.66	T	19.3669
7.376	0.36	U	0.0726
8.584	106.61	T	20.1124
9.179	81.88		15.2952
10.747	0.18	U	0.0352
11.312	0.08	T	0.0158
11.637	0.18	U	0.0340

Fig. 8.16 Annotated chromatogram and reports from data processing system: (a) area per cent report with annotated chromatogram.

(b)

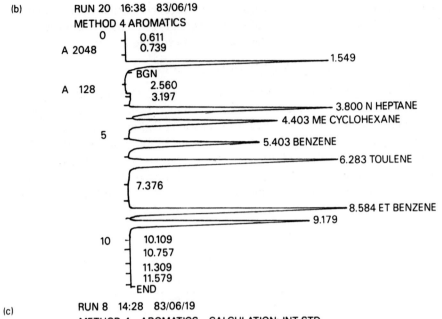

RUN 20 16:38 83/06/19

METHOD 4 AROMATICS

0 — 0.611
          0.739
A 2048
                                              1.549
       BGN
A 128   2.560
          3.197
                                    3.800 N HEPTANE
                              4.403 ME CYCLOHEXANE
5   5.403 BENZENE
                              6.283 TOULENE
       7.376
                                    8.584 ET BENZENE
                              9.179
10 — 10.109
        10.757
        11.309
        11.579
      END

(c)   RUN 8 14:28 83/06/19
          METHOD 4   AROMATICS   CALCULATION: INT STD

RT	AREA	BC	RRT	RF	AMOUNT	NAME	GRP
3.851	118.20	T	0.703	1.1102	0.0234	N HEPTANE	1
4.383	87.66	T	0.814	1.1050	0.0173	ME CYCLOHEXANE	1
5.442	94.75	T	1.000	1.0520	0.0159	BENZENE	2
6.269	135.45	T	1.162	1.0000	0.0242	TOLUENE	0
8.552	147.06	T	1.588	0.9850	0.0259	ET BENZENE	2

5 MATCHED COMPONENTS 99.99% OF TOTAL AREA
5 PEAKS > AREA/HT REJECT

2 GROUP 1 PEAKS TOTAL AMOUNT 0.0407
2 GROUP 2 PEAKS TOTAL AMOUNT 0.0418

(d)   RUN 6 12:16 83/06/19   METHOD 4   AROMATICS   CALCULATION: CALIB AUG OF 1

RT	RRT	RF	STD AMT	NAME	GRP
3.85	0.703	1.1102	0.9875	N HEPTANE	1
4.38	0.814	1.1050	1.0058	ME CYCLOHEXANE	1
5.44	1.000	1.0520	1.0045	BENZENE	2
6.26	1.162	1.0000	1.0258	TOLUENE	0
8.55	1.588	0.9950	0.9877	ET BENZENE	2

Fig. 8.16 (*Contd.*) (b) Annotated chromatogram with component labelling; (c) peak identification and example report printout; (d) calibration report. (Reproduced by permission of Perkin-Elmer Ltd.)

Z-shaped peak, the zero crossing point corresponding to the peak maxima. The second derivative produces a central peak which is narrower than the first-order peak and coincident with it (Fig. 8.18). Thus a second derivative time-domain display of a chromatogram shows the constituent peaks in a sharpened form and has been successfully applied in drug analyses [12]. Other routines such as Fourier transforms are being used for removing low and high frequency noise from chromatograms and to improve signal quality generally.

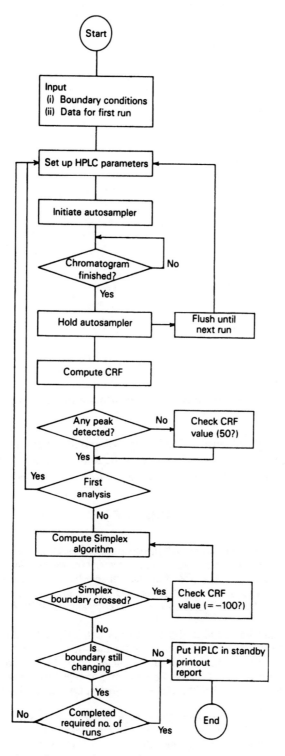

Fig. 8.17 Flow diagram for simplex optimization computer program.

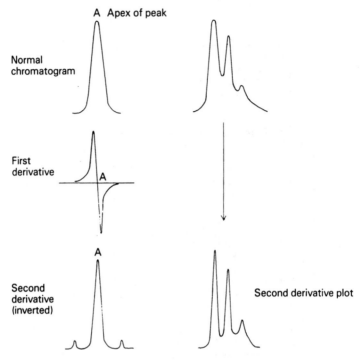

Fig. 8.18   Derivatization method of peak enhancement.

Data processing and evaluation using computers offers the analyst the flexibility and capabilities needed to extract the maximum of information from the analytical data and also to enhance the performance of instruments.

REFERENCES

1. Carrick, A. (1979) *Computers and Instrumentation*, Heyden, London: Malcome-Lawes, D. J. (1984) *Microcomputers and Laboratory Instrumentation*, Plenum Press, London: Leventhal, L. A. (1978) *Introduction to Microprocessors*, Prentice-Hall, New York: Meadows, R. and Parsons, A. J. (1983) *Microprocessors: Essentials, Components and Systems*, Pitman, London: Braithwaite, A. (1983) *Eur. Spect. News*, **51**, 24–27.
2. Tarroux, P., and Rabilloud, J. (1982) *J. Chrom.* **248**, 249–262: Braithwaite, A. and Smith, B. (1984) *Computer Applications in the Laboratory*, No. 3, 190–194.
3. Lyne, P. M. and Scott, K. F. (1981) *J. Chromatogr. Sci.*, **19**, 547, and 599: Bishop, D. (1982) *Interfacing to Microprocessors and Microcomputers*, Newnes Butterworth, London: Titus, J. A. *et al.* (1981) *Apple Interfacing*, Osbourne McGraw-Hill, New York.
4. Spencer, W. A. *et al.* (1980) *Anal. Chem.* **52**, 950: Kaiser, R. E. and Rackstraw, A. J. (1983) *Computer Chromatography*, Afréd Huthig, Heidelberg: Lee, J. D. and Lee, T. D. (1982) *Statistics and Computer Methods in BASIC*, Van Nostrand Reinhold, New York.

5. Massart, D. L., Dijkstra, A. and Kaufman, L. (1978) *Evaluation and Optimisation of Laboratory and Analytical Procedures*, Elsevier, Amsterdam: Bunday, B. D. (1984) *Basic Optimisation Methods*, Edward Arnold, London: Daniels, R. W. (1978) *An Introduction to Numerical Methods and Optimisation Techniques*, Elsevier, North Holland.
6. Ryan, P. B., Barr, R. L. and Todd, H. D. (1980) *Anal. Chem.*, **52**, 1460–1467, Berridge, J. C. (1980) *J. Chromatogr.*, **202**, 469; Berridge, J. C. (1982) *Chromatographia*, **16**, 172; Berridge, J. C. (1984) *Trends Anal Chem.*, **3**, 1.
7. Grant, J. R., Dolan, J. W. and Snyder, L. R. (1979) *J. Chromatogr.*, **185**, 153.
8. Demming, S. N. and Morgan, S. L. (1973) *Anal. Chem.*, **45**, 278, and (1974), **46**, 1170.
9. Nelder, J. A. and Mead, R. (1965) *Comp. J.*, **7**, 380.
10. Carr, P. W. and Watson, M. W. (1979) *Anal. Chem.*, **50**, 1835.
11. Atkinson, D. J. and Linnett, L. M. (1980) *J. Chromatogr.* **197**, 1.
12. Fell, A. F. (1980) *Anal. Proc.* **17**, 512–519, and (1979) *UV Spectrom. Bulletin*, **7**, 5–26.

9 MODEL OR PRACTICAL EXPERIMENTS IN CHROMATO-GRAPHIC TECHNIQUES

It has been the objective of the text to provide theory at a level adequate for an understanding of the underlying principles of chromatographic techniques. However, chromatography is very much an applied and practical subject and a 'hands on' approach provides much insight into the fundamentals of chromatographic methodology.

The experiments described in this chapter are a few of those which have been found by the authors to be useful in teaching the fundamental techniques of chromatography to technician, diploma and undergraduate students and to members of short courses in practical chromatography. The experiments have been chosen to give an example of each of the main procedures, and all have been found to work well in the hands of the inexperienced. No particular originality is claimed, although it is not always possible to quote original sources, because several published methods may have been blended, and then further adapted, by the present authors or their colleagues. In many cases the experiments are designed for use with a particular material or apparatus, often merely because that happened to be available. It is usually not difficult to modify the methods so that other similar equipment can be used. All the experimental figures and chromatograms reported have been determined by the authors (or their students) for the conditions described.

Some experiments in paper chromatography, electrophoresis, thin layer and open column chromatography have been included to illustrate the types of separations possible as well as to give practice in the different techniques.

A greater number of experiments have been included on GC and HPLC to reflect the importance of these techniques in the modern chromatography laboratory. The experiments in these sections may be performed on the majority of commercially available chromatographs with little or no modification.

9.1 LIST OF EXPERIMENTS

Section A. Paper chromatography

1. Ascending and horizontal methods: separation of cobalt, manganese nickel and zinc.
2. Quantitative separation of copper, cobalt and nickel.
3. Ascending chromatography on ion-exchange paper.
4. Separation of amino acids by two-way development.
5. Separation of amino acids using Kawerau technique.

Section B. Electrophoresis and related techniques

6. Horizontal low-voltage electrophoresis of amino acids.
7. Cellulose acetate and polyacrylamide gel electrophoresis of proteins.
8. Analytical fractionation of proteins according to isoelectric point by gel electrofocusing.

Section C. Thin-layer chromatography

9. Preparation of microplates and separation of aromatic amines.
10. Separation of simple organic compounds on fluorescent silica plates.
11. Separation of sugars on bisulphite and acetate modified silica.
12. TLC of analgesics by multiple development.

Section D. Column chromatography

13. Separation of dichromate ion and permanganate ion on alumina.
14. Determination of the exchange capacity and exchange efficiency of a cation exchange resin.
15. Complex elution of iron and copper using a cation-exchange resin.
16. Purification of proteins on DEAE-cellulose.
17. Gel filtration of Dextrans and vitamin B_{12}.

Section E. Gas chromatography

18. Gas chromatography of alcohols.
19. Determination of ethanol in an aqueous solution.
20. Analysis of barbiturates.
21. Qualitative analysis using retention data from two columns.
22. The determination of chlorinated insecticides using an ECD.
23. A study of some important parameters in gas chromatography
    (a) column temperature
    (b) injection port temperatures
    (c) sample size
    (d) carrier gas flow rate

Section F. High Performance liquid chromatography

24. Analysis of barbiturates by reverse-phase isocratic chromatography
25. Ion pair chromatography of vitamins.
26. Techniques in HPLC analysis of analgesics.
27. Analysis of amino acids as their DNP derivatives.
28. Analysis of inorganic anions using conductimetric detection.

9.2 SECTION A. PAPER CHROMATOGRAPHY

Standard tubes are available for applying accurate volumes $(1-10\,\mu l)$ of sample solutions to chromatographic paper and TLC plates. Alternatively a Pt loop, 3 mm in diameter or an extruded melting point tube can be used for spotting the sample solutions.

9.2.1 Experiment 1. Ascending and horizontal methods: separation of cobalt, manganese, nickel and zinc

Object

To illustrate the use of gas jars for ascending development and to compare with horizontal methods. To compare the sensitivity of three different locating reagents and different papers.

Introduction

For basic information on development techniques and visualization of spots in paper chromatography, see Chapter 3.

Materials and equipment

Solution A:	mixture of the chlorides of the four metals (about 0.05 g of each metal in $100\,cm^3$).
Solvent:	acetone/conc. HCl/water (87:8:5 v/v).
Paper:	No. 1, No. 3 MM, (reels 3 cm wide, or cut from sheets) No. 1, No. 2, and No. 4 (12.5 cm circles) Whatman chromatography papers,
Locating reagents:	(a) rubeanic acid/salicylaldoxime/alizarin (RSA); (b) diphenylcarbazide. (c) soldium pentacyanoammine ferrate(II)/rubeanic acid (PCFR).
Developing apparatus	(a) gas jars 7 cm × 30 cm, with suspension hooks; (b) Petri dishes 11 cm in diameter.

Method

(a) Ascending development

Cut three strips of No. 1 paper 24 cm long. Apply 10 μl of solution A (about 2.5 μg of each metal) to the centre of the strip about 2 cm from one end. Place the solvent in the gas jars to a depth of 3 cm and roll the jars round to wet the walls with solvent. Suspend the paper strips, sample spots to the bottom, in the sealed gas jars just clear of the solvent. Allow to stand for a few minutes, to equilibrate the liquid and vapour phases, and then lower the strips so that the ends are 1 cm below the liquid surface. When the solvent front has risen 12–15 cm remove the strips from the jars, mark the solvent front and hang to dry. Spray one strip with each of the locating reagents (a), (b) and (c). Repeat the experiment with No. 3 MM paper.

(b) Horizontal development

Locate through the centre of the paper disc a small wick formed from a piece of the same type of paper. The wick should be long enough to reach the bottom of the petri dish and have a diameter not more than one thickness of paper. Draw a circle of 1.5–2.0 cm diameter and apply 10 μl of the samples at 1.5 cm intervals. Allow to dry, put the paper on a Petri dish containing solvent, cover with a second dish, and develop, dry, and spray as before.

The horizontal methods should be tried with Nos. 1, 2, and 4 papers.

Remarks

The order of elution of metals and the approximate R_f values for the ascending method are:

$$Ni, 0.05; \ Mn, 0.30; \ Co, 0.50; \ Zn, 0.90$$

The visible solvent front is the 'dry' front. The 'wet' front has an R_f value of about 0.75, and a pale yellow band may be seen at this point (before application of the locating reagent) due to traces of iron (Fig. 9.1). It should be noted that traces of the iron (very soluble in the wet solvent) impurity and the zinc (very soluble in the dry solvent) give rather diffuse zones, whereas the other metals give much more compact spots.

9.2.2 Experiment 2. Quantitative separation of copper, cobalt and nickel [1] by ascending development

Object

To evaluate quantitatively the composition of a mixture of metal ions by visual comparison of the coloured spots with standards. An accuracy of $\pm 5\%$ is possible if the procedure is carefully followed, and the standards accurately made up.

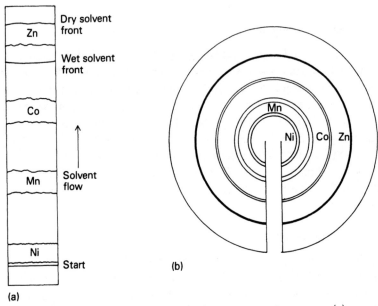

Fig. 9.1   Separation of metals on Whatman no.1 paper: (a) ascending
separation; (b) horizontal separation.

Introduction

The range of visualization techniques and procedures for quantitations in paper
chromatography have been detailed in Chapter 3.

Materials and equipment

Solutions: (a) Standard solutions: S1, 4.0 µg; S2, 2.0 µg; S3, 1.0 µg; S4,
0.50 µg; S5, 0.25 µg of each metal per 0.01 ml. Solution S1
is made up of the following: $CuCl_2.2H_2O$ 282 mg,
$CoCl_2.6H_2O$ 395 mg, $NiCl_2.6H_2O$ 395 mg made up to
250 ml in water with the minimum amount of hydrochloric acid. S2–S5 are made by quantitative dilution of
S1.
(b) Solutions containing an unknown amount of each
metal; the concentrations should fall within the limits of
S1 and S5.

Solvent: butanone/conc. HCl/water (75:15:10 v/v).
Paper: CRL/1, No. 1. chromatography papers
Locating reagent: rubeanic acid.
*Development
apparatus:*   1 l beaker and clock glass.

Method

Make up some solvent mixture and put 25 ml into the 1 l beaker. Roll the solvent round the walls and cover with the clock glass. Put about 2 ml of each standard solution and one unknown into labelled test tubes; to each add 0.5 g of potassium hydrogen sulphate, warm, and then cool to room temperature.

Apply 10 μl quantitatively to each paper strip with a pipette, in the order S1, u, S2 ... u, S5 (u is the unknown). Label each strip. Make the sheet into a cylinder by means of a paper clip at the top, and put it in a 600 ml beaker suspended in a boiling water-bath. Leave it for three min. to dry, and then immediately put it into the beaker containing the solvent. Replace the cover, and allow to run until the solvent front is just above the top of the slots (about 50 min).

Remove the sheet, allow to dry in the air for five min., and then stand it in an atmosphere of ammonia for two min. (a convenient way is to put it in a covered 600 ml beaker, in the bottom of which is a 25 ml beaker containing 0.880 ammonia). Immediately open out the cylinder and spray the paper evenly on both sides with rubeanic acid solution; dry and estimate the concentration of the unknown solution by visual comparison of the spots.

9.2.3 Experiment 3. Ascending chromatography on ion-exchange paper [2]

Object

To illustrate the use of ion-exchange papers for the separation of metals. A strong and a weak acid cation-exchange modified cellulose paper are used, in the form in which they are supplied.

Introduction

The principles underlying the separation of ions on paper have been presented in Chapter 3. The method of development is as Experiment 2; only the sorption mode differs.

Materials and equipment

Solution:	iron, copper, and nickel, as chlorides (aqueous, about 2 mg of each metal per ml.).
Eluting solution (buffer):	1.0 mol l^{-1} $MgCl_2.6H_2O$.
Paper:	(a) cellulose phosphate (P81) in the monoammonium form.
	(b) carboxymethylcellulose (CM82) in the sodium form.
	Supplied as sheets in each case – cut strips as required.
Locating reagent:	sodium pentacyanoamminoferrate(II)/rubeanic acid (PCFR)
Tanks:	gas jars as used in Experiment 1.

Method

Prepare two tanks, and one strip 3 cm wide of each paper as described for Experiment 1. Apply 10 μl of the test solution as a streak; there is no need to dry the spot. Put the paper in the tank and start the run immediately. For comparison, run a strip in a third gas jar using No. 1 paper, and the solvent used in Experiment 1. Allow a run of 10–15 cm, and then remove the sheets, dry, and apply the locating reagent.

Remarks

Note that the strong acid paper gives a better separation than the weak acid type. The order of elution on the ion-exchange paper is opposite to that in normal chromatography (Fig. 9.2). Notice also that on P81 paper the iron does not move, because of the high stability of the iron-phosphate complex.

The approximate R_f values are given in Table 9.1

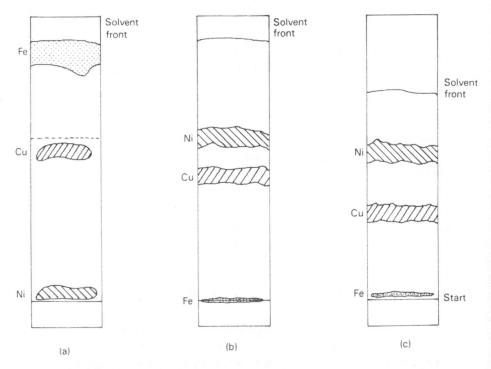

Fig. 9.2   Separation of metals on Whatman papers: (a) no.1 paper; (b) P81 paper; (c) CM 82 paper.

Table 9.1 R_f values for Experiment 3

Paper	P81	CM82	No. 1
Iron(III)	0.00	0.06	0.75
Copper(II)	0.60	0.27	0.65
Nickel(II)	0.75	0.75	0.05

9.2.4 Experiment 4. Separation of amino acids by two-way development [3–5]

Object

To illustrate the advantages of two-way development techniques in the separation of complex mixtures, for instance amino acids.

Introduction

The classical paper separation of amino acids is the two-dimensional method. As an example of the technique a synthetic mixture of amino acids is used rather than protein hydrolysates which require a number of sample preparation steps. The ascending frame methods of Dent and of Smith are used in this experiment.

Materials and equipment

Solutions:	Reference solutions of individual amino acids (in water, dilute hydrochloric acid, or 10% propan-2-ol), and solutions of mixtures. Suitable mixtures are listed below; each acid should be present in a concentration of about 0.25% w/v.
Solvents:	1. butan-1-ol/acetic acid/water 12:3:5 v/v.
	2. phenol/water 500 g:125 ml. This solvent is made up by adding 125 ml of water to a normal 500 g bottle of phenol and leaving to stand in a warm place until a homogeneous liquid has been formed.
Paper:	No. 1, Whatman chromatosheets; 25 cm square with corner holes.
Locating reagents:	(a) ninhydrin; (b) isatin; (c) Ehrlich reagent.
Development apparatus	cubic tanks 30 × 30 × 30 cm, with dural frame and solvent tray, each accommodating five paper sheets.

Method

It is essential to handle the paper with the fingers as little as possible, especially when it is wet with solvents, as finger prints may show up on treatment with ninhydrin.

Take eight sheets of paper and draw two lines at right angles 2 cm from the edges. With the intersection (the origin) at the lower left-hand corner, mark the solvent flow directions – solvent 1 upward, and solvent 2 horizontally. On four further sheets of paper draw a line 2 cm from one edge, and mark seven points at equal intervals along it. These sheets are for one-way reference chromatograms of single amino acids. Label all the sheets and origins.

Apply $10 \mu l$ of an amino acid mixture solution at the origin; the spot should not exceed 0.5 cm in diameter. Apply the same mixture to the next sheet. Repeat with the third and fourth sheets, but using a second mixture. The fifth should be one of the one-way sheets; apply $5 \mu l$ of each of seven individual amino acid solutions to the marked positions.

Prepare two frames in this manner, using the same two mixtures, and the same seven acids as on the one-way sheet. See that in the second frame the start line of the one-way sheet is correctly placed for running in solvent 2. Allow all the spots to dry.

Put 150 cm³ of solvent in the tray in each tank (solvent 1 in one tank and solvent 2 in the other). Put the sheets in the trays with the appropriate starting lines lowermost, and replace the lids. It will be observed that no equilibration time is necessary. An overnight run of 12–16 h. should be allowed.

Remove the sheets from the tanks, and dry. Sheets which have been in solvent 1 will be dry in 1 h, but those from solvent 2 must have a least 4 h drying time.

When the sheets are dry, carefully unscrew the panel nearer to the one-way sheet, and remove that sheet. Replace it by a second one, ensuring that its starting line is located correctly at right angles to the starting line of the sheet removed, and apply one spot of each of seven other amino acids; replace the side panel. Repeat for the second frames, using the same seven acids.

Put fresh solvent in each tank and repeat the above procedure for the next solvent. Ensure that the sheets are turned through 90°, so that the correct starting lines are lowermost. Remove and dry as before.

The following chromatograms have been obtained:

Two sheets containing one-way chromatograms of fourteen amino acids run in solvent 1;

Two sheets containing one-way chromatograms of the same acids run in solvent 2;

Two sheets each containing a chromatogram of a mixture, run first in solvent 1, and then in solvent 2;

Two sheets each containing a chromatogram of the same mixture, run first in solvent 2, and then in solvent 1; and

Four sheets containing chromatograms of a second mixture, run under the same conditions.

The amino acids are located by spraying when dry, as follows:

One-way sheets: ninhydrin
Two-way sheets for a particular mixture:

First sheet:	(1) ninhydrin
	(2) Ehrlich reagent
Second sheet:	(1) isatin
	(2) Ehrlich reagent.

After treatment with ninhydrin and with isatin, heat the sheet in the drying oven at 105° C for 4 min; mark all the spots which appear, examine the sheet under ultraviolet light, and identify as many of the amino acids as possible before applying the second reagent.

Determine R_f values (Table 9.2) for the individual amino acids from the one-way sheets; from those, and the 'standard map' (Fig. 9.3) identify the constituents of the mixture.

Remarks

Notice that the one-way chromatograms only form a rough guide to the position of the substances on the two-way sheets, and also notice how the order in which the two solvents are used affects the two-way results. Suggested mixtures which give good two-way chromatograms are:

1	2	3
alanine	glutamic acid	2-aminobutanoic acid
arginine	glycine	leucine
glutamic acid	hydroxyproline	phenylalanine
proline	lysine	taurine
serine	proline	threonine
tyrosine	serine	tyrosine
valine		

Table 9.2 R_f values for amino acids

	Solvent 1 $BuOH/AcOH/H_2O$	Solvent 2 $PhOH/H_2O$
Alanine	0.24	0.55
2-Aminobutanoic acid	0.28	0.58
Arginine	0.13	0.60
Glutamic acid	0.25	0.33
Glycine	0.20	0.40
Hydroxyproline	0.21	0.67
Leucine	0.58	0.82
Lysine	0.12	0.55
β-phenylalanine	0.50	0.86
Proline	0.39	0.88
Serine	0.19	0.34
Taurine	0.12	0.33
Threonine	0.21	0.49
Tyrosine	0.38	0.62
Valine	0.40	0.74

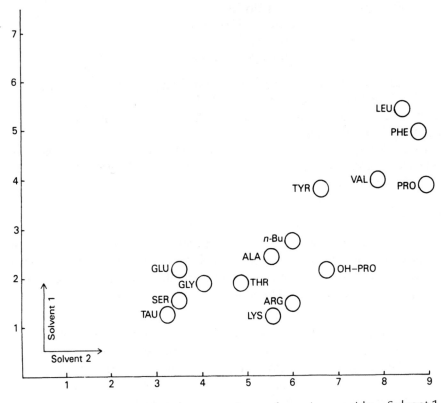

Fig. 9.3 Standard map for separation of amino acids: Solvent 1, BuOH/AcOH/H₂O; solvent 2, PhOH/H₂O; *n*-Bu, 2-aminobutanoic acid.

9.2.5 Experiment 5. Separation of amino acids using Kawerau technique

Object

To illustrate the use of the Kawerau apparatus for horizontal development, and the improved speed and resolution of the method compared with ascending and descending techniques.

Introduction

The principles underlying the improved resolution and increased speed of analysis afforded by 'Kawerau' development have been presented in Chapter 3. Useful comparison can be made with results obtained in previous experiments by ascending development techniques.

Materials and equipment

Solutions:	cystine, hydroxyproline, β-phenylalanine, and mixtures of two or all (about 0.25% w/v of each acid in water).
Solvent:	butan-1-ol/acetic acid/water 12:3:5 v/v.
Paper:	No. 4, type KCT, 14.5 cm (circles with five radial slits).
Locating reagent:	isatin.
Development apparatus:	Kawerau apparatus.

Method

Apply 5 µl of the test samples (five in all: three reference solutions and two mixtures) at the inner apex of each sector of the paper. Allow the spots to dry. Put enough solvent in the dish to give a depth of about 0.5 cm; see that the capillary is running freely, and adjust its height to be just above the edge of the dish. Put the paper in place with its centre touching the capillary. If flow does not start, put a drop of solvent on the centre of the paper. When flow is established, replace the lid, and allow to run until the solvent front reaches the ends of the slits.

Dry the paper and develop by dipping in the isatin solution then drain, dry, and heat in the oven at 105° C for 4 min. The three amino acids give characteristic colours with the reagent; their order from the centre is cystine, hydroxyproline, β-phenylalanine (Fig. 9.4).

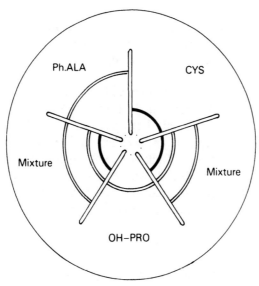

Fig. 9.4   Horizontal separation of amino acids.

Remark

This separation can be carried out by the ascending method, using CRL/1 papers
in the manner of Experiment 3.

9.3 SECTION B. ELECTROPHORESIS AND RELATED TECHNIQUES

9.3.1 Experiment 6. Horizontal low voltage electrophoresis of amino acids

object

To illustrate the separation of amino acids using horizontal low-voltage
electrophoresis.

Introduction

Electrophoresis is more often used to separate proteins than amino acids. The
degree of separation obtained for amphoteric electrolytes depends on the pH of
the buffer and on the isoelectric point of the substances. This experiment
illustrates the use of a horizontal low-voltage paper method, which separates
acidic, basic and neutral amino acids but is not satisfactory for separating the
members of one group from each other.

Materials and equipment

Solution:	a mixture of arginine, aspartic acid, and glycine $(0.04 \, mol \, l^{-1}$ of each, in water).
Electrolyte (buffer):	1 mol l^{-1} acetic acid.
Paper:	No. 1, reels 3 cm wide.
Locating reagents:	(a) ninhydrin; (b) isatin; (c) Sakaguchi reagent.
Apparatus:	Horizontal electrophoresis tank. This experiment was originally designed for the Shandon Horizontal Electrophoresis Tank No. 2508, which is now superseded by the Model U77. Any horizontal electrophoresis apparatus could be used: in all cases manufacturers provide instructions for the use of their products.

Method

Cut four strips of paper of exactly the same length and mount them in the support
frame. Number the strips and draw a line just clear of the paper support, across
the end of the strips to be located in the anode compartment.

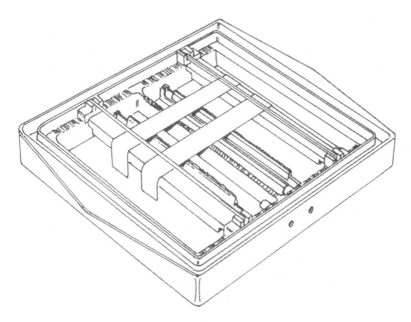

Fig. 9.5   Shandon horizontal electrophoresis apparatus U77

Fill the tank with buffer solution and put the frame in position. Moisten the strips by gently dabbing with pieces of paper dipped in the buffer solution, or with a small soft brush. Mop up any solution spilt on the tank or frame. Adjust the tension of the strips by easing into position and then apply $10 \mu l$ of the test solution with a capillary tube along the lines to within 5 mm of the edges.

Replace the lid, connect up the electrodes to the power pack, and apply a potential of 200 V for 4 hours; the current will be about 2 mA. Display a safety notice on the tank while the current is on, and do not touch the tank or connections without switching off.

At the end of the run, switch off, lift out the frame, and dry quickly. Remove the strips from the frame, and dip two strips in ninhydrin solution and heat at 105° C for 4 min. All three acids are thus revealed, and the strips should appear identical. Dip the third strip in isatin solution and heat at 105°C for 4 min to detect aspartic acid, and treat the fourth strip with Sakaguchi reagent to detect arginine. The order of migration from the start position is aspartic acid, glycine, arginine.

9.3.2 Experiment 7. Cellulose acetate and polyacrylamide gel electrophoresis of proteins

Object

The following practicals enable two electrophoretic techniques on different solid supports for the separation of serum proteins to be studied.

Introduction

Cellulose acetate has a lower solvent and adsorptive capacity than paper. Thus higher voltages can be used with cellulose acetate electrophoreto media, giving sharper bands and improved resolution. Polyacrylamide gels have additional advantages in that the degree of cross-linkage and hence porosity of the medium can be varied; also, if required, the gels can be solubilized after electrophoresis thus facilitating recovery of the separated components.

(1) Cellulose acetate electrophoresis

Materials

Human serum
Cellulose acetate strips (3 × 20 cm) CAM;
Sodium barbitone buffer (0.07 M) pH 8.6;
Lissamine green staining reagent (0.3 g dissolved in 15% (v/v) acetic acid);
1% (v/v) Acetic acid (Destaining reagent).
Whatman No. 1 paper

Method

Place 150 ml of barbitone buffer in each of the two inner compartments of the electrophoresis tank and 200 ml of buffer in each of the two outer compartments. Take 3 CAM strips from the box and lay them with the 'Oxoid' label uppermost on a clean sheet of filter paper. Draw a faint pencil mark across each strip (leaving a 3 mm gap at each side) 5 cm from one end. Label the strips with suitable identification marks at the end of each strip. *Float* the marked strips, 'Oxoid' label down, on the surface of the buffer in the tank so that they are wetted from below by capillary action. This avoids the occlusion of air in the pores of the membrane. When the strips have been wetted completely (a few s) they can be submerged in the buffer. Remove the wetted strips from the tank and blot *lightly* to remove the excess buffer. Place the two curved shoulder pieces in the slots in the outer compartments so that their inner edges are 16 cm apart. Cut two 23 cm strips of Whatman filter paper from the sheets provided and moisten them in the barbitone buffer. Place the moistened strips of filter paper on the perspex shoulder pieces with one edge of the strip running along the top edge of the shoulder piece and the other edge of the strip dipping into the buffer in the outer compartment. These filter paper strips act as wicks to conduct the current from the buffer to the CAM strips. Place the moistened-blotted CAM strips in the tank at right angles to the shoulder pieces with their ends overlapping the filter paper wicks and the borders of the centre of each strip supported by the pins in the tank partitions. Pull the strips taut and secure the ends of the strips with the curved strip holders. Place the transparent cover over the tank to minimize evaporation. From this point on, do not remove the tank cover for longer than is necessary.

Apply 10 μl of the serum samples to the strips in the form of a streak to within 3 mm of the edges. Replace the lid. Connect the leads to the tank so that the origins (pencil lines) are nearer to the cathode (black) than the anode (red). Connect the red and black plugs to the positive and negative terminals of the power pack respectively. Turn on the power supply and run the electrophoresis for 60–90 min at 150 V; the meter should register a current of 4–10 mA. A current of approx. 0.4 mA cm^{-1} width of strip is required.

(a) Staining of serum strips

After the required time turn off the current and remove the strips. Immerse them in the Lissamine green staining reagent for 5 min. Wash the strips 3 times in 1% (v/v) acetic acid to remove the excess dye and blot dry. Dry the strips in a stream of warm air. Record your results both quantitatively and qualitatively. The dry strips may be rendered glass clear by immersion in Whitmore oil if required.

(2) Polyacrylamide gel electrophoresis

Materials

Human serum in 10% (w/v) sucrose;
5% (w/v) sucrose
Solution A: gel buffer (Tris-HCl buffer pH 8.9 containing tetramethylethy-lenediamine (TEMED) 0.17 ml/100 ml of buffer).
Solution B: 33% (w/v) solution of acrylamide in distilled water.
Solution C: 2.25% (w/v) solution of methylene-bisacrylamide in distilled water;
Solution D: an aqueous solution of amonium persulphate (7.5 mg ml^{-1}) prepared just prior to use;
Solution E: tank buffer (Tris-glycine buffer pH 8.2);
Bromophenol Blue: a 0.05% (w/v) solution in 10% (w/v) sucrose;
Staining solution: Coomassie brilliant blue.
TCA staining solution: 10% TCA in water

Method

(a) Preparation of gels (7.5% acrylamide)

N.B. Acrylamide is a nerve toxin – do not ingest or allow solutions of the monomer to touch your skin.

Cap four gel tubes and stand vertically. Into a Buchner flask add 3 ml of solution A, 2.25 ml of solution B, 0.5 ml of solution C and 3.25 ml of distilled water. Cap the Buchner flask and evacuate for 30s. Add 1 ml of the ammonium persulphate solution, mix, then add the prepared solution to the gel tubes with a Pasteur pipette to within 1 cm of the top of the gel tube. Using a hypodermic syringe gently overlay the top of the gel with distilled water, taking care not to cause any mixing, this prevents oxygen (an inhibitor of polymerization) being absorbed and also gives a gel with a flat surface. The gels will polymerize in 10–20 min. After polymerization leave for 30 min. and then remove the water from the top of the gels using a Pasteur pipette.
    Place the gel tubes in the apparatus and add 20, 30, 40 and 50 μl of the serum

into the four gel tubes. Add 5 μl of bromophenol blue to each of the tubes and gently overlay with 5% sucrose to the brim of the tube.

Place solution E in the lower and upper compartments of the electrophoresis apparatus. The lower compartment is the anode compartment (connect to red leads) and the upper compartment the cathode compartment (connect to black leads). Switch on the power supply and adjust to give a current of 3–4 mA per gel tube. Follow the progress of the blue bromophenol band until it reaches 1 cm from the bottom of the tube (30–40 min.).

(b) Staining the gels

Remove the gel columns from the glass tubes by pushing water from a hypodermic syringe between the gel and the glass tube. Cut the gels at the bromophenol blue marker, place two in two separate test tubes of TCA staining solution (anode to the bottom) and heat at 60° C for 15–20 min. When the protein bands are visible rinse the gels in tap water and note your observations.

The other two gels should be placed in two separate test tubes containing 'normal' Coomassie blue staining solution and left for 1 h. The gels can then be removed and destained in a mixture of methanol/acetic acid/water. The transfer of the gels to staining solution should be performed as quickly as possible in each case.

9.3.3 Experiment 8. Analytical fractionation of proteins according to isoelectric point by gel electrofocusing [6]

Object

(a) To analyse a protein mixture by gel electrofocusing and to examine the pH gradient in the gel:
(b) To determine the total protein and lactate dehydrogenase activity of human serum by gel electrofocusing.

Introduction

Gel electrofocusing can be used to determine isoelectric points, analyse protein mixtures, concentrate protein solutions and for protein isolation.

The principles of the technique were first investigated by two Japanese chemists who developed a system in which glutamic acid in protein hydrolysates became concentrated near the anode on electrolysis in a multicompartmental cell. Although several efforts were made to improve on their method the pH gradients produced all lacked stability. Vesterberg and Svensson [7, 8] developed a technique to produce stable pH gradients using carrier ampholytes in a sucrose density gradient. (The density gradient reduces mixing by convection.) The ampholytes used were saturated aliphatic compounds substituted to varying extents with carboxyl acid amino groups. The compounds, with molecular weights in the range 300–600, formed a continuous spectrum of isoelectric points. These carrier ampholytes are now commercially available from LKB Produkter AB Stockholme (trade name *Ampholine*).

Isoelectric focusing on density gradients is slow (days) and expensive in reagents particularly where isolation is not required.

pH gradients can be stabilized in gels. Polyacrylamide is the gel most frequently used and several variants of the technique were reported more or less simultaneously in 1968 – see for instance Wrigley [9], Leaback and Rutter [10], Riley and Coleman [11] and Awden et al. [12]. This technique has the advantage of much faster analysis times.

Acrylamide gels containing ampholine acid samples can be made and the gels set up as shown in Fig. 9.6. The H_2SO_4 and ethanolamine protect the ampholine from anodic oxidation and cathodic reduction respectively.

Initially the pH through the gel is the mean of the pH range of the ampholine being used (in this case 6.5). Under the influence of the applied potential those ampholytes that carry a negative charge, i.e the more acidic, migrate towards the anode. Eventually those molecules find themselves in a region where the pH is at their isoelectric point and no further migration can take place. In this way a stable pH gradient is established. The sulphuric acid stays in the anodic compartment because sulphate ions are discharged at the anode. The acid above the gel neutralizes the negative charge on the ampholyte and thus confines it to the gel. A similar situation exists at the cathode.

Protein molecules, being much larger than the ampholyte molecules, migrate more solwly. For the protein molecules with isoelectric point at pH 6.5 the following applies:

1. molecules in acidic parts of the gradient will be protonated and migrate towards the cathode;
2. molecules in basic parts of the gel will be deprotonated and migrate towards the anode;
3. protein molecules at pH 6.5 carry no charge and therefore will not migrate.

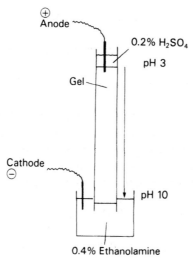

Fig. 9.6   Gel electrofocusing apparatus.

After electrofocusing the protein bands cannot be detected with normal stains because ampholine strongly binds most protein dyes. The following detection methods are used:

1. direct visualization of coloured proteins;
2. precipitation of the protein with 5% trichloroacetic acid (TCA)
3. the dyes Fast Green FCF and Light Green SF can be used directly but their colour yield is low;
4. the ampholyte can be removed by repeated washing with TCA (5%) or by electrophoresis followed by normal staining;
5. the proteins can be viewed by UV scanning (280 nm);
6. procedures dependent on enzymic activity can be used for staining;
7. immunological techniques.

Materials

Solutions required:	(a) acrylamide solution: 30 g acrylamide and 1 g of NN'-methylenebisacrylamide in 100 ml of distilled water;
	(b) ampholine pH 3–10: 40% solution as provided by LKB;
	(c) ammonium persulphate: a freshly prepared 1% ammonium persulphate solution;
Samples:	solution of cytochrome C and haemoglobin (both at 1 mg ml^{-1}), and catalase (5 mg ml^{-1}); 0.2% solution of orcein in 10% acetic acid; human serum;
Electrolytes:	0.2% H_2So_4, 0.4% ethanolamine.

Methods

Method A

Acrylamide is *toxic* by skin absorption – wear gloves when handling solutions of the monomer – the polymer is non-toxic.

High potentials are used in this experiment; make sure that the apparatus and bench are dry and tidy.

Prepare eight gel tubes by sealing one end with parafilm and standing them in a vertical position. Mix the following solutions for each of the samples: water (3.6 ml), sample (0.6 ml), acrylamide (1.5 ml), ampholine (0.15 ml), persulphate (0.3 ml). There will be sufficient for two 65 × 8 mm gels for each sample. Degas the solutions. (Air slows or prevents polymerization and may form bubbles in the gel during electrophoresis). Carefully transfer the solutions into the gel tubes. Layer water over the top of each gel without causing mixing at the interface. The gels should set in about 30 min. Pour the water off the gels and insert them in the apparatus. The electrolysis should be carried out under constant current conditions at not more than 2 mA/tube. Ensure that the potential does not increase beyond 350 V. It takes about 20 min. to establish the pH gradient and a further 30–60 min. to focus the proteins. The process can be followed visually. When focusing has been achieved switch off the current and remove the tubes from the apparatus. Remove the gels from the tubes either by water pressure or by rimming with a fine needle lubricated with water. Cut out the protein bands with a razor blade and place them in distilled water (2 ml). Leave them for about 1 h and then measure the pH of the solution using a previously standardized pH meter. Cut one of the gels into 2–3 mm slices and use these to measure the pH gradient in the gel.

Method B

In the second experiment the total protein and lactate dehydrogenase (LDH) activity of human serum are investigated. If possible compare LDH from serum with LDH from another source. Make gels according to the table below.

Water	Sample	Acrylamide	Ampholine	Persulphate	No. gels required
4.2 ml	10 μl	1.5 ml	0.15 ml	0.3 ml	2
4.2 ml	25 μl	1.5 ml	0.15 ml	0.3 ml	4

Carry out the electrofocusing as in the previous experiment but reduce the current to 1.5mA/tube and allow two hours for focusing. Develop one 10 μl and one 25 μl tube by precipitation with 5% TCA. Wash the second 10 μl tube repeatedly with 5% TCA and stain with amido black. Assay the remaining three 25 μl tubes for LDH activity.

Remark

The staining solution (amido black) should be made just before required by mixing the following in a brown bottle; sodium lactate (3 ml), NAD (3 ml), NaCl (3 mg), $MgCl_2$(3 mg), phosphate buffer (7.5 ml), nitroblue tetrazolium (NBT) (75 ml) and phenazine methosulphate (PMS) (0.75 ml). Place the gel in the staining solution and leave until deep purple bands develop (45–120 min.), wash the gels with water and store in 7.5% acetic acid.

9.4 SECTION C. THIN-LAYER CHROMATOGRAPHY

9.4.1 Experiment 9. Preparation of microplates and separation of aromatic amines

Object

To illustrate a method of preparation of microchromatoplates and to use the prepared plates to identify the aromatic amines in a simple mixture by comparison with standards.

Introduction

This technique for the analysis of mixtures employs an active adsorbent spread as a layer (0.05–1 mm in depth) on a planar surface, e.g. glass. Samples are applied to the base of the plate in volatile solvents ('spotting') and the chromatogram is then developed with an ascending solvent. Components are detected by spraying or exposing to the vapours of reagents which yield coloured spots.

Small scale thin-layer chromatography, a convenient procedure for such uses as the rapid preliminary examination of the composition of a crude product from a reaction, is based on the use of microscope slides as the support (microchromatoplates). Greater resolution can sometimes be obtained by the use of larger plates and separations on a preparative scale can be achieved with thick-layer chromatography.

Materials and equipment

Solvents: methanol, chloroform and toluene;
Standard solutions: p-phenylene diamine, m-phenylene diamine, aniline, p-chloroaniline and o-nitroaniline (all 1% w/v in toluene);
Unknowns: two or more of the above components at the same concentration in toluene;
silica gel G;
calibrated solution applicators;
microscope slide, beakers, watchglasses.

Method

(a) Preparation of microchromatoplates

Microscope slides must first be cleaned by wiping, washing with a detergent, then water and then alcohol. Do not touch the clean surfaces as this will prevent satisfactory coating.

Place a mixture of 50 g silica gel G (a mixture of silicic acid and plaster of Paris), 66 ml chloroform and 33 ml methanol in a 125 ml bottle, the cover of which is lined with aluminium foil. Shake for 5–10 s to bring the silica into suspension. Remove the stopper, and dip a microscope slide into the suspension to within 5 mm of the top of the slide. Withdraw the plate slowly and let any excess of solvent drain back into the jar. The dipping-withdrawal operation should normally take 1–2 s; the more quickly the plate is withdrawn, the thinner the deposit of silica. Lay the plate on a clean surface. Coat additional plates until the silica suspension starts to settle (say 30–40 s). Then suspend the silica again by shaking.

The plates dry quickly (3–4 min.) and are then ready for use. Carefully remove the silica adhering to the nearside of the plate by wiping with a clean tissue. Plates should be usable for several weeks.

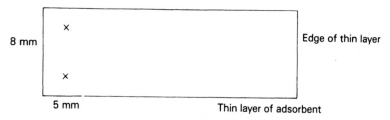

Fig. 9.7 Silica chromatoplate.

(b) Sample Application

Apply 10 μl of test solution from a calibrated capillary by very lightly touching the plate about 5–6 mm from the bottom; the development solvent (see below) should *not* come up to the level of the spot. Each spot should be as small as possible, if possible < 1 mm in diameter. Gently blowing on the capillary as it touches the plate reduces the spread of the spot.

(c) Development

Line the inside of a beaker with a strip of filter paper, then pour in the developing solvent to moisten the paper and give a depth of 2–3 mm on the bottom of the beaker. Place the chromatoplate upright in the beaker (the end with spots on at the bottom). Cover the beaker with a watchglass. When the solvent has risen 5–6 cm up the plates, remove the plate from the beaker and immediately mark the solvent front, then allow the solvent to evaporate.

In general, in choosing a developing solvent so that a separation of the components of a mixture is achieved, it is usual to start with a relatively non polar solvent like petroleum ether. If the compounds do not move on the chromatoplate use a more polar solvent, e.g. toluene, chloroform, ethyl acetate, methanol or acetic acid in that order. Frequently a mixed solvent is valuable. Thus if the compound moves only slightly with toluene, try a 9:1 mixture of toluene: chloroform.

(d) Detection of spots

To visualize the compounds after chromatography expose the plate to iodine vapour. Place the solvent free plate in a sealed jar containing a few crystals of iodine. Within a few minutes reddish brown spots will appear (which are relatively permanent), warming the jar accelerates this staining process. Observe the initial colour of the spots as this often aids in the identification of unknowns.

Exercise

Make up thin layer plates as described above. Chromatograph the standards and the unknown(s) in toluene and locate the spots by iodine staining. Calculate the R_f values and hence determine which of the five standard compounds the unknown(s) contain. Confirm your conclusions by running a further chromatogram using the unknown mixture as one spot and the suspected mixture as a second spot. (The R_f-values may vary with the quality of the TLC plate and hence comparisons between the unknown and the standard must finally be made on the *same* plate).

9.4.2 Experiment 10. Separation of simple organic compounds on fluorescent silica plates

Object

This procedure describes the location of spots on adsorbent plates containing a fluorescent indicator.

Introduction

Plates are available commercially, which use an indicator which absorbs light at 254 nm and re-emits or fluoresces light at the green end of the spectrum, thus the plate when irradiated at 254 nm takes on a striking green colour. If a spot of compound is present which itself absorbs at 254 nm this will quench the fluorescence and the component will show up as a dark spot against the green background. Thus the spots can be located on the developed chromatoplate by irradiating with UV light of 254 nm. This technique has the advantage that as the indicator is insoluble in the common solvents and the location is non-destructive, it allows the isolation of resolved components for subsequent spectroanalytical study.

Other reagents can be added to the silica which fluoresce when irradiated at 370 nm.

Materials

Standard solutions: *m*-dinitrobenzene, fluorenone, acetone-2,4-dinitrophenyl-hydrazine, benzylidene acetone and azobenzene (all 1% w/v in toluene);

Unknowns: two or more of the above components at the same concentration in toluene;

UV lamp radiating at 254 nm;
Calibrated solution applicators.

Method

The procedures regarding sample application and development are as previously described (Experiment 9). The component spots are located by irradiating the developed plates with short wave (254 nm) UV light. The spots can be outlined in pencil and subsequently stained with iodine if desired.

Exercise

Chromatograph the standards and the unknown(s) in toluene and locate the spots by UV detection. Calculate the R_f values of the standards and hence determine which of the five standard compounds the unknown(s) contains.

Remarks

Typical R_f values for the compounds listed are 0.46, 0.32, 0.28, 0.10 and 0.60 respectively. The absolute values may be significantly different due to the quality of the TLC plate and solvent used. However the relative order should be the same.

9.4.3 Experiment 11. Separation of sugars on bisulphite and acetate modified silica

Object

This procedure describes two possible methods of pre-treating silica gel TLC sheets to provide a modified layer which is effective for the separation of sugars.

Introduction

The adsorptive properties of silica gel can be modified by incorporating substances such as bases or buffers, thus enabling gels with accurately defined pHs to be prepared. Admixtures of silica gel with sodium bisulphite and sodium acetate prove useful for the chromatography of sugars giving distinctive R_f ranges.

Materials and equipment

Sugar solutions:	fructose, glucose, maltose and sucrose (all 1% w/v in chloroform);
Unknown(s):	containing two or more of the above sugars prepared as above;
Solvents:	methanol, ethanol, acetone, acetic acid, chloroform and ethyl acetate;
Chemicals:	sodium bisulphite and sodium acetate;
Spray:	5% aniline hydrogen phthalate freshly prepared in glacial acetic acid;

Filter papers (Whatman No. 1):
Shallow tray or dish and oven (at 100° C).

Methods

(a) Method A (sodium bisulphite)

A solution is prepared as follows: 4 g sodium bisulphite is dissolved in 80 ml distilled water, then 120 ml ethanol are added slowly while stirring. The chromatogram sheet is submerged for 1 min. in a tray containing this solution, then removed, drained and allowed to air dry on a clean piece of filter paper. It is then activated in an oven at 100° C for 30 min. prior to spotting with the sugar solutions. When spotted, the sheet is eluted in the usual way and the eluent is allowed to travel approximately 8 cm up the sheet. The sheet is then removed from the apparatus and dried.

The eluent consists of: ethyl acetate, methanol, acetic acid and water in the ratio of 12:3:3:2

(b) Method B (sodium acetate)

A solution is prepared as follows: 1.6 g sodium acetate is dissolved in 10 ml distilled water, then 190 ml ethanol are added slowly while stirring. The chromatogram sheet is submerged for 1 min. in a tray, then removed, drained and left to air-dry on a clean piece of filter paper. It is then activated in an oven at 100° C for 30 min. prior to spotting with the sugar solutions. When spotted, the sheet is eluted in the usual way and the eluant is allowed to travel approximately 8 cm up the sheet. The sheet is then removed from the apparatus and dried.

The eluent consists of: acetone, chloroform, methanol and water in the ratio of 16:2:2:1.

Detection

The sheet is sprayed with 5% aniline hydrogen phthalate freshly prepared in glacial acetic acid and this is followed by gentle heating at 85° C to produce the spots. Some of these spots tend to fade rather quickly.

Exercise

Chromatograph the sugar standards and the unknown(s) on the prepared sheets using the solvent systems detailed above. Calculate the R_f values of the standards and hence determine which of the standard components are in the unknown mixture(s). Account for the different R_f values in the two systems.

Remarks

The sugars will separate according to the table below. By comparison with the behaviour of known sugars, an unknown one may sometimes be identified by running it in both the systems described.

	Approximate R_f values	
Sugar	Bisulphite layer separation	Acetate layer separation
Maltose	0.22	0.11
Glucose	0.38	0.25
Sucrose	0.39	0.25
Fructose	0.44	0.30

9.4.4 Experiment 12. Thin-layer chromatography of analgesics by multiple development

Object

The following procedure is a general method for the separation of salicy-lamide, aspirin, *o*-ethoxybenzamide, *p*-acetophenetidide, caffeine and *p*-hydroxyacetanilide.

Introduction

It should be noted that while some analgesic mixtures will separate quite well after one development, others require several additional developments for acceptable resolution of the components of the mixture. When a number of developments are performed, care should be taken to avoid developing the sheet in areas of high humidity which will tend to deactivate it. When this type of deactivation occurs in adsorption chromatography, the R_f values of the compounds are higher and separations are not as sharp. When humid conditions cannot be avoided, the addition of cyclohexane to the developing solvent will help to correct the deactivation of the sheet.

Several specific spray reagents can be used to form coloured zones with certain analgesics. This will lower the limits of their detection. The non-destructive method of UV detection described here is more useful since the separated spots may be cut from the sheet and the pure material eluted with ethyl alcohol for subsequent spectrophotometric or other confirming analyses.

Materials

Analgesic solutions:	solutions of the analgesics identified above (2% w/v in ethanol);
Unknown(s):	powdered drug preparation, for instance a proprietary analgesic formulation, containing two or more of the identified analgesics;
Eluents:	system 1 comprising dichloroethane and acetic acid in the ratio of 120:1;
	system 2 comprising cyclohexane, dichloroethane and acetic acid in the ratio of 40:60:0.8;

silica gel sheets UV sensitized (254 nm);
UV lamp radiating at 254 nm;
development tanks and calibrated solution applicators.

Method

Use 10 mg of powdered drug preparation and extract the analgesics with 0.5 ml of warm ethanol. Spot 1 μl of each of the analgesic standards and the test solution on to the base line of the TLC plate, noting their positions. Develop the chromatogram to a distance of at least 10 cm using system 1. Remove the sheet, warm and completely dry off the solvent. Run the solvent up the sheet a second time to the same distance, again remove, dry and run a third time.

View the fully developed chromatogram under short wavelength UV light (254 nm) and mark the separated zones.

Repeat the above process using system 2.

Calculate the R_f values and determine the components of the drug preparation.

9.5 SECTION D. COLUMN CHROMATOGRAPHY

9.5.1 Experiment 13. Separation of dichromate ion and permanganate ion using an alumina column

Object

To undertake the separation of dichromate ion and permanganate ion on an alumina column and to examine the absorbance of the eluant fractions with a colorimeter.

Introduction

As in paper chromatography, the principle of column chromatography is the separation of a mixture into its components. The mixture is distributed between a stationary phase – alumina – and a moving phase – the eluent. The solid stationary phase competes with the liquid mobile phase for the substrate and a variety of organic and inorganic liquids are used to bring about an effective separation. The eluting power of the solvent is approximately proportional to its polarity i.e. hexane < benzene < ethyl acetate < acetone < methanol < water.

The two main types of elution are known as elution development and gradient elution. The former type of chromatography is used when the components of a mixture only differ slightly in polarity. The eluent is kept constant throughout the separation. In the case of gradient elution, the components usually differ widely in ease of elution. Different solvents showing increasing polarity can be used to effect a separation.

Materials and apparatus

mixture of dichromate and permanganate (~ 0.2 M) made in 0.05 M H_2SO_4; colorimeter;
glass column, e.g. a burette.

Method

Wash the alumina with 0.5 mol l^{-1} nitric acid and decant off any fine particles. Insert a loose glass-wool plug at the bottom of the column and half-fill with dilute nitric acid. Carefully pour in the alumina in the form of a slurry so that the column is evenly packed. The column should be about 12 cm in length. Ensure that the level of the nitric acid in the column is just above the level of the alumina. It is very important to prevent the liquid level falling below the alumina level, otherwise air-pockets are formed in the alumina which greatly restricts the flow rate through the column.

Using a graduated pipette, add 10 ml of the given mixture of permanganate and dichromate ion mixture to the top of the column. Adjust the flow-rate through the column to about $2 \, ml \, min^{-1}$ and collect the eluent in 2 ml fractions. When the level of the liquid just falls to the level of the alumina, carefully add $0.5 \, mol \, l^{-1}$ nitric acid in small portions until all the first coloured band has been eluted from the column. Change the eluent to $1 \, mol \, l^{-1}$ sulphuric acid, and collect 3 ml fractions.

Take the most intensely coloured dichromate sample and, using the colorimeter, determine the absorbance of the sample. Use the special sample tubes provided and ensure that it is correctly located in the cell compartment. If you get a full-scale reading, dilute the sample by an appropriate amount to bring the reading back on scale. Note the dilution required and dilute the remaining samples by the same amount. Measure the absorbance of each sample.

Likewise for the permanganate fractions. Plot the absorbance against the fraction number and comment on the shape of the absorbance curve.

9.5.2 Experiment 14. Determination of the exchange capacity and exchange efficiency of a cation-exchange resin

Object

To determine the ion exchange capacity of a sulphonic acid resin in the H^+ form, and then to determine the exchange efficiency of the resin.

Introduction

The ion-exchange capacity of a resin is a quantitative measure of its ability to take up exchangeable ions. This property and exchange efficiency reflects the accessibility of the ionogenic groups to the exchanging ions.

The determination of the exchange capacity of a resin is essential for any quantitative work. The exchange capacity is defined as the number of moles of univalent cation exchanged per kilogram of resin.

Materials and equipment

ZeoKarb 225 resin;
sodium hydroxide standard solution (0.1 M);
hydrochloric acid (2 M);
analar sodium chloride and copper sulphate pentahydrate;
glass column e.g. a burette.

Method

(a) Exchange capacity of resin

The resin ZeoKarb 225 is of the sulphonic acid type (strong cation exchanger) and the hydrogen (H^+) form. Take about 15 g of the resin in a large beaker, add twice the volume of distilled water, shake, allow to settle and then decant off the liquor. Repeat until the liquor is clear (usually three times). Now wash the resin by decantation into the glass column which should have a glass wool plug. From this point on the resin must always be covered with liquid to avoid air bubbles getting into the column. Leave 2 or 3 mm of water above the column.

Wash the prepared resin column with a small volume of dilute hydrochloric acid to ensure that resin is in the H^+ form, then wash with distilled water until the effluent is neutral to litmus paper. Remove approximately 0.5 g resin and dry thoroughly between filter papers, weigh accurately and then place in a conical flask, add 50 cm³ of distilled water containing approximately 3 g of sodium chloride. The large excess of Na^+ ions ensures that the hydrogen ions are brought into solution. Shake gently for 5–10 minutes. Add phenolphthalein indicator (three drops), titrate slowly with standard sodium hydroxide (0.1 mol dm⁻³). An early end-point which fades slowly may be due to the last traces of exchange still going on.

Calculate the capacity of the resin.

(b) Exchange efficiency of resin

(i) Introduction

Using the hydrogen ion form of the ZeoKarb 225 in the column, copper(II) ions are exchanged for hydrogen ion from copper sulphate in aqueous solution yielding sulphuric acid.

$$Cu^{2+} + 2R^-H^+ \rightleftharpoons 2H^+ + (R^-)_2Cu^{2+}$$

The acid effluent is titrated with standard alkali, and thus the efficiency of analytical exchange can be evaluated.

(ii) Method

Dissolve about 0.3 g, accurately weighed, of copper sulphate pentahydrate in 25 ml of water and slowly pass this solution through the cation exchange column, collecting the effluent at the rate of about 1–2 drops s⁻¹. Then wash the column with water until the effluent is neutral to litmus paper. Titrate the total effluent against the standard alkali solution. Assume the copper sulphate to be 100% pure.

Calculate the efficiency of analytical exchange for your column.

9.5.3 Experiment 15. Complex elution of iron and copper using a cation-exchange resin

Object

To separate a mixture of copper(II) and iron(III) on a cation-exchange resin by elution using the technique of phosphate complexation.

Introduction

The separation involves the stepwise elution of iron(III) by phosphoric acid and then of copper(II) by hydrochloric acid, from a strongly acidic cation-exchange resin such as ZeoKarb 225, Amberlite IR-120 or Dowex 50. If hydrochloric acid alone is used the order of removal of the ions from the column is reversed, and a poorer separation is obtained.

The phosphoric acid eluant modifies the activities of the ions, possibly by complex formation, giving improved resolution. The order of elution is also reversed with a phosphate eluant, iron having the smaller retention volume.

Materials and equipment

Analar copper sulphate pentahydrate and ferric nitrate;
ZeoKarb 225;
hydrochloric acid (0.5 M);
phosphoric acid (0.2 M);
potassium cyanoferrate indicator solution;
two glass columns.

Method

Make up two columns about 1.5 cm in diameter and 10–15 cm long using ZeoKarb 225 (in the sodium form) mesh size 52–100 (8% DVB). Slurry the resin with water, allow to settle, and decant the supernatent. Repeat until the washings are clear, then pack the column, and wash with water until the eluate is no longer acid. The column is then in the hydrogen form.

Load each column with a solution containing about 0.5 g each of copper sulphate and ferric nitrate. Wash the column with about 100 ml of water to remove the acid liberated in the exchange process.

Elute one column 0.5 M HCl at a rate of $\sim 100\,\mathrm{ml\,h^{-1}}$. Collect the column effluent in 5 ml fractions. Estimate in a semi-quantitative manner the amount of copper and iron present in each fraction by transferring to a test tube and comparing with a solution of known concentration.

Elute the second column with 0.2 M H_3PO_4 at $\sim 100\,\mathrm{ml\,h^{-1}}$. Collect 2 ml fractions, and, since the phosphate complex is colourless, test each fraction with potassium cyanoferrate. When no more iron can be detected change the eluting agent to hydrochloric acid (equal volumes of concentrated acid and water); the copper is rapidly removed from the column. Collect fractions as before and test for copper with the same reagent ($K_4[Fe(CN)_6]$).

Note (a) the volume eluted before iron first appears; (b) the volume which contains iron; (c) the volume collected after all the iron has been eluted, and before copper first appears: and (d) the volume which contains copper.

Remarks

Average values are: (a) 15 ml, (b) 100 ml, (c) 20 ml and (d) 10 ml.

Metals which readily form complexes with the eluent will tend to be eluted first. In the above experiment iron complexes strongly with phosphate whilst copper hardly complexes at all. Hence the iron is readily eluted.

9.5.4 Experiment 16. Purification of proteins on DEAE-Cellulose

Object

The aim of the experiment is to separate glucose oxidase and catalase by ion-exchange chromatography on DEAE-cellulose.

Introduction

The first ion-exchangers designed for the separation of biological molecules utilized a cellulose matrix. Although cellulose, due to its hydrophilic properties, had little tendency to denature proteins, these packings suffered from low sample capacities and poor flow characteristics, both defects stemming from the irregular shape of the particles. It was not until the mid-60s that cellulose gels were produced in the optimal bead form. In the production of commercial gels the polysaccharide gel is broken down and during the bead regeneration process it is cross-linked for added strength with epichlorohydrin. The resulting macroporous bead (40–120 μm diameter) has good hydrolytic stability with an exclusion limit of $\sim 1 \times 10^6$ for proteins. The only commercially available material, DEAE (diethylaminoethyl) Sephacel can be used in the pH range 2–12. However, hydrolysis can occur in strongly acidic solutions while strongly alkaline media can cause breakdown of the macromolecular structure. These packings have

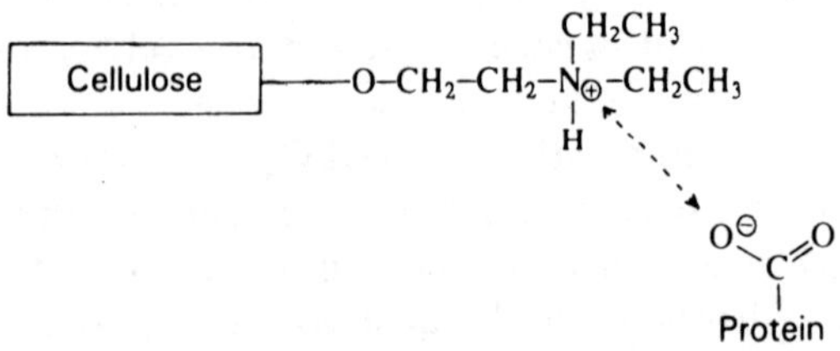

Fig. 9.8 Binding of protein to DEAE-cellulose.

excellent flow characteristics and increased physical strength and stability arising from the cross-linked bead structure. Re-equilibration is also facilitated as the bed volume is stable over a wide range of ionic strength and pH. The above material is used in the ion-exchange separation of proteins, nucleic acids, hormones and other biopolymers. Proteins bind to this material due to electrostatic interactions between carboxylate groups on the protein and the positively charged tertiary amine.

Materials

Buffer solutions: B1 (20 mM sodium acetate and 8 mM acetic acid);
B2 (40 mM sodium acetate and 40 mM acetic acid);
B3 (100 mM sodium acetate and 100 mM acetic acid);
B4 (105 mM sodium acetate and 105 mM acetic acid to pH 5.6);

Other solutions: glucose solution (0.7 M); hydrogen peroxide solution (3% v/v);
catalase standard solution (100 units ml^{-1}); glucose oxidase stock solution (0.03 mg ml^{-1} B4); enzyme test solution containing glucose oxidase 'contaminated' with catalase;

DEAE Sephacell;
UV-vis. scanning spectrophotometer;
glass column.

Method

Pour a slurry of DEAE-cellulose in B1 into the column and allow it to settle. The final bed height should be about 4 cm. Wash the column with 10 ml of B1. Do not allow the column to run dry. The top of the DEAE-cellulose should be flat.

Filter the enzyme test solution if it is not clear and carefully add 5 ml of it to the column. The flow rate should be adjusted so that it is no greater than 1 ml min^{-1}. When the sample has run on to the column commence washing with 10 ml of B1 and collect the eluant in 3 ml fractions. After the B1 wash is complete, wash the resin with 10 ml of B2 and finally 15 ml of B3.

Monitor the eluant for protein (absorbance at 280 nm). Assay those fractions which contain protein for glucose oxidase and catalase. Record your observations. Determine the recovery and purification of glucose oxidase. Select your purest fractions of glucose oxidase and catalase and determine their spectra in the range 200–500 nm. Record your observations and comment on your results.

Enzyme assays

(a) Glucose oxidase

The basis of this assay is summarized below.

1. Rate limiting step:
β-D-glucose + β-FAD → β-FADH$_2$ + D-gluconic acid

2. $\beta\text{-FADH}_2 + O_2 \rightarrow \beta\text{-FAD} + H_2O_2$

Peroxidases

3. $H_2O_2 + \text{guaiacum} \longrightarrow \text{guaiacum} + H_2O$

(reduced form)   (oxidized form blue λ_{max} 600 nm)

Prepare solution A freshly as follows: peroxidase/guaiacum (60 ml), acetate buffer B4 (15 ml) and glucose solution (5 ml).

Make 1/2, 1/4, 1/8, 1/16 and 1/32 dilutions of the glucose oxidase stock solution using buffer B4 (1 ml of each dilution is sufficient for the assay).

Add 1 ml of 1/32 enzyme dilution to 5 ml of solution A, mix thoroughly, pour into a cell and measure the absorbance at 600 nm at 3 min intervals against a control prepared by adding 1 ml of acetate buffer to 5 ml of solution A. Repeat this for each of the standard enzyme solutions. Construct a calibration graph of rate (Absorbance min^{-1}) against enzyme concentration.

Assay the enzyme test solution and the protein-rich fractions. Dilute these 1/500 and 1/2500 respectively with buffer B4 before assay to take account of their high activities.

(b) Catalase

In this assay a filter disc is first soaked in a catalase solution and then placed in a solution of H_2O_2. The oxygen produced within the filter disc causes it to float to the surface. The higher the catalase activity the more rapidly the oxygen is produced and hence the more quickly the filter floats.

Set up a series of test tubes containing 5 cm^3 of 3% H_2O_2. Prepare catalase solutions from the standard provided as shown below.

Tube no.	Catalase solution (ml)	Water (ml)
1	2.0	–
2	1.0	1.0
3	1.0	2.0
4	0.5	2.0
5	0.5	4.5

Soak the filter disc in the enzyme solution for 2 min. and transfer it to a test tube contaning H_2O_2. Using a stop watch measure the time from when the disc was placed in the test tube until it reaches the surface. Assay each dilution of the standard catalase in duplicate and construct a calibration graph transforming the data as necessary.

Assay the enzyme test solution and the protein-rich fractions.

9.5.5 Experiment 17. Gel filtration of Dextrans and vitamin B_{12}

Object

To prepare a sephadex column for the separation of a sample containing blue dextran, yellow dextran and vitamin B_{12}.

Introduction

The principles of gel chromatography have been presented in Chapter 4. The nature and structure of sephadex gels has also been discussed in detail.

Materials

Column K/9/30 and fittings;
Sephadex G-25 and G-100;
Blue Dextran ($\bar{M}_w$ 2×10^6);
Yellow Dextran ($\bar{M}_w$ 2×10^4);
Vitamin B_{12} (MW 1357);
Freeze dried solutions containing $3\,mg\,ml^{-1}$ of blue and yellow dextran and $0.09\,mg\,ml^{-1}$ of vitamin B_{12}.
(All the above items are available from Pharmacia Fine Chemicals [13]).

Method

(a) Swelling the gels

In order that the experiments described here be completed within a normal laboratory period, it is essential that the gels be swollen in appropriate eluants well before use. The minimum swelling times for the gels are given on page 46 of the booklet, 'Sephadex – gel filtration in theory and practice' [13]. For the column, K/9/30, the amounts of dry Sephadex required are approximately 5 g Sephadex G-25, 1.2 g Sephadex G-100.

(b) Preparation of the column

The preparation and packing of the column and sample application are described on pages 46–49 and 52, 53 of the above mentioned booklet [13]. A knowledge of these procedures is thus assumed in the following instructions. As with other chromatographic techniques, the need for care in all stages of Sephadex gel filtration cannot be over emphasised.

The following is intended to give, in outline only, a simple procedure for gel filtration experiments.

Set up the column and ensure that it is vertical with the aid of a spirit level. Remove air from under the bed supporting net by forcing eluant back and forth through the net with a syringe attached to the outlet tubing; fill the column with gel slurry. Pack the gel as described in the booklet, 'Sephadex – gel filtration in theory and practice' [13]. When this has been done an eluant reservoir should be connected to the top of the column, which can then be run under varying pressures (and therefore varying flow rates). The 'pressure head' or 'operating pressure' is indicated in Fig. 4.13. After two or three bed-volumes of eluant have been run through the column, at the flow rate to be used in the experiment, the column may be stopped, the eluant reservoir disconnected, and the sample applied. Elution may then be carried out.

Calculation of results

V_i, the 'inner volume' of the gel may be calculated from the equation:

$$V_i = mW_r$$

where m = weight of dry Sephadex in grams, W_r = water regain value in ml g^{-1} if the weight of dry Sephadex is known. Otherwise V_i must be calculated from the equation:

$$V_i = [W_r d/(W_r + 1)](V_t - V_0)$$

where V_0 = 'void volume', V_t = 'total volume' of the gel and d = density of the wet gel. V_t the 'total volume' of the gel, may be calculated from the height and cross-sectional area of the bed. The measurement of V_t may also be made directly either by calibrating the column before use or after use by marking the position of the top of the gel bed, emptying out the Sephadex, filling to the mark with water and running this water into a measuring cylinder.

K_d, the partition coefficient between the mobile liquid phase and the stationary liquid phase, should be calculated from the equation:

$$K_d = (V_e - V_0)/V_i$$

where V_e is the 'elution volume'.

K_{av}, the partition coefficient between the liquid phase and the gel phase, should be calculated from the equation:

$$K_{av} = (V_e - V_0)/(V_t - V_0)$$

Assume that K_d and K_{av} are zero for Blue dextran 2000.

The dilution factors should be calculated from the equation:

Dilution factor = total volume of eluted component (ml)/sample volume (ml)

For Sephadex G. 25, $W_r = 2.5 \pm 0.2$ ml H$_2$O g^{-1} dry Sephadex, $d = 1.13$ g ml^{-1}.

For Sephadex G. 100, $W_r = 10.0 \pm 1.0$ ml H$_2$O g^{-1} dry Sephadex, $d = 1.04$ g ml^{-1}.

Recording results

The layout below is presented as a guide to assist in the accurate and clear recording of data.

GEL TYPE	weight	g	$W_\mu = $ ml/g $d = $ ml/g
COLUMN	type: internal diameter: bed height:		$V_t =$
ELUANT			
FLOW RATE	ml min^{-1}	ml h^{-1}	
SAMPLE	composition		Sample volume
component I		mg ml^{-1}	
II		mg ml^{-1}	
III		mg ml^{-1}	

ELUTION DATA

Void volume $(V_0) = V_e$ of Blue Dextran	2000		$V_0 = $ ml
Elution volumes (V_e): component I	ml		$V_t = $ ml
II	ml		
III	ml		
			Dilution factor
Volumes of eluted components I	ml		I
II	ml		II
III	ml		III

K_{av} and K_d values	K_{av}	K_d	
component I			
II			
III			

9.6 SECTION E. GAS CHROMATOGRAPHY

The experiments described in this section were developed by the authors using a Perkin-Elmer F33 gas chromatograph with a Hewlett-Packard HP3390A computing integrator for data collection and presentation. The set-up parameters quoted in the text refer to these instruments. The experiments, however, can readily be performed on the majority of commercially available gas chromatographs.

9.6.1 Experiment 18. Gas chromatography of alcohols

Object

The object of the experiment is to analyse a mixture of alcohols both qualitatively and quantitatively and also to relate the retention data to molecular structure.

Introduction

The separation of the alcohols is effected by the retention, to a varying degree, of the different alcohols by the liquid stationary phase (PEG 1000) coated on to a solid support (Chromosorb W – ratio 10:90 respectively). The small differences in the structures of the alcohols are sufficient to cause differences in the association (H-bonding, dipole–dipole interaction, etc.) between the liquid stationary phase and the alcohol (solute) molecules. Thus the compound having least association is eluted first followed by the others in order of the degree of the association. The retention time is a characteristic of the compound under the conditions used.

Materials and equipment

Standards:	Analar ethanol, *n*-propanol, *n*-butanol, *n*-pentanol and *t*-butanol;
Unknown(s):	mixture(s) of ethanol and *n*-butanol;
Column:	10% PEG 1000 on Chromosorb-W (2 m);

Gas chromatograph fitted with FID (Flame Ionization Detector);
Computing integrator or chart recorder.

Method

For the PE F33 the instrument settings are as follows:

Nitrogen carrier gas	$30 \, \text{ml min}^{-1}$
Hydrogen	$50 \, \text{ml min}^{-1}$
Air	$300 \, \text{ml min}^{-1}$
Column temperature	$95°\text{C}$
Injection port temperature	$150°\text{C}$
Attenuation	$10^3 \times 256$

(a) Qualitative experiment under isothermal conditions

Injecting 1 μl samples of ethanol, *n*-propanol, *n*-butanol, *n*-pentanol and tertiary butanol in turn on to the column followed by a 3 μl sample of a mixture of the first four alcohols. Note the sequence of elution and obtain the retention times for each alcohol. Plot a graph of $\log_{10}$ retention times against the number of carbon atoms in the molecule; note the position of tertiary butanol and suggest a reason for the discrepancy.

(b) Quantitative experiment, conditions as for (a)

The area of the peak for any particular compound is proportional to the amount of that compound in the mixture injected, though not necessarily with the same proportionality factor.

Prepare the following mixtures:

EtOh(ml) :		BuOH(ml)
1	:	2
1	:	3

At the end of the chromatogram the integrator will print out retention time and peak area data from which the percentage composition of the mixture can be calculated.

Note: The flame ionization detector does not have the same response or sensitivity to all compounds (see Chapter 5). Some compounds produce larger detector signals than others (for a given amount) and it is therefore necessary to apply correction factors to the peak areas obtained above.

$$\text{Corrected area} = \text{Observed area/Response factor}$$

Typically for butanol the factor is 1.67. Analyse the unknown mixture provided.

(c) Qualitative experiment using temperature programming

The influence of temperature programming on the resolution and analysis time of the alcohols can be investigated using the following temperature profile:

Initial column temperature: $90°C$
Final column temperature: $150°C$
Rate of temperature increase: $10°C\,min^{-1}$

Repeat the analysis of the mixture of ethanol, *n*-propanol, *n*-butanol and *n*-pentanol ($3\,\mu l$ injection). Compare the retention times with those for the isothermal analysis and note the improved resolution and peak shape, particularly *n*-pentanol.

9.6.2 Experiment 19. Determination of ethanol in an aqueous solution

Object

The object of the experiment is to determine the ethanol content of an aqueous solution using *n*-propanol as an internal standard.

Introduction

The analysis of alcohol solutions has become very important due to the implications of the 'Road Traffic Act (1972)' which required the estimation of small amounts of ethanol in blood and/or urine. This experiment demonstrates the most frequently used method – gas–liquid chromatography using an internal

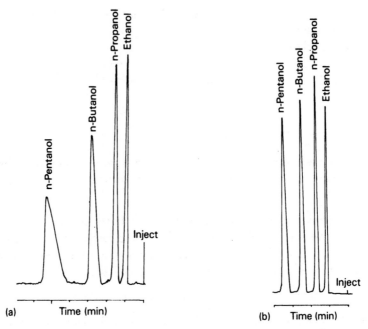

Fig. 9.9   Gas chromatograms of alcohol mixture: (a) Isothermal operation at 90° C; (b) temperature programmed from 90–150° C at 10° min⁻¹ with initial temperature held for 1 min.

standard. Before the advent of GLC the method most frequently used involved the chromate oxidation of ethanol.

The most satisfactory method of quantitative analysis in GC involves the calibration of the detector response for the compound of analytical interest against a reference compound. This 'internal standardization' technique involves adding a known amount of reference compound to both sample and standard solutions.

The response factor (R) of the detector to an analyte component relative to the internal standard (IS) can be evaluated by running a sample containing the internal standard and each of the sample components, all in accurately known concentration. Thus the response factor R_A for compound A can be calculated as follows:

$$R_A = (Peak\ area_A / Peak\ area_{IS}) \times (Amount_{IS} / Amount_A) \qquad (1)$$

Similarly the response factors for the other components in the calibration mixture, relative to the internal standard, can be calculated.

An accurately measured quantity of the internal standard is then added to the analysis sample and the mixture is run through the chromatograph. From equation (1) the concentration can be expressed as:

$$Conc_A = (Peak\ area_A / Peak\ area_{IS}) \times (Amount_{IS} / R_A) \qquad (2)$$

Thus by substitution in this equation of the peak areas from the chromatogram, the relative response factors derived from the calibration analysis, and the concentration of the internal standard added to the sample, the concentration of the components in the sample can be calculated. Since this method involves ratios of peak areas rather than absolute values, it should be noted that the precision of analysis is not dependent on the injection of an accurately known amount of sample. However, the accuracy does depend on the accurate measurement of peak area. Although these can be measured by manual means, the best results are obtained using electronic, peak-area integrators.

Assay and quantitation by the internal standard is often the preferred method as it takes account of variable compound response and removes potential errors due to variation in sample injection.

Materials and equipment

Standard solutions: 80 and 200 mg% aqueous ethanol;
                        25 mg% aqueous *n*-propanol (internal standard);
Unknown(s):   simulated urine sample;
Column: 15% PEG 400 on Supasorb 60–80#(2 m);
Gas chromatograph fitted with FID;
Computing integrator or chart recorder.

Method

For the PE F33 the instrument settings are as follows:

Nitrogen carrier gas	25 ml min^{-1}
Hydrogen	50 ml min^{-1}
Air	300 ml min^{-1}
Column temperature	90° C
Injection port temperature	150° C
Attenuation	10 × 8

Into a small container pipette carefully 2 ml 80 mg% ethanol and 5 ml of the *n*-propanol solution. Stopper the container and mix thoroughly. Inject 1 μl. The chromatogram will consist of three peaks due to (i) ethanol, (ii) propanol, and (iii) water. The latter is a broad low intensity peak.

Repeat the above sequence using the 200 mg% ethanol.

For each analysis calculate the response factors for ethanol relative to the *n*-propanol standard solution using equation (1) and hence the average value.

Repeat the above procedure using 2 ml of the simulated urine or blood and 5 ml of the *n*-propanol solution.

Substitution of the appropriate values in equation (2) will give the ethanol content of the urine or blood sample. In practice each solution (80 mg%, 200 mg% EtOH and unknown) should be analysed in triplicate to establish the accuracy and precision of the analysis.

Note: 80 mg% ethanol = 80 mg ethanol/100 ml.

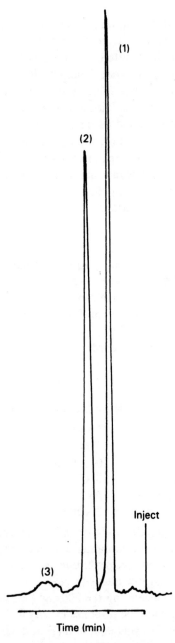

Fig. 9.10 Chromatogram of standard mixture of ethanol and *n*-propanol. Conditions as detailed in text. Signals: (1) ethanol; (2) *n*-propanol; (3) H_2O.

9.6.3 Experiment 20. Analysis of barbiturates

Object

The object of the experiment is to analyse a mixture of barbiturates both qualitatively and quantitatively by GC using the internal standardization technique.

Introduction

Barbiturates are a class of drugs that act as depressants of the central nervous system. They are readily synthesized from urea and substituted malonic esters and are 5,5-disubstituted pyrimidones, e.g.

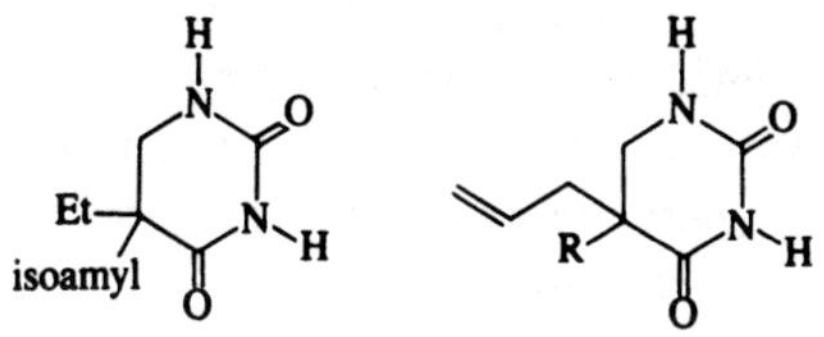

amobarbitone   secobarbitone (R = 1—methylbutyl)

The first barbituric acid derivative was introduced into clinical practice in 1903 and the use and misuse of this group of hypnotics has steadily increased. They are now the most commonly encountered agents in suicide attempts and much effort has been expended in developing methods to determine barbiturates in biological fluids. Many very delicate analytical techniques involving the whole range of spectroscopy, chromatography and other physico-chemical methods, e.g. polarography have been established. With the introduction of partition chromatography not only could a quantity of barbiturate be determined, but also identification could be quickly established, the latter being all important if the correct treatment of an overdose is to be instigated. With the advent of gas chromatography both rapid identification and quantitation have become a reality.

Materials and equipment

Solutions:	0.2% w/v barbitone in water (internal standard);
Barbiturates:	butobarbitone, amobarbitone, pentobarbitone and secobarbitone;
Unknown(s):	containing two or more of the above components;
Column:	10% Apiezon L on DMCS chromosorb W; (2 m);

Gas chromatograph fitted with FID;
Computing integrator or chart recorder.

Method

For the PE F33 the recommended instrument settings are:

Nitrogen carrier gas	$\sim 30\,ml\,min^{-1}$
Hydrogen	$\sim 50\,ml\,min^{-1}$
Air	$\sim 300\,ml\,min^{-1}$
Column temperature	$210°\,C$
Injection temperature	$260°\,C$

Procedure

Barbiturates readily adhere to glass and glass columns; liners and other glassware used in this analysis should be silanized with dimethyldichlorosilane prior to use. Pretreatment of the packing by *in situ* silanization and with successive 100 μg barbitone injections improves the column performance. If there is an initial lack of resolution it can be overcome by following the injection of barbiturate with 2 μl of 2% dimethyldichlorosilane so that the silane chromatographs through the barbiturate. The silane will appear on the solvent front providing the injection was within ten seconds of the barbiturate injection.

Prepare the following solutions:
(a) solutions of amobarbitone, butobarbitone, pentobarbitone and secobarbitone with internal standard, barbitone, as follows. Dissolve 50 mg of barbiturate in ethanol, add 50 ml of barbitone stock solution and dilute to 100 ml with ethanol. (Solutions A, B, C, D);
(b) solution of unknown as detailed in (a) (solution E).

Using solutions A, B, C and D determine the retention times of the barbiturates and their response factors with respect to barbitone as internal standard (see Experiment 19). Using this data identify and quantify the barbiturates in the unknown.

Inject 1 μl of each solution in duplicate. Wash syringe thoroughly with ether between injections.

9.6.4 Experiment 21. Qualitative analysis by GC using retention data from two columns

Object

To determine the components in an unknown mixture by comparison of retention data with that of standard components obtained on polar (Carbowax 20M) and non-polar (SE30) stationary phases.

Introduction

In addition to being a highly efficient separation technique, gas chromatography supplies much qualitative and quantitative information about sample constitu-

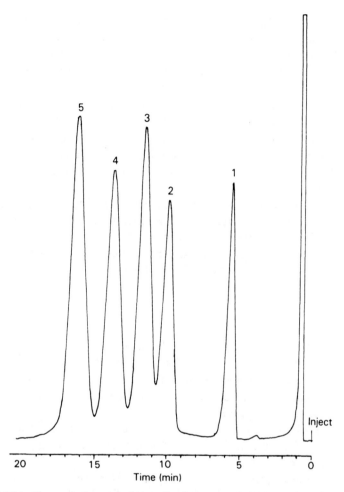

Fig. 9.11   Chromatogram of standard mixture of barbiturates, column and
conditions as detailed in text. Peaks: (1) barbitone; (2) butobarbitone; (3) amo-
            barbitone; (4) pentobarbitone; (5) secobarbitone.

ents. With the use of general-type detectors the single piece of information which
best describes the qualitative nature of the sample is the retention time, t_r. Within
a homologous series it is expected that retention time would be linearly related to
the boiling point of the component. Such relationships are very useful in
identification of particular sample components. For many types of compounds
the boiling point is directly related to the length of the carbon chain (number of
carbon atoms) and a plot of retention time *vs.* the number of carbon atoms can be
used for identification purposes. This approach, however, requires that the basic
type (i.e. alkane, alcohol, etc.) of compound whose retention time is being
measured is known. In cases where this may be uncertain or with mixtures of
solutes a two-column plot is necessary.

Two components belonging to different homologous series may have identical retention times on a particular column. However, if the same two components are examined with a very different column it is extraordinarily unlikely that the same retention times will again be encountered. Standard plots of retention times of column 1 *vs.* retention times on column 2 for various homologous series are commonly used. An unknown, similarly chromatographed on the two columns, will have retention times which simultaneously fit only one of the lines, thus identifying the homologous series. Identification of the compound itself can also be made from the plots. The usual procedure is to use columns of substantially different properties in order to get a wide separation of slopes for the different homologous series.

The range of compounds within a homologous series which can be identified from such a two-column plot is usually quite small (three or four compounds per series) because of the very large differences in retention times. Thus pentane may have a retention time of 0.5 min on an SE30 column and under the same conditions may have a retention time of several min. on a polar column.

Materials and equipment

Alkanes:	pentane, hexane, heptane and octane;
Esters:	methyl, ethyl, n-propyl and n-butyl acetate;
Alcohols:	methanol, ethanol, n-propanol and n-butanol;
Unknown(s):	containing three of the above components e.g. heptane, methyl acetate, n-propanol;
Columns:	(i) 10% Carbowax 20 M on 60–80#chromosorb W (2 m);
	(ii) 15% Apiezon L on 80–100#chromosorb W (2 m);

Gas chromatograph fitted with dual FID;
Computing integrator (An electronic integrator is essential to enable the retention times of the compounds which are rapidly eluted to be accurately measured);

Method

For the PE F33 the recommended instrument settings are:

Nitrogen	$35 \, ml \, min^{-1}$
Hydrogen	$50 \, ml \, min^{-1}$
Air	$300 \, ml \, min^{-1}$
Column temperature	$95° \, C$
Oven temperature	$150° \, C$

Inject 1 μl of each member of the above homologous series on each column in turn and record the retention time data. Inject 5 μl of the unknown(s) on each column and record the retention time data.

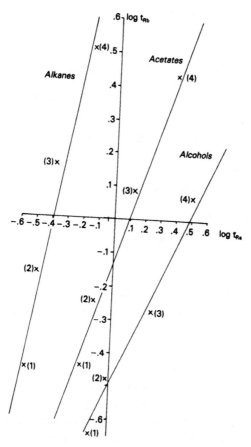

Compound number in homologous series		1	2	3	4
n-Alkanes	t_{R_a}	0.29	0.33	0.44	0.66
	t_{R_b}	0.39	0.70	1.47	3.19
Alcohols	t_{R_a}	0.76	0.95	1.74	3.37
	t_{R_b}	0.23	0.32	0.55	1.10
Esters	t_{R_a}	0.61	0.83	1.36	2.42
	t_{R_b}	0.36	0.58	1.18	2.55

Fig. 9.12 t_{R_a}, t_{R_b}: retention times on columns (a) and (b) respectively. *n*-alkanes: (1) pentane; (2) hexane; (3) heptane; (4) octane. *n*-alcohols: (1) methanol; (2) ethanol; (3) propanol; (4) butanol. Acetates: (1) methyl; (2) ethyl; (3) *n*-propyl; (4) *n*-butyl.

Calculations

1. Obtain the retention time for each compound on each column and tabulate.
2. On the same graph, plot retention time on the non-polar column *vs.* retention time on the polar column for each homologous series.
3. Repeat 2 but plotting log retention times.
4. Identify the components of the mixture.
5. Which graph (2 or 3) gives the best plot and why?
6. What factors influence retention times?

9.6.5 Experiment 22. The determination of some chlorinated insecticides using an electron capture detector (ECD)

Object

The exercise is designed to investigate the separation and sensitivity limits of the analysis of a range of organochlorine pesticides using GC with EC detection.

Introduction

Pesticides are a group of substances which are used extensively, with new and varied formulations constantly being marketed. This expanding usage has resulted in the growing need and interest in analyses for the presence of their residues in water courses and food and agricultural products. The analysis of these materials by GC is well documented and offers short analysis times and good sensitivity. The electron capture detector (ECD) is extremely sensitive to molecules containing electronegative substituents, such as chlorine, while being relatively insensitive to hydrocarbons. This selective sensitivity makes the detector especially valuable for the analysis of chlorinated pesticides. The sample injected onto an ECD system should contain about 1 ng of dry individual component. Amounts greater than 50 ng may give poor results since the ECD may start to operate in the ionization mode rather than the normal electron capture mode.

Materials and equipment

Pesticide standard containing:	α-BHC, γ-BHC, heptachlor, aldrin, heptachlor epoxide, endosulphate, dieldrin and p, p-TDE;
Unknown:	for instance a riverwater or effluent sample;

Anhydrous sodium sulphate (heated at 600° C for 5 h),
n-Hexane: fractionally distilled over potassium hydroxide pellets;
Aluminium oxide, neutral, Brockmann type 4: heated at 800° C for 5 h, deactivated by adding 10% w/w distilled water;
25 ml graduated flask

Column: 2.5% OVl, 2.5% H_3PO_4 on Chromosorb
                                         G-AW DMCS 80–100#(2 m)

Gas chromatograph fitted with ECD;
Computing integrator or chart recorder.

Method

All glassware should be washed with detergent, rinsed in distilled water, soaked
in chromic acid and rinsed with distilled water again then dried.
For the PE F33 the recommended settings are as follows:

Nitrogen carrier gas	$\sim 60\,\text{ml min}^{-1}$
Column temperature	200° C
Injection temperature	250° C
Detector temperature	250° C
Attenuation	64;
ECD	pulse 4–6

(a) Sample preparation

The sample is extracted by shaking gently with 20 ml hexane (added by pipette)
for 2 min. After marking the level of water sample in the flask, distilled water
is added to raise the hexane layer into the neck and 5 ml of hexane is removed.
For sewage effluents, the hexane is 'cleaned up' by passing down a column consisting of approximately 1 g of alumina topped by 0.5 g of anhydrous sodium
sulphate. The column is washed with a further 15 ml hexane and the total
eluate concentrated to 5 ml.

A 4 μl aliquot of the hexane extract is injected into the chromatograph and the
resulting chromatograms compared with those obtained from similar injections
of the standard solution of known pesticides. The concentration of the pesticides
in the unknown may be determined by comparison of peak areas and the internal
standard method for quantitative analyses. (See experiments 19 and 20 and
Chapter 2.)

9.6.6 Experiment 23. A study of some important parameters in gas chromatography

Object

This series of experiments examines the influence of various parameters on gas
chromatography performance. The parameters under study are:

(a) column temperature;
(b) injection port temperature;
(c) sample size;
(d) mobile phase flow rate.

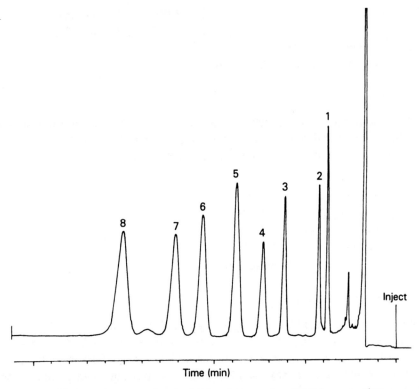

Fig. 9.13 Chromatogram of standard mixture of pesticides, conditions and column as detailed in text. Peaks: (1) α-BHC (25 pg); (2) γ-BHC (25 pg); (3) heptachlor (50 pg); (4) aldrin (25 pg); (5) heptachlor epoxide (50 pg); (6) endosulphate (50 pg); (7) dieldrin (50 pg); (8) p, p-TDE (100 pg).

The effects of these parameters on the chromatographic system to be used are significant. These experiments demonstrate the effect on the recorded chromatogram and the need for optimizing the above variables for better separations.

(a) The effect of column temperature

Introduction

Chromatograms obtained at constant temperature have early peaks which are sharp but closely spaced or even overlapping (peaks 1–4 in Fig. 9.14) and peaks eluted after a long time are broad but well separated (peaks 6–8). To obtain well-resolved sharp peaks for each compound we can systematically vary the column temperature whilst the separation is progressing. This technique is called 'temperature programming'. The column oven is set at a low temperature to enable the low-boiling compounds to be resolved; once these are eluted the temperature is increased at a predetermined rate according to the boiling point spread of the remaining components of the mixture. This will progressively

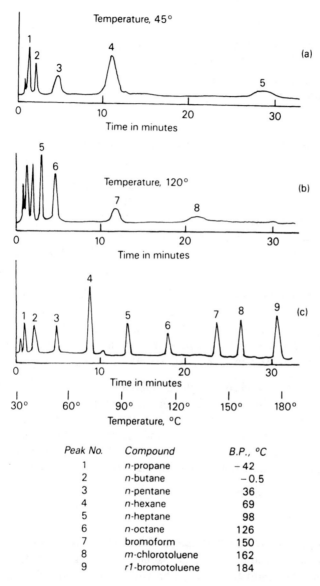

Fig. 9.14   Chromatograms of a mixture: (a), (b) isothermal; (c) programmed temperature. [From Habgood and Harris (1960) *Anal. Chem.*, **32**, 450].

increase the rate at which the higher boiling components pass through the column thus decreasing the retention time. Careful oven design and elaborate control electronics are required for accurate reproducible results. Careful design of the instrumentation and choice of suitable detectors usually overcomes the problem of base line drift associated with the increased volatility of the stationary phase.

Materials and equipment

n-Alkanes: pentane, hexane, heptane, octane, nonane, decane and dodecane;
Column: 3% SE30 on Chromosorb W;
Gas chromatograph fitted with FID;
Computing integrator.

Method

For the PE F33 the recommended instrument settings are as follows:

Nitrogen carrier gas	25 ml min^{-1}
Hydrogen	50 ml min^{-1}
Air	300 ml min^{-1}
Injection temperature	150° C
Column temperature, isothermal	135° C
programmed	initial 50° C–hold 1 min:
	20° C min^{-1} increase to 250° C.

Ensure that the column has been 'cleaned' up at 250° C. Reduce the temperature to 130–140° C and then inject 5 μl of a mixture of equal amounts of the above alkanes. They will be eluted in order of boiling point. Next reduce the oven temperature to 50° C and set the temperature programme for an initial period of 1 min. followed by a 20° min^{-1} increase to 250° C. Repeat the injection.

1. Compare the two chromatograms, tabulate the retention data and the peak widths at half height for each component.
2. Plot the log retention time *vs.* boiling point and *vs.* molecular weight.
3. Obtain the area of each peak and determine the ratios for each chromatogram with respect to pentane. Would you expect the ratios to be the same? Also note the varying detector response to each alkane.

(b) Injection-port temperature

Introduction

The injection port is a relatively simple device which must efficiently introduce the sample on to the column. The sample is injected through the septum quickly and vaporized very rapidly to produce a narrow 'plug' or band of sample on the column. A narrow band of sample will give the best resolution and efficiency. The latter is determined by calculating the number of theoretical plates N of the column for each injection.

Materials and equipment

As in part (a).

Method

Chromatograph settings are as described above in part (a).
Inject 1–5 μl samples of a mixture containing equimolar amounts of octane,

nonane and decane with the injection port set to 50° C then 100° C, 150° C and 200° C. Ensure that the gas chromatograph has a column packed with a suitable stationary phase (e.g. SE30 silicone oil).

1. Calculate the number of theoretical plates (N) from one of the peaks and plot N vs. port temperature.
2. Comment on the effect of injection port temperature and decide on a general rule for choosing the optimum value. The boiling points of the components of the mixture are required.

(c) Sample size

Introduction

For optimum performance the sample size should be such that only the first theoretical plate in the column is saturated. Since a theoretical plate has a very small capacity, large samples will overload the column. The optimum size is that which gives the sharpest symmetrical peaks with adequate sensitivity. The limit is thus a function of column capacity and detector performance.

Materials and equipment

As in part (a).

Method

Chromatograph settings as detailed in part (a) except column temperature 250° C and injection port 275° C. Inject 1, 5, 10, 20, 50, 100, 200 μl samples of an equimolar mixture of octane, nonane and decane on to the column.

1. Determine the number of theoretical plates (N) for each peak and plot N vs. sample size.
2. Comment on the effect of sample size on the resolution.

(d) Selection of carrier gas and flow rate in gas chromatography

The experiment aims to determine the effect of carrier gas flow rate on the efficiency of a given column. A plot of H, the height equivalent of a theoretical plate (HETP) in mm vs. u (flow rate) ml min^{-1} is obtained as detailed below.

The choice of carrier gas is usually based on detector response and sensitivity, column efficiency and convenience in terms of availability, cost and safety.

Flow rate markedly influences column efficiency. At low flow rates the HETP is high, i.e., efficiency is low. As the flow rate increases the HETP decreases, passes through a minimum and then slowly increases. Operation of the instrument at the flow rate which corresponds to minimum HETP for a particular column would give maximum efficiency. The slope of the curve representing column efficiency is given by:

$$H = L/N = A + B/u + C/u$$

L = column length; N = number of theoretical plates for the column; u = time averaged mean carrier gas velocity.

The above equation is often called the van Deemter Equation (See Chapter 2). A, B and C are coefficients representing various parameters affecting gas flow through the column. The multiple path effect is a major contribution to A, molecular diffusion to B, and resistance to mass transfer to C.

Materials and equipment

As part (a).
Standard mixture: hexane, heptane and octane (equimolar).

Method

For the PE F33 the recommended instrument settings are as follows:

Nitrogen carrier gas	25 ml min^{-1}
Hydrogen	50 ml min^{-1}
Air	300 ml min^{-1}
Injection temperature	150° C
Column temperature	110° C

Optimize the column and injector temperature to give good resolution and peak shape for the components of the standard mixture. Then inject the mixture (1–5 μl) at various carrier gas flow rates.

Determine the value of N for various values of the flow rate over the range 5 ~ 150 ml min^{-1}. Obtain at least eight readings and take extra readings in the region of the minimum valve of H. Construct a plot of H vs u and hence determine the optimum flow rate of carrier gas for the column.

Note: It may be necessary to measure the flow rate using a soap bubble flow meter.

9.7 SECTION F. HIGH PERFORMANCE LIQUID CHROMATOGRAPHY (HPLC)

9.7.1 Experiment 24. Analysis of barbiturates by reverse-phase isocratic chromatography

Object

(i) To investigate the influence of solvent strength on the degree of resolution and analysis time for a range of barbiturates.
(ii) To determine the composition of a mixture of barbiturates.

Introduction

High efficiency column performance is achieved by the use of small diameter packing material (2–10 μm). The small size of the packing has the following consequences:

1. the solvent must be pumped through under high pressure;
2. the stationary phase must be chemically bonded to the support material.

The most common stationary phase used is octadecylsilane (ODS) (see Chapter 6).

Commonly a two component solvent system is employed comprising a buffered aqueous solvent with methanol or acetonitrile added to enhance the solubility of non-polar organic sample components in the eluent. This is an example of reversed-phase chromatography. Using a solvent of constant composition for development of the chromatogram is called isocratic elution. If no single isocratic solvent mixture can be found effective for a mixture of components then solvent programming or gradient elution techniques may be used. Here elution is begun with a weak solvent and solvent strength is increased with time. The overall effect is to elute successively the more strongly retained substances and to achieve a reduction in the analysis time.

The properties and uses of barbiturates have previously been discussed (see Experiment 20).

The following exercise in quantitation uses the internal standard technique; it should be appreciated however that improved precision and accuracy may be obtained in HPLC using external standard calibrations (see Chapter 6).

Materials and equipment

Standard mixture:	containing equal weights of barbitone, butobarbitone, phenobarbitone, amobarbitone and secobarbitone;
Unknown(s):	containing a known weight ($\%$w/w) of barbitone and two or more of the above barbiturates;
Column:	Spherisorb-10 ODS, 250 mm × 4.6 mm i.d.;
Mobile phase:	solvent A–acetonitrile, solvent B–2 mM KH_2PO_4;
Chromatograph:	Pye-Unicam gradient system comprising 4010 pump, LC-XP gradient programmer and 4020 variable wavelength UV detector;
Integrator:	Hewlett-Packard 3390A;
Injector:	Rheodyne valve fitted with 20 μl loop.

Method

The system should be set up as follows:

mobile phase flow rate	2 ml min^{-1}
detector wavelength	225 nm.

Take 50 mg of the standard mixture, dilute with 20 ml of acetonitrile and make up to final volume of 25 ml with 2 mM KH_2PO_4. Find the optimum solvent composition for the separation of these components, i.e. that which requires the minimum analysis time but gives the necessary resolution of peaks ($< 10\%$

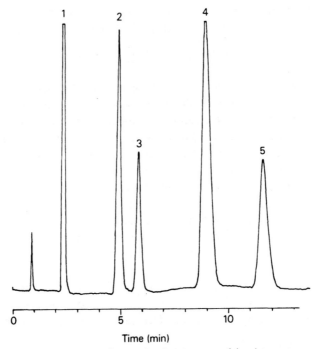

Fig. 9.15 Chromatogram of standard mixture of barbiturates, column and conditions as detailed in text. Eluent 25% solvent A/75% solvent B. Peaks: (1) barbitone; (2) butobarbitone; (3) phenobarbitone; (4) amobarbitone; (5) secobarbitone.

overlap). Isocratic elution should be used with solvent mixtures of varying composition starting with 70% A, 30% B and decreasing A in steps down to about 25%.

The response factors of the barbiturates should be calculated relative to barbitone. The order of elution of the components is:

1. barbitone;
2. butobarbitone;
3. phenobarbitone;
4. amobarbitone;
5. secobarbitone.

Hence, determine the composition of the unknown by taking 50 mg and diluting to 25 ml as detailed for the standard solution.

9.7.2 Experiment 25. Ion-pair chromatography of vitamins [14, 15]

Object

To investigate the changes in retention times of vitamins caused by varying the proportion of counter-ions in the eluent.

Introduction

A vitamin has been defined as a biologically active compound which acts as a controlling agent for an organism's health and growth. Vitamins are generally labile compounds and are susceptible to oxidation and breakdown when exposed to heat, oxygen and light; thus HPLC (in preference to GC) has proved to be the method of analysis for such compounds.

Vitamins may be classified as fat or water soluble. Chromatography of the former is generally achieved using reverse-phase systems. Development of a general elution procedure for the latter class, however, has proved difficult due to the range of polarities encountered; for example, thiamine is strongly ionic while riboflavin has little tendency to ionize. Ion-pair chromatography is a technique with which ionized compounds can be made to favour the organic stationary phase by using suitable counter-ions to form ion pairs according to the equation:

$$A^+ + B^- \longrightarrow [A^+B^-]$$

$$\underset{\text{ion}}{\underset{\text{counter-}}{}} \qquad \text{ion pair}$$

The ion pairs behave as if they are non-ionic neutral species. For reverse-phase ion-pair chromatography, a non-polar surface (eg. C_8 or C_{18}) is used as a stationary phase and an ionic alkyl compound is added to the aqueous mobile phase as a modifier. For the separation of acids, an organic base (e.g. tetrabutylammonium phosphate) is added to the eluant; for the separation of bases an organic acid (e.g. octane sulfonate) is used.

The application of reverse-phase ion-pair chromatography to the separation of charged solutes has gained wide acceptance mainly because of the limitations of ion exchange in separating both neutral and ionic samples and because of the difficulty in separating ionic components by the reversed-phase techniques of ion suppression.

The combination of varying mobile phase strength and type of ion-pairing reagent is often sufficient to enable the analyst to develop a separation. In addition to these parameters, it is also possible to mix two ion-pairing reagents having different chain lengths to 'fine tune' or 'tailor' a separation. In some situations, when dealing with mixtures of ionic and non-ionizable compounds, mixing ion-pair reagents to control retention is the only way to approach the development of a separation. For example, when a five-carbon alkyl chain is used to separate water-soluble vitamins, insufficient retention is observed. Changing the mobile phase counter-ion to a compound containing a seven-carbon alkyl chain increases the retention, particularly of the most strongly ionic compound. A mixture of counter-ions added to the mobile phase produces a retention proportional to the concentration of each counter-ion and is the approach by which the best separation can be achieved. The separation of water-soluble vitamins, niacin, pyridoxine, riboflavin, and thiamine, can be used to illustrate this approach.

Materials and equipment

Solvents: (i)   methanol and 1% acetic acid in distilled water;
              (ii) 2.5 mM pentane sulphonic acid ⎫ in methanol: 1% acetic
              (iii) 2.5 mM heptane sulphonic acid ⎭ acid (25:75)
Solutions: (1) riboflavin (4 mg 100 ml^{-1} of methanol: 1% acetic acid (25:75))
              (2) thiamine (20 mg), riboflavin (4 mg), pyridoxine (6 mg) and niacin
              (4 mg) in 100 ml of methanol: 1% acetic acid (25:75);
Column: μ-Bondapak column; 5 μm silica-ODS, 250 mm × 4.6 mm i.d.;
Chromatograph, detector, integrator and injector system as for Experiment 24.

Method

The recommended instrument settings are:

Mobile phase flow rate	2 ml min^{-1}
Detector Wavelength	270 nm.

Thiamine, pyridoxine and niacin are ionic, and riboflavin is non-ionic at the pH used to pair the ions of the ionic samples. The development of a separation of these compounds requires a two-step procedure.

First, adjust the methanol/water ratio (polarity of the mobile phase), to obtain good retention, approximately 6 min, of the non-ionic compound riboflavin (solution 1). Second, optimize, the separation of the components in solution 2 by varying the relative proportions of pentane and heptanesulphonic acids in the eluent while keeping the acid strength constant (5 mM). The base solvent for the acids is the methanol: 1% acetic acid composition established for the 6 min elution of riboflavin.

Construct a graph of retention time *vs.* counter-ion composition for each component of the mixture.

9.7.3 Experiment 26. Techniques in HPLC analysis of analgesics [16, 17]

Object

This experiment demonstrates the techniques of solvent selection, gradient elution, pH control and ion-pairing in the analysis of an analgesic mixture using reversed-phase HPLC on an octadecylsilane (ODS) column.

Introduction

Typical analgesic formulations contain components with a wide range of pK_a values. The HPLC analysis of such diverse samples can be aided by using techniques such as gradient elution, ion suppression and ion pairing. The underlying principles of these techniques have been discussed in detail in Chapter 6.

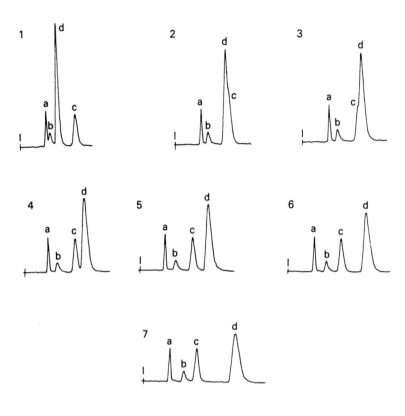

Chromatogram	Solvent %A:%B	Compound a	b	c	d
1	100:0	2.34	2.70	4.99	3.33
2	75:25	2.38	3.00	Sh.>4.53	4.53
3	60:40	2.40	3.14	Sh.<5.23	5.23
4	50:50	2.40	3.20	4.80	5.64
5	40:60	2.42	3.37	4.85	6.20
6	25:75	2.42	3.50	4.82	6.98
7	0:100	2.43	3.66	4.75	8.10

Fig. 9.16   Chromatograms and solvent data for standard mixture of vitamins. Solvent A; 2.5 mM pentane sulphonic acid in 25% MeOH/75% 1% HoAc. Solvent B; 2.5 mM heptane sulphonic acid in 25% MeOH/75% 1% HoAc. Peaks: (a) niacin; (b) pyridoxine; (c) riboflavin; (d) thiamine. Other details in text.

Materials and equipment

Solvents:	(i) phosphate buffers containing AR Na_2HPO_4 and NaH_2PO_4 (0.025 M), pH adjusted to requirements using NaOH or H_3PO_4; (ii) tetrabutyl ammonium phosphate (0.005 M) buffered to pH 7.6; (iii) 1% HoAc;
Mixture A:	acetylsalicylic acid (86 mg); paracetamol (5.1 mg); salicylamide (87.8 mg); caffeine (28.1 mg); phenacetin (11.4 mg) in 50 cm³ of methanol;
Mixture B:	acetylsalicylic acid (86 mg) and salicylamide (87.8 mg) used as above. Salicylic acid (6 mg) is included because of the likelihood of its presence as an impurity in aspirin;
Column:	Spherisorb-10 ODS, 250 mm × 4.6 mm i.d.;
Chromatograph:	Waters 6000 solvent delivery module with 660 solvent programmer, variable wavelength UV detector;
Integrator:	Hewlett-Packard 3390A;
Injector system:	Rheodyne valve fitted with 10 µl loop.

Method

The recommended instrument settings are:

mobile phase flow rate $2\,cm^3\,min^{-1}$;
detector wavelength   254 nm.

(a) Solvent selection and determination of an unknown

Isocratic elution of the analgesics may be investigated using a methanol/phosphate buffer (pH 7) and methanol/1% HoAc eluent. The methanol composition should be varied between 20–55%. For the optimum solvent composition the peaks can be identified by injecting the individual analgesics.

The technique of gradient elution is demonstrated by injection of mixture A using the following conditions: initial solvent composition approximately 15:85 MeOH:pH 7 buffer, final solvent composition approximately 60:40 MeOH:pH 7 buffer, convex gradient (No. 3 of Waters Model 660 Solvent Programmer) using a run time of 12 min. When a suitable solvent composition has been determined the relative response factors of the individual components can be calculated as in experiment 24. An analgesic tablet may then be analysed quantitatively by crushing the tablet, extracting with methanol, making up to a known volume (e.g. 10 ml) and injecting the resulting solution into the HPLC sample valve via a luer filter.

(b) pH effects

Solvents are prepared with the composition approximately 45:55 MeOH: buffer using phosphate buffers of pH 5.0, 7.0 and 9.0. After allowing the column to equilibrate to the solvent by flushing for 15 min, mixture A is injected and the peaks identified by injection of the individual solutes.

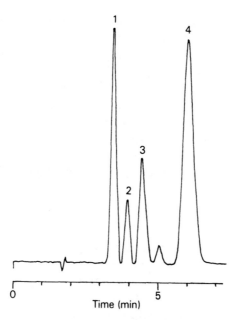

Fig. 9.17 Chromatogram of standard mixture of analgesics, column and conditions detailed in text. Eluent 40% methanol/60% 1% HoAc. Peaks: (1) salicylamide; (2) aspirin; (3) caffeine; (4) phenacetin.

(c) Ion-pairing

The use of ion pairing in HPLC is investigated using tetrabutylammonium phosphate (TBAP) (solution ii), combined with methanol to give a solvent composition of approximately 45:55 MeOH:TBAP. For comparison purposes, a solvent not containing TBAP is prepared using pH 7.6 phosphate buffer mixed with methanol in the same proportions as above. Mixture B is injected using both of the above solvents and the peaks are identified by comparison with chromatograms of the single analgesics obtained using the same solvents.

9.7.4 Experiment 27. Analysis of amino acids as their DNP derivatives

Object

To derivatize the amino acids of a protein hydrolysate with dinitro-phenylhydrazine and to identify and quantify by comparison with external standards containing the appropriate DNP amino acid derivatives.

Introduction

Derivatization of samples in HPLC is undertaken principally for two reasons. First, there is no detector for HPLC with universally high sensitivity for all

solutes; hence a suitable chemical transformation of the solute can greatly extend
the sensitivity and versatility of a selective detector.

Second, sample derivatization may be undertaken to enhance the detector
response to sample bands relative to overlapping bands of no analytical interest.

This experiment involves the precolumn derivatization of sample with
dinitrofluorobenzene so enhancing the spectrophotometric response of the
sample, i.e., the amino acids from a protein hydrolysate. The conversion of the
amino acids to their apolar DNP derivatives allows them to be analysed using
reverse-phase chromatography. Thus polar DNP-amino acids, such as DNP-
aspartate, will elute early whereas apolar DNP-amino acids, such as DNP-
alanine, will elute later.

Materials and equipment

Solvents:	A-methanol; B-water;
Stock solutions:	DNP-alanine, DNP-aspartate, DNP-serine and DNP-threonine in methanol (1 mg ml^{-1});
Unknown:	protein sample;
Derivatizing reagent:	fluorodinitrobenzene (FDNB);
Column:	Spherisorb-10 ODS, 250 mm × 4.6 mm i.d.;

Chromatograph, detector, integrator and injector system as for experiment 24.

Method

The recommended instrument settings are as follows:

solvent flow	2 ml min^{-1};
isocratic elution	80% methanol, 20% H_2O;
detector wavelength	365 nm.

From the stock solutions of DNP-alanine, DNP-aspartate. DNP-serine and
DNP-threonine provided make up working standards containing 0.05 mg ml^{-1}
MeOH of each of the DNP-amino acids. Inject 5 μl of each of these working
standards and record the retention of each DNP-amino acid.

Make up the following calibration mixtures containing the following volumes
(μl) of each of the primary standards.

Mixture	DNP-Alanine	DNP-Aspartate	DNP-Serine	DNP-Threonine
I	10	50	10	50
II	20	40	20	40
III	30	30	30	30
IV	40	20	40	20
V	50	10	50	10

To each calibration mixture add 1 ml MeOH. Inject $5\,\mu l$ of each calibration mixture.

Identify the terminal amino acid of the protein sample as follows. React the protein with FDNB and then hydrolyse the derivative (6 M HCl, 110°C, 2h). Extract the hydrolysate with diethyl ether (3 × 5 ml) and evaporate to dryness; take up the residue in 1 ml of methanol. Chromatograph these solutions using the conditions established above.

1. Report the retention time of each DNP-amino acid and determine its reproducibility.
2. Construct calibration graphs.
3. Identify the N-terminal amino acid of the unknown protein.

9.7.5 Experiment 28. Analysis of inorganic anions using conductimetric detection

Object

To analyse qualitatively and quantitatively the inorganic anion contaminants in aqueous samples using an ion chromatograph system fitted with a suppressor column and conductivity cell.

Introduction

Initially application of ion exchange to modern LC depended upon the analyte having a specific property, such as ultraviolet absorbance, fluorescence or radioactivity. Conductivity detectors could not be used without modification, as the eluants used in ion exchange often contained complexing agents (citrate, EDTA), buffer solutions (carbonate, phosphate) and other various electrolytes required to achieve the desired resolution; thus the eluent itself produced an extremely high background conductivity making that due to analyte species undetectable. This restriction was overcome by the work of Small, who developed a general technique for the removal of background electrolytes. The technique uses a secondary column, the scrubber column, which effectively removes ions arising from the background electrolyte leaving only the species of analytical interest, as the major conducting species in deionized water. Further detail on the principles and uses of such systems is presented in Chapter 6.

Materials

Standard solution containing:	fluoride (2 ppm), chloride (5 ppm), nitrite (10 ppm), bromide (10 ppm), phosphate (15 ppm) nitrate (30 ppm) and sulphate (30 ppm) in deionized water;
Unknown:	river water sample;
Eluant:	0.022 M Na_2CO_3/0.0028 M $NaHCO_3$;

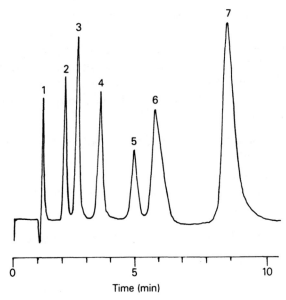

Fig. 9.18   Chromatogram of standard mixture of anions, column and conditions as detailed in text. Peaks: (1) fluoride; (2) chloride; (3) nitrite; (4) bromide; (5) phosphate; (6) nitrate; (7) sulphate.

Regenerant:	0.0125 M H_2SO_4;
Instrument:	Dionex Ion Chromatograph (QIC);
Detector:	Conductivity;
Integrator:	Spectraphysics 4270;
Columns:	Anion Separator (HPIC AS4);
	Anion Guard (HPIC AG4);
	Anion Suppressor (AFS);
Injector:	Multiport valve, air actuated, with 50 μl loop.

Method

The recommended instrument settings are as follows:

eluant flow rate	2 ml min^{-1};
regenerant flow rate	3 ml min^{-1};
detector range	10–30 μS.

All dilutions of standards and samples must be made with deionized water of conductivity $< 20\,\mu$S or better. A set of standards covering the following concentration range should be prepared:

F^-	2–0.2 ppm
Cl^-	5–1 ppm
NO_2^-	10–1 ppm
Br^-	10–1 ppm

PO_4^{3-} 15–4 ppm
NO_3^- 30–5 ppm
SO_4^{2-} 30–5 ppm

Aqueous samples can be diluted such that the analyte levels lie within the calibration range.

1. Report the retention times of the analyte species.
2. Construct calibration graphs.
3. Analyse the sample provided, taking account of any dilution factors required.

REFERENCES

1. Hunt, E. C., North, A. A. and Wells, R. A. (1955) *Analyst*, **80**, 172.
2. Jakubovic, A. O. and Knight, C. S. (1960) *Chromatographic and Electrophoretic Techniques*, (ed. I. Smith), Heinemann, London **1**, 559.
3. Consden, R., Gordon, A. H. and Martin, A. J. P. (1944), *J. Biochem.*, **38**, 224.
4. Dent, C. E. (1948) *J. Biochem.*, **43**, 169.
5. Jepson, J. B. and Smith, I. (1953) *Nature*, **171**, 43 and **172**, 1100.
6. Wrigley, C. W. (1972) *Biochem. Education*, **1**, 10.
7. Vesterberg, O. and Svensson, H. (1966) *Acta Chem. Scand.*, **20**, 820.
8. Vesterberg, O. *et al.* (1967) *Biochim. Biophys. Acta*, **133**, 435.
9. Wrigley, C. W. (1968) *J. Chromatogr.*, **36**, 362.
10. Leaback, D. H. and Rutter, A. C. (1968) *Biochim. Biophys. Res. Commun.*, **32**, 447.
11. Riley, R. F. and Coleman, M. K. (1968) *J. Lab. Clin. Med.*, **72**, 714.
12. Awden, Z. L. *et al.* (1968) *Nature*, **219**, 66.
13. *Gel Filtration Theory and Practice*, Pharmacia Ltd., 351, Midsummer Boulevard, Central Milton Keynes MK9 3YY, Pharmacia Fine Chemicals AB, Box 175 S-751 04 Uppsala 1, Sweden.
14. Wills, R. B. H., Shaw, C. G. and Day, W. R. (1977) *J. Chromatogr. Sci.*, **15**, 262.
15. Conrad, E. C., (1975) *Food Product Development*, **9**, 97.
16. Kagel, R. A. and Farwell, S. O. (1983) *J. Education*, **60**, 163.
17. Haddad, P., Hutchins, S. and Tuffy, M. (1983) *J. Education*, **60**, 166.

INDEX

ABBREVIATIONS USED IN THE INDEX

Expt.   Experiment
GC   Gas chromatography
GC—IR   Gas chromatography—infrared
GC—MS   Gas chromatography—mass
   spectrometry
GSC   Gas solid chromatography
HETP   Height equivalent to a theoretical
   plate
HPLC   High performance liquid
   chromatography
HPLC—IR   High performance liquid
   chromatography—infrared
HPLC—MS   High performance liquid
   chromatography—mass spectrometry
HPLC—UV   High performance liquid
   chromatography—ultraviolet

HPTLC   High performance thin layer
   chromatography
IEC   Ion exchange chromatography
IR   Infrared
LC   Liquid chromatography
LLC   Liquid liquid chromatography
LC—MS   Liquid chromatography—mass
   spectrometry
PC   Paper chromatography
PEI   Polyethylene imine
PLOT   Porous layer open tubular (column)
RI   Refractive index
SCOT   Surface coated open tubular
   (column)
WCOT   Wall coated open tubular (column)
UV-visible   Ultraviolet-visible

A

Absorbance ratioing techniques in HPLC 239
Acylation of samples for GC   149
Adsorbents
   for columns in LC   92
   for GSC   200
   for thermal desorption in GC   153
   for TLC   26, 127
   in LC   92
Adsorption
   in HPLC   214
   isotherms in LC   93
   sampling for GC   153
Adsorption chromatography
   in LC   90
   in HPLC   258
Advances in TLC   49
Affinity chromatography   129
Affinity methods in HPLC   217
Agarose for electrophoresis   77
Agarose gels for
   gel LC   123
   ion exchange LC   114

Alkali bead flame ionization detector for
   GC   167
Alkylation of samples for GC   150
Alumina for TLC   29
Alumina adsorbent for
   GSC   200
   LC   94
Analog to digital converters   327, 328
Application of
   samples in TLC   34
   GC   191
   gel LC   126
   HPLC   285
   microcolumn HPLC   285
   PC   69
   PC, solvent systems   59
Application examples of partition LC
   97
Applications, head space analysis in
   GC   191
Argon ionization detector for GC   178
Ascending development in TLC   38
Atmospheric pollutants analysis by GC
   197
Atomic absorption for GC and HPLC
   320

E

T